The Shadows of

EUROPE, EAST ASIA, AND

1919–1939

The period between the two world wars of the twentieth century was one of the most exciting in the history of war. In anticipation of another conflict, military planners and civilian thinkers struggled after 1918 with the painful implications of World War I. Given its scope, the wholesale mobilization of civilian populations, and the targeting of civilians via blockades and strategic bombing, many observers regarded this titanic conflict as a "total war." They also conluded that any future conflict would bear the same hallmarks; and they planned accordingly. The essays in this collection, the fourth in a series on the problem of total war, examine the interwar period. They explore the lingering consequences of World War I, the intellectual efforts to analyze this conflict's military significance, the attempts to plan for another general war, and several episodes in the 1930s that portended the war that erupted in 1939.

Roger Chickering is Professor of History at the BMW Center for German and European Studies at Georgetown University. His publications include *Imperial Germany and the Great War, 1914–1918* (Cambridge 1998) and *Karl Lamprecht (1856–1915): A German Academic Life* (1993).

Stig Förster is Professor of History at the University of Bern in Switzerland. His publications include *Der doppelte Militarismus: Die deutsche Heeresrüstungspolitik zwischen Status-quo-Sicherung und Aggression, 1890–1913* (1985) and *Die mächtigen Diener der East India Company: Ursachen und Hintergründe der britischen Expansionspolitik in Südasien, 1793–1819* (1992).

PUBLICATIONS OF THE GERMAN HISTORICAL INSTITUTE
WASHINGTON, D.C.

Edited by Christof Mauch
with David Lazar

The German Historical Institute is a center for advanced study and research whose purpose is to provide a permanent basis for scholarly cooperation among historians from the Federal Republic of Germany and the United States. The Institute conducts, promotes, and supports research into both American and German political, social, economic, and cultural history; into transatlantic migration, especially in the nineteenth and twentieth centuries; and into the history of international relations, with special emphasis on the roles played by the United States and Germany.

Recent books in the series

Norbert Finzsch and Dietmar Schirmer, editors, *Identity and Intolerance: Nationalism, Racism, and Xenophobia in Germany and the United States*

Susan Strasser, Charles McGovern, and Matthias Judt, editors, *Getting and Spending: European and American Consumer Societies in the Twentieth Century*

Carole Fink, Philipp Gassert, and Detlef Junker, editors, *1968: The World Transformed*

Roger Chickering and Stig Förster, editors, *Great War, Total War: Combat and Mobilization on the Western Front*

Manfred F. Boemeke, Gerald D. Feldman, and Elisabeth Glaser, eds., *The Treaty of Versailles: A Reassessment After 75 Years*

Manfred Berg and Martin H. Geyer, eds., *Two Cultures of Rights: The Quest for Inclusion and Participation in Modern America and Germany*

Manfred F. Boemeke, Roger Chickering, and Stig Förster, eds., *Anticipating Total War: The German and American Experiences, 1871–1914*

The Shadows of Total War

EUROPE, EAST ASIA, AND THE UNITED STATES, 1919–1939

Edited by
ROGER CHICKERING
Georgetown University

STIG FÖRSTER
University of Bern, Switzerland

GERMAN HISTORICAL INSTITUTE
Washington, D.C.
and

CAMBRIDGE UNIVERSITY PRESS
Cambridge, New York, Melbourne, Madrid, Cape Town, Singapore, São Paulo, Delhi

Cambridge University Press
32 Avenue of the Americas, New York, NY 10013-2473, USA

www.cambridge.org
Information on this title: www.cambridge.org/9780521812368

First published 2003
Reprinted 2007
This digitally printed version 2008

A catalog record for this publication is available from the British Library

Library of Congress Cataloging in Publication data

The shadows of total war : Europe, East Asia, and the United States, 1919-1939 / edited by
Roger Chickering and Stig Förster.
p. cm. – (Publications of the German Historical Institute)
Paper presented at a conference held Aug. 1999, Münchenwiler, Switzerland as the
forth of a series of five collections.
Includes bibliographical references and index.
ISBN 0-521-81236-4
1. World War, 1914-1918 – Influence – Congresses. 2. Military art and
science – History – 20th century – Congresses. 3. World War, 1939-1945 –
Diplomatic history – Congresses. 4. Europe – Foreign relations – 1918-1945 – Congresses.
5. United States – Foreign relations – 1935-1945 – Congresses. 6. East Asia – Foreign
relations – Congresses. 7. War aid society – History – 20th century. I. Chickering, Roger,
1942- II. Förster, Stig. III. Title.
HG4028.M4B335 1998
D727 .S5 2002
940.3-dc21 2002020163

ISBN 978-0-521-81236-8 hardback
ISBN 978-0-521-10039-7 paperback

Contents

List of Contributors

Timo Baumann is a Research Fellow in the History Department at the University of Bern, Switzerland.

Roger Chickering is Professor of History at Georgetown University.

Deborah Cohen is Assistant Professor of History at American University, Washington, D.C.

Wilhelm Deist is a retired historian living in Freiburg im Breisgau.

James M. Diehl is Professor of History at Indiana University.

Stig Förster is Professor of History at the University of Bern, Switzerland.

Bernd Greiner is a researcher at the Institute for Social Research, Hamburg.

Edgar Jones is Senior Research Fellow in the Department of Psychological Medicine at Guy's, King's and St. Thomas' School of Medicine, London.

Giulia Brogini Künzi is a Research Fellow in the History Department at the University of Bern, Switzerland.

Hartmut Lehmann is Director of the Max Planck Institute for History, Göttingen.

Klaus A. Maier was a researcher at the Office of Military History Research, Potsdam.

Hans-Heinrich Nolte is Professor of History at the University of Hannover.

Markus Pöhlmann is print and photograph researcher at the Deutsche Verlags-Anstalt, Stuttgart.

Thomas Rohkrämer teaches history at the University of Lancaster.

Daniel Marc Segesser is a Research Fellow in the History Department at the University of Bern, Switzerland.

Dennis E. Showalter is Professor of History at Colorado College.

Hew Strachan is Professor of Modern History at the University of Glasgow.

Benedikt Stuchtey is a Research Fellow at the German Historical Institute, London.

Gerhard L. Weinberg is a retired historian living in Chapel Hill, North Carolina.

Simon Wessely is Professor of Psychological Medicine at Guy's, King's and St. Thomas' School of Medicine, London.

Louise Young is Professor of History at New York University.

Introduction

ROGER CHICKERING AND STIG FÖRSTER

At the beginning of the twenty-first century it appears as if the age of total war may be over. Military history, let alone "history" itself, has admittedly not come to an end.[1] The so-called new world order, in which a single superpower remains, has failed to provide global peace or stability. Wars continue with unabated frequency. Nonetheless, the character of international conflict, at least in its organized form, seems to have moved away from the patterns that dominated the first half of the twentieth century.[2]

During the recent war in Kosovo, NATO officials routinely offered public regrets about the "collateral damage" that the alliance's airplanes had inflicted inadvertently on civilians in the Balkans. The destruction of a single bus by NATO bombs resulted in an international outcry and consternation among Western leaders. By contrast, the same officials proudly announced that one of their pilots had avoided a target after he had determined that it lay close to a church. Fifty-five years earlier, during World War II, political and military leaders would have found this kind of warfare difficult to comprehend. They would not have been troubled by the destruction of a bus in the course of a bombing sortie. The wholesale killing of civilians was a common and essential part of their strategies, for the distinction between soldiers and civilians had ceased to matter much.

Today, however, wars are evidently fought for more restricted aims with more limited, albeit sophisticated, means. Unconditional surrender no longer represents the conventional conclusion to warfare. Mass, conscripted armies are found today primarily in less developed countries, where they

1 Cf. Francis Fukuyama, *The End of History and the Last Man* (New York, 1992).

2 Martin van Creveld has suggested a different "retreat" from total war. He argues that organized warfare is being replaced by low-intensity wars waged by terrorists and resistance movements. See Martin van Creveld, *The Transformation of War* (New York, 1991); cf. Ulrich Bröckling, "Am Ende der grossen Kriegserzählungen? Zur Genealogie der 'humanitären Intervention,'" Arbeitskreis Militärgeschichte, *Newsletter* 11 (2000): 7–10.

usually bring unhappy economic and political consequences. The strategies of modern armed forces are designed to reduce their own casualties – if possible (as in Kosovo) to eliminate them altogether. After Vietnam, as Hew Strachan has recently remarked, "both the public and politicians were re-educated to expect wars to be short, victorious, and comparatively bloodless."[3] The future of warfare seems to belong to highly trained, well-equipped professional soldiers, whose mission is, as the public hand-wringing over collateral damage in Kosovo suggested, to remove their business as far as possible from civilian affairs.

Has the "age of total war" really passed? Has warfare returned to a "normal" state? Was total war but a momentary aberration in the long history of warfare? Did it emerge in specific historical circumstances during the nineteenth century, come to fruition in the early twentieth century, and then disappear?

John Keegan has recently lent support to this view. He has restated an old argument that early human societies fought only limited wars – that they avoiding mass-killings and large-scale destruction. In this perspective, limited warfare appears to be the natural form of armed conflict among human groups. The radicalization of warfare, its extension to all the members of the participating groups, commenced only with the emergence of modern states and sophisticated armies.[4]

The paleo-anthropologist Lawrence Keeley has painted an altogether different picture.[5] He concludes that prehistoric societies often fought wars in which destruction was limited only by the means at the disposal of the combatants. Mobilizing all able-bodied men – and sometimes women – these "primitive" groups set out to subjugate or annihilate one another. In this light, *total war* – waged to the limits of a society's capabilities – has been the "normal" pattern, the basic historical form of intergroup conflict. Only when states could no longer afford the strains and costs of conflict in this pattern did the limitation of warfare begin.

If Keeley is right, the total wars of the twentieth century represented no historical aberration. Limiting warfare depended on the ability of states and societies to control the use of military violence, to employ it with limited means for limited aims. One could then argue that historical circumstances in the nineteenth and twentieth centuries brought the breakdown of these control mechanisms and opened the road to total war. Warfare returned to its

3 Hew Strachan, "Essay and Reflection: On Total War and Modern War," *International History Review* 22 (2000): 347.

4 John Keegan, *A History of Warfare* (London, 1993).

5 Lawrence Keeley, *War Before Civilization* (New York, 1996).

basic nature, albeit in much more destructive form, which corresponded to the expanded capacities of modern industrial societies. The principal question then relates to the causes of the disastrous disappearance of constraints on warfare in the modern era.

This question has posed the underlying theme in a series of conferences of which this volume represents a part. "Total war" became a popular topos during the period between the two world wars of the twentieth century. It was coined during the first of them, and it subsequently played an important role in deliberations everywhere about the future of warfare. Even as it entered the popular vocabulary, though, a compelling definition of the term eluded contemporaries; and it has continued to frustrate historians. Accordingly, one of the principal goals of the conference series has been to explore the definition and historical meaning of the concept of total war. The first three conferences demonstrated the difficulties of the undertaking.[6] Participants found it hard to agree on the dimensions of total war, the origins of the phenomenon, the conflicts that might lay claim to the label, and whether total war ever fully materialized. In fact, doubts have lingered over whether the concept of total war has occasioned more confusion than insight and ought best to be abandoned.

One of the difficulties lies in the expanding purview of warfare in the modern epoch. The idea of total war implies the breakdown of the distinction between organized combat and the societies, economies, and political systems that support it. Analyzing this phenomenon in turn has broad methodological implications, which are captured in the proposition that "total war requires total history."[7] If the idea of total war has any utility for historians, it requires the investigation of warfare in its many historical dimensions, an effort that extends to the fields of military, political, social, economic, and cultural history. This realization has brought a significant expansion in the scope of the conference series, as historians from other areas have joined the ranks of military historians in examining the history of warfare in the modern era.

The series began with the hypothesis that a phenomenon called total war could claim its immediate origins in the American and French Revolutions. As the revolutionaries in both lands invoked the idea of a "people's war"

6 Stig Förster and Jörg Nagler, eds., *On the Road to Total War: The American Civil War and the German Wars of Unification, 1861–1871* (New York, 1997); Manfred F. Boemeke, Roger Chickering, and Stig Förster, eds., *Anticipating Total War: The American and German Experiences, 1871–1914* (New York, 1999); Roger Chickering and Stig Förster, eds., *Great War, Total War: Combat and Mobilization on the Western Front, 1914–1918* (New York, 2000).

7 Roger Chickering, "Total War: The Use and Abuse of a Concept," in Boemeke, Chickering, and Förster, eds., *Anticipating*, 27.

as a response to the professional armies that they faced, they called on the support of the general public for their war effort. At the end of the eighteenth century, warfare increasingly involved entire societies. One might thus argue that the ideological foundations of total war were laid in these revolutions, once it became theoretically compelling and plausible to mobilize every citizen for war.

Industrialization later in the nineteenth century offered the material means to put the ideology of people's war into practice. Mass armies of volunteers and conscripts could be transported to the battlefields and provided with weapons, munitions, equipment, and food. These requirements attached enormous significance to the exertions of civilians on the home front. Non-combatants produced the essential material provisions for soldiers in the field; the moral and political support of non-combatants was consequently hardly less vital to the prosecution of war than were the efforts of the soldiers. Civilians became directly implicated in the fighting, hence legitimate targets of military action, as the conceptual distinction between them and soldiers began to erode.

At the same time, the aims for which wars were being fought themselves lost their constraints. As belligerent societies began to cast one another as threats to their own survival, the destruction of the enemy's basic social or political institutions seemed to offer appropriate redress. Finally, as mass mobilization for warfare reached its zenith in the industrial wars of the twentieth century, populations grew accustomed to mass slaughter. This experience reduced popular resistance to the employment of every means available to achieve victory.

Given the hypothesis that total war grew out of the combined military implications of what Eric Hobsbawm has called the "dual revolution" of popular sovereignty and industrialization,[8] it seemed appropriate to begin the conference series in the middle of the nineteenth century, with a comparison between the American Civil War and the German Wars of Unification. These were the first large-scale wars in which many of these new features of warfare could be observed. The participants in the first conference could not agree, however, whether any of these mid-century wars might legitimately be called "total." The America Civil War in particular was the object of an extended debate. While James McPherson argued that this conflict turned total in 1862, Mark Neely disagreed.[9] On the other hand, no one claimed

8 Eric Hobsbawm, *The Age of Revolution, 1789–1848* (New York, 1962).

9 James M. McPherson, *Battle Cry of Freedom: The Civil War Era* (New York 1988), 490; Mark E. Neely Jr., "Was the Civil War a Total War?" in Förster and Nagler, eds., *On the Road*, 29–52; James M. McPherson, "From Limited War to Total War in America," in ibid., 295–310.

that the German Wars could remotely lay claim to this label, although some argued that the Franco-German War showed tendencies in this direction.[10] In all events, the conference resulted in no consensus. Disagreements grew primarily out of the paradoxical characters of these wars, which exhibited both "modern" and "traditional" characteristics. The conference did make clear, however, that any attempt to define total war would have to accommodate several dimensions of analysis, although the blurring of distinctions between combatants and non-combatants, the extension of warfare to include civilians as well as soldiers, impressed many as the most basic.

The next conference was devoted to the experiences of the United States and Imperial Germany in the era between the mid-century wars and the outbreak of World War I. This conference achieved more consensus. Although signs of the loosening of constraints on warfare could be detected in the writings of German and American observers, as well as in the practices of colonial warfare, it was clear that few contemporaries in either country foresaw the wars of the early twentieth century. While some military and civilian theorists in Germany envisaged a long, catastrophic war, even they failed to anticipate a war of such comprehensive impact that it might legitimately be called total.[11] The conference laid bare so many alternative visions of future war that it became difficult to contend that the road to total war led straight from the middle of the nineteenth century to the Great War.

The third conference was the first to confront a conflict that has conventionally enjoyed the designation "total war." By virtually every index, World War I was the most extensive and comprehensive ever fought. Its sheer magnitude defied the limits of a single conference and made necessary a focus on the principal powers that were engaged on the western front. Although disagreements surfaced once again, the conference did yield some general conclusions. Despite the ghastly extent of the slaughter at the front, leaders in all the belligerent countries persisted in conducting the war as "business as usual," at least until 1916, which proved to be a turning point. As the terrible battles of this year failed to break the military deadlock on the western front, conceptual limits on war began to break down. Unrestricted submarine warfare, the introduction of new technologies, and the grim attempt to achieve the full mobilization of society, cost what it might, all suggested that warfare had undergone a significant modulation.

10 Stig Förster, "The Prussian Triangle of Leadership in the Face of a People's War: A Reassessment of the Conflict Between Bismarck and Moltke, 1870–71," in ibid., 115–40; Robert Tombs, "The Wars Against Paris," in ibid., 541–64.

11 Stig Förster, "Dreams and Nightmares: German Military Leadership and the Images of Future Warfare, 1871–1914," in Boemeke, Chickering, and Förster, eds., *Anticipating*, 343–76.

The Hindenburg Program in Germany and Lloyd George's policy of conscription and full mobilization in Britain were the most salient markers of this process. By this time, the belligerent states had resolved to fight to the bitter end, to subvert if necessary one another's institutions by revolutionary means, and to disdain all thoughts of a compromise peace.

Did the Great War in fact represent a total war? Contemporaries such as Erich Ludendorff and Ernst Jünger denied that it did. After the war they charged that the German leadership had failed to implement total mobilization. German society had not, they argued, devoted itself unconditionally to the war effort. The conference demonstrated, however, that this charge could have been leveled as well at France, Britain, and the United States. Nor, judged by the victimization of civilians, did the Great War present an unambiguous picture. Britain's naval blockade was admittedly directed against Germany's civilian population, while the German U-boats were deployed to repay the British in kind. But, as Strachan emphasized, the static character of the front, which turned the Great War into a protracted siege, spared most civilians from the direct impact of military action.[12] Still, civilian targets were bombed from the air on both sides. German atrocities against Belgian civilians at the beginning of the war and the subsequent deportation of Belgian labor to Germany were also pertinent in this respect. In the end, though, the argument of Ludendorff and Jünger seemed compelling: although tendencies in this direction were detectable, total war did not materialize during the Great War.

But should one even pose the problem in these terms? This basic methodological question has hung over all the conferences. It has to do with what one might call the ontological status of total war. Is total war something real, a potentiality awaiting its realization in history? This conception of the problem draws on Carl von Clausewitz's idea of "absolute war," although the military philosopher himself was convinced that for several practical reasons the potential of absolute war, which inhered in every act of violence, would not be fully realized in historical fact. Defining total war in these "realist" terms has invited discussion of the specific indices or measures of "totality." How unrestrained must military violence become to deserve the label "total"? How radical must war aims be? How total was World War I?

The difficulties of answering this order of questions suggested the possibilities of posing the problem in different terms. "Total war," in an alternative

12 Hew Strachan, "From Cabinet War to Total War: The Perspective of Military Doctrine, 1861–1918," in Chickering and Förster, eds., *Great War, Total War*, 19–33; cf. Gerd Krumeich, "Kriegsfront – Heimatfront," in Gerhard Hirschfeld et al., eds., *Kriegserfahrungen: Studien zur Sozial- und Mentalitätsgeschichte des Ersten Weltkrieges* (Essen, 1997), 12–19.

reading, might be better conceived as an "ideal type," in the sense that Max Weber understood the term – as a heuristic device, an intellectual construction that lays claim itself to no independent historical reality but serves instead as a conceptual model, which allows the observer to abstract from empirical phenomena in order to analyze broader tendencies or categories of events. By this definition, "totality" in warfare has never been achieved historically; it can be only approximated. As an "ideal type," however, total war draws the attention of historians to specific dimensions of warfare, and it provides categories of meaningful comparison among historical cases.

If the conference series has failed to resolve issues like these, it has hardly ignored them. Roger Chickering has warned of the pitfalls that lurk in the teleologies of total war as a "master narrative."[13] The conferences have demonstrated that the "plot line" of this narrative did not lead directly or ineluctably from the French revolutionary armies to Hiroshima. Portraying historical developments in light of such narrative logic obscures a host of contingencies, accidents, alternatives, and counter-tendencies that have figured prominently in all the recent conferences.

The concept of total war was contrived only during the interwar period, so anyone who wishes to use it to characterize earlier conflicts must be sensitive to charges of anachronism. Neither Lincoln nor Bismarck, Moltke nor even Ludendorff had conceived of total war before 1916. Employing the standards of one era to judge another is a dangerous exercise, which requires considerable caution. In this spirit, the conference series has suggested that productive structural comparisons require careful attention to the question why constraints on warfare that prevailed in one historical era broke down in another.

The conferences marked out a number of analytical dimensions or axes along which any definition of total war must be framed, however the concept is understood. One has to do with war aims. Pursuing the destruction or complete subjugation of an enemy, let alone the genocidal annihilation of its population, was rare before the modern era. It occurred primarily on the peripheries of Europe, as in the Spanish Reconquista. More commonly, defeated powers needed only to accede to the victors' limited demands in order to be left alone. Wars ended usually in some sort of negotiation. This state of affairs survived into the wars of Napoleon, who, at least when he fought other great powers, did not as a rule seek their destruction.

During the American Civil War this pattern changed. The Confederacy admittedly fought for limited aims, insofar as it wished only to gain

13 Chickering, "Total War," in Boemeke, *Anticipating*, 15–28.

independence. As Jefferson Davis pleaded, "All we ask is to be left alone."[14] As the war dragged on, however, Lincoln raised the stakes, defining the Union's goal as nothing less than the revolutionary recasting of the South with the elimination of slavery, its basic social institution. "The character of the war will be changed. It will be one of subjugation," he declared. "The South is to be destroyed and replaced by new propositions and ideas."[15] Thus, even if Lincoln were prepared to negotiate on details, the term "unconditional surrender" now well described the Union's war effort. A similar tendency surfaced in the Franco-German War several years later. After Léon Gambetta's *guerre à outrance* had caused enormous difficulties for the German armies as they sought to bring the war to an end, Moltke demanded the complete occupation and subjugation of France. The Prussian crown prince was horrified by this call for "a war of extermination," and Bismarck refused to agree to it.[16] Both cases suggested that the radicalization of war aims was becoming a feature of war in the industrial era.

During the Great War, the French and Germans envisaged their mutual dismemberment and the destruction of one another's great-power status. That extreme war aims were seriously meant was demonstrated in the peace treaty of Brest-Litovsk. During much of the proceedings at the Paris peace conference in 1919, the French called for radical measures against Germany, before the influence of the Anglo-Saxon powers moderated the terms of the treaty. In World War II, unlimited aims were an even more prominent feature. The Germans planned to destroy the Soviet Union and to enslave or eradicate the population of the conquered territories. At the Casablanca conference, Churchill and Roosevelt made unconditional surrender officially the goal of their war against the Axis.

The radicalization of war aims reflected the changing attitudes of belligerent states toward one another. Political and military leaders, as well as large segments of their peoples, tended to regard their enemies as threats to their existence. Such beliefs blocked the path to negotiations and directed wars against an enemy's political system or its entire people. This trend was partly due as well to the enormous collective effort and sacrifice that mass mobilization demanded in industrial warfare. Limited war aims seemed incongruent with the exertions required.

A second dimension of total war pertains to the methods of war. It is difficult to argue that wars were more humane in premodern times. The conventions that were negotiated early in the twentieth century at The Hague

14 Quoted in McPherson, *Battle Cry*, 310.
15 Ibid., 558.
16 Förster, "Prussian Triangle," 133.

and in Geneva were thought to be necessary precisely because warfare had not historically observed international rules.[17] Nonetheless, belligerents in both world wars of the twentieth century disregarded even the conventions that they themselves had negotiated. German submarine warfare constituted a flagrant breach of international law. So did the aerial bombing, scorched-earth tactics, and the use (by the Japanese) of chemical and biological weapons in World War II. Some of the worst abuses befell prisoners of war. During World War I the treatment of POWs was generally consistent with internationally accepted rules, although prisoners from both sides were occasionally killed behind the front lines.[18] In World War II the maltreatment of POWs was far more extensive and brutal. The Germans murdered most of the Red Army soldiers who fell into their hands, and the Japanese often behaved in similar fashion. This phenomenon suggested the radicalization of the methods of war, and it extended to measures undertaken against partisans, whether real or imagined. The spectacle began with the German atrocities in Belgium 1914 and reached a climax in the *Partisanenbekämpfung* of the SS and Wehrmacht in occupied Soviet territory during World War II. One might well argue that the genocide of the European Jews in the same war was itself an aspect of the radicalization of warfare. The Nazi leadership itself regarded its campaign against the Jews in this light.

Signs of this radicalization could be seen during the American Civil War and the Franco-German War, albeit to less an extent. Aerial bombardment was not yet technologically feasible, but the shelling of Vicksburg, Strasbourg, and Paris suggested that it would have encountered few moral barriers. Sherman's march through the South and Sheridan's destruction of the Shenandoah Valley were like aerial bombardments by foot, although they usually spared the lives of civilians. In similar fashion, warfare against guerillas in the South and West during the American Civil War, like the German war against the *franc-tireurs*, foretold things to come. The treatment of POWs in the Civil War was often brutal, although the horrors of Andersonville were less the product of intent than incompetence.[19] POWs from both sides in this war were randomly murdered behind the lines, especially when black soldiers fell into the hands of Confederate units. In the Franco-German War, by contrast, POWs were as a rule treated better.[20]

17 Jost Dülffer, *Regeln gegen den Krieg? Die Haager Friedenskonferenzen 1899 und 1907 in der internationalen Politik* (Frankfurt am Main, 1981).

18 See Niall Ferguson, *The Pity of War* (London, 1998), 367–94.

19 Reid Mitchell, "'Our Prison System, Supposing We Had Any': The Confederate and Union Prison Systems," in Förster and Nagler, eds., *On the Road*, 565–86.

20 Manfred Botzenhart, "French Prisoners of War in Germany, 1870–71," in ibid., 587–95.

In several cases the radicalization of the methods of warfare corresponded to the radicalization of war aims. During the Civil War the destructive raids of Sheridan and Sherman were geared to the principle of unconditional surrender; they were calculated to bring the horrors of war directly to the enemy's civilian population. The German atrocities in Belgium in 1914 were likewise designed to force an enemy population into submission. So was Allied aerial bombing in World War II, and it, too, was an integral part of a strategy to force unconditional surrender.

Unrestricted submarine warfare and the use of poison gas were more complex, for they grew out of technological developments in the means of warfare. Between 1861 and 1945 the destructive power of weapons increased immensely. This era was marked at the one end by the rifle and at the other by the atomic bomb. The results of technology were ambiguous, however, for it was no foregone conclusion that technological development would result in the kind of massive, comprehensive conflicts that are invoked by the term *total war.*[21] If technological development be taken as the gauge of "modernity," total war, as Strachan has recently written, "need not be modern; a modern war need not be total."[22] Many observers argued persuasively at the end of the nineteenth century that more destructive weapons would in fact shorten wars. A classical case was Bismarck's insistence on shelling Paris in order to bring the Franco-German War to a rapid end, before it got out of control. Advocates of strategic airpower in the interwar period resorted to similar reasoning in order to justify their visions of war. The effect was nevertheless to lower the moral threshold to employing all available weapons against civilians as well as soldiers.

Another important dimension of total war was the creation of mass armies. In the American Civil War and Franco-German War, the belligerent powers put hundreds of thousands of soldiers into the field. In the two world wars, the contending armies counted in the tens of millions. All of these forces could be moved, equipped, and provisioned only by industrial means. Keeping mass armies under control and in fighting spirit was also an organizational achievement. The sheer size of these forces made it difficult to defeat them. In addition, the million-man armies enjoyed the passionate support of their societies, if only because families had fathers, sons, husbands, and other male relatives in the field. Defeating armies thus increasingly implied defeating the societies that supported them.

21 Strachan, "From Cabinet War to Total War"; and Dennis E. Showalter, "Mass Warfare and the Impact of Technology," both in Chickering and Förster, eds., *Great War, Total War.*

22 Strachan, "Essay and Reflection," 351.

Any analysis of total war must emphasize the mobilization of the belligerent societies. This phenomenon was not unique to the twentieth century. Stone-age groups, as well as the Germanic tribes that invaded Roman territory, appear to have practiced it. However, the larger and more complex societies grew, the more difficult became the effort to mobilize large portions of their human resources for war. In less-developed societies, mobilization was usually restricted by gender. Large-scale recruitment of women for war was rare. Young men under the command of elder men usually bore the brunt of the fighting, although male children were also often recruited, as was common during the Thirty Years War. Particularly during the eighteenth century in Europe and large parts of Asia, warfare became primarily a matter of professional soldiery, as states sought a monopoly of organized force. In these circumstances, it became common to distinguish between the armed forces and civilian society. Unless it was subjected to "collateral damage" or enemy raids from the fighting zones, civilian society was, as a rule, expected to supply and finance wars, not to fight them.

During the French Revolutionary Wars, however, the distinction between combatants and non-combatants broke down. In the words of Clausewitz, "Suddenly war again became the business of the people – a people of thirty millions, all of whom considered themselves to be citizens."[23] But the enthusiasm of the masses was apparently not sufficient; it had to be organized. Hence the Jacobin regime introduced conscription for males between 18 and 25. All other citizens were also called on to join the war effort. Married men were to produce weapons, women to produce clothes and tents, children were to make bandages, and the elderly were to assemble in public places to rally morale.[24] The idea of total mobilization of state and society for war was born. However, the history of Revolutionary and Napoleonic France thereafter demonstrated the practical difficulties of implementing this idea. Beyond popular resistance, the necessary institutions were difficult to establish and sustain, with respect either to the army or the economy.

These lessons were subsequently confirmed, as capitalist economies proved particularly difficult in principle to coordinate. For all his remarkable achievements, Gambetta learned as much when, in 1870–1, he tried to organize a *levée en masse* to fight the Germans after the defeat of the French

23 Carl von Clausewitz, *On War*, ed. Michael Howard and Peter Paret (Princeton, N.J., 1976), 592.
24 Albert Soboul, *Die Grosse Französische Revolution* (Frankfurt am Main, 1973), 294–5.

regular armies.[25] In the American Civil War the Confederacy attempted to mobilize all its resources for the war effort, as women were called on to play an essential role. The degree of mobilization in the Confederacy far exceeded that in the more populous and industrialized North, but even in the South, mobilization never approached the degree of thoroughness achieved later by belligerents in the wars of the twentieth century.[26]

In fact, even during these great wars, mobilization remained well within limits. The German authorities tried ruthlessly during World War I to mobilize society and economy behind the war effort, particularly after 1916. At the same time, the British government sought to extend its control in a similar direction, while in the United States the Wilson administration pursued a policy of state control that clashed in significant ways with American traditions. But full mobilization was never realized. In Germany the Hindenburg Program failed largely in its aims, and in fact undermined morale on the home front. With this lesson in mind, the Nazi regime hesitated to introduce full social and economic mobilization at home during World War II. Only in 1944–5, against a moral backdrop announced in Goebbels' famous "total war speech," did anything like full mobilization begin to take place. By then, however, Britain and the Soviet Union had already mobilized much more comprehensively.

Perhaps the most challenging and problematic aspect of total war is its suggestion of total control. Total mobilization in advanced societies implied the need for total organization. Resistance was to be crushed.[27] Civilian enthusiasm was to be sustained by propaganda. As the supply of volunteers diminished, the supply of military manpower had to be organized in conscription. Hence, total war implied centralized government control over virtually every phase of life. Such control has been impossible to achieve. The Jacobins tried to do so by means of terror, and they failed. During the American Civil War both sides used coercion as well as propaganda to rally their citizens. Censorship, arbitrary arrests, and conscription were all essential parts of the effort, but they had mixed results.[28] Institutional control of society was both more prominent and effective in the world wars.

25 Stéphane Audoin-Rouzeau, "French Public Opinion and the Emergence of Total War," in Förster and Nagler, eds., *On the Road*, 393–412.

26 Donna Rebecca D. King, "Women and War in the Confederacy," in ibid., 413–48; Stanley L. Engerman and J. Matthew Gallman, "The Civil War Economy: A Modern View," in ibid., 217–48.

27 See Francis L. Carsten, *War Against War: British and German Radical Movements in the First World War* (London 1992).

28 See Mark E. Neely Jr., *The Fate of Liberty: Abraham Lincoln and Civil Liberties* (New York 1991); Jörg Nagler, "The Home Front in the American Civil War," in Förster and Nagler, eds., *On the Road*, 329–56; Phillip S. Paludan, "'The Better Angels of our Nature': Lincoln, Propaganda, and Public Opinion in the North During the Civil War," in ibid., 357–76.

Conscription became the rule, even in Britain after 1916. Censorship and propaganda were staples of these wars. During World War II, terror became standard practice in Nazi Germany and the Soviet Union. Attempts to control the economy were also part of this story. Ludendorff's "war socialism" provided an early model, which was emulated to a degree in Albert Speer's economy of total war. The Soviet Union established a command economy in the 1930s, and the results looked like an attempt to institutionalize a total-war economy in time of peace. In this respect at least, the transition to war was comparatively smooth in the Soviet Union.

One is tempted to see in these developments an inherent paradox of total war. The attempt to establish total control has encouraged total chaos. The failure of Ludendorff's policy ultimately led to Germany's collapse in 1918; and it followed a more fundamental breakdown of state and society in Russia the year before. Much of the rubble with which the Soviet Union and the two Germanies had to contend after 1945 was arguably the product of measures undertaken by the red and brown dictatorships during the war.

Each of these dimensions of total war has its own history, although they are interconnected in important ways. Perhaps the most central aspect has been the erosion of the distinction between the military and civilian society. The growing, deliberate implication of civilians in war constituted in this light the principal feature of the age of total war. Without the direct support of civilian society, the massive industrial warfare that was the hallmark of this period would have been inconceivable. But the same truth turned civilians into targets of military violence. The true symbols of total war were burning villages and cities and the other countless civilian casualties of calculated military violence. The bloody road to total war led from the American South through Strasbourg and Paris, Belgium, Guernica, and Nanking, through Lidice, Oradour, and countless Greek, Serbian, and Soviet villages, to Babi Yar, Auschwitz, Dresden, and Hiroshima. The plight of civilians in modern war, one might conclude, is the central theme in the age of total war.

This book examines the period between World War I and World War II. It resembles the second volume in the series insofar as it focuses on an interlude between major wars, when military experts and popular writers alike attempted to anticipate the next war in light of the last. The second volume documented the near-complete failure of these observers to draw accurate lessons from the past or to anticipate the operational impact of social and industrial change at the end of the nineteenth century. The conclusions of this volume are more tentative in this regard; and they must remain so until a final volume in the series can turn to World War II.

The theme of this volume differs from that of the second in several other respects. In the first place, the interval between the major wars was shorter. The Paris peace settlement bequeathed a legacy of bitterness and international instability, which lent an aura of urgency to military planning from almost the moment the treaties were signed. In addition, the war that ended in 1918 set a powerful agenda for military planners in all the former belligerent countries, winners as well as losers. The shadow of the last war loomed large over thinking about the next one. The prospects were as frightening as they were general that the Great War had established basic patterns that no future European conflict could escape, that the next war would require the wholesale mobilization of economies and societies to feed the insatiable demands of land armies that could not defeat one another in battle. In some quarters, this conclusion led to political resignation. It suggested that the demographic and social costs of another war were too high to justify fighting. In other quarters, particularly in the defeated countries, the same conclusion bred invention and receptivity to military reform, as it suggested that the means had to be found to fight a different kind of war. In the eyes of some planners, the Great War appeared itself to offer these means, above all in the proper operational exploitation of armor and air power.[29] The discourse on war in the 1920s and 1930s was governed by these imperatives. They surfaced in prolonged debates in both the military and civilian literature over directions of technological development, terms of military service, and the organization and training of armed forces.

One other theme – an additional shadow of the Great War – figured centrally in these debates, and it occupies a privileged place in this volume. The term *total war* gestated during the interwar period, the child of intensive discussions about the challenges, consequences, and implications – both political and military – of civilian mobilization for war. This historical fact emphasizes the ideological freight that attached to the concept of total war from its birth, and it recommends still greater caution in employing this term as a tool of historical analysis.[30] As a spate of memoirs from military and political leaders made clear in the 1920s and 1930s, its immediate point of reference was the Great War. Ludendorff and Lloyd George could agree that the outcome of the conflict had reflected ultimately the superior ability of the allies to exploit human and material resources, and that the Allies' success had had as much to do with moral determination and organizational skill as with the extent of these resources.

29 See Williamson Murray and Allan R. Millett, eds., *Military Innovation in the Interwar Period* (Cambridge, 1996).

30 Fabio Crivellari, "Der Wille zum Totalen Krieg," Arbeitskreis Militärgeschichte, *Newsletter* 12 (2000): 10–14.

Agreement reigned further that the outcome of the next war would likewise depend on the effective moral and material organization of the home front. The public debates about strategic air power only underlined this truth, as they portrayed home fronts as at once the most crucial and the most vulnerable facet of any state's capacity to make war. So central was home-front mobilization in discussions of future war that it emerged as the underpinning of theories of state in the interwar period. In the new Soviet Union, War Communism was the product of civil war, but it owed inspiration to the Hindenburg Plan in Germany, and its imprint was basic in the institutional development of the new Soviet state after the conclusion of the Civil War.[31] In Italy, a similar experiment took place in the name of Fascism; here, too, it featured an attempt in peacetime to refashion politics and society to the organizational requirements of war. The propagandists of the Italian model included the neo-Hegelian scholar Giovanni Gentile, who invoked the word "totalitarian" to describe the Fascist experiment.[32] Even as Mussolini deployed it in the struggle to consolidate the new regime, the idea of "totalitarian" rule attracted the interest of political theorists elsewhere. In Germany, another group of neo-Hegelians around the jurist Carl Schmitt fanned the fierce ideological struggles of the Weimar era, as they laid claim to the word "total" and cast the lessons of mobilization during the Great War within the authoritarian theoretical framework of a "total state." From here, the conceptual advance of the German right toward a theory of total war was brief.[33]

A fifth and final volume in this series will address the question whether Nazi Germany and the other participants in World War II put this theory into practice – and whether this conflict offers in the end a paradigmatic instance of total war. The chapters in this book explore the conceptual and practical preparations for the second great war of the twentieth century. The emphasis falls on two dimensions of these preparations. The first is the enormous influence of the Great War in shaping deliberations about the next war. The second is the question whether those who planned the next war envisaged anything like World War II. The concept of total war provides an analytical bridge between these two themes. Employing the concept in this capacity hardly evades the methodological difficulties that have troubled the earlier volumes in the series; but it can claim some solid justification, insofar as the contemporary discourse on war began itself to feature the term

31 Olando Figes, *A People's Tragedy: The Russian Revolution, 1891–1924* (New York, 1996), 613; see also the chapter by Heinz Heinrich Nolte in this volume.

32 See Abbot Gleason, *Totalitarianism: The Inner History of the Cold War* (New York 1995), 13–50.

33 See Hans-Ulrich Wehler, "'Absoluter' und 'totaler' Krieg: Von Clausewitz zu Ludendorff," *Politische Vierteljahresschrift* 19 (1969): 220–48; see also Roger Chickering's chapter in this volume.

total war both in its analysis of the last Great War and its projections about the next.

The first group of chapters provides general reflections on the problems of war, politics, and international relations in the interwar period. Gerhard Weinberg emphasizes that the devastation wrought by the Great War impaired the ability of the Western powers to respond to the threat of another even more destructive conflict, even as the leaders of Japan, Italy, and Germany actively prepared for it. Strachan examines military doctrines of the interwar period. He emphasizes the general search for alternatives to mass armies of foot soldiers, whose immobility had turned the Great War into an operational nightmare. In these circumstances, the advocates of armor, air power, and elite, professional armies offered a credible vision of more mobile warfare in the future. However, the key to the next war, Strachan suggests, lay ultimately in efforts to marry these new formations to the military institutions – mass infantry armies and effective home-front mobilization – that had dominated the Great War. Dennis Showalter's broad survey of "strategic cultures" in interwar Europe also addresses the attempts of military planners to devise a more palatable way to wage war in the future. He argues that these cultures were based on five strategic concepts, which he identifies as "paralysis," "management," "mass," "shock," and "compensation." His chapter then charts the differential appeal of these paradigms in European armed forces during the interwar period. While all these concepts were designed to keep the next war within limits, each in fact, Showalter concludes, "interacted with the other four, and combined in a total war out of civilization's worst nightmares."

The next section addresses several ways in which the shadow of the Great War colored the contexts in which thinking about warfare took place, as the conflict's lingering effects unsettled European politics and preoccupied leading thinkers. Hartmut Lehmann investigates the career of the Protestant theologian Paul Tillich, whose experience of the Great War set an intellectual agenda that led first to religious socialism and pacifism. This was a difficult position for a German theologian to hold even in the Weimar era, and the Nazi seizure of power forced him into American exile. Here he continued to ponder the problem of war, but as Lehmann shows, he retreated from his earlier utopian views to embrace the responsible use of force within an effective international order. James Diehl's chapter documents the enduring impact of the Great War in another sphere. The militarization of domestic politics in several European countries, particularly in Germany, can be traced directly to the war, not the least because those who drove this process were in most cases veterans. Diehl writes of politics in a "new, martial key," for "domestic politics became a continuation of war by other means." Deborah Cohen writes of another category of veterans, whose plight represented one of the most painful agendas that the Great War bequeathed. In a comparative analysis of policies for supporting disabled veterans in Great Britain and Germany, she arrives at a paradoxical conclusion. German policies, which provided generous support through a centralized public regime, created far more disaffection among their beneficiaries than did British policies, which were miserably funded and relied primarily on volunteerism and private philanthropy. That battered bodies did not alone define the disabled of the Great War is abundantly clear in the chapter by Edgar Jones and Simon Wessely. They note that some 65,000 British veterans were awarded pensions for neurasthenia and related conditions. The meager efforts of the Ministry of Pensions to deal with this challenge matched the failure of British psychiatrists and, to a lesser degree, neurologists to comprehend the intellectual and diagnostic implications of the phenomenon. Only the next total war, write Jones and Wessely, brought an effort to repair the problem, principally because the psychological traumas of World War II affected civilian participants to a much greater extent than they had in 1914–18.

The next section of chapters explores several attempts to forecast the next war in light of the last. Roger Chickering seeks to situate Erich Ludendorff's famous book on total war in the context of the author's troubled intellectual and political biography after the German defeat in 1918. Thomas Rohkrämer then analyzes the cloudy vicissitudes that Ernst Jünger's thinking about technology and war underwent before it arrived at a point not far from Ludendorff's. The other three chapters in this group survey the writings of military writers in Britain, France, Germany, and the United States, as these professionals sought to assimilate the lessons of the last war in anticipation of the next one. Timo Baumann and Daniel Segesser analyze the British and French cases. They document a lively debate in both lands, which resulted in agreement that any future war would be a long ordeal and require the thoroughgoing mobilization of national resources. Baumann and Segesser also suggest, however, that the French and British military writers entertained different visions of the operational specifics of such a conflict – differences that were aggravated by the inability of the separate services in either country to agree about a common scenario. While the French anticipated a war in which a mass army would again bear the principal burden, the emphasis in the British literature fell on the strategic role of the air force. Markus Pöhlmann examines the German official history of the Great War. He looks carefully at the political pressures that shaped the work, but he argues that a close reading of the entire opus reveals that it was by no means confined to operational history. Instead, he writes, it contained many "glimpses of total war," for its authors were sensitive to the global dimensions of the conflict and the broad impact of industrial war on the home front. Finally, Bernd Greiner examines military periodicals in the United States, particularly the *Infantry Journal*. Like Baumann and Segesser, he documents a vigorous controversy over the lessons to be drawn from the Great War. In the United States, however, the discussion was dominated throughout by anxieties about the military fitness of soldiers drawn from a society, like the United States', with a deep suspicion of military institutions and values. In the 1930s, Greiner suggests, these anxieties acquired broader relevance, as American military writers began to envisage a "total" war that would extend the ordeal of combat to civilian society itself.

The final segment of the volume investigates several attempts during the 1930s to institutionalize or otherwise to put new "total" visions of warfare into practice. Benedikt Stuchtey's chapter examines the efforts of military and political leaders in the British Commonwealth to plan effectively for a global conflict. He argues that it was one thing to celebrate the rhetoric of imperial cooperation and common loyalties, but quite another to translate these sentiments into effective military force against the challenges posed simultaneously by Germany, Italy, and Japan. Wilhelm Deist's chapter explores the institutional problems, not to say contradictions, that arose when the German leadership began to plan for a war that Ludendorff or Jünger might recognize. Deist argues that the German military could never define a "strategic vision" of such a conflict, as he lays bare the interservice rivalries, competing military and economic pressures, and the conflicting political goals that the military and civilian leadership brought to the planning process. Klaus Maier then turns to the performance of the German Condor Legion in the Spanish Civil War. He looks carefully at the circumstances in which the Germans decided to employ air power systematically against civilian targets, most notably in Guernica in April 1937. In his investigation of Soviet agricultural collectivization, Hans-Heinrich Nolte then argues that the Soviet experience offered a dramatic precedent for the waging of warfare against a large group of civilians who had been defined as enemies. In this case, however, the Soviet government conducted "total social war" against a select category of its own people, the *kulachestvo*, as the distinction between military and civilian affairs lost all meaning. Giulia Brogini Künzi shows that these distinctions also lost meaning in the war that Fascist Italy undertook in East Africa in 1935–6. Despite the vast disparities of force that the two sides could deploy, she documents a number of features of the

Italo-Ethiopian War that did seem to portend the great war of the next decade. Among these were the Italians' calculated use of massive military violence (including chemical weapons) against civilians, their invocation of racist stereotypes to justify this kind of warfare, and their careful managing of the war's representation in the media. Louise Young's chapter paints a similar picture of war's pervasive cultural consequences in Asia. Under the rubric of "total empire," she analyzes the impact of Japan's war in China on the metropolitan culture and economy. The repercussions of colonial conquest, she argues, entailed the mobilization of the home front and marked in significant ways the onset of total war years before Pearl Harbor.

Together, the chapters in this book make clear the extent to which planning for war in the 1920s and 1930s took place in the twin "shadows of total war." The Great War everywhere cast its imprint on thinking about the next war. Consensus thus reigned in most quarters that the next war would likewise require the wholesale mobilization of the home front, the subjection of civilians to military violence, and the remorseless prosecution of war until the full defeat of the enemy. The character of World War I had surprised those who had planned for it. As the final installment in the series will demonstrate, this proposition was less true of World War II.

PART ONE

Reflections on the Interwar Period

1

The Politics of War and Peace in the 1920s and 1930s

GERHARD L. WEINBERG

Two factors must be kept in mind at all times when the 1920s and 1930s are under review: the dominating memory of the "Great War" – as what we call World War I had come to be called – and the reality of continued conflict in some portions of the world. In Europe, where most of the fighting had taken place, there was hardly a family without a member who had been killed or wounded in the recent conflict; those individuals were now either conspicuously missing from the family circle or were carrying the physical scars of the fighting. And the family members who had been at the front and survived were generally careful to keep their most awful experiences to themselves; what was the point of upsetting loved ones with accounts of terrors they could neither understand nor alter? The general nature of the fighting and its horrors for participants were well enough known and needed no reciting.

No one anywhere needed to be told that it had all been terrible. Photography was sufficiently advanced by this time to enable anyone interested to obtain some appreciation of the devastation – if they had not seen it in person. Furthermore, certain new developments in the conduct of warfare had aroused horror at the time, and these continued to haunt the memory of the past and reinforce fears for the future. The introduction of poison gas and of the bombing from the air of towns far distant from the actual fighting, both originally German contributions to warfare, were feared as signs of ever more horrible features of fighting if it ever took place again.

The armistice of November 1918, however much commemorated, had not, however, brought peace to all portions of the globe. Civil war and attendant upheavals characterized the situation in Russia, China, and Ireland. People who were not directly affected by these conflicts could certainly hear about them on the radio, read about them in the newspapers, or, perhaps most frequently, see images in the newsreels that now increasingly accompanied feature films in the movie theaters.

Adding to the dangers people saw about them were aspects of a whole host of new countries that had emerged in Europe in the immediate aftermath of the war. Most of them were internally unstable and simultaneously often dissatisfied about their new borders; obviously they would need years to develop even moderately stable forms. Outside Europe, the colonial empires had begun to dissolve. The emergence of the British dominions as independent actors on the international scene was the politically most obvious harbinger of a world far different from the European-dominated globe before 1914. And if people took the trouble to think back to the fighting on the western front, they would come to realize that both Britain and France had been obliged to draw on their respective colonial empires for soldiers to fight in Europe as opposed to the prior pattern of sending some of their own soldiers from the home country to defend colonial possessions and perhaps add to them.

Although often ignored, it can be argued that the most fateful development of the immediate postwar years in terms of its impact on the maintenance of the peace that had just been constructed was the refusal of two of its major authors to abide by the very provisions they had themselves insisted on including in it. The United States and Great Britain had pressured the French delegation at the peace conference into accepting guarantee treaties in place of a separation of the German territory on the left bank of the Rhine from Germany as a shield against any possible future German aggression. Having received this concession from the French, they had quickly gone back on their part of the bargain: the United States had refused to ratify such a guarantee treaty, and the British had utilized the American refusal to justify a similar procedure of their own. An exhausted France was thus left alone to uphold a settlement that did not include the safety provision the French delegation had thought essential; that under these circumstances French governments shifted uneasily between complaisance and defiance in subsequent years should hardly have surprised – as it did – those countries that were responsible for creating the situation in the first place.

There is an aspect of the interrelationship of the development of total war and the endless and agitated interwar discussion of the so-called war guilt issue that requires our attention. Precisely because no one could conceive of the possibility that anyone in any country had actually wanted what had happened to take place, there was both furious debate about who was responsible for causing the war and an increasing tendency toward the concept that no one had wanted it. Many came to argue, and some came to believe, that nations had slithered into it the way an individual might slip on a wet pavement and fall into the gutter.[1] The converse of this thought was that if sufficient care were taken, such an accident caused by miscalculation or misunderstanding could be prevented in the future.

In this connection, the letter sent by British Prime Minister Neville Chamberlain to German Chancellor Adolf Hitler as soon as he heard of the Nazi-Soviet Pact of August 23, 1939, is worth quoting:

> It has been alleged that, if His Majesty's Government had made their position more clear in 1914, the great catastrophe would have been avoided. Whether or not there is any force in that allegation, His Majesty's Government are resolved that on this occasion there shall be no such tragic misunderstanding.
>
> If the case should arise, they are resolved, and prepared, to employ without delay all the forces at their command, and it is impossible to foresee the end of hostilities once engaged. It would be a dangerous illusion to think that, if war once starts, it will come to an early end even if a success on any one of the several fronts on which it will be engaged should have been secured.[2]

Chamberlain thus tried to make sure that the Germans miscalculate neither the effect of an attack on Poland nor a quick victory on that front.

Although the memory of the war made it inconceivable to most that anyone could possibly deliberately start another one, it must be noted that during the 1920s there was a substantial inclination to move into precisely that direction in two countries: Italy and Japan. In both there were elements arguing for a continuation of pre-1914 expansionist policies; in both cases the pursuit of traditional imperialist objectives looked attractive to some. Since whatever could be grabbed from Germany and Austria-Hungary had already been taken, this would mean a reversal of fronts: from now on one could end the independence of the few states left so in Africa and Southeast Asia, namely Abyssinia and Siam, as Ethiopia and Thailand were then called; try to impose one's power on other independent countries, namely those of Southeast Europe and China; or attempt to steal the colonial possessions of one's allies in the preceding war.

In the case of both countries, the new wars into which they threw themselves, that against Abyssinia by Italy and that against China by Japan, should be seen and can only be understood as continuations of pre-1914

1 For a study quite explicitly directed against this thesis, see Fritz Fischer, *Juli 1914: Wir sind nicht hineingeschlittert; das Staatsgeheimnis um die Riezler-Tagebücher, eine Streitschrift* (Reinbeck bei Hamburg, 1983). For a recent survey of the relevant literature, see John W. Langdon, *July 1914: The Long Debate, 1918–1990* (New York, 1991).

2 Chamberlain to Hitler, Aug. 22, 1939, in *Documents on British Foreign Policy, 1919–1939*, 3d ser., vol. 7 (London, 1954), no. 145. It is most likely that Chamberlain's reference to a continuation of hostilities, even if Germany quickly defeated Poland, had a major impact on the refusal of Italy to join Germany in 1939.

expansionist policies, but in both cases with the utilization of at least some of the new weapons developed in large part during the war. Both Japan and Italy relied heavily on terrorizing enemy populations by attacks from the air, both employed poison gas, and Japan killed thousands of Chinese and other victims in the process of developing a variety of bacteriological weapons. It is of great importance for an understanding of the inability of the two countries to work effectively with Germany in World War II that neither ever understood that they had not only reversed alliances but had now allied themselves with a state that had fundamentally different objectives and was fighting a basically new kind of war.

In the 1920s the government of Germany for most of the time perceived diplomacy as a continuation of war by other means. Determined to reverse the verdict of 1918, the emphasis was on the dissolution of the system created by the treaties of 1919 and the restoration of Germany to its prewar status. Practically no one in leadership positions in the country recognized that the peace settlement had left Germany in a relatively stronger position than the one that it had occupied before the war.[3] Neither the acceptance into the League of Nations with a permanent seat on the Council – a position Germany has not secured more than fifty years after World War II – nor the early end of military inspection and of military occupation were ever understood for what they actually represented. Defeat in war had come in a manner few inside the country could accept, and defeat, a despised and misunderstood peace treaty, and the mess inherited by the inexperienced leaders of the new republic were all blamed on the latter rather than on those responsible for the war, the defeat, and the constitutional system that had barred political parties and their leaders from the experience and responsibilities of power. In the competition for leadership in Germany among those who hoped to go beyond any signs of acceptance of the postwar situation to an entirely new position for Germany, the advocate of the most extreme line was called to lead the country in 1933.

Adolf Hitler had seen directly and personally what war was actually like, especially for those who participated at the front in combat themselves. It was in this context that he derided those of his rivals for power who wanted to return to the borders of 1914, a return that would be possible only if Germany went to war for them. Here was a clear sign of their utter stupidity: they were prepared to conduct wars for aims that, given the cost of modern wars in lives, were guaranteed to be hopelessly inadequate since they would merely return Germany to the situation of 1914 when she had been unable to feed her population from her own soil. Referring to them as mere

3 See Gerhard L. Weinberg, *Germany, Hitler, and World War II* (New York, 1995), chap. 1.

Grenzpolitiker, border politicians, he designated himself as a *Raumpolitiker*, a politician of space. He would conquer vast spaces for German settlement; these in turn would enable Germans to raise children and control resources for further conquests, until Germany conquered the globe and that globe was inhabited or controlled exclusively by Germans. Only for *such* wars could the sacrifices modern war required be justified; and he assured his listeners in the 1920s that he would be willing to lead them to shed their blood in that type of conflict.[4]

It is not possible to understand what happened after 1933 unless one considers the Nazi revolution as a racial or demographic revolution with worldwide aims from its very beginnings and pays close attention to its aims even when these were not reached. A revolution halted in its tracks cannot be comprehended without attention to where those tracks were supposed to go in the eyes of those in charge: individuals who not surprisingly expected success, not failure, in their efforts, and who attuned their policies and actions as far as possible to the attainment of their goals. The racial measures inside Germany which were inaugurated in 1933 – marriage loans to encourage lots of the "right" kind of children and compulsory sterilization of those deemed likely to have the "wrong" kind of children, to mention only two – must be seen in this context.

Rearmament measures that were also begun in 1933 pointed in the direction of new wars of the sort Hitler considered appropriate, with the focus on design and production of weapons systems attuned to the anticipated needs of the wars that were intended. The simplest way to see this is in the orders for armaments. Tanks were ordered for the wars against the Western Powers; it is too often forgotten that the conquest of the USSR was expected to be so easy that the first tanks for war in the East were ordered *after* the invasion of the Soviet Union. The single-engine dive bomber was ordered with France in mind; the two-engine dive bomber was designed for service against England; and when these had been developed and ordered into production, the long-range intercontinental bombers, sometimes called "America bombers," sometimes referred to as "New York bombers," were ordered in 1937.[5] Naval preparations followed a similar trajectory. Most of the warships ordered completed in 1933 and 1934 could be seen as rounding out a small contingency fleet. The first major warships to fight England were ordered in 1935 in violation of the Anglo-German Naval Agreement signed that year and were therefore expected to surprise the British once completed and when they appeared in action. The super-battleships for war

4 Ibid., chap. 3.
5 Jochen Thies, *Architekt der Weltherrschaft: Die "Endziele" Hitlers* (Düsseldorf, 1976), 136ff.

with the United States were ordered designed in 1937, with construction begun in early 1939.[6]

Although we know today that the Germans did not employ poison gases during World War II, this had not been the intent. Not only gases of the kinds employed in the "Great War" were being stockpiled after trials in the Soviet Union with the cooperation of that country in the 1920s, but a series of nerve gases was also developed in the 1930s.[7] The hope and expectation was that these gases would provide Germany with a massive advantage in the war against the Western Powers. The original work on long-range rockets, the project that eventuated into the A-4 or V-2 ballistic missile, was actually designed for the accurate delivery of poison gas.[8] It all turned out differently from what the Germans anticipated during their preparations for the wars they expected to fight as they worked on them during the 1930s, but it is the direction and nature of those preparations that must be considered. They expected to fight wars with some weapons developed further from those employed in the most recent conflict together with some radically new ones. Certainly the direction in which their preparations pointed was one in which war would surely be even more destructive than recent experience might have led anyone else to expect.

Furthermore, Hitler had repeatedly explained in his writings and speeches that conquered peoples were to be expelled or exterminated, not Germanized. One could not alter the inferior racial characteristics of non-Germans by insisting they learn the German language; education would simply make them more dangerous, not more German. The expansion of Germany, therefore, was to take a form in many ways different from that of prior wars in which conquered provinces or colonies might see substantial destruction and human losses, primarily during the course of the fighting, but afterward, the prior population was expected to be controlled, not replaced. Why did so few understand or expect this at the time, and why are so few willing to recognize reality even today?

Two factors may explain the failure of contemporaries to recognize and the refusal of so many in subsequent years to understand the worldwide aims of the Nazi government. In the first place, as already mentioned, the idea that

6 Ibid., 128ff.; Jost Dülffer, *Weimar, Hitler und die Marine: Reichspolitik und Flottenbau 1920 bis 1939* (Düsseldorf, 1973). There is some evidence that the construction of the *Panzerkreuzer*, the so-called pocket battleships, was pushed by the navy with war against Britain in mind – these were to be commerce raiders on the open oceans.

7 Rolf-Dieter Müller, "Die deutschen Gaskriegsvorbereitungen 1919–1945: Mit Giftgas zur Weltmacht," *Militärgeschichtliche Mitteilungen* 21, no. 1 (1980): 25–54.

8 Michael J. Neufeld, *The Rocket and the Reich: Peenemünde and the Coming of the Ballistic Missile Era* (New York, 1995), chap. 1.

anyone could, after the experience of the Great War, seriously contemplate the deliberate initiation of another vast conflict looked so preposterous that it was simply not taken into consideration as a plausible possibility. The efforts to appease Germany in the 1930s can only be understood in the context of an assumption that some sort of European settlement that involved peaceful adjustments – if necessary with colonial concessions in Africa thrown in – was a real possibility and would in any case be preferable to another war that was certain to be even more costly and destructive than the last one. The details of such a settlement replacing that of 1919 might be good, bad, or mediocre; but it would still be less dangerous for those involved than another major war.

The second element of incomprehension then and now is the general cynicism which keeps people from considering the possibility that political leaders for the most part believe what they say and actually intend what they propose. It was assumed then – and is frequently assumed now – that political leaders neither believe nor intend what they say, or at least those things they say that seem preposterous. Here I should insert a piece of evidence from personal experience. Almost every time I refer to a document of 1927 describing Hitler's aims as being worldwide, a copy editor asks whether this is not an error for 1937. Each time I have to explain that the document is indeed dated 1927 and that the original may be found in the National Archives.[9] People project their own views onto others and forget that others act on *their* assumptions and beliefs, not on those held by later observers or by contemporaries with differing perceptions.

Ironically, Hitler appears to have understood this common misperception. He quite deliberately counted on the reluctance of others to take his moves toward war seriously. Other powers would shrink from hostilities just as long as possible, thereby providing him with time for rearmament initially and concessions extorted by threats thereafter. But there were self-imposed limits on this process. One such limit was personal: Hitler did not expect to live long and repeatedly made explicit his preference for starting war at a younger and more vigorous age than at a later time. The earliest such reference with mention of a specific age that can be found in contemporary records dates from 1938, when he referred to preferring war at age 49 than when older.[10]

9 Weinberg, *Germany, Hitler, and World War II*, chap. 2, contains the full text of this document.

10 The key document on this is the telegram of Charles Carbon, the French ambassador to London, on a conversation with British Foreign Secretary Lord Halifax on Sept. 17, 1938, in *Documents diplomatiques français 1932–1939*, 2d ser., vol. 11 (Paris, 1977), no. 188. Although Lord Halifax had not been present at the Chamberlain-Hitler meeting, and although none of the reports on Chamberlain's other discussions of the meeting contains a reference to Hitler's mentioning his age,

The 1938 situation will be examined further subsequently, but there is the other time factor, that inherent in the German armaments program. It was clear to Hitler that after an interval of a few years, Germany's prospective enemies were likely to react by beginning to rearm themselves. Then their broader resource base would enable them to overtake Germany – and with more modern weapons since they would have standardized their production models later than Germany. Hitler argued that Germany would, therefore, have to utilize its head start in armaments before too long lest it lose that advantage. In 1937, Hitler placed that final time limit into the years 1943–5.[11] From these perspectives, it may be easier to understand why Hitler came to see the Munich agreement of 1938 as the biggest mistake of his career, regretted having drawn back from war in 1938, and made certain that there would be no repetition of such a development in 1939; it was peace, not war, that he feared.[12]

There was, it should be noted, one further misconception about Germany's movement toward war. Hitler himself and most of those in his government actually believed the stab-in-the-back legend. Because they believed that Germany's home front had collapsed under the strains of war, strains that internal enemies had taken advantage of, they were very hesitant about imposing excessively heavy burdens on the German home front both before and during World War II. Not only ideological preconceptions about the proper role of women but a general reluctance to risk a collapse of morale at home restrained the German government from imposing total mobilization on economy and people until the later stages of World War II.

Germany's World War II enemies, on the other hand, assumed that the supposedly efficient, thorough, and well-organized Germans had fully mobilized their human and material resources for war already in the 1930s. From this they would draw the equally erroneous conclusion that the German war economy was severely strained in the first years of World War II and could be badly damaged by blockade and bombing. They were therefore greatly surprised by the lack of effect from the bombing and blockade in the early stages of World War II and were astonished to see the increases in production of which the Third Reich proved capable once the turning tide at the fronts suggested to those in charge of Germany that greater effort and a higher level of sacrifices would be necessary after all.

this is assuredly not the sort of thing either Chamberlain or Lord Halifax would have fabricated. The most likely explanation is that Chamberlain mentioned it to Lord Halifax – who was one of his few close friends – in a personal conversation along the lines: "Edward, you will not believe what that man said to me."

11 This was one of the main themes of the so-called Hossbach Conference; see Gerhard L. Weinberg, *The Foreign Policy of Hitler's Germany: Starting World War II, 1937–1939* (Amherst, N.Y., 1993), 37.

12 Ibid., chaps. 12–14.

What this meant in practice was that the Allies of World War II moved toward a more complete mobilization of their resources earlier than Germany once they had concluded that there was no alternative to fighting. Until that time, however, their inclination had been in the opposite direction. They had substantially reduced their military forces during the 1920s, and under the impact of the world depression, both Great Britain and the United States initially reduced their military expenditures. By the early 1930s, both had brought their armies down approximately to the size prescribed for Germany by the Treaty of Versailles. Rearmament began slowly and haltingly in both countries. The British looked back in horror at the experience of committing large land forces to the continent in the Great War and were quite determined not to do so again. They would instead build up an air force, both to defend against any new and expanded version of the raids they had suffered the last time and to bring such attacks home to the Germans. Those on the British political Left opposed all such measures. It is too often forgotten that in the last election in Britain before World War II, that of 1935, Chamberlain was attacked as a warmonger. It is from that perspective that all members of Parliament from the Labour and Liberal Parties voted against the first peacetime conscription in British history when Chamberlain reversed course and called for the creation of a substantial army in May of 1939.

In France, the later impact of the world depression brought fiscal constraints to the fore somewhat after the analogous situation in Britain and the United States, but then there was a far more substantial rearmament effort than has generally been recognized.[13] The Soviet Union was, in the 1920s and 1930s, building the industrial basis for a modern military structure; but in the later 1930s Joseph Stalin was eviscerating the Red Army, Navy, and Air Force by systematic purges.[14] From the perspective of the Germans, this only reinforced their concept of a state consisting of racial inferiors ruled by incompetents. In the eyes of the Western Powers, bolshevism was seen as an internal menace, not an external threat.

If people in Britain thought that the commitment of a large army to the continent had been a mistake of the Great War that should not be repeated, the public in the United States became increasingly convinced in the 1920s and 1930s that their very entrance into the war had been an error. As they saw increasing dangers of conflict in Europe and East Asia in the 1930s, their reaction for the most part was to try to devise means by which a repetition

13 The most recent treatment is Eugenia C. Kiesling, *Arming Against Hitler: France and the Limits of Military Planning* (Lawrence, Kans., 1996). For further detail, see Ernest R. May, *Strange Victory: Hitler's Conquest of France* (New York, 2000).

14 A fine analysis is given in David M. Glantz, *Stumbling Colossus: The Red Army on the Eve of World War* (Lawrence, Kans., 1998).

of the supposed mistake of 1917 could be avoided. Not only would they not participate again; they would try to insulate themselves by a series of neutrality laws designed to prevent a repetition of those developments that had, in their eyes, caused the country to enter the preceding war. It is entirely possible that if these laws had been in effect in 1914–17, they would indeed have had that result; the problem of course was that one cannot stay out of a war one has already been in. The challenge of the 1930s was fundamentally different, but most Americans then, and very many still today, failed to see that.

Unable to understand then, as many cannot understand now, that the converse of belief in the stab-in-the-back was that the military role of the United States in making it possible for the Allies to hold in the West and move toward victory in 1918 then became a legend, Americans simply found it impossible to grasp that war with the United States was a central part of Hitler's outlook from the 1920s on. There could be, in other words, no sense for the United States to plan for a contingency that most of its people thought impossible. That the Germans would act on *their* beliefs, not on the beliefs of Americans, seemed inconceivable then; and as the repeated references to the German declaration of war on the United States in December 1941 as an incomprehensible act show, is hard for Americans to understand now.

From the German perspective, of course, a conquest of the globe necessarily implied war with the United States. Americans could not be expected to surrender their independence just because the Germans were so good looking. And since America's military role the last time was believed negligible, such a war was not expected to be particularly difficult; it was just that the right weapons systems had to be ordered. That process had been initiated in 1937, as mentioned above, while the vast quantities of oil needed to fuel those planes and ships were expected to become available to Germany as a result of the rapid and easy conquest of the Soviet Union between the defeat of the British and French and the war against the United States. That in this context of assumptions – crazy but widely shared by the authorities in Berlin – there should be *less* criticism of going to war with the United States and fewer warnings against such a step from those in the German military and political leadership than against any other war measure of Hitler has been, but really should not be, difficult to comprehend.[15]

It was under these circumstances, and in view of the widely held American misconceptions, that only the growing danger at the end of the 1930s began to reverse the trend toward disarmament in the United States.

15 Weinberg, *Germany, Hitler, and World War II*, chap. 15.

In 1937 there was the initiation of a naval construction program; at the end of 1938 President Franklin Roosevelt ordered a substantial air force buildup; and in 1940, under the impact of the German victory in the West, the United States initiated the raising of a large army. Once the attack by the Japanese followed by the German and Italian declarations of war on the United States had forced the country into hostilities, however, the public shifted its perceptions dramatically. Unlike Germany, but much more like Great Britain and the Soviet Union, the United States moved in the direction of a total war effort relatively quickly. It can certainly be argued that the war did not reach into the lives of its citizens to the extent true for the two other major Allies, but this was more the result of available resources and the minimal impacts of direct Axis attacks than of any reluctance in the government or the population at large to harness people and funds to the needs of war. The way in which the United States was precipitated into the conflict created an atmosphere in the country that was conducive to both the most extreme measures of mobilization and to an almost unlimited willingness to employ the weapons that would pour forth from the "arsenal of democracy."

The assumption of many in the interwar years that any new war was likely to be terrible was based on a fundamentally sound understanding of what had happened in the Great War. The evidence of experience showed that the social mechanics of the modern state enabled it to draw out of societies at war vast human and material resources and to throw them into all-consuming battle. The technological developments of the late nineteenth century and the innovations of the last prewar years had made war more destructive in a physical sense, and the further enhancements of weapons technology during the conflict as well as the new weapons introduced during hostilities had only accelerated the process.

There had been, on the other hand – and in part precisely because of the experience of 1914–18 – some substantial attempts to contain and perhaps reverse the trend toward ever greater destructiveness. The Washington naval treaties of 1922 and treaties outlawing the use of poison gas and even war itself were steps in this direction. In retrospect it is easy to overlook these contrary trends that were overtaken by events, but they were a significant aspect of international relations in the interwar years, attracted massive public attention at the time, and gave many the hope that another disaster like the most recent one could be avoided. All the measures taken to restructure international relations and to contain the horrors of any war, however, assumed a peaceful world, as did the self-imposed land disarmament of the Western powers.

An unwillingness in the United States and Britain to uphold their commitment to France and a general reluctance to risk the lives and treasure of one's citizens in defense of others – such as the Chinese and the Ethiopians – who might be attacked, opened up the possibility for Japan and Italy to resume prior expansionist policies and for Germany to embark on the new road toward world conquest. Only supreme exertions would suffice to thwart these new challenges to the world's peace. Almost by definition, the very nature of the challenge to the world order posed by the aggressors of World War II would oblige the Allies to respond with escalating vehemence and violence.

2

War and Society in the 1920s and 1930s

HEW STRACHAN

World War I's static nature was a major factor in preventing it from becoming a total war. The trenches, at least in northwestern Europe, acted as a geographical brake on what modern military analysts would call high-intensity conflict. This was less true elsewhere; in East Prussia, Poland, Galicia, Eastern Anatolia, and in almost all the extra-European theaters, the more mobile the operations the greater the suffering of the civilian population. This is not a claim that the peoples of France, Germany, and Britain were not profoundly affected by the war. They were psychologically manipulated by propaganda, they were rationed, their labors were directed toward the war effort, their family lives were disrupted; but only very rarely were they in direct physical danger.

There is, however, one obvious qualification to that introduction. In World War I the idea of the nation in arms found its fullest practical expression. The French revolution may have made the mass army theoretically and politically possible: by conferring citizenship the state could levy military obligations, and by transforming the machinery of government it could carry those obligations into effect. But in 1793 the state could not yet deploy the mass army: it would need the railway to do that. Nor could it arm it; that would require the application of precision engineering to series production. By 1914, most of Europe was industrialized. France could not only call up but also equip and move almost 90 percent of its adult males of military age. Germany conscripted a smaller proportion, not least in deference to the inherent dangers of democratization. But the arms race of 1912–14 and the manpower requirements of the general staff's war plans had begun to convince the Prussian ministry of war that it had to embrace the nation in arms. The war itself effected the change. In 1916, even Britain adopted conscription. Over 63 million men were mobilized for military service in World War I, 12 million of them from Russia, 11 million from Germany,

8.9 million from Britain, 8.4 million from France, and 7.9 million from Austria-Hungary. The military participation rate averaged out at 12 percent of the total populations, and for some countries (notably Serbia) it was two or even three times that. The manpower requirements of the armies, and to a lesser extent the navies, were what drew society and the war together. It was the crucial component in its "totalizing" effect.[1]

And yet the war seemed to show that the mass army was of doubtful strategic value. Operations had increasingly lost the coherence given them by the concepts derived from the Napoleonic wars. Dominated instead by tactics, fighting became an end in itself. Particularly in Germany it acquired a vocabulary – *Heldenkampf* (heroic struggle) and *Durchhaltung* (holding on) – that made a virtue not of victory, not of war's purpose, but of the nature of combat. Means were elevated over ends. In this self-contained world, the experience of the individual in an industrialized conflict, the level caught by Ernst Jünger, the war was total. It was ended, according to a prevailing interpretation, not by one side winning but by the refusal of the other to carry on. The civil population may not have been stormed at with shot and shell, but it was its ability, or inability, to hold out that determined the war's outcome.

Victory was not, apparently, achieved in an operational sense. The mass army had failed to deliver a result. The conduct of the war had thus lost the Clausewitzian, rationalizing shape that was the greatest constraint on its inherent violence. It required the peace settlement to reclothe it in political objectives. And so Versailles, for all the harshness of its terms, was at least limiting in one respect: by defining what the war had been for it placed it within bounds, and ensured its characterization as either victory or defeat.

The mass army had proved to be of dubious operational value for two reasons. First, the railway could not supply it beyond the railhead. Once industry had converted itself to war production, as by and large it had by late 1915, armies were no longer constrained by the output of munitions. But the effect of increased output, and of greater reliance on heavy artillery, was deepening logistic dependence in the field. The Allied advance slowed in the autumn of 1918 for this very reason. Second, the problems of communication, particularly the lack of man-portable radios, meant that the mass army could not be commanded from the top down. General headquarters became primarily administrative centers. Command was exercised at lower

1 These figures do not represent detailed analysis, and may stand in need of correction. They are derived from Hoffmann Nickerson, *Can We Limit War?* (Bristol, U.K., 1933), 123. Nickerson was a major opponent of the mass army: see his *The Armed Horde, 1793–1939: A Study of the Rise, Survival, and Fall of the Mass Army* (New York, 1940).

and lower levels of authority. Thus, its effectiveness was tactical, and its coordination at an operational or strategic level correspondingly problematical.[2]

One obvious way to restore decisiveness to the conduct of war seemed therefore to be to reject the mass army. A forceful and early exponent of this conclusion was J. F. C. Fuller in *The Reformation of War* (1923). World War I had occurred at a cross-over point, when tactics were still based on massed infantry but when the introduction of the machine, particularly the internal combustion engine, promised to decrease the reliance on muscles and men. Furthermore, if demoralization had ultimately proved more decisive than physical destruction, then the intangibles of courage, training, and discipline were more important in machine warfare rather than less so. In other words, quality would triumph over quantity. The mechanized, armored elite army would defeat the horde.[3]

More vociferous and less equivocal in his condemnation of the mass army was the man who borrowed Fuller's ideas, Basil Liddell Hart. Even more than Fuller, Liddell Hart reacted to the losses and suffering of World War I. Fuller believed that conscription would still be needed in wartime, not least in order to get a rational division of labor.[4] Liddell Hart rejected compulsion, even in 1939. By then Fuller had of course become a fascist; Liddell Hart was a liberal. Both wanted to restore greatness to command. In World War I, "generalship became the slave" of the nation in arms: "The artist of war yielded place to the artisan."[5] Both anticipated that in a future war the carefully organized mobilizations of 1914 would be disrupted by air attack. The result would be chaos.

> The larger the armies that are mobilized, the more they will contribute to that chaos. The concentration of forces, according to accepted military principles, will precipitate a state of rapid congestion, hopeless to relieve. The overburdened arteries will give a multiplied effect to the enemy's air attacks in producing a paralytic stroke. And the effects may put an unbearable strain on the bonds of discipline. One can picture swarms of starving soldiery pouring over the countryside – their own countryside – which otherwise might have been able to live on its own local supplies until the flow of traffic was restored.[6]

2 I have felt it necessary to summarize an argument which I developed at greater length in "From Cabinet War to Total War: The Perspective of Military Doctrine, 1861–1918," in Roger Chickering and Stig Förster, eds., *Great War, Total War: Combat and Mobilization on the Western Front, 1914–1918* (New York, 2000).

3 J. F. C. Fuller, *The Reformation of War* (London, 1929), esp. 229. For summaries of Fuller's thinking on the mass army, see Brian Holden Reid, *J. F. C. Fuller: Military Thinker* (Basingstoke, U.K., 1987), 68, 143–4; see also Reid, *Studies in British Military Thought: Debates with Fuller and Liddell Hart* (Lincoln, Neb., 1998), 17.

4 J. F. C. Fuller, *Towards Armageddon: The Defence Problem and Its Solution* (London, 1937), 92.

5 B. H. Liddell Hart, *Paris, or the Future of War* (London, 1925), 69, 87.

6 B. H. Liddell Hart, *When Britain Goes to War: Adaptability and Mobility* (London, 1932), 56.

In such circumstances only the tank-dominated "new model army," "the concentrated essence of fighting power," would be able to maneuver. "The new mobility," Liddell Hart concluded, "threatens to convert mass into a boomerang for the user. Thus, we may reach the paradoxical result that the larger the balance, the heavier the deficit; the bankruptcy of large armies may do more to hasten their limitation than any pacific propaganda for disarmament."[7]

Even within the senior ranks of the British army, conscription was seen as at best a wartime expedient. Colonial campaigning had taught it to maximize its numbers, frequently inferior in the wars of imperial conquest, by the exploitation of technological advantage.[8] "The general view," the secretary of state for war declared in 1921, "is that mechanical means of fighting must be developed to the fullest extent."[9] By 1939 the British army, for all its problems with tanks, was the most fully motorized in the world. In some respects Liddell Hart was preaching to the converted. Sir Ian Hamilton, who as adjutant general had written an officially inspired rejection of conscription before World War I, and who significantly did not serve on the western front during it, continued to condemn the mass army after it. He cited examples of smaller but better equipped armies defeating larger ones, and pointed out, not unreasonably, that Napoleon's declaration that God was on the side of the big battalions had been the precursor to the *Grande Armée*'s decline. "Do character and courage hold their own," he asked, "or, are we going to put our trust in the fertility of our females?" He went on to answer his own question by averring that "efficiency can, must and will learn how to cope with numbers before numbers can overthrow efficiency."[10] A Staff College text of 1932 stressed the inverse relationship between manpower and equipment levels. "For the exercise of command at its best," it went on, "armies must not be too large to be easily moved and handled; otherwise their powers of maneuver are hampered by the resultant excessive demand on the administrative machine, without which no army of today can fight and live; and the high standard of training necessary for efficiency in open warfare can with difficulty be attained in the case of million-strong armies."[11] The general staff itself believed it would need conscription in the

7 Ibid., 72.

8 I have developed these arguments in relation to World War I in "The Battle of the Somme and British Strategy," *Journal of Strategic Studies* 21 (1998): 79–95.

9 Rolland A. Chaput, *Disarmament in British Foreign Policy* (London, 1935), 277; on the general background, see above all Brian Bond, *British Military Policy Between the Wars* (Oxford, 1980).

10 Ian Hamilton, *The Soul and Body of an Army* (London, 1921), 180–4.

11 E. W. Sheppard, *Military History for the Staff College Entrance Examination: A Brief Summary of the Campaigns, with Questions and Answers* (Aldershot, U.K., [1932]), 70, 84.

event of a British commitment to a war in Europe, but it entertained neither hope nor expectation of its application in anything short of that.[12] In the debates on disarmament in 1924–5, when the British government proposed the abolition of conscription, the army did not object.[13] The same happened in 1934.

What Liddell Hart believed, but the general staff did not, was that the British army had become the victim of a European approach to war, what he called the "Napoleonic fallacy." Its constituent element, the conscript army apart, was a belief that "the national object in war can only be gained by decisive battle and the destruction of the main mass of the enemy's armed forces."[14] In *The Ghost of Napoleon* (1933) he developed this argument. Napoleon had been defeated because he had violated "the law of economy of force, which rested on mobility and surprise, factors to which density was anathema." In particular Liddell Hart assaulted Clausewitz – whom he saw not as the exponent of war as an instrument of politics (and hence of war's utility and inherent limitation) but as "the Mahdi of the mass."[15]

Liddell Hart's anticontinentalism and British liberalism's anti-conscriptionism suggest a polarity between the Anglo-American approach to the mass army in the 1920s and that of the European powers. Such an impression is not false, but nor is it wholly accurate, for doubts about the military utility of the nation in arms emerged in Germany and France as well.

"Perhaps the principle of the levy in mass, of the nation in arms has outlived its usefulness, perhaps the *fureur du nombre* has worked itself out," Hans von Seeckt wrote in 1928. "Mass becomes immobile; it cannot manoeuvre and therefore cannot win victories, it can only crush by sheer weight."[16] Seeckt was not a theorist operating on the fringes, as Fuller and Liddell Hart were; he was the German army's de facto commander-in-chief between 1920 and 1926. Current German historiography, preoccupied with civil-military relations and with the subsequent Nazification of the Wehrmacht, sees Seeckt's separation of army from state as a pinnacle of professionalism.[17] But Seeckt's own concept of professionalism was not so narrow: it linked industrial capability, recruitment, and tactical utility. A mass army could not be fully equipped with modern weapons because of the demands it would

12 Peter Dennis, *Decision by Default: Peacetime Conscription and British Defense, 1919–1939* (London, 1972).

13 Dick Richardson, *The Evolution of British Disarmament Policy in the 1920s* (London, 1989), 34–5, 49.

14 B. H. Liddell Hart, *The Remaking of Modern Armies* (London, 1927), 88.

15 B. H. Liddell Hart, *The Ghost of Napoleon* (London, 1933), 103, 127–8.

16 Hans von Seeckt, *Thoughts of a Soldier* (1928; English ed., London, 1930), 55.

17 See, e.g., the essays in Rolf-Dieter Müller and Hans-Erich Volkmann, eds., *Die Wehrmacht: Mythos und Realität* (Munich, 1999).

generate for a peacetime economy. Nor could it be properly trained. Neither constraint would affect a professional force. "The whole future of warfare," Seeckt concluded, "appears to me to lie in the employment of mobile armies, relatively small but of high quality."[18]

Seeckt's concepts were in direct opposition to those of Erich Ludendorff. The former First Quartermaster General was clear that the war had been lost because the Entente had commanded superior resources of manpower. "The totalitarian war," he asserted in 1935, "demands the incorporation in the Army of every man fit to bear arms."[19] By then Hitler had reintroduced conscription, and Seeckt's apologists were quick to argue that their hero's support of a professional army had been the product of the circumstances of the Versailles treaty rather than of any intellectual conviction. Restricted to a force of 100,000 men, Seeckt could not embrace the *Volksheer* (nation in arms), but had to create an army of leaders, a cadre for expansion modeled on the *Krümper* (short-service training) system adopted by Prussia after the convention of Königsberg in 1808.[20]

It can be argued that Seeckt's thinking was politically pragmatic rather than militarily utilitarian, a reflection of what the Germans had to accept given their defeat. The fact that he first advocated a voluntarily enlisted army in February 1919, before the terms of the Versailles treaty had been settled, does not necessarily undermine this argument. His proposed target of 200,000 men was consonant with what he expected the Allies to demand. It does, however, ignore Seeckt's own World War I experience.[21] Much of it had been on the eastern front, where he had seen a mass army, that of Russia, overcome by better-equipped but smaller forces. Moreover, mobile and offensive operations had brought decisive battlefield success, notably at Tannenberg. In retirement in 1927, Seeckt still regarded an army of 250,000 as perfectly adequate for a first-rank power.[22] He never abandoned conscription as an ultimate goal, but he became increasingly persuaded that the *Führerheer* (army of leaders) would have to stand in its own right and not be, as he had at first thought in 1919–21, a bridging device to the mass army. A *Volksheer*'s morale would be fragile, and technical progress demanded higher training standards. Thus, the conscript army would be designed for defensive purposes only; the operational army, voluntarily enlisted men serving for six years, would achieve a quick victory before the enemy's mass army could be

18 Seeckt, *Thoughts of a Soldier*, 62.

19 Erich Ludendorff, *The Nation at War* (1935; English ed., London, 1936), 89.

20 Hans von Seeckt, *Aus seinem Leben*, 2 vols. (Leipzig, 1938–41), 2:461–4.

21 Ibid., 2:43; see also James S. Corum, *The Roots of Blitzkrieg: Hans von Seeckt and German Military Reform* (Lawrence, Kans., 1992), 29–33.

22 Gaines Post Jr., *The Civil-Military Fabric of Weimar Foreign Policy* (Princeton, N.J., 1973), 163.

deployed.[23] As late as 1935 Friedrich von Rabenau, who would edit Seeckt's posthumous memoirs, published a didactic collection of studies designed to reinforce his chief's case, *Operative Entschlüsse gegen eine Anzahl überlegener Gegner* (operational decisions against a number of superior opponents).

In 1929 Wilhelm Groener, the imperial army's last chief of staff, became minister of war. He took the first steps in rupturing the fabric of the Seecktian settlement, especially in the area of civil-military relations. However, although he had thought Seeckt wrong on the issue of conscription, his approach to numbers was incremental rather than gargantuan. In 1919 he had favored a comparatively small army, 350,000, and in 1920 he wrote that "the era of making war with mass armies is finished, for Germany."[24] Seeckt's case against the mass army was tactical (and therefore potentially universal); Groener's was economic, and specifically national. The implication was that Germany's recovery could moderate his position. But the maximum field army he favored in 1930 – twenty-one divisions and a tripling of its manpower to 300,000 – was no more than the ideal mobilization strength harbored under the Seecktian regime. It remained diminutive by the standards of 1914.[25]

Similarly, General Ludwig Beck, chief of the general staff when conscription was reintroduced, was no lover of numbers per se. "It is not true," he wrote in his 1934 memorandum on the army's future shape, "that a quickly assembled army possesses more as a power-instrument of the state than an army half or a third smaller which is more solidly constructed."[26] Beck believed that a larger army was only worth having if it retained the quality of a smaller one. His acceptance of universal conscription was driven by the army's domestic political needs rather than by operational considerations. The SA's promotion of itself as a defensive citizen force challenged the army's monopoly in the profession of arms. In opposing the SA, Beck found an ally in Hitler, whose offensive ambitions required an army that was modernized and effective. And so Beck endeavored to apply Seecktian

23 Hans Meier-Welcker, *Seeckt* (Frankfurt am Main, 1967), 529–32, 636; see also the discussion in Jehuda L. Wallach, *Das Dogma der Vernichtungsschlacht. Die Lehren von Clausewitz und Schlieffen und ihre Wirkung in zwei Weltkriegen* (Munich, 1970), 326–33.

24 Quoted by Berenice A. Carroll, *Design for Total War: Arms and Economics in the Third Reich* (The Hague, 1968), 54.

25 Ibid., 59–60; Harold J. Gordon Jr., *The Reichswehr and the German Republic, 1919–1926* (Princeton, N.J., 1957), 261, 284. Wilhelm Deist sees Groener's arrival as a much more significant break with Seeckt; see Deist, *The Wehrmacht and German Rearmament* (London, 1981), 5–7, 13; Wilhelm Deist, in Militärgeschichtliches Forschungsamt, ed., *Germany and the Second World War* (Oxford, 1990–) 1: 375–92; Corum, *Roots of Blitzkrieg*, 53–5. See also Wilhelm Deist's contribution to this volume.

26 Klaus-Jürgen Müller, *General Ludwig Beck: Studien und Dokumente zur politisch-militärischen Vorstellungswelt und Tätigkeit des Generalstabschefs des deutschen Heeres 1933–1938* (Boppard am Rhein, 1980), 351; see also 165–6, 169, 339–44, 350–4.

standards in training and equipment while endorsing a force of sixty-seven divisions, twice as large as that favored by Groener.

The fact that less divided Groener – and even Beck – from Seeckt than might at first appear confirms the degree of consensus in Germany surrounding Seeckt's condemnation of the full nation in arms. The idea of an elite mechanized force appealed to fascism. Hitler himself, although anxious to conscript, still said in the early 1930s: "The next war will be quite different from the last world war. Infantry attacks and mass formations are obsolete."[27] In *Das Wäldchen 125* (1925) Jünger – possibly influenced by reading J. F. C. Fuller – declared that the next war would be a machine war, in which "sheer mass" would have little influence.[28] The embryonic fascism of Jünger's veneration of the stormtrooper occurred also in Georg Soldan's attack on the mass army, discussed elsewhere in this book by Markus Pöhlmann. Soldan argued that the fighting in World War I had been sustained by small numbers of battle-hardened warriors: he preferred to have eighty tested men rather than a full company made up of doubtful replacements. For Soldan, the experience of 1918 confirmed not only the military unwisdom of the mass army but also its political unreliability. He cited the writings of the *Action française* and of Oswald Spengler for prewar anticipations of the nefarious consequences of citizen armies.[29] Spengler himself now reckoned that the popular disillusionment with war made the ideal of the nation in arms useless. But, more than that, the idea of the citizen army was positively dangerous in a period of civil strife.[30] The army's role as a buttress to domestic order was an argument to which Seeckt himself was particularly susceptible. Truly universal service had, by the end of World War I, exposed the army to the fissures of civilian society. In the context of the revolutions of 1918–19 and of the early days of the Weimar republic, professionalism's attractions included its promise to divide army from society.[31]

This was precisely why France looked askance at a professional force. Having reconciled the differences between army and nation in the crucible of war, the Third Republic had no desire to reactivate them. The concept of total war, of whose utility not only Fuller and Liddell Hart but also Seeckt and Groener were doubtful, had a politically unifying function within

27 Carroll, *Design for Total War*, 18.

28 Azar Gat, *Fascist and Liberal Visions of War: Fuller, Liddell Hart, Douhet and Other Modernists* (Oxford, 1998), 83–5; see also Ernst Jünger, *Feuer und Blut* (1925), in *Sämtliche Werke* (Stuttgart, 1978), 1:449–50.

29 Georg Soldan, *Der Mensch und die Schlacht der Zukunft* (Oldenbourg, 1925), 38–9, 79, 82, 87–8.

30 Walter Struve, *Elites Against Democracy: Leadership Ideas in Bourgeois Political Thought in Germany, 1890–1933* (Princeton, N.J., 1973), 257.

31 Seeckt, *Aus seinem Leben*, 2:614–15.

France. Its rejection of Britain's proposal to abolish conscription as part of the process of disarmament was unequivocal. In doing so it employed the vocabulary of the Enlightenment to argue that compulsory military service was the corollary of universal suffrage.[32] In 1922 Raymond Poincaré reckoned that France needed between 690,000 and 725,000 men, and in 1923 the term of service was fixed at eighteen months. By 1930, with the latter reduced to a year, the French army was effectively a massive training establishment. The Jaurèsian concept of the nation in arms was extended, beyond the males of military age, to embrace France's entire population: the role of women and children in war was underpinned by a concept of total war that derived its logic from the experience of 1914–18 but its rhetoric from 1793.

France's soldiers accepted the consequences of short service as the lesser of two evils: better that than domestic political isolation. The war had disseminated the military spirit throughout France and had hallowed the military credentials of the citizen soldier. For Joseph Joffre, the mass army had become the agent of victory.[33] But this did not mean that France's generals were oblivious to the arguments in favor of elite forces voiced by military pundits elsewhere. Both Foch and Pétain were entirely persuaded of the potential trade-off between man and machine. In 1930 Foch's wartime chief of staff, Maxime Weygand, secured the endorsement not only of Pétain but also of the *conseil supérieur de guerre* for a ten-year plan to develop mobile forces made up exclusively of professional elements.[34] Furthermore, the military effectiveness of a long-service professional army, both in its own right and as a cadre for expansion, was precisely what roused Foch's opposition to Seeckt's proposals for the restructured German army in 1919. He was prepared to accept a German army of 200,000 men, but wanted it to be formed of short-service conscripts, because he deemed them to be inefficient. The reduction to 100,000 was a corollary of long service and professionalism. If Foch had had his way, the result would have been the creation of a massive reserve, a prospect ironically that aroused the adamant opposition of Britain, which did not have one, but which was treated with equanimity by France, which did.[35]

32 Denis Hayes, *Conscription Conflict: The Conflict of Ideas in the Struggle for and Against Military Conscription in Britain Between 1901 and 1939* (London, 1949), 349.

33 Joseph Montheilhet, *Les institutions militaires de la France (1814–1932): de la paix armée à la paix désarmée* (Paris, 1932), 405–6; see also Richard D. Challener, *The French Theory of the Nation in Arms, 1866–1939* (New York, 1955); Robert Allan Doughty, *The Seeds of Disaster: The Development of French Army Doctrine, 1919–1939* (Hamden, Conn., 1985), 14–40.

34 Elizabeth Kier, *Imagining War: French and British Military Doctrine Between the Wars* (Princeton, N.J., 1997), 77; see also 58–65; Monteilhet, *Institutions militaires*, 422; H. Bouvard, *Les leçons militaires de la guerre* (Paris, 1920), 41–2.

35 Chaput, *Disarmament in British Foreign Policy*, 256–7, 266–8.

France's formal endorsement of its own mass army was therefore equivocal. In 1919–20 the perceptive military critic, Emile Mayer, called for a professional army for France of 200,000 men. Articles by Liddell Hart advocating a professional army for France and published in the *Daily Telegraph* in January 1927 were circulated on Pétain's orders in 1928.[36] The law of that year, designed to prepare for the introduction of one-year service, fixed the establishment of 106,000 regular soldiers as a minimum rather than (as in the past) as a maximum.[37] The fact that in practice the army struggled to reach this target increased its apprehension as the qualities of the *Reichswehr* were borne in on them. Long before Germany reembraced the mass army, the French looked with concern at their neighbor's ability to launch an attack in a matter of hours. In 1930 Stéphane Lauzanne called for "a technical army of 250,000 . . . serving seven or eight years, and able in a few hours to be concentrated on this or that frontier without the enormous machinery required to put the national levée en masse in operation."[38]

The protection of France's frontiers and the screening of its mobilization – the doctrine of *couverture* – could best be performed by counterstrokes carried out by armored divisions. Thus, alongside the small group of soldiers who advocated a professional army stood a larger group who pushed the cause of the tank. Most of these did not necessarily see the abandonment of conscription as the corollary of mechanization. Therefore, the importance of Charles de Gaulle's *Vers l'armée de métier*, published in 1934, lay not in its advocacy of a force of six armored divisions, but in its allying this concept to that of professionalism. De Gaulle used vocabulary that in the circumstances of the Third Republic was frankly inflammatory. He stressed the need to isolate the professional army from the values of civilian society and to inculcate a military ethos. He called these picked troops "the aristocrats of war."[39] When Paul Reynaud popularized de Gaulle's arguments in the chamber of deputies on March 15, 1935, Léon Blum was quick to dismiss them as praetorian and antidemocratic.

De Gaulle's defenders have been anxious to stress that his professional army was a supplement to the nation in arms, not a substitute for it.[40] But the army's senior officers, notably Gamelin, Weygand, Debeney, and Pétain

36 Jean-Charles Jauffret, "L'armée de métier: un siècle de débats, 1871–1972," in Bernard Boëne and Michel Louis Martin, eds., *Conscription et armée de métier* (Paris, 1991), 212–14.

37 Monteilhet, *Institutions militaires*, 407–9.

38 Ibid., 441; on reactions to Seeckt, see also Shelby Cullom Davis, *The French War Machine* (London, 1937), 83–4, 208, 212.

39 Charles de Gaulle, *The Army of the Future* (London, 1934; reprinted, 1941), 35, 102; see also Robert A. Doughty, "De Gaulle's Concept of a Mobile Professional Army: Genesis of a French Defeat?" in Lloyd J. Matthew and Dale E. Brown, eds., *The Parameters of War: Military History from the Journal of the U.S. Army War College* (Washington, D.C., 1987).

40 Alain Levy, "De Gaulle et Jaurès," in *Jaurès et la défense nationale, Cahiers Jaurès*, no. 3, n.d., 163–75.

were quick to condemn him for reopening the divisions between the army and the nation, as well as between the regular army and the nation in arms. The consequence was to associate mechanization with elite forces, and so to vitiate Gamelin's efforts on behalf of tactical modernization. Moreover, the professional suspicions of the left were not without foundation. In 1936 de Gaulle's case for a professional army included its possible value in the maintenance of internal order.[41]

De Gaulle declared that it was "certain that future French victories will no longer be those of big battalions."[42] Germany's decision to adopt conscription in 1935, when balanced by France's numerically inferior and declining population, made the nation in arms a greater necessity but a less obvious asset. Although Gamelin crushed any debate in the interests of civil-military fusion, de Gaulle's message that a smaller army could, if it was properly trained and equipped, triumph over a bigger one was one way out of a desperate dilemma. As an American commentator writing in 1937 observed (admittedly more in hope than expectation), "France is not yet convinced of the value of more numbers, but is content to see a smaller force lavishly and perfectly equipped. New guns, new machine-guns, new tanks, new aeroplanes, coupled to a wise production organization, may render France's smaller striking army a more formidable force than Germany's *Millionheer* [mass army]."[43]

Implicit here is the relationship between industrial capability and military efficiency. If France traded high numbers for advanced machinery, then it increased its reliance on a sizeable and sophisticated manufacturing capability. Dependence on manpower, rather than on equipment, was a manifestation of comparative economic backwardness. Moreover, the soldiers of a professional army required higher pay: a reason advanced by the Italians for opposing the abolition of conscription in 1919. Thus, the Jaurèsian definition of conscription, in which the citizen did indeed become a soldier, was no more than a political rallying cry. The concept of the nation in arms which France embraced in the 1920s and which Germany adopted in the 1930s reflected the awareness that war production was itself a form of national service. The mechanization of armies, whether they were conscript or professional, increased the state's dependence on industry in wartime and helped erode the distinction between front and rear. In the process of becoming smaller, armies widened their circles of support.

41 Martin S. Alexander, *The Republic in Danger: General Maurice Gamelin and the Politics of French Defence, 1933–1940* (Cambridge, 1992), 34–42, 87; Philip C. F. Bankwitz, *Maxime Weygand and Civil-Military Relations in Modern France* (Cambridge, Mass., 1967), 125–54.

42 De Gaulle, *Army of the Future*, 79.

43 Davis, *French War Machine*, 212.

The advocates of the elite army, Fuller, Liddell Hart, and Seeckt included, argued that the first phase of the next European war would be an air attack. Moreover, its purpose would be not just to disrupt the intricate mobilization timetables of the mass army; it would be aimed against the civilian population for reasons that were both moral and material. If the home front was cowed into submission, then an army of citizens would be robbed of support; if production was disrupted, then an army would lack the munitions with which to fight.

Therefore, the advocates of elite mechanized forces tended also to be advocates of air forces. The mass army was characterized as infantry-dominant; creating head room for artillery and armor itself implied modification. Adding in an air arm – assuming a constant allocation of resources – carried a further reduction in the army. This was Giulio Douhet's message in *Command of the Air* (1921), and it was Italo Balbo's intent when he aspired to move from Italy's air ministry to its supreme general staff in 1933.[44] But the support of air power had a much more fundamental purpose: it was designed to restore political utility to war. If the mass army had failed to deliver a decision in 1918, then faith for the future should reside in air forces. Aerial attack was therefore not only a means of widening war into the third dimension, and of forcing fronts to be deep as well as lateral; it was also intended to achieve results in shorter order, and – in the most optimistic scenario – through demoralization rather than through destruction.

Air power doctrine was a product of compromise and confusion. For some it was a weapon of precision and discrimination, capable of hitting targets that were of direct military significance. For others its mission was terror. In this scenario the civilian population, which was to be spared the manpower demands of the mass army, would instead be the subject of direct rather than indirect attack. However, all the attention devoted to the bomber, both in the rhetoric of the interwar period and in the historiography since, tends to neglect the fact that in the context of the 1920s and 1930s an air attack on a scale sufficient to be decisive was undeliverable. Air forces were too small, they lacked heavy bombers, and their targeting systems were rudimentary. The only independent air arm in the world in 1918, the Royal Air Force, acknowledged many of these weaknesses in 1931.[45]

44 Gat, *Fascist and Liberal Views of War*, 66–9.

45 Philip Meilinger, "Clipping the Bomber's Wings: The Geneva Disarmament Conference and the Royal Air Force, 1932–1934," *War in History* 6 (1999): 309; see also Philip Meilinger, "Trenchard and 'Morale Bombing': The Evolution of R.A.F. Doctrine Before World War II," *Journal of Military History* 60 (1996): 243–70.

Nor could the airplane intercept contraband. The proven weapon for attacking the home front after the Great War seemed to be maritime blockade. But to call it that, as one of its prime advocates, Admiral Sir Herbert Richmond, pointed out, was legally inaccurate. The Royal Navy had not mounted a close watch on German ports; instead it had stood off, shifting the focus from military application to economic pressure.[46] In the interwar years Germany and Britain colluded to confirm that what had decided the outcome of World War I was economic warfare. The German army, anxious to argue that it had not been defeated in the field, blamed the nation's collapse on the revolution. This had in turn been provoked by a combination of socialism and Allied propaganda, which had flourished on the back of the material privations to which the civilian population had been subject. British analysts, notably but not only Liddell Hart, were happy to fall in with this interpretation. It rendered redundant the continental commitment, and, with it, the mass army.

The evidential base for the argument that the blockade had won the war was shaky. It formed the conclusion but not the content of Liddell Hart's own history. The British official account, by A. C. Bell, was completed in 1937 but not made publicly available until 1961. The secrecy reflected the fact that by then the methods evolved for the conduct of economic war in 1914–18 formed a blueprint for British strategy in the next war with Germany. Significantly, the first elements of Bell's work to be published appeared not in English but in a German translation in 1943.

Bell's book was largely diplomatic history: a description of how Britain had secured the cooperation of the border neutrals and of the United States. His analysis of the blockade's effect focused almost exclusively on food supply, which he reckoned to have fallen to 1,000 calories per adult per day in 1917, and on mortality rates, which he claimed had increased 37 percent between 1913 and 1918. He attributed almost 700,000 deaths to the blockade.[47]

These figures were themselves culled from German sources produced in the 1920s with three objectives. First, they affirmed the stab-in-the-back argument. Second, they impressed on Germany that preparation for total war implied the preparation of a war economy. And, third, they demonstrated the immorality of Britain's conduct of war. In setting aside the declaration of London and its definitions of contraband, Britain had waged war on Germany's women and children rather than on its soldiers. The effects of

46 Herbert Richmond, *Sea Power in the Modern World* (London, 1934), 101–8.

47 A. C. Bell, *A History of the Blockade of Germany and of the Countries Associated with Her in the Great War, Austria-Hungary, Bulgaria, and Turkey* (London, 1937; reprinted, 1961), 671–3.

World War I on the civilian population may have been indirect but they were nonetheless lethal.

The fact that Avner Offer has recently argued that Germany did not starve in World War I is less important in this context than the fact that in the 1920s and 1930s many people believed that it had and that its doing so had brought the war to a decisive conclusion.[48] In 1920 Arthur Dix, significantly using the same figures as those employed by Bell in 1937, went on to calculate Germany's demographic loss to be four million.[49] By 1933 Hoffmann Nickerson quoted, at second hand and without explanation, the conclusion that the total civilian losses for all belligerents in World War I equaled, if they did not exceed, those of the armies in the field. He put them at thirteen million, so challenging (although even then I would argue not undermining) a fundamental premise of this chapter.[50]

Dix and others characterized the allied blockade as a *Hungerblockade*. In other words, its primary purpose was to deprive the civilian population of food; resistance having been lowered, death followed from disease. And this was the image of blockade which British naval theory refurbished in the 1930s. Bell, a retired Royal Naval officer, may have been denied public recognition for his history of the blockade, but in 1938 he was able to lay out his principal conclusions in *Sea Power and the Next War*. This was emphatically not another consideration of fleet action. "A study of sea warfare," he averred, "is, in large measure, a study of economic war." He gave seven rules for economic warfare, the second of which was that its principal target should be the enemy's food supply. By being directed against the entire nation, and by causing "universal want and suffering," economic warfare achieved its aims less through its primary effects (shortages of food and fuel) than through its secondary consequences, "the disappointments, unhappiness, and depression of the civil population."[51]

This was also the message of the official history. "What, indeed, could be more frivolous," the latter had asked with heavy irony, than so much effort over so long a period by so many allies and their forces, "to execute an operation of war against hospital patients; to increase the sufferings of phthistic, asthmatical, and bronchitic persons; and to raise the number of women who miscarry in childbirth?"[52] The answer was that blockade undermined the morale of the nation. Thus, even on the admission of its practitioners,

48 Avner Offer, *The First World War: An Agrarian Interpretation* (Oxford, 1989), 45–53.

49 E.g., see Arthur Dix, *Wirtschaftskrieg und Kriegswirtschaft: Zur Geschichte des deutschen Zusammenbruchs* (Berlin, 1920), esp. 12, 294–5.

50 Nickerson, *Can We Limit War?* 125.

51 A. C. Bell, *Sea Power and the Next War* (London, 1938), 14, 80–2.

52 Bell, *History of the Blockade*, 673.

blockade had been an imprecise weapon, with no direct military consequences, and had almost certainly violated the traditional principles of just war. Furthermore, it had taken a long time to have effect.

The problem for Britain in the 1930s, therefore, was not just that Germany had taken the injunctions of Dix and others to heart and had recognized the wartime values of autarchy and the management needs of a war economy. It also resided in the derogation of the mass army. If the advocates of mechanized forces were right, military operations might achieve their objectives, particularly if they were limited, in short order. Blockade as defined by Bell was an instrument for a long and "total" war. Even potential supporters of blockade, like Liddell Hart and Admiral Sir Herbert Richmond, found themselves modifying their claims on its behalf. It failed to curb Italy in 1936. Liddell Hart's recognition of the porousness of Germany's land frontiers led him to be deeply despondent about the prospects for a British strategy after Munich.[53] Richmond's appreciation of the naval difficulties in the application of blockade led him to stress the margin of superiority on which its implementation would depend.[54]

During World War I blockade had little, if any, direct influence on the equipment levels of the field armies. After it, nobody, not even in Germany, argued that the German army had been defeated in 1918 because economic warfare had exhausted its stocks of guns and shells. But in the 1930s British strategies for the next European war were buoyed by the fact that elite, mechanized forces contained their own vulnerabilities. The reliance of armies on metals and oil was increased, not diminished. Thus, blockade could, if it was targeted against strategic raw materials rather than against food supplies, be an instrument of greater precision and speedier effect than its lumbering predecessor of 1914–18.

In 1927 Sir Maurice Hankey, the secretary of the Committee of Imperial Defence, enlisted Richmond's aid in his successful bid to persuade the Foreign Office to defend the belligerent rights of a blockading power against the revisionism of the United States.[55] Throughout his thirty years at the center of British strategy, from the origins of World War I to the origins of World War II, Hankey was a continuous advocate of the role of sea power in a British strategy of economic warfare. Persuaded of its centrality in Britain's contribution to the outcome in 1918, he had no intention of forfeiting it in the 1930s. His principal ally in this endeavor was neither Liddell Hart nor

53 Gat, *Fascist and Liberal Views of War*, 194–7; see Liddell Hart, *Paris*, 38.

54 Herbert Richmond, *Economy and Naval Security* (London, 1931), 56–61; see also *National Policy and Naval Strength and Other Essays* (London, 1928), 64.

55 Stephen Roskill, *Hankey: Man of Secrets*, 3 vols. (London, 1970), 2:451–5.

Richmond but Desmond Morton, a soldier attached to the Foreign Office, who was given the task of studying industrial mobilization in wartime under the auspices of the Committee of Imperial Defence. Morton's Industrial Intelligence Centre collected information on German stockpiles of essential raw materials, particularly iron ore and petroleum, and by 1937 was predicting that war with Germany would end owing to Germany's "inability to continue manufacturing armaments as soon as stocks of the essential raw materials had been used up."[56] By this time the C.I.D. had established an Economic Pressure on Germany sub-committee, which the Industrial Intelligence Centre serviced and through which Morton shaped policy. At one level the faith in blockade with which Britain approached the crises of 1938–9 was a direct consequence of World War I and its lessons for the mobilization of the entire population, a British reflection of France's definition of the nation in arms and Ludendorff's of totalitarian warfare. But at another level, it was profoundly different. For Morton the target was less food and the effects of starvation on the civil population, but the "constant stream of highly mechanized weapons and large quantities of relatively precision-made material" on which the front line would depend.[57] Furthermore, by 1939, although reluctant to be precise, the Industrial Intelligence Centre doubted whether Germany had sufficient stockpiles to last a year and thought that economic warfare could take effect within fifteen months. In other words, the Industrial Intelligence Centre had rendered blockade a means for a type of warfare less total and less targeted on civilians than had been the case in World War I.

Criticisms of Britain's military unpreparedness in 1939 are not appropriate in relation to blockade. Thinking and analysis, much of it secret (and that confidentiality was in itself an indication of its importance) had been continuous throughout the interwar years. The C.I.D. sub-committees provided the nucleus for the Ministry of Economic Warfare, created in July 1939, and at the war's outbreak blockade, rather than the dispatch of the British Expeditionary Force to France, was Britain's primary strategy both in the immediate and in the long term.

The German navy was not unmindful of the danger. Spurning Groener's determination that it should focus on the Baltic and reject plans for a major war, Erich Raeder and the naval leadership looked to the Atlantic and the

56 Wesley K. Wark, *The Ultimate Enemy and Nazi Germany, 1933–1939* (London, 1985), 177.

57 Ibid., 160; for what follows, see also W. N. Medlicott, *The Economic Blockade* (London, 1952), 1:12–40; Patrick Salmon, "British Plans for Economic Warfare Against Germany, 1937–1939: The Problem of Swedish Iron Ore," *Journal of Contemporary History* 16 (1981): 53–71; Robert J. Young, "Spokesmen for Economic Warfare: the Industrial Intelligence Centre in the 1930s," *European Studies Review* 6 (1976): 473–89.

need to keep open Germany's sea lanes. He told Groener in 1929 that the greatest threat which Germany confronted was a blockade by Britain – "the simplest and safest way, without any bloodshed, of defeating us."[58] The political solution was to appease Britain; the technological was to emulate Britain's battle-cruisers by the construction of pocket-battleships in order to break the blockade. Wolfgang Wegener believed the remedies should be geographical. The Helgoland Bight was "a dead angle in a dead sea";[59] the German navy needed direct access to the Atlantic through mastery either of the French coast or of Norway. Hitler gave it both.

Although Raeder planned to operate offensively, his grand strategy remained essentially defensive. The German navy's own plans for economic warfare were remarkably ill-developed given the near success of the U-boat campaign in 1917–18. At Geneva in 1932, the United States, the Soviet Union, and Italy all supported Britain in demanding the submarine's restriction or abolition. But the Germans, speaking for its retention, maintained that it was their defense against a British surface fleet.[60] This was the view of the Marinearchiv's historian of the U-boat campaign, Arno Spindler. For him, as for Raeder, the essential point was that submarine warfare had failed, not that it had come as close as Germany ever came throughout the war to inflicting a decisive defeat on Britain. On this point too Raeder and Wegener were agreed. The latter made virtually no mention of the U-boat in his analysis of the naval strategy of World War I. The belief that Britain's development of asdic (sonar) was more successful than it was confirmed Raeder in his conviction that cruiser warfare should be conducted by a mixed force containing also surface vessels and aircraft. The lesson he drew from the war was one derived from the missed opportunities of 1914, not of 1917: oceanic cruiser warfare should be coordinated with battle fleet action in the North Sea. With this variation only on Tirpitzian thought, the German navy elected to dog the footsteps of the great sea powers with a surface fleet rather than to pursue a *guerre de course*. In 1939 Germany had fifty-seven submarines, when Dönitz reckoned three hundred could have been decisive.[61] To all intents and purposes, Germany had renounced its

58 Werner Rahn, "German Naval Strategy and Armament During the Inter-War Period, 1919–1939," in Phillips Payson O'Brien, ed., *Preparing for the Next War at Sea: Technology and Naval Combat in the Twentieth Century* (London, 2001); Rahn, *Reichsmarine und Landesverteidigung 1919–1928: Konzeption und Führung der Marine in der Weimarer Republik* (Munich, 1976), 281–6. See also Militärgeschichtliches Forschungsamt, ed., *Germany and the Second World War*, 1:390, 456–62; Deist, *Wehrmacht and German Rearmament*, 69–76.

59 Wolfgang Wegener, *Die Seestrategie des Weltkrieges* (Berlin, 1929), 8.

60 Meilinger, "Clipping the Bomber's Wings," 311–13.

61 The figure of 57 is given in Militärgeschichtliches Forschungsamt, *Germany and the Second World War*, 1:480; see also Holger Herwig, "Innovation Ignored: The Submarine Problem – Germany,

capacity to use naval means to wage a war of starvation against the civil population.

The bombed cities of Warsaw and Rotterdam, the columns of refugees on the roads of northern France – there is plenty of evidence that Germany's conduct of the war between 1939 and 1941 did not spare civilians. But in a sense they were accidental casualties. The resources of the Wehrmacht were concentrated toward two objectives – the destruction of the enemy armed forces in the field and the securing of the raw materials which would render Britain's blockade strategy redundant. Dubbing the first year of the war "phoney" obscures the intensity of the economic war. Germany's imports by weight fell 57 percent in the last months of 1939; by March 1940 raw material imports were 13 percent of their 1938 total.[62] Furthermore, although the Allies did not launch their bombers against civilian targets, their efforts at sea were not directed just against strategic raw materials. Foodstuffs were declared conditional contraband, and, although they were only a small proportion of the goods seized, the winter in Berlin in 1939–40 was described by one resident as "Spartan."[63]

Hitler's attack in the west in May 1940 was an effort to break the stranglehold of blockade – just as the British expedition to Norway was a bid to reinforce it. At one level, furthermore, the German victory was Seecktian: the breakthrough of the Panzer divisions could be construed as the triumph of the highly equipped elite army over the nation in arms. Casualties were light.[64] Foch's 1919 characterization of short-service conscripts as militarily inefficient seemed proven in 1940. But, however doctrinally seductive, such an interpretation glosses over the impact of the reintroduction of conscription to Germany. Elite forces, to be sure, were vital to the German victories of 1939–41; not only the armored divisions but the airborne troops and the Luftwaffe were at the cutting edge of the Wehrmacht. But behind them was a mass army, logistically almost as ponderous as those of 1914.

The implications, as well as the weaknesses, of such structures became evident after 1941. In the West, critics of Fuller and Liddell Hart had stressed that modern industrial states would opt for both a mechanized and a mass

Britain, and the United States, 1919–1939," in Williamson Murray and Allan R. Millett, eds., *Military Innovation in the Interwar Period* (Cambridge, 1996), 231–41; Joseph A. Maiolo, *The Royal Navy and Nazi Germany, 1933–39: A Study in Appeasement and the Origins of the Second World War* (Basingstoke, U.K., 1998), 67–83.

62 Williamson Murray, *The Change in the European Balance of Power, 1938–1939: The Path to Ruin* (Princeton, N.J., 1984), 326–34.

63 R. J. Overy, *War and Economy in the Third Reich* (Oxford, 1994), 285; see also Medlicott, *Economic Blockade*, 1:70, 85.

64 This was the line taken, predictably, by Nickerson, *Armed horde*, x, 366, 392–3, but also more interestingly by Frido von Senger und Etterlin (see Wallach, *Dogma der Vernichtungsschlacht*, 333).

army. "The net result of 'mechanization,'" V. W. Germains wrote in a balanced, effective, but neglected critique of the tank's advocates, "is not to eliminate the man, but to enhance his fighting power." For him "the greatest strategic surprise of the [first world] war" was the formation of the Kitchener armies (about which he wrote a book). "If we can have mechanization *plus* a well thought-out and elastic system of raising reserve armies, then mechanization is worth having." The foreword to Germains's book was by Sir Frederick Maurice, director of military operations until May 1918, when he publicly accused the government of misleading the House of Commons, significantly, on the issue of manpower. Maurice devoted his postwar career to developing the general staff approach so reviled by Liddell Hart and embodied in Maurice's wartime superior, Sir William Robertson, chief of the imperial general staff. "Our little regular army," he warned, "is but the advanced guard of our national army."[65]

But this sort of language found little resonance in Britain in the late 1920s. Moreover, even if it had, it would have been sublimated in schemes similar to those of Seeckt or de Gaulle – a two-tier army, the small professional part for offense and the large, comparatively untrained element for defense. Only in the Soviet Union was real progress made toward the fusion of these two components, resulting in the creation of a mass army that was also fully mechanized.

The merits of the nation in arms as opposed to a professional, regular force were debated at the ninth party congress in 1920. Leon Trotsky favored a working-class militia, A. A. Svechin stressed its inefficiencies. Trotsky's deputy and then in 1925 commissar for war, M. V. Frunze, took up the cudgels on behalf of mobile warfare and embraced a mixed military system embracing elements of both approaches. Frunze appreciated that bourgeois states might reject the mass army, but that "in the final resort for us we must not conceive of a future clash being such that we will be able to win through with numerically small armed forces and without involving the broad mass of the population and without employing in this undertaking all the resources at the states's command."[66]

In 1925 the Soviet Union's greatest resource, as it had been Russia's in 1914, was manpower. Frunze's mixed army was therefore an infantry force, with its capability for maneuver provided – as Frunze's operations in the civil war had been – by cavalry. But in 1929 V. K. Triandafillov, who was close to

65 Victor Wallace Germains, *The "Mechanization" of War* (London, 1927), xiv, 184–8, 193, 249; see Gat, *Fascist and Liberal Visions of War*, 37–8.

66 John Erickson, *The Soviet High Command: A Military-Political History 1918–41* (London, 1962), 211; see also 115–38, 179–200.

both Svechin and Frunze, went further. He condemned "the idea that small, albeit motorized, forces can conquer modern states" as naive: "Such an army, having invaded deep into an enemy country, risks becoming isolated if it is not immediately supported by a stronger army." Capitalist theorists like Fuller were being gulled by their own fears of the masses. The consequences of their policies, if they were adopted (and he acknowledged that so far they had not been), would be that they could not conduct "a large war." To do that, "the best conditions for free maneuver, for extensive tactical and operational art, will be achieved not through a return to the small armies of the armchair warriors, but by the corresponding increase in the mobility of modern million-man armies by improving the technology of transportation assets."[67]

This was the army which Tukhachevsky set about creating in 1934. Building on the first five-year plan, he fused mass and mechanization, devising an instrument capable of deep attack in the furtherance of revolutionary objectives.[68] What essentially Tukhachevsky had done was reject the opportunity costs which limited the conceptions of warfare entertained in the west. The alternative between the mass army and the mechanized army was shown to be a false choice. But so too was that between the Jaurèsian nation in arms and the full mobilization of the economy. A state convinced of its ideological objectives could do both things. Thus, war was not limited in the ways which Fuller and Liddell Hart hoped. Moreover, the very mobility they had worked so hard to restore meant that civilian populations, which had been comparatively untouched in 1914–18, now found themselves in the paths of military operations themselves. Ironically, as the war lengthened, maritime blockade loomed less in the popular consciousness than the raids of air forces and the movements of armies. And the strong points on which those armies foundered were all too often cities, like Stalingrad and Berlin, rather than natural obstacles, like rivers and mountains. If Europe has experienced total warfare, it did so between 1941 and 1945.

67 V. K. Triandafillov, *The Nature of the Operations of Modern Armies* (London, 1994), 26–9.
68 Erickson, *Soviet High Command*, 308–9, 321, 349–52, 372.

3

Plans, Weapons, Doctrines

The Strategic Cultures of Interwar Europe

DENNIS E. SHOWALTER

It may be a canard that armed forces always prepare for the previous war. It is, however, true that certain forces at the end of certain conflicts look back and congratulate themselves. The Prussian army in 1763, the Royal Navy in 1815, the (re-)United States in 1865 – all remembered flaws of conceptualization and execution, but each could congratulate itself on its overall performance. World War I, however, was an exception. The defeats had been catastrophic; the victories archetypes of "winning ugly." The military establishments of the Western world looked back on the years since 1914 with a single emotion: Never Again – at least not in the same way![1]

International relations were equally dysfunctional. The much-maligned Versailles Treaty and its counterparts were less responsible for that condition than the general lack of restraint that emerged in Europe after 1914.[2] Political climates in general had been significantly brutalized by four years of war. The Little Entente; France's network of Eastern European alliances; and Italy's Balkan ambitions encouraged unstable successor states to threaten each other with armies they could not afford. Postwar economic relationships developed in zero-sum contexts well before the Great Depression.[3] Great-power policy became the conduct of war by other means. The new Soviet Union regarded itself in a state of war with its capitalist counterparts. Germany and Russia were entirely excluded from the peace negotiations.

1 See the contributions to *Military Effectiveness*, vol. 2: *The Interwar Period*, ed. Allan Millett and Williamson Murray (Boston, 1988); and Williamson Murray and Allan Millett, eds., *Military Innovation in the Interwar Period* (Cambridge, 1996).

2 On the treaties and their consequences, see particularly Manfred F. Boemeke, Gerald D. Feldman, and Elisabeth Glaser, eds., *The Treaty of Versailles: A Reassessment After 75 Years* (New York, 1998).

3 Cf. Gyorgy Ranki, *Economy and Foreign Policy: The Struggle of the Great Powers for Hegemony in the Danube Valley, 1919–1939* (New York, 1983); and Steven A. Schuker, *The End of French Predominance in Europe: The Financial Crisis of 1924 and the Adoption of the Dawes Plan* (Chapel Hill, N.C., 1976). David A. Kaiser, *Economic Diplomacy and the Origins of the Second World War: Germany, Britain, France, and Eastern Europe, 1930–1939* (Princeton, N.J., 1980), carries the story forward.

The Allies blockaded Germany for a year after the armistice. Low- and mid-level armed conflict persisted into the mid-1920s: Germany, everywhere in Eastern Europe, Russia and Poland, Turkey and Greece. Even the League of Nations developed into a forum for expressing antagonisms. Woodrow Wilson's principle of "open covenants openly arrived at" too often became "overt hostilities publicly expressed."[4]

In previous eras, such compound-complex antagonisms would have led either to resolution by war or to substantive negotiations undertaken from fear of war.[5] After 1918, however, the second was unviable because the first was impractical. The Great War left few precedents on which to build future conflicts. At one end of the spectrum, the experience of 1914–18 seemed to argue the necessity of total, permanent mobilization of the state's material, human, and spiritual resources. In his postwar writings, Germany's Erich Ludendorff presented the purest model of a comprehensively militarized society under a leader with dictatorial power. War plans, according to Ludendorff, must integrate foreign and domestic policies, economic and operational planning, tactical doctrine and psychological conditioning. Internal critics faced silencing or incarceration.[6]

The problem with such dystopian visions lay in their implementation. The experiences of Europe's major belligerents between 1914 and 1918 indicated above all the *limits* of national mobilization, even in a contest for mortal stakes. No permanent balances could be struck among the armed forces, or within them. The Royal Navy successfully insisted on top priority for steel. In consequence, British tanks went into battle in 1917 armored in boiler plate.[7] Civilian needs continued to exist apart from the war effort. Triage might be useful in field hospitals, but its principles could not be universally applied. Parallel military administrations like the "Deputy Corps Commands" in Germany were short-war institutions. They had never been expected to function much longer than it took the Kaiser's proverbial leaves to stop falling. Their best young officers were combed out as the war

4 Case studies of this pattern in different contexts include Bastiaan Schot, *Nation oder Staat? Deutschland und der Minderheitsschutz: Zur Völkerbundpolitik der Stresemann-Ära* (Marburg, 1988); Ingeborg Plettenberg, *Die Sowjetunion im Völkerbund, 1934 bis 1939* (Cologne, 1987); and Michael D. Callahan, "Mandates and Empire in Africa: Britain, France, and the League of Nations Mandates System 1914–1931," 2 vols., Ph.D. diss., Michigan State University, 1995.

5 See, e.g., Paul W. Schroeder, *The Transformation of European Politics, 1763–1848* (Oxford, 1994).

6 Erich Ludendorff, *Kriegführung und Politik* (Berlin, 1921); and *Der Totale Krieg* (Munich, 1935). Cf. Azar Gat, *Fascist and Liberal Visions of War: Fuller, Liddell Hart, Douhet, and Other Modernists* (Oxford, 1998).

7 Cf. Jon Sumida, "British Naval Operational Logistics 1914–1918," *Journal of Military History* 57 (1993): 447–80; and David J. Childs, *A Peripheral Weapon? The Production and Employment of British Tanks in the First World War* (Westport, Conn., 1999).

endured. Most of the seniors had been retired for a good few years before returning to duty in 1914. Four years later they were still at their desks, making decisions and implementing policies so infuriating to civilians that it became questionable whether total mobilizations, wherever attempted, had not been disruptive rather than productive – at best, efficient rather than effective.[8]

At the spectrum's other end, in the micro-world of operations, the Great War had witnessed the steady replacement of industrial by artisanal models.[9] At company levels the homogenized infantryman with rifle and bayonet had given way to a synergy of specialists: light machine gunners, rifle grenadiers, hand bombers. Battalions and regiments had infantry guns, one-pounders, trench mortars. Tactics grew correspondingly complicated and command correspondingly demanding. Even sergeants now led small combined-arms teams.[10] What did not show up on the ground, however, was the tendency of these New Models to become perpetual-motion machines – again, more efficient than they were effective. The clearest indication of this is the German image of the "front fighter." The stormtrooper remains in many quarters a myth-dominated study in military *virtu*. Put to a large-scale test in March 1918, however, these vaunted shock soldiers showed the limits of their methods. Able to break *in* to enemy positions, they could neither break *through* nor break *out*.[11]

Artisanal patterns were demonstrated as well in the combined-arms, corps-level, semi-mobile style of war furthest developed in the British Expeditionary Force (BEF) during the war's final months. Infantry, artillery, engineers, tanks, and close-support aircraft harmonized their specific qualities in the context of communications systems insufficiently developed to permit systematic control. The result was a pattern of lurching forward, regrouping, then lurching forward again, always at the price of heavy

8 Gerald D. Feldman, *Army, Industry, and Labor in Germany, 1914–1918* (Princeton, N.J., 1966), is still the best overview. See also Richard Bessel, *Germany After the First World War* (Oxford, 1993), 4, passim; and Karl-Ludwig Ay, *Die Entstehung einer Revolution: Volksstimmung in Bayern während des Ersten Weltkrieges* (Berlin, 1968).

9 On this development in a German context, see Dennis E. Showalter, "Niedergang und Zusammenbruch der deutschen Armee 1914–1919," in Dietrich Papenfuss and Wolfgang Schieder, eds., *Deutsche Umbrüche im 20. Jahrhundert* (Cologne, 2000), 39–69.

10 Paddy Griffith, *Battle Tactics of the Western Front: The British Army's Art of Attack, 1916–1918* (New Haven, Conn., 1994), is a case study of this development in the BEF. Cf. James W. Rainer, "Ambivalent Warfare: The Tactical Doctrine of the AEF in World War I," *Parameters* 13 (Sept. 1983): 34–46.

11 Cf. Bernd Hüppauf, "Schlachtenmythen und die Konstruktion des 'Neuen Menschen,'" in G. Hirschfeld et al., *Keiner fühlt sich hier als Mensch* (Essen, 1993), 43–84; Thomas Rohkrämer's chapter in this book; and Bruce I. Gudmundsson, *Stormtroop Tactics: Innovation in the German Army, 1914–1918* (New York, 1989).

casualties.[12] The approach was state-of-the-art, the best solution possible given the limits imposed by terrain, technology, and the casualties of the previous three and a half years.[13] It was not, however, the kind of warmaking that generated complacency in General Staff circles.

One possible alternative was pacifism. Another involved disarmament: negotiating mutual efforts to reduce military capacities. While both approaches influenced general policy making in the interwar period, Europe's armed forces developed a third: finding more effective ways to fight. Reaction to political frustrations exacerbated by military gridlock encouraged the development in Europe during the 1920s and 1930s of five new strategic concepts: paralysis, management, mass, shock, and compensation. Each produced its own operational and technological infrastructures. Each also generated a "strategic culture," a comprehensive way of viewing and making war. Each was intended to enable its host system to make war by averting the Great War's spiral into ineffective efficiency. They had in common an emphasis on focusing material and moral mobilization in ways seen as making military decisions possible. Yet each strategic culture was also autarkic, divorced from its counterparts and from the policy and the political considerations of grand strategy. The result was an unintended consequence, as the "conflict facilitators" marked out despite themselves the path to total war.

I

The first alternative to the Great War's legacy involved paralysis: striking an enemy's moral and material resources at their roots, from the air. In the 1920s, however, even specialized journals like *Rivista Aeronautica* and *Revue de l' Aeronautique militaire* provided at best limited forums for discussion of strategic air power. A French air force that achieved institutional independence only in 1933 did no more than dally with the concept. Italy had too many other competitors for scarce resources, and an air force strongly influenced by Fascist vitalism had little patience with doctrinal abstractions. Germany's theorists did not ignore strategic bombing, but gave it a distinctly lower priority than a land-oriented, combined-arms approach

12 Cf. J. P. Harris, *Amiens to the Armistice: The BEF in the Hundred Days' Campaign* (London, 1998). Jonathan Bailey, "The First World War and the Birth of the Modern Style of Warfare," SCSI Occasional Paper (Camberley, 1996); and Shane Schreiber, *Shock Army of the British Empire: The Canadian Corps in the Last 100 Days of the Great War* (Westport, Conn., 1997).

13 For a counterargument, see Timothy E. H. Travers, "Could the Tanks of 1918 Have Been War Winners?" *Journal of Contemporary History* 27 (1992): 389–406.

extending the battlefield to an enemy's rear zones, as opposed to flying over them. Russia's vast spaces conditioned thinking in the long-distance terms required by strategic bombardment. Soviet strategists nevertheless saw future war primarily in terms of combined-arms operations – especially after their experiences in the Spanish Civil War. The formidable heavy bomber fleet the USSR built in the 1930s reflected less a commitment to sending revolution down Europe's chimneys than an economy so devoted to military production that prioritizing was unnecessary.[14]

It was Britain's Royal Air Force that began institutionalizing strategic bombardment. Britain had embarked on a strategic air offensive under the auspices of the Royal Navy as early as 1916, responding to German Zeppelin attacks on London. The material results of the early raids were so difficult to determine that reports devoted increasing attention to their moral effect. By late 1917 the army's Royal Flying Corps picked up the argument, insisting that regular and repeated bombing attacks would disrupt German production and undermine German confidence. In effect, every bomb counted no matter what it hit.

This early form of cost-effectiveness was particularly congenial to airmen, given the difficulty of hitting anything from any altitude with the technologies available even in the war's final year. It struck a snag when, with the end of the war, the newly created RAF and the U.S. Air Service sent assessment teams into Germany. Their reports reached similar conclusions, finding no significant correlation between effort expended and damage inflicted. As for moral consequences, German civilians were more incensed at slow payment of damage claims than intimidated by the bombing that inflicted the damage.[15]

These reports were processed, however, by an Air Ministry anxious to justify its existence in a postwar era of tight budgets and a "Ten Year Rule" assuming no major war for a decade. Civil servants as well as officers insisted on the Royal Air Force's unique, indispensable role of mounting continuous direct attacks against enemy factories and morale. Even the best home

14 Cf. Williamson Murray, "Strategic Bombing: The British, American, and German Experiences," in Murray, ed., *Military Innovation in the Interwar Period*, 96–143; James S. Corum, *The Luftwaffe: Creating the Operational Air War, 1918–1940* (Lawrence, Kans., 1997); L. Robineau, "French Air Policy in the Interwar Period and the Conduct of the Air War Against Germany from September 1939 to June 1940," in H. Boog, ed., *The Conduct of the Air War in the Second World War* (Oxford, 1992), 85–107; and Thierry Vivier, "Le Douhetisme française enter tradition et innovation (1933–39)," *Revue Historique des Armées* 184 (1991): 89–99. A common subtext of strategic bombardment's continental critics was that conventional bombs took too much time to be acceptable in modern strategic contexts, while even the hardest-core air warriors were reluctant to proclaim openly the military virtues of gassing masses of civilians.

15 George K. Williams, *Biplanes and Bombsights: British Bombing in World War I* (Maxwell, Ala., 1999).

defense was an offense. Limited funds were better spent on bombers than fighters, on aerial explosives rather than antiaircraft guns.[16]

Despite its interest-group origins, warmaking from above was attractive in British policy contexts for three reasons. It fit the postwar concept of a limited liability strategy vis-à-vis Europe, reflecting in turn a growing acceptance of the concept of "imperial overstretch." Bombers bade fair to replace warships in enabling Britain to take as much or as little of a particular situation as it willed. They provided as well a high-tech element considered unavailable to continental powers constrained to devote most of their spending to ground forces.

In a similar context, air power assumed the deterrent function historically assigned to a Royal Navy now checked, if not mated, by the automobile torpedo. Strategic bombardment, indeed, extended that function by offering deterrence through apocalypse. Citizens of a democracy or subjects of a dictatorship, subjected to sufficient bombing, would either compel their governments to make peace or run wild in the streets in the kind of entropic disorder that had destroyed three of the Great War's major European participants.

Aerial bombardment also promised quick results. Even if some of its claims were clearly overoptimistic, destroying the factories that made guns was easier than destroying the guns one by one. Moreover, a logic that dared not speak openly suggested that women, children, and old people were easier to demoralize than were young, fit men under military discipline.[17]

The policy of air bombardment paid more attention to concept than to execution. It asserted long-distance air raids would do in the future exactly what the RAF's own records demonstrated they had not done in the past: destroy the capacity to make war and the will to fight. Because the effectiveness of bombardment was already postulated, technological and scientific tools to facilitate strategic air operations could not be emphasized in budgets. Nor could squadron-level training seriously and comprehensively address navigation, accuracy, and all the other problems that eviscerated Bomber Command during the first eighteen months of World War II.[18]

16 John Ferris has recently shown that even in this context, the grounds of an effective strategic air defense of Britain were laid in the 1920s. "Fighter Defence Before Fighter Command: The Rise of Strategic Air Defence in Great Britain, 1917–1934," *Journal of Military History* 63 (1999): 845–84.

17 Harford M. Hyde, *British Air Policy Between the Wars, 1918–1939* (London, 1976); Barry D. Powers, *Strategy Without Slide-Rule: British Air Strategy, 1914–1939* (New York, 1976); Uri Bialer, *The Shadow of the Bomber: The Fear of Air Attack and British Policies, 1932–1939* (London, 1980); and Philip Meilinger, "Trenchard and 'Morale Bombing': The Evolution of RAF Doctrine Before World War II," *Journal of Military History* 60 (1996): 243–70.

18 Cf. Neville Jones, *The Beginnings of Strategic Air Power: A History of the British Bomber Force, 1923–1939* (London, 1987); and Max Hastings, *Bomber Command* (New York, 1979), 54 passim.

What began as a doctrine evolved into a mantra, "the bomber will always get through." Should that prove to be less than the case in a next war, it was theoretically possible to rethink comprehensively Britain's national policy. Under stress, however, the predictable reaction would be to improve incrementally the RAF's capacity to smash things and kill people at long range. Destroying an enemy by attrition is not an exact description of total war – but it is close enough for government work.

II

The second paradigm of interwar warmaking was management. Here France took pride of place. Victor in 1918, the continent's principal status quo power, France nevertheless devoted significant effort to analyzing its Great War experience. That experience showed above all the limits of improvisation. At regimental levels the French army went to war with *élan* and *cran* as its principal force multipliers. When those proved insufficient, the generals threw men and shells at the *Boche*. As men and shells ran out, economic and social mobilization was implemented on an emergency basis, with corresponding waste of human and material resources epitomized in 1918 by a nearly empty treasury and all too crowded cemeteries.[19]

Unless Marshal Foch's *jeu d'esprit* about castrating twenty million Germans were taken literally, France was unlikely to have a numerical edge in a second round. Nor was a French economy still dominated by middle-sized family firms going to achieve a sudden takeoff in either Rostow's or the Tofflers's sense of that concept. Permanent peacetime mobilization along Ludendorff's lines was inconceivable in the context of a public and political opinion that could not establish a consensus on the best way of dealing with even a weakened, disoriented, post-1918 Germany.[20]

The solution developed and implemented in France between the World Wars began by creating a centrally controlled grand matrix. Foreign policy was aimed at simultaneously conciliating Germany, extending diplomatic connections in Central Europe, and increasing French influence in the League of Nations. Military budgets were sustained at a higher percentage

19 Jean-Baptiste Duroselle, *France et le Français, 1914–1920* (Paris, 1972), is a useful overview. Cf. R. G. Nobecourt, *L' année du 11 novembre* (Paris, 1968); and Jean Jacques Becker, *Victoire et frustrations, 1914–1929* (Paris, 1990).

20 On this last, cf. Nicole Jordan, *The Popular Front and Central Europe: The Dilemmas of French Impotence, 1918–1940* (Cambridge, 1992); Vincent J. Pitts, *France and the German Problem: Politics and Economics in the Locarno Period* (New York, 1987); Marc Trachtenberg, *Reparations in World Politics: France and European Economic Diplomacy* (New York, 1980); and Walter A. McDougall, *France's Rhineland Diplomacy, 1914–1924* (Princeton, N.J., 1978).

of GNP than in any other interwar great power – Nazi Germany included. By 1938 French military spending in constant francs was over two and a half times what it had been in 1913. Beginning in the 1920s successive governments established institutions of national mobilization needing only final touches and final authorization for implementation as coordinators of strategic planning, economic mobilization, and resource allocation.[21] Compartmentalization, the thinking and acting in the context of a particular service or ministry that was a defining characteristic of the Third Republic, was challenged by the creation of the Conseil Superieur de la Defense Nationale. While hardly a complete success, it nevertheless put France twenty years and another World War ahead of the rest of the great powers in establishing a permanent authority for managing a nation at war. The College des Hautes Etudes de la Defense National was similarly ahead of its time in defining the concept of national security strategy.[22]

Morale factors were not quite so susceptible of calculation. The Great War had left a great weariness, a population strained to physical and psychological breaking points. The dissonances of interwar French society are aphorized in Maurice Chevalier's 1939 hit song satirizing the spectrum of opinions and ailments represented in the mobilized French army.[23] Belief in French fragility contributed significantly to the fundamental postulate of French planning after 1918 that France's next war, no matter how it might be conducted operationally, must be psychologically defensive: "the fatherland again in danger!" In that context what was important above all was time – not years, or even months, but enough weeks to make the nation's war the focus of the people's consciousness. After all, Chevalier's ditty ends with the couplet that the diversity it satirizes nevertheless makes "excellent Frenchmen, excellent soldiers," however unaccustomed they might be to marching in step.

Economic geography set a high price on the time France needed. Most of the country's heavy industry lay within the Metz-Verdun-Strasbourg triangle. Two of those reference points had been part of Germany until 1918; the third was the site of one of the Great War's most destructive battles.

21 Cf. Anthony Adamthwaite, *Grandeur and Misery: The French Bid for Power in Europe, 1914–1940* (London, 1995); Steven Ross, "French Net Assessment," in Allan Millett and Williamson Murray, eds., *Calculations, Net Assessment and the Coming of World War II* (New York, 1992), 136–74; and Robert Frankenstein, *Le prix du rearmament français* (Paris, 1982).

22 Eugenia Kiesling, "A Staff College for the Nation in Arms: The College des Hautes Etudes de Defense Nationale, 1936–1939," Ph.D. diss., Stanford University, 1988, is an excellent analysis of this institution.

23 Annette Becker, *La guerre et la foi: De la mort a la memoire, 1914–1930* (Paris, 1994). Cf. Eugen Weber, *The Hollow Years: France in the 1930s* (New York, 1994).

Losing, even temporarily, the natural resources and manufacturing facilities in this region would negate the planning, the management, on which French national strategy depended. Trading land for time violated both the army's and the Republic's postwar "social contracts" with the people of France. More pragmatically, delay left the frontier zone vulnerable to gas attack.[24]

Couverture, therefore, was best implemented on the far side of the frontier. The French army's initial postwar plans all involved advancing into Germany. The most comprehensive of them, Plan A, introduced in 1924, projected a rapid invasion by as many as thirty divisions in order to occupy key industrial areas and disrupt mobilization and concentration.[25] This was by no means theoretical speculation. In the final months of 1918 the French army had demonstrated increasing skill at both tactical and operational levels in using maneuver instead of frontal attack. The generals believed they could replicate that performance – until a series of political decisions reduced the length of active peacetime service from the three years instituted in 1918 to two in 1921, one and a half in 1923, and a single year in 1928.

Short service was not a partisan issue. In 1922 only eight deputies voted to retain the two-year term; 546 voted against it. But in its wake the number of active French divisions sank from forty-one in 1920 to thirty-two in 1923, and only twenty when the term of service was cut to a year. That was well below the number deemed necessary simultaneously to maintain the forward-leaning strategy of Plan A and to provide an institutional framework adequate for training the biennial intake of draftees. Something had to give. A high command solidly Republican in behavior and conviction opted to concentrate on mobilizing a national army.[26]

In general terms the decision was a logical consequence of the earlier commitment to managed mobilization. Carefully crafted tables of organization eventually allowed most French active units to triple themselves immediately on mobilization. That administrative achievement, however, meant reconceptualizing the notion of even small-scale and limited offensives from a standing start, since all the mobilized formations would require some time to shake down. In that context the Maginot Line was neither a Chinese Wall nor a strategic icon, but an economy of force measure, designed to channel any major German attack north of the Ardennes Forest

24 Robert C. Doughty, *The Seeds of Disaster: The Development of French Army Doctrine, 1918–1940* (Hamden, Conn., 1985), 42ff.

25 Paul-Emile Tournoux, *Haut-commandement: Gouvernement et defense des frontieres du nord et de l'est, 1919–1939* (Paris, 1960).

26 The best analysis by far of this process is Eugenia Kiesling, *Arming Against Hitler: France and the Limits of Military Planning* (Lawrence, Kans., 1996).

and into Belgium – where it would encounter the mobile forces that were an increasing part of French war planning.

Belgium might be no more interested in being a glacis for the French than a highway for the Germans. After 1930, and particularly after 1933, however, the French army expected Germany would make the issue moot by striking first. The French response would be to engage as far forward in Belgium as possible. The army began motorizing the best of its active divisions – no fewer than seven of them by 1939. They were intended to advance in company with another new unit: the light mechanized division. France began the war with three, equipped with the best medium tank in Europe. French strategy, it must be emphasized, was not based on a decisive engagement in Belgium. Instead the motorized/mechanized formations were to draw *Boche* teeth, disrupt *Boche* schedules – and above all buy time for the national army to find its feet and prepare the massive counterattack, itself armor-tipped, that would ultimately decide the war.

Victory was not expected to be easy. To the French, modern war offered no shortcuts. Neither technology, genius, or zeal were likely to end a great-power conflict quickly, or with a small number of casualties. French doctrine correspondingly emphasized four factors. First was the ability to mass artillery, then to concentrate and shift its fire. That depended on durable communications and reliable ranging. Second came infantry able to maneuver effectively against modern defensive systems. That was contingent not only on tactical skill, but on coordinated support by mortars, light infantry guns, tanks, and, increasingly, aircraft as well. Third was supply: ensuring the steady movement of men and shells to forward positions. That required an administrative organization incorporating both "pull" and "push," meeting the needs of the front while keeping the pipelines clear. Fourth came isolating the zone of operations by aerial interdiction. The French Army had organized an entire air division, tactical bombers and escorting fighters, in 1917; and had grown increasingly sophisticated in using it against rear areas and choke points. Its successors, equipped with exponentially more capable aircraft, could achieve even greater success in the next round – if air and ground operations were synergized.[27]

27 Eugenia Kiesling, "Resting Uncomfortably on Its Laurels: The Army of Interwar France," in Harold Winton, ed., *The Challenge of Change: Military Institutions and New Realities, 1918–1941* (Lincoln, Nebr., 2000), 1–24; and "'If It Ain't Broke, Don't Fix It': French Military Doctrine Between the Wars," *War in History* 3 (1996): 90ff. Judith Hughes, *To the Maginot Line: The Politics of French Military Preparation in the 1920s* (Cambridge, Mass., 1971); and Michel Forget, "Cooperation Between Air Force and Army in the French and German Air Forces During the Second World War," in Boog, ed., *Conduct of the Air War*, focus on specific aspects of planning.

All four doctrinal foci depended on management. The "managed battle" and the "managed campaign" were designed to address the exponentially increased killing power of modern weapons and the correspondingly reduced fighting power of modern conscripts. The French interwar aphorism that "fire kills" is often cited to illustrate a static, retrograde approach to military planning. But what else caused the losses of World War II, Vietnam, and the Gulf Wars? By 1945 British infantry in northwest Europe were such a scarce commodity that they were riding into battle in tanks converted to personnel carriers. A Red Army that attacked through minefields as if they were not there also counted its artillery in divisions and corps, and numbered its ground support aircraft in thousands.

Nor, in a broader context, did the experience of World War II challenge the French perception that citizen soldiers and citizen officers were unlikely to manifest in any predictable fashion either tactical skill or leadership proficiency. The managed battle provided supervision to guard against disastrous mistakes. It assumed that initiatives undertaken by men with minimal training and little experience were unlikely to produce worthwhile results. Neither Russians, British, nor Americans exactly proved masters of small-unit combat between 1940 and 1945. The often-celebrated German skills in that sphere also declined exponentially as losses mounted and enemies grew less obliging.

The essence of management was coordinating the disparate elements of modern warfare, producing a whole greater than the sum of its parts. Throughout World War II, military electronics were better suited to control than to communication. It was easier and more certain to transmit information and adjust movements in rear echelons than in battle zones; and to do so vertically rather than laterally.[28]

Management was not button-pushing. A French commander was not a bureaucrat but a symphony conductor, expected to bring his own inspiration to bear on the "score" of the plan and the "musicians" executing it. The managed approach to war was also a measure of limiting war by controlling and focusing the application of force, as opposed to hastily building, then indiscriminately swinging, ever-larger hammers. The self-defined benchmark of French military effectiveness was its ability to manage successfully: to improve the training of its mobilized reservists; to maintain the communications systems demanded by its doctrine; to provide senior officers

28 These lines of argument are developed in Dennis E. Showalter, "Le que l'armée française avait compris de la guerre moderne," in Maurice Vaïsse, ed., *Mai–Juin 1940: Défaite française, victoire allemand, sous l'oeil des historiens étrangers* (Paris, 2000), 29–58.

whose battle symphonies would drown out the Germans' military jazz.[29] Should management fail and the system unravel, France's slide into total war could be quick – and potentially fatal, for a system conditioned at all levels to think *inside* the box.

III

A third culture of war built itself around mass – or, better said, mass multiplied by impulsion. Experience from 1914 to 1918 had shown the limitations of everyman in uniform. Neither his skill in arms nor his enthusiasm for the nation's cause were enough to generate victory. They *were* sufficient to sustain a gridlock that made the citizen soldier a citizen victim, floundering to his doom in the mud of Verdun or Passchendaele, waiting to pick up the rifle of a fallen comrade on the eastern front. On the other side of the equation, elite forces of techno-warriors like the German stormtroopers, or heroic vitalists like Italy's *arditi*, were too small either to shape the outcome of mass war or to infuse those masses with martial qualities.[30]

What, however, might be the military prospects of a people infused with a transcendent idea and given the tools and skills to fight for it? In the disarmed Germany of the early 1920s, General Walther Reinhardt argued for a national militia whose moral strength would complement the small professional Reichswehr mandated by the Versailles treaty. The Franco-Belgian occupation of the Ruhr in 1923 generated a related recommendation for *Volkskrieg* in the style associated with the nineteenth-century Wars of Liberation. Sabotage and guerrilla warfare directed against an invader's vulnerable points, military or civilian, would exhaust him to the point where withdrawal would be a preferred alternative.[31]

These lines of reasoning suffered from the weakness of postulating, as opposed to demonstrating, popular readiness to assume the assigned roles of warrior or guerrilla. They did, however, encourage the Reichswehr to consider affirmatively the concept of *Volksbewegung* subsequently proclaimed

29 Cf. Martin Alexander, *The Republic in Danger: General Maurice Gamelin and the Politics of French Defence, 1933–1940* (Cambridge, 1992); and Claude Paillat's survey, *La guerre immobile (Avril 1939–10 Mai 1940)* (Paris, 1984). Robert Doughty, *The Breaking Point: Sedan and the Fall of France, 1940* (Hamden, Conn., 1990); and Jean Vidalnec, "Les divisions de serie 'B' dans l'armée française pendant la campagne de France, 1939–1940," *Revue Historique des Armées* 1 (1980): 106–26, are case studies.

30 Gudmundsson, *Stormtroop Tactics*; and Giorgio Rochat, *Gli arditi della grande guerra*, rev. ed. (Gorizia, 1990).

31 Cf. Walther Reinhardt, *Wehrkraft und Wehrwille*, ed. E. Reinhardt (Berlin, 1932); and Helm Speidel, "1813–1814: Eine militärpolitische Untersuchung," Ph.D. diss., University of Tübingen, 1924.

by the National Socialists and the possible value of Adolf Hitler as its "drummer."[32]

In the war's immediate aftermath, Italy's army considered reorganizing along the lines of Switzerland's militia. A small regular cadre and truly universal training could produce a mobilized force of over sixty divisions. Generals and politicians, however, dismissed a Swiss-style army as impossible without Swiss-style citizens. Benito Mussolini approached the issue from a slightly different angle. In theory at least, his Blackshirt militia was pre-infused with zeal for the new Italian order. Organized in battalions and regiments, the Blackshirts were expected to serve alongside the conscript army in war, fleshing out and invigorating the small "binary divisions" created in the 1930s for the sake of flexibility.

When put to the test in Ethiopia and Spain, the Blackshirts showed themselves willing enough to fight. The militia "legions," however, possessed neither the cohesion, the training, or the equipment to perform first-line missions against a reasonably effective enemy. And an Italy strained to its limits by trying simultaneously to create modern land, sea, and air forces while engaging in "total colonial warfare" had few material or human resources to spare upgrading Mussolini's amateurs. In short, the "vitalizing" or "fascistizing" of the Italian armed forces had significant practical limits.[33]

It was the Soviet Union that did the most to develop the synergies of mass and impulsion. The Red Army was from its inception an ideological institution. Its roots lay in the Red Guards, the revolutionary formations that emerged from Tsarist regiments and factory militias. Throughout the Civil Wars, the Soviets depended on communist volunteers, workers or peasants, soldiers or students, to revitalize their armed forces at times of crisis. At the same time the Red Army's commanders increasingly perceived the operational limits of politicized enthusiasm both at the front and behind the lines. By the end of the organized fighting, the USSR was committed to a regularized, conscript military system – but one essentially different from its capitalist counterparts.[34]

32 Most recently, this is the argument (significantly overstated) of Carl Dirks and Karl-Heinz Janssen, *Der Krieg des Generals: Hitler als Werkzeug der Wehrmacht* (Munich, 1999).

33 Giorgio Rochat, *L' esercito italiano da Vittorio Veneto a Mussolini* (Bari, 1967), is still a useful introduction. See also Brian R. Sullivan, "The Italian Armed Forces, 1918–1940," *Military Effectiveness*, 2:169–217; Sullivan, "A Thirst for Glory: Mussolini, the Italian Military, and the Fascist Regime," Ph.D. diss., Columbia University, 1984; and Giulia Brogini Künzi's chapter in this book.

34 Curtis S. King, "Victory in Red: An Analysis of the Red Commanders on the Southern Front of the Russian Civil War, 1918–19," Ph.D. diss., University of Pennsylvania, 1999, is excellent on the Red Army's professionalization. Cf. Rex A. Wade, *Red Guards and Workers' Militias in the Russian Revolution* (Stanford, Calif., 1984).

The new Red Army was intended to incorporate Communist Party members at all levels, accept the supervision of political commissars, and be penetrated by the secret police. In a military context the purpose of these innovations was to develop and increase the class consciousness necessary for war against the external class enemy: the capitalist states that surrounded the USSR and sought its destruction because of their own objective dynamics. For the Soviet Union future war was not a contingency, but a given. Preparing for it was not a theoretical exercise, but a pragmatic imperative.[35]

That preparation in turn required the Red Army to be a cutting-edged instrument of social and cultural modernization. From a Soviet perspective, the two missions were synergistic. The regime continued to view the peasants who made up the vast majority of its potential soldiers as unreliable, to the point of being potential raw material for counterrevolution. Yet to exclude peasants from military service was impossible. To accept them conditionally was to invite permanent domestic instability. The Red Army met that challenge by developing an organization that combined active divisions with full-time conscripts and territorial divisions of part-time soldiers, with small cadres of regulars as instructors and specialists. Both types of division mixed workers and peasants as far as possible in an effort to create a community that would produce New Soviet Men on assembly lines.[36]

Such an army, however politically correct it might be, was most likely to succeed militarily in defensive, attritional contexts; trading space and lives for the time needed to mobilize Russia's resources. An emerging generation of communist military specialists regarded that form of total war as unnecessary. It invited regression to the irregular, partisan-warfare amateurism of the Civil Wars. It incorporated social risks, should the peasants' commitment to the New Order prove evanescent. It also invited replicating the hecatombs of a Great War the Red Army's young Turks perceived as the apotheosis of capitalism.

A rising generation of revolutionary technocrats like M. V. Tukhachevsky called for the development of a mass mechanized army supported by a comprehensive industrial base. In the mid-1920s N. E. Varfolomeev, who held the chair of "operations" at the Red Army Military Academy, was describing the total destruction of enemy forces by a series of deep operations.

35 Cf. James J. Schneider, *The Structure of Strategic Revolution: Total War and the Roots of the Soviet Warfare State* (Novato, Calif., 1994); Jacob W. Kipp, "The Militarization of Marxism," *Military Affairs* 49 (1985): 184–91; and Walter D. Jacob, *Frunze: The Soviet Clausewitz* (The Hague, 1969).

36 Cf. Roger R. Reese, *Stalin's Reluctant Soldiers: A Social History of the Red Army, 1925–1941* (Lawrence, Kans., 1996); and Mark von Hagen, *Soldiers in the Proletarian Dictatorship: The Red Army and the Soviet Socialist State, 1917–1930* (Ithaca, N.Y., 1990).

Initially these depended on "shock armies" for breakthrough and successive echelons of cavalry for exploitation and pursuit – a concept particularly appealing to the *Konarmya* veterans who exercised an influence in the Red Army similar to airborne officers in the United States after 1945.

A "New Model" army could export the revolution as well as defend it. It could preempt wavering and suppress doubt by delivering early victories. It would validate the ideology that was the Soviet Union's ultimate source of legitimacy. Commissars' reports demonstrated that the army's ranks included many "reluctant soldiers." They would be transformed into enthusiasts not by compulsion or indoctrination, but directly – by experiencing what the Soviet regime could do to its enemies. Even the USSR's adversaries – at least their proletarian elements – might well be sufficiently impressed to join the future.[37]

Mechanization received a decisive boost as Stalin began implementing large-scale, forced-draft industrialization focused on military production. The Soviet dictator repeatedly insisted that to fall behind in modernization was to be defeated: the USSR must make up a fifty-year gap in a decade. In 1930 Tukhachevsky called for eight thousand planes, twenty thousand guns, fifty thousand tanks, to meet the Red Army's future needs. Appointed Deputy Commissar for Military and Naval Affairs in 1931, he initiated the design and production of integrated families of weapons systems, intended to facilitate all phases of continuous operations. High-velocity direct-firing field guns were complemented by light howitzers for high-angle fire and medium-caliber pieces to saturate enemy rear areas. The air force received air superiority fighters, ground attack aircraft, medium and heavy bombers, transports for the newly created deep-penetration airborne units. The USSR fielded tanks designed to support infantry, tanks designed for breakthroughs, tanks designed for exploitation – and counted each category not in hundreds but in thousands.

Tukhachevsky and his supporters insisted that mechanization vitalized, rather than negated, mass war. The projected mobilized strength of the Soviet Union was over two hundred fifty divisions. Nor did machines challenge the revolutionary aspects of the Red Army. Only class-conscious proletarians, the mechanizers argued, could make optimum use of the technologies created under communism. This approach facilitated the proletarianization

37 Cf. the English translation of V. K. Triandafilov, *The Nature of the Operation of Modern Armies* (London, 1994). Secondary analyses include Jacob Kipp, "Soviet Military Doctrine and the Origins of Operational Art, 1917–1936," in Philip S. Gillette and Willard C. Frank, eds., *Soviet Military Doctrine from Lenin to Gorbachev* (Westport, Conn., 1992), 85–133; and, most recent and comprehensive, Richard W. Harrison, *The Russian Way of War: Operational Art, 1904–1940* (Lawrence, Kans., 2001).

of military technology: the privileging of numbers over quality that did much to shape the Soviet Army for the rest of its history. It also linked the army's high command with Josef Stalin, who translated the generals' visions into assembly-line realities.[38]

Ironically, the emergence of this revolutionary juggernaut in the mid-1930s diminished the credibility of Stalin's simultaneous attempts at developing collective-security policies against Adolf Hitler's suddenly resurgent Germany.[39] The size and the structure of the Red Army made it an objective threat impossible to ignore in Paris and London, much less the capitals of central Europe. Domestically, Stalin feared an imbalance of power in favor of the army at the expense of the other elements of the Soviet troika, the Party and the secret police. He responded by organizing a fictitious plot of senior officers against himself, complete with an elaborate supporting structure of forged documents.[40] In the context of the purges already underway, it was a short and logical series of steps from the decapitation of the allegedly treasonous high command to the decimation of the officer corps – a process that continued as late as 1941.

These purges significantly checked the increasing focus of Soviet identity on the armed forces. Another of their results was to transform Tukhachevsky's mechanized mass vanguard of revolution into a blinded, hamstrung, emasculated giant, compelled to seek with brute force what it could no longer hope to achieve with technique. The Red Army had always been conceived as an instrument of total war. But by 1940 it was an instrument of total attritional war – which in turn it waged badly, because that was not part of the institutional and doctrinal structure developed over the previous fifteen years.[41]

IV

The fourth paradigm of interwar warmaking was shock. The German offensives of 1918, despite their limited strategic consequences, attracted

38 Lennart Samuelsson, *Plans for Stalin's War Machine: Tukhachevskii and Military-Economic Planning, 1925–1941* (Basingstoke, U.K., 1999); and Jacob Kipp, "Military Reform and the Red Army, 1918–1941: Bolsheviks, Voyenspetsy, and Young Commanders," in Winton, ed., *The Challenge of Change*. Cf. Walter Dunn, *The Soviet Economy and the Red Army, 1930–1945* (Westport, Conn., 1995).

39 Jiri Hochmann, *The Soviet Union and the Failure of Collective Security, 1934–1938* (Ithaca, N.Y., 1984).

40 The best updates are Igor Lukes, "The Tukhachevsky Affair and President Edvard Benes: Solutions and Open Questions," *Diplomacy and Statecraft* 7 (1996): 505–29; and "Stalin, Benesch und der Fall Tuchatschewski," *Vierteljahrshefte für Zeitgeschichte* 44 (1996): 527–47.

41 David M. Glantz, *Stumbling Colossus: The Red Army on the Eve of World War II* (Lawrence, Kans., 1998); and Beth M. Gerard, "Mistakes in Force Structure and Strategy on the Eve of the Great Patriotic War," *Journal of Slavic Military Studies* 4 (1991): 471–86.

significant postwar attention. Some Italian military planners – once again at the cutting edge of innovation theory – considered reorganizing the army into only a dozen or fifteen divisions. Kept at full strength; given state-of-the-art training, heavy firepower, and high mobility; they would be unleashed offensively at the beginning of Italy's next war. Institutional conservatism arguably did less to discredit the idea than its projected costs – combined with the problem of getting the elite mobile strike force over the mountains separating Italy from its obvious major enemies.[42]

In Great Britain as well, theorists like J. F. C. Fuller and B. H. Liddell Hart called for new approaches to warfare based on small, mechanized forces. Fuller in particular argued that combined-arms coordination as practiced by the BEF in 1918 meant an unacceptable sacrifice of momentum. Instead, he advocated concentrating on an all-armored force with the tank as its common denominator.

The British army had by no means regressed after 1918 to "huntin', shootin', and fishin'," plus the occasional spot of native-bashing in remote imperial corners. It accepted in principle that its core mission involved preparing for conventional war in a great-power context on the continent of Europe. Such preparation involved accepting a high-tech matrix focusing on mechanization. Even the army's old guard rejected the firepower/attrition model of 1916–17. By 1926 theory and practice combined to produce a brigade-strength Experimental Armored Force, with Fuller the designated commander. A combination of operational, financial, and political factors led to its disbanding two years later. Britain continued both to experiment with armored warfare and to extend mechanization and motorization at the expense of mass. The second BEF initially had only four divisions, but it embarked for France in 1939 without a single horse in its order of battle. British acculturation to shock warfare may have been incomplete, but its shortcomings were doctrinal rather than paradigmatic.[43]

"Incomplete" is an adjective that fits Germany's experience as well. The reduction of the Reich's armed forces to 100,000 men without reserves, aircraft, or heavy weapons had limited direct consequences. By the mid-1920s few senior officers took seriously the right-wing image of France

42 Vincenzo Gallinari, *L' esercito italiano nel primo dopoguerra, 1918–1920* (Rome, 1980), 169ff.; and John Sweet, *Iron Arm: The Mechanization of Mussolini's Army, 1920–1940* (Westport, Conn., 1980).

43 Cf., among others, Harold Winton, *To Change an Army: General Sir John Burnett-Stuart and British Armored Doctrine, 1927–1938* (Lawrence, Kans., 1988); J. P. Harris, *Men, Ideas, and Tanks: British Military Thought and Armoured Forces, 1903–1939* (Manchester, 1995); Peter Dennis, *Decision by Default: Peacetime Conscription and British Defense, 1919–1939* (London, 1972); Brian Bond, *British Military Policy Between the Two World Wars* (Oxford, 1980); and David French, *Raising Churchill's Army: The British Army and the War Against Germany, 1939–1945* (Oxford, 2000), 12–47.

seeking only a pretext to finish off its wounded foe. Czechoslovakia built fortifications at the expense of offensive military capacity. The Polish army was a foe the Reichswehr always knew it could beat. Nevertheless, Weimar's diplomatic behavior and military planning drew their basic inspiration from Thucydides. Natural harmony among states is a fiction. International institutions may fine-tune power relationships but cannot replace them. War is the last argument of kings and democracies alike.[44]

From this "realist" perspective, the drastic military imbalance between Germany and its neighbors invited coercive diplomacy, based on compelling assent by negative incentives. In developed forms, a "bullying influence strategy" may not even require overt pressure: the weaker power conforms without prodding. The capacity to challenge such a strategy – or better yet, prevent its employment altogether – is a major component of an effective foreign policy.[45] From the perspective of the Reichswehr that emerged from the collapse of the monarchy and the establishment of the Republic, Germany faced circumstances making the effective waging of war impossible. Germany therefore must avoid war and moderate behaviors and policies having war as a probable outcome.

For military planners, the general disarmament advocated by Foreign Minister Gustav Stresemann in the mid-1920s responded to a truth no less fundamental for being unpleasant. If the military clauses of Versailles were simply abolished, Germany's condition would become worse. A program of expansion designed to raise the Reichswehr to the level of even Poland or Czechoslovakia was likely to generate a ripple effect, forcing Germany into a competition that it had no chance of winning.[46] The de facto military dictatorship of 1916–18 had demonstrated that in practice the High Command lacked the skill and will to wage a war, manage an economy, and manipulate a political system simultaneously. Germany's wartime experience suggested instead the *limits* of the armed forces' capacities outside their areas of professional specialization. The bright young colonels who sought contacts in the business, political, and intellectual communities during the Weimar years were thinking in terms of synergy rather than subordination.[47]

44 Dennis E. Showalter, "Past and Future: The Military Crisis of the Weimar Republic," *War & Society* 14 (1996): 49–72.

45 Cf. Russell Leng and Henry Wheeler, "Influence Strategies, Success, and War," *Journal of Conflict Resolution* 23 (1975): 655–84; and Glenn H. Snyder and Paul Diesing, *Conflict Among Nations: Bargaining, Decision Making, and System Structure in International Crises* (Princeton, N.J., 1977).

46 Michael Geyer, *Aufrüstung oder Sicherheit? Die Reichswehr in der Krise der Machtpolitik 1924–1936* (Wiesbaden, 1980).

47 Cf. Gaines Post, *The Civil-Military Fabric of Weimar Foreign Policy* (Princeton, N.J., 1983); Ernst Hansen, *Reichswehr und Industrie* (Boppard, 1977); and from the military perspective, Johannes Huerter, *Wilhelm Groener: Reichswehrminister am Ende der Weimarer Republik* (Munich, 1993).

It was nevertheless axiomatic in military circles that in any future conflict, Germany's mobilized energy must be channeled through the armed forces. Between 1920 and 1935 the Reichswehr implemented and developed man-management techniques significantly different from any in Europe. The principal gulf in the old Imperial army had not been between aristocrats and commoners, but between short-service conscripts and professionals who trained and commanded them. A small, self-selecting body like the Reichswehr instead fostered stable personal relationships based on common values. Recruit training was designed to engage and socialize the young soldier. Relationships among officers, NCOs, and junior enlisted men tended increasingly toward task orientation and mutual cooperation in common enterprises. Routine and boredom were deadly sins in an army whose rank and file served for twelve years and officers a quarter-century. All ranks were given wide opportunities for increasing varieties of professional development and cross-training, as much to maintain their alertness as to provide cadres for some nebulous future expansion.[48]

By the mid-1920s the Reichswehr was less an army restored than an army reborn. The performance of its professional soldiers on maneuvers as well as the willingness of its officers to experiment with new ideas and new tactics were arousing general admiration in Europe and the United States. Germany's soldiers had never accepted the attrition/breakthrough battles of World War I as anything but a last resort. Their postwar emphasis on mobility, maneuverability, and initiative also reflected an absence of alternatives. The underlying principle of the Reichswehr's operational art was less to seek victory than to buy time for the diplomats to seek a miracle. That meant keeping the army as a force in being, not wearing it down in frontal attacks or hopeless stands. The *Truppenamt*, successor to the now-banned General Staff, was convinced that the next war would be decided by campaigns of maneuver involving large, mobile, regular forces. In other words, like their counterparts elsewhere on the continent, German generals proposed to work with what they had, and they wanted more of it.[49]

"More" meant of necessity something different in a Germany restricted by the Versailles Treaty than it did in Russia, France, or even Britain. The internal-combustion engine was a Reichswehr force multiplier from the beginning. By 1926 training emphasized developing mobile forces

48 Cf. James S. Corum, *The Roots of Blitzkrieg: Hans von Seeckt and German Military Reform* (Lawrence, Kans., 1992); and Adolf Reinicke, *Das Reichsheer 1921–1934* (Osnabrück, 1986).

49 Cf. Wilhelm Meier-Dornberg, "Die grosse deutsche Frühjahrsoffensive 1918 zwischen Strategie und Taktik," in Militärgeschichtliches Forschungsamt, ed., *Operatives Denken und Handeln in deutschen Streitkräften im 19. und 20. Jahrhundert* (Bonn, 1988), 73–96; Robert M. Citino, *The Evolution of Blitzkrieg Tactics* (Westport, Conn., 1987).

complementing the foot-marching infantry. Armored units, represented by dummy tanks and a few improvised armored cars, were an integral part of these formations. The Treaty of Versailles allotted each infantry division a motor transport battalion that usually was underemployed once the peacetime garrisons stabilized. These trucks developed into an increasingly valuable mobile-warfare supplement to the cavalry that – again by Allied design – made up almost a third of the army's combat strength. By 1929 the Reichswehr was even developing theoretical training schedules for as yet nonexistent but operationally independent tank regiments.

Cavalry officers in particular became increasingly involved with ideas for improving the striking and staying power of their arm. Unlike their counterparts in France and Britain, Germany had no armored force to challenge the cavalry's position and foster branch rivalry. Germany's horsemen, in contrast, were likely to find motor vehicles appealing precisely because they were deprived of them. In 1927 the maneuver report of one cavalry division dismissed battle without tanks as "obsolete." If lances were not abolished as field issue until 1927, the cavalry did not drag its feet and hooves with the assiduity of some of their counterparts, Western and Eastern.[50]

After 1930 German war games and maneuvers became increasingly abstract, postulating artificial force structures, troop levels, and political conditions in order to give participants wider chances to learn from the exercises. In turn, this approach encouraged acceptance of the concept that quality could overcome numbers, if "quality" was understood as a comprehensive concept. Mobility, surprise, concentration: these had begun as keys to the Reichswehr's tactical survival. In the 1930s they became the bases of operational-level power projection. Training, staff and line alike, stressed balancing time and space, thinking ahead of the enemy, giving clear, concise orders. Victory depended on the offensive; the successful offensive was a product of a mind-set emphasizing surprise, initiative – and above all, the courage to take risks against odds.[51]

The German army mechanized in reverse. Rearmament added tanks and motor vehicles to already existing doctrines and force structures that stressed the combination of mobility and striking power. Reichswehr and Wehrmacht shared a belief that capacities should be adjusted to doctrines, rather than the other way around – a mind-set contributing to the eventual Hobbesian competition for resources that helped drive Germany into

50 Citino, *Evolution*, 173ff.; Corum, *Blitzkrieg*, 185ff.; and Richard T. Burke, "The German Panzerwaffe, 1920–1939: A Study in Institutional Change," Ph.D. diss., Northwestern University, 1969.

51 Karl-Volker Neugebaur, "Operatives Denken zwischen dem Ersten und Zweiten Weltkriege," in Militärgeschichtliches Forschungsamt, ed., *Operatives Denken und Handeln*, 97–122.

war in 1939. Those capacities, moreover, should focus on winning the decisive victories that would reaffirm the military's privileges of class and calling in the egalitarian, populist Reich that came to power in 1933. Colonel General Ludwig Beck, appointed Chief of a retitled General Staff in October 1933, was a particular advocate of rapid, large-scale rearmament – rearmament with an offensive emphasis. Beck may not have seen the potential of mechanized warfare, or understood its ramifications, as clearly as Heinz Guderian. He nevertheless quickly grasped the new methods' utility as a strategic, as well as an operational, force multiplier.

However complicit they may have been in the rise and survival of the Third Reich, Beck and his colleagues conceived of neither war nor victory in the apocalyptic terms of Adolf Hitler. Instead they processed the Führer's visions in the paradigm of "hard war for limited objectives" that had shaped Prussian/German strategic thinking since the eighteenth century. The General Staff of the Third Reich sought to redraw Europe's map and rebalance its power relationships to Germany's advantage. Its attitude to Poland, Czechoslovakia, and the other Central European successor states owed much to Frederick the Great: frontiers in this region were evanescent, to be adjusted according to the interests of the great powers. Franco-German relations similarly reflected traditional patterns in which force was an ultimate, if not quite an inevitable, arbiter. The *Kriegsmarine*, obsessed with its own short history, was eager to reissue Tirpitz's challenge to the Royal Navy, whether on the sea or under it.[52]

In its developed form, the way of war called *Blitzkrieg* by those who faced it was not predicated on a small professional force as conceived across the Rhine by Charles de Gaulle. Nor did it involve a homogenized mass army in the imperial German style. Its offensives were carried out by high-tech specialized formations within a mass – a functional elite based neither on ideology nor race, but on learned skills. That elite faced the risks of fine-tuning: overheating, exhaustion, attrition. These, however, would become neither strategic nor political problems if "the craft of war" and "the art of policy" synergized as they had in the days of Moltke and Bismarck.

It was in that context that Hitler's apparent approach to foreign policy appealed to Germany's senior officers. Initially the generals gave over to Hitler a *Wiederwehrhaftmachung* beyond their professional concerns and capacities. Now they projected onto him the military's beliefs on the subjects

52 Cf. Wilhelm Deist, *The Wehrmacht and German Rearmament* (Toronto, 1981); Klaus-Jürgen Müller, *Das Heer und Hitler: Armee und Nationalsozialistisches Regime* (Stuttgart, 1969); and Karl-Heinz Janssen, "Politische und militärische Zielvorstellungen der Wehrmachtsführung," in Rolf-Dieter Müller and Hans-Erich Volkmann, eds., *Die Wehrmacht: Mythos und Realität* (Munich, 1999), 75–84.

of national interest, national aggrandizement, and national security. Hitler described the Third Reich as resting on "two pillars": the army and the party. The German military, taking him at his word, assigned to the Nazi leader the role exercised by Bismarck, the policy half of the job done by Frederick the Great. In the minds of the generals, the Führer would establish the political and diplomatic matrices. The Wehrmacht would win the wars – and in the process give the "Bohemian corporal" a badly needed lesson in manners. But should shock not be enough, should Germany's enemies choose to fight rather than capitulate or negotiate – the generals' planning files were as empty as they had been in October of 1914. And the chances for a different course of events were correspondingly slim.[53]

V

The final interwar strategic perspective involved compensation: adjusting Europe's balances by involving the rest of the world. At its most basic level, this involved a new wave of traditional imperialism. Fascist Italy's extension of its influence in North Africa, its conquest and occupation of Ethiopia, its development of a navy and an air force able to secure the new African Empire – all provided indirect leverage in Europe. Its overseas successes positioned Italy to challenge militarily the African positions of Britain and France, to threaten the Suez Canal, to cut British communications in the Indian Ocean. All these things in turn – and at least in principle – made Italy a better friend and a worse enemy than it had been in 1914.[54]

There was nothing particularly unusual in Italy's attempt to use imperial growth to enhance European power. France took a long step further by stationing soldiers from its overseas possessions in the *metropole* during peacetime. The concept of a "Black army," a *force noire* compensating for Germany's larger population, had been dismissed before 1914 as too radical a step.[55] After 1918, however, it became the means of bridging, at least partially, the gap between France's force structure and its commitments.

By 1930 over a fifth of the infantry regiments in the metropolitan army's order of battle came from North and sub-Saharan Africa, Madagascar, and

53 Dennis E. Showalter, "German Grand Strategy: A Contradiction in Terms?" *Militärgeschichtliche Mitteilungen* 48 (1990): 65–102. Cf. Karl-Heinz Frieser, "Die deutschen Blitzkriege: Operativer Triumphstrategische Tragödie," in Müller and Volkmann, eds., *Die Wehrmacht*, 182–96.

54 Cf. Robert Mallett, *The Italian Navy and Fascist Expansionism, 1935–1940* (London, 1998); McGregor Knox, *Mussolini Unleashed, 1939–1941: Politics and Strategy in Fascist Italy's Last War* (Cambridge, 1982); and R. Quartararo, *Roma tra Londra e Berlino: La politica estera fascista dal 1930 al 1940* (Rome, 1980).

55 Marc Michel, "Un Mythe: La 'Force noire' avant 1914," *Relations Internationales* 1 (1974): 83–90.

Indochina. The actual proportion was higher, since the metropolitan regiments were essentially training cadres while the non-European formations were fully manned, with high percentages of volunteers. Without the colonials, France's defense policy would have been unsustainable. As much to the point, the non-Europeans were widely regarded by the rest of the army as elite troops – so long as their French officers and cadres survived to lead and set an example.[56]

They were correspondingly welcome. A navy that since the century's turn had grown increasingly vestigial now found itself tasked with maintaining communications with the empire, securing the systematic – or "managed" – transportation of men and material from the colonies to the continent. Class after class of first-quality ships joined its order of battle. From 4 percent of the military budget in 1918, the navy's share increased to over 20 percent in 1938 – at the expense of an army needing every *sou* it could obtain. No clearer material proof can be offered of the importance of compensation to French strategy.[57]

There were other kinds of proof as well. Never in the history of any modern European state had so many armed men of color been seen for so long in its cities and villages. Their experiences combine in a useful case study of necessity overcoming prejudice. The North African soldiers frequently experienced less discrimination in France proper than at the hands of *colons* across the Mediterranean. Many among the Malagaches and North Africans in particular believed that military service would lead to political reform. The Senegalese had been essentially adopted as human pets during the Great War. That pattern continued afterward, with the *tirailleur*'s purported childish sense of wonder at the marvels of French civilization furnishing material for cartoons, jokes, stories – and sometimes more. Official policy sought to limit strictly any contact between African soldiers and French women. A postcard of the war years nevertheless featured a white rabbit in an apron and a black rabbit wearing a *tirailleur* fez. In *tirailleur* patois, the black rabbit tells the white rabbit that after the war he will take her to Senegal and they will have many *café au lait* bunnies. A second postcard shows a Frenchwoman dressed in the height of fashion and a *tirailleur* in

56 During the interwar period, one-fourth of the personnel of a North African regiment stationed in France were Europeans. About 70 percent of the *tirailleurs* were volunteers, the rest conscripts. The specialized literature on the Africanization of the French interwar army is significantly thin – which, upon reflection, is not surprising. Anthony Clayton, *France, Soldiers, and Africa* (London, 1988), 152ff., 217ff., presents the structural details.

57 Cf. William G. Perrett, "French Naval Policy and Foreign Affairs, 1930–1939," Ph.D. diss., Stanford University, 1977; and Ronald Chalmers Hood, *Royal Republicans: The French Naval Dynasties Between the World Wars* (Baton Rouge, La., 1985).

full kit smiling warmly, if not possessively, at each other. Analyzing the layers of meaning in these artifacts is best left to poststructuralists. It is, however, appropriate to note that possession of such material would for a black man have been a substantial risk in not a few U.S. states until recently.[58]

Armed multiethnicity represented a significant escalation of the position of empire. In principle, Europeans were supposed to be protecting the "lesser races." Now the situation was reversed. Meanwhile, the Germans fulminated about the "Black disgrace," the French use of non-European troops in occupation roles; and bided their time until they could sterilize the few mixed-race children that resulted.

It was Britain, however, that developed the most comprehensive application of compensation. However much Liddell Hart and his fellow blue-water strategists might deplore the "continental commitment," after 1918 it was a fact of military and diplomatic life – only accepted *faute de mieux*, should deterrence fail, but no more to be ignored than gravity.[59] The question was how Britain could best implement the policy in a context of diminished GNP, reduced budgets, and general war weariness.

The general importance of Britain's global commercial and financial networks may safely be stipulated. It was understood from the corridors of Whitehall to the desk of George Orwell that the United Kingdom could neither feed itself nor maintain itself at great-power levels from its own resources. Working together under direction from London, however, Britain, its dominions, and its colonies, had at least a rhetorical claim to superpower status.[60] "Compensation" in the sense of this essay, however, has a narrower, more directly military focus. One of its major elements was the search for a formal security relationship with – and among – the "settlement colonies": Canada, Australia, New Zealand, and South Africa. Their participation in the Great War had been decisive. Each in its own way made plain afterward that the unquestioning response of 1914 could no longer be expected. Britain, despite desperate efforts, was unable to create even a comprehensive system of Imperial defense, to say nothing of cooperative commitment to a European war. Indeed, particularly in the cases of Australia and

58 The postcards are reproduced in Marc Michel, *L' Appel a l'Afrique. Contributions et reactions a l'éffort de guerre en AOF* (Paris, 1982). For a cross-section of contemporary scholarship on images of France's sub-Saharan soldiers, see J. Riesz and J. Schultz, eds., *Tirailleurs Senegalais* (Frankfurt am Main, 1989). For the North Africans, see Recham Belkacem, *Les Musulmans algeriens dans l' armée française, 1919–1945* (Paris, 1996). There are useful insights as well in Jonathan Gosnell, "The Politics of Frenchness in Colonial Algeria, 1930–1954," 2 vols., Ph.D. diss., New York University, 1998.

59 Michael Howard, *The Continental Commitment* (London, 1972).

60 Anthony Clayton, *The British Empire as a Superpower, 1919–1939* (London, 1986).

New Zealand, the commitment was in the other direction, with Britain offering guarantees of support whose fulfillment was at best problematic.[61]

Those guarantees initially reflected concern for the Far Eastern ambitions of a Japan rapidly developing into a major potential enemy. Italy as well began emerging as an objective threat as its Mediterranean and African positions improved. As a consequence, the Royal Navy in particular began concentrating its mind on the sine qua non of defending the empire: a blue-water perspective in many ways more congenial than the previous three decades of littoral emphasis. The army put more attention – and a disproportionate amount of its limited resources – into imperial security commitments.[62] The appeasement policies of the 1930s were in good part driven by the repeated insistence of the Services that there were no feasible military solutions to the problems they were currently tasked to address, let alone preparing to fight a war in Europe. Ergo, since we can't lick them, we must lick their boots – at least temporarily.[63]

Compensation was problematic for Britain in other ways as well. As developed during the interwar years, it depended heavily on maritime blockade: starving out future continental enemies as Germany had been starved in the Great War. Yet here as in so many other areas, interwar scholarship and policy stressed both the moral and practical shortcomings of wartime behavior. Even the official history asked what sense it made to make war on hospital patients and pregnant women.[64] As much to the point, blockade took too long to take effect. Its use seemed a corresponding step toward the "war of long duration" compensation was intended to avoid.

That last point was reinforced because the experience of the 1914–18 blockade had also been seared into Germany's strategic consciousness. The general importance of autarky to Nazi planning was recognized in Britain

61 Cf. Roy F. Holland, *Britain and the Commonwealth Alliance, 1918–1939* (London, 1987); John Robertson, "The Distant War: Australia and Imperial Defence, 1919–41," in Michael McKernan and Margaret Browne, eds., *Australia; Two Centuries of War and Peace* (Canberra, 1988), 223–44; and David Day, *The Great Betrayal: Britain, Australia, and the Onset of the Pacific War* (North Ryde, New South Wales, 1988).

62 Cf. Orest Babij, "The Royal Navy and the Defence of the British Empire, 1928–1934," in Keith Neilson and Greg Kennedy, eds., *Far Flung Lines: Studies in Imperial Defence in Honour of Donald Mackenzie Schurman* (London, 1996), 171–89; Larry Pratt, *East of Malta, West of Suez: Britain's Mediterranean Crisis, 1936–1939* (Cambridge, 1975); and T. R. Moreman, "'Small Wars' and 'Imperial Policing': The British Army and the Theory and Practice of Colonial Warfare in the British Empire, 1919–1939," *Journal of Strategic Studies* 19 (1996): 105–31.

63 Williamson Murray, *The Change in the European Balance of Power, 1938–1939: The Path to Ruin* (Princeton, N.J., 1984).

64 A. C. Bell, *A History of the Blockade of Germany During the Great War* (London, 1937; reprinted, 1961), 73.

almost from the beginning. As much to the point, German naval theorists like Admiral Wolfgang insisted on the importance of gaining control of Scandinavia's Atlantic coastline as a preliminary to a comprehensive campaign against the shipping on which Britain's military effectiveness ultimately depended. After 1933 strategic concepts took operational form. In the next war, German aircraft and surface raiders, pocket battleships and submarines, would attack merchantmen until the Z Plan provided a surface navy strong enough to challenge Britain – and the United States if necessary – directly. A British blockade of Germany, in other words, would have to be implemented in the face of an immediate, massive threat to whatever support the empire provided.[65]

In a context of the "long duration," Britain's interwar policy makers continued to perceive empire as a source of strength. Whatever the specific problems of defending it, no serious discussion of reducing that commitment was undertaken in the interwar years. Yet to the extent that imperial military potential – in men, material, or resources – was more than wishful thinking, its mobilization and focus would above all take time. This was particularly true as during the 1930s the United States increasingly came to be regarded as an adoptive member of the Empire – albeit as yet unaware of its projected status and responsibilities.[66]

That last was less a final flowering of turn-of-the-century Anglo-Saxonism than a sober recognition that Britain needed more than its own immediate resources to keep its place at the table of the great powers. The supplements might be African or Indian, Canadian, Australian, or American. But bringing them to bear would both lengthen and globalize the next war. Compensation, at least in its developed, British form, would in the event prove an ultimate doomsday machine for Europe's mastery of the world.

VI

Between 1918 and 1939, "total war" was a phrase that dominated Europe's discourse on military questions. Yet the semantics of the phrase were anything but literal at the point where theory and policy interfaced. To "managers" it meant "long war." To proponents of shock, it meant "intense

65 Cf. Wolfgang Wegener, *Die Seestrategie des Weltkrieges* (Berlin, 1929); Carl-Axel Gemzell, *Raeder, Hitler und Skandinavien: Der Kampf für einen maritimen Operationsplan* (Lund, 1965); and Jost Dülffer, *Weimar, Hitler und die Marine: Reichspolitik und Flottenbau 1920–1939* (Düsseldorf, 1973).

66 On the projected role of the United States in British security policy, see particularly David Reynolds, *The Creation of the Anglo-American Alliance, 1937–1941: A Study in Competitive Co-operation* (London, 1981).

war." In the aerial-bombardment paradigm, "total war" was a synonym for stunning an enemy. The concept of vitalized mass developed in the Soviet Union came closest to incorporating a developed concept of replacing a defeated enemy's system with one's own. And even that vision was designed to be implemented at minimal cost to the Red Army.

In short, all five of the paradigms discussed in this essay, and the strategic cultures they spawned, were intended to enable making war by restoring decision, averting the Great War's spiral into the ineffective efficiency that resulted in gridlock, mutual exhaustion, and eventual entropy. They represented efforts to reassert normative and temporal constraints. The wars they postulated were horrible beyond most pre-1914 projections, but their horrors would occur within limits. Yet in a paradox that would have delighted Hegel, eventually and increasingly after 1939, each of the interwar "conflict facilitators" broke its banks, interacted with the other four, and combined in a total war out of civilization's worst nightmares. That, however, is a subject for another presentation at another conference.

PART TWO

Legacies of the Great War

4

Religious Socialism, Peace, and Pacifism

The Case of Paul Tillich

HARTMUT LEHMANN

In the late 1950s and early 1960s Paul Tillich was celebrated in the Federal Republic of Germany as an apostle of international understanding and peace. In 1956 the city of Frankfurt awarded him its Goethe Medal. In order to appreciate the significance of this distinction, one must first recall that in postwar Germany, Goethe symbolized not only German idealism but also the best features of the German tradition of humanism and cosmopolitanism – values that stood diametrically opposed to the chauvinism of the Nazi regime. In 1958 Tillich was again honored by the city of Hamburg with the prestigious Goethe Prize; and in 1962 he received the even more prestigious Friedenspreis des deutschen Buchhandels, the peace prize of the Society of German Publishers, which was awarded in a public ceremony in the Paulskirche. These events testified to the desire of Germans to demonstrate that they had learned the lessons of recent history and from the experience of Nazi terror and aggression. Tillich, the distinguished theologian and philosopher, now served as a German crown-witness to international peace.

The remarkable role that Tillich played in postwar Germany raises questions about his views on peace and pacifism during the interwar period. It is fitting to begin with an episode that changed the life of one of Weimar's leading Religious Socialists. On November 6, 1928, Pastor Günther Dehn lectured in Magdeburg's Ulrichskirche on "The Church and International Reconciliation."[1] Here Dehn declared that Christians should not regard the Fifth Commandment as a strict principle, but rather as a guideline to be discussed and redefined as the political situation changed. He then questioned whether national interest was a valid justification for going to war. Although he acknowledged the right of nations to defend themselves if attacked, he

1 The best account of the Dehn controversy is by one of his colleagues, Ernst Bizer, "Der Fall Dehn," in Wilhelm Schneemelcher, ed., *Festschrift für Günther Dehn* (Neukirchen/Moers, 1957), 239–61.

expressed doubts about whether Christians should as a rule take part in such wars. He argued that Christians could decide to defend themselves by force of arms; but he added that they could also refuse to participate in military conflicts. Dehn's statements legitimated the position of conscientious objectors. He believed that many varieties of pacifism were shallow and thoughtless, yet he also denied the parallel between death for the fatherland and death as a Christian sacrifice. Therefore, he explained, war memorials to those who had lost their lives should be erected in public spaces and not in churches. The office of military chaplains should be abolished because clergymen who served in this capacity could not preach freely. Finally, Dehn called for educating children to respect other nations and not to admire the deeds of war heroes.

Predictably, a lively discussion followed Dehn's remarks. A few days later, some in the congregation sent a critical account of the pastor's lecture to the Brandenburg consistory, which in turn asked him for an explanation. Without investigating the charge (denied by Dehn himself) that he had called German soldiers "murderers," the consistory reprimanded him for not having chosen his words more carefully.

Two years later, in December 1930, Dehn was appointed to a professorship in practical theology at the University of Heidelberg. As soon as the appointment was announced, Dehn's right-wing opponents circulated reports about the incident in Magdeburg to members of Heidelberg's theological faculty, which then resolved by a vote of 6–1 that Dehn was "not suited" for the position. The dissenting vote was cast by Martin Dibelius, a renowned scholar of the New Testament. In 1945, Dibelius was one of the few professors in Heidelberg whom the American occupation forces considered qualified to rebuild the university.[2]

As soon as he learned of the resolution, Dehn declined the appointment. In the meantime, he had received another offer, which he accepted, to a professorship at the University of Halle. After notice of his appointment was made public, the Nazi student association issued a pamphlet on February 4, 1931, denouncing Dehn as a pacifist who supported conscientious objection, had called for the removal of war memorials from churches, and advocated educating German children in a spirit of "cowardly pacifism." As he prepared for his lectures in Halle, Nazi students staged a massive protest. They spread slanderous rumors about Dehn and threatened to boycott the university. This time, however, university officials did not succumb to

2 Jürgen C. Hess, Hartmut Lehmann, and Volker Sellin, eds., *Heidelberg 1945* (Stuttgart, 1996), 63–5, 120, 284–6, 398–401, 415.

the pressure. Dehn was given police protection for his first lecture, on November 3, 1931, which was extended for the following weeks.

Shortly before Christmas in 1931, Dehn explained his position once more in an open letter, and he suggested prophetically that what he had himself endured was a prelude to an impending battle between modern nationalism and true Christian beliefs. Distorted idealism was demonic, he charged, provoking yet another round of protest. By early 1932 Dehn's opponents in Halle were joined by Nazi students from Jena and Leipzig, as well as by the Göttingen theologians Hermann Dörries and Emanuel Hirsch. After a difficult summer semester in 1932, when student protests against him continued, Dehn asked for, and received, a one-year sabbatical. Officially it was announced that he needed the time for his scholarship. However, everyone in Halle knew that university officials were anxious to put an end to the student unrest. In April 1933, before he could resume his academic duties, Dehn was dismissed from his academic post by the new Nazi regime. He joined the Confessing Church and was imprisoned by the authorities before he was banished to a small village in Württemberg, where he remained until 1945. In 1946 he was hired by the University of Bonn.

The Dehn episode illustrates two truths. First, the ideas of Religious Socialists like Dehn were much disputed in Weimar Germany. Second, Religious Socialists, who were a small minority, could make themselves heard only in German states where Social Democrats ruled and offered protection. By the spring of 1933 this protection had disappeared. These truths also bore on the career of Paul Tillich, who taught *Religionswissenschaft* (religious studies) at the Technische Hochschule in Dresden from 1925 to 1929 before moving to a chair of philosophy and sociology at the University of Frankfurt in 1929.[3]

Tillich's post-1918 thinking about peace and pacifism had its roots in the era before World War I. In 1914 he was a twenty-eight-year-old pastor, and, like many of his friends, he volunteered for the German war effort. He was assigned to the western front as an army chaplain. His letters and sermons during the war revealed the degree to which he was torn between patriotism and horror. He experienced what he called the spirit of aggressiveness, which helped soldiers endure all kinds of hardship.[4] He also was well aware of the devastation caused by the war. He wrote to his father that after only a few

3 The best brief introduction to Tillich's life and thought is Renate Albrecht and Werner Schüssler, *Paul Tillich: Sein Leben* (Frankfurt am Main, 1993).

4 "Der Aggressiv-Geist, der über alle Strapazen hinweg hilft": Paul Tillich to his Father, Mar. 9, 1915, in Renate Albrecht and Margot Hahl, eds., *Paul Tillich: Ein Lebensbild in Dokumenten: Briefe, Tagebuchauszüge, Berichte, Ergänzungs- und Nachlassbände zu den gesammelten Werken* 5 (Stuttgart, 1980), 87.

hours of combat healthy young soldiers turned pale and gray and could hardly speak. Once the nobility of war, the inspiring passion of the first few weeks, had disappeared, he remarked in 1915, one was left only with the burden and the terror of war.[5] He was horrified by what he saw. War was at once mechanization and disorganization, he wrote in 1917. The individual was destroyed, pressed into the service of machines.[6]

The same tensions and contradictions surfaced in Tillich's sermons during the war. He preached that Germans should rejoice because the "Lord had done great things" for them.[7] He recalled the heroic deeds of Germans in the past,[8] and he admonished soldiers not only to believe in the greatness of the German nation, but also to honor the German emperor.[9] Yet in 1916 he prayed openly for peace.[10] He characterized the losses of war in unembellished terms.[11] When he buried young soldiers in 1918, he reminded his comrades that the Kaiser's proclamations had not brought peace but renewed struggles, hatreds, and hostilities. Genuine peace, he preached, could only be found in Christ:

> Our Kaiser's words of peace have died away amid the din of new battles, the din of hate and enmity. And these comrades of ours, too, have hoped in vain. Strife did not release them until the last moment. Disquiet and labor day and night, fighting and watching, hardship and burdens, and added to all this the restless yearning of the heart, the thoughts of home, the daily familiarity of death; and finally they have been swallowed by strife, having become its victims. Our heart is shocked at what we see every day and at every new grave – the triumph of strife.[12]

These were not the words of a pastor who was trying to give meaning to death for the fatherland, nor were they even words of consolation. The fallen soldiers were victims of a world of hardship and hostility, Tillich concluded, and peace was no part of it.

Looking back on his war experience in 1919, Tillich remarked that he had early come to see the war as the doom of European culture and the product of extreme social injustice, and that he had become increasingly angry over this realization. He wrote that he had learned in particular to see the limits of national loyalties during the war and the curse that nationalism, if carried to the extreme, brought upon people. After the war, he wished to contribute to a new society, which would be born of the spirit of both

5 Ibid., 88.

6 Letter to members of his fraternity, Aug. 19, 1917; ibid., 108.

7 Sermon, Aug. 1, 1915, in Erdmann Sturm, ed., *Paul Tillich: Frühe Predigten (1909–1918)* (Stuttgart, 1994), 402.

8 Sermon, 1915 (no exact date), ibid., 415.

9 Sermon, Jan. 27, 1916, ibid., 433.

10 Sermon, Aug. 1916 (no exact date), ibid., 494–7.

11 Sermon, 1918 (no exact date), ibid., 642.

12 Sermon, 1918 (no exact date), ibid., 651.

Christian love and socialism – a society in which capitalism and nationalism alike had been overcome.[13]

This letter was one of the documents that signaled Tillich's conversion to Religious Socialism. Before the war, this movement had been propounded mainly by the Württemberg Pietist Johann Christoph Blumhardt and his Swiss disciples, Leonhard Ragaz and Hermann Kutter. After the war, some former students of Ernst Troeltsch and former adherents of German "cultural Protestantism" (*Kulturprotestantismus*) joined the movement. They formed what might be called the Berlin chapter of Religious Socialism, and Tillich soon became one of its leading voices.

Tillich set out to elucidate the program of Religious Socialism in the early years of the Weimar republic. In 1923 in his *Principles of Religious Socialism* (*Grundlinien des Religiösen Sozialismus*), he argued that the demonic power of nationalism had led nations to ignore the right of others to exist. Nationalism, he wrote, had been born as theocratic imperialism. The European nation-states were not imperialistic because of any primitive or natural will to power and expansion, but instead because they embodied theocratic ideas. To overcome nationalism, a dual strategy was necessary. It was essential not only to fight the demonic side of nationalism, Tillich insisted, but also to strengthen international law and cooperation. The natural anarchism of war was despicable, but the mystical anarchism of religious pacifism, which counseled nonresistance against those who broke the law, offered no convincing alternative. The solution lay instead, he concluded, in the will to safeguard the law and respect for those who enforced the rule of law within and among societies.[14]

In 1926, in a treatise titled *The Religious Situation of Our Time* (*Die religiöse Lage der Gegenwart*), Tillich spelled out the difference between bourgeois pacifism and socialist pacifism. He argued that the strongest of the driving forces of bourgeois pacifism was economic gain. By contrast, socialist pacifism was rooted in the ideal of humanity. After 1918, he noted, these varieties of pacifism complemented each other, as both Anglo-American bourgeois pacifism and socialist pacifism supported the establishment of an international order to encourage the progress of humankind.[15]

In yet another treatise, which he published in 1931 on *The Problem of Power* (*Das Problem der Macht*), Tillich touched on another important idea:

13 Letter to students of his fraternity, Sept. 1919, reprinted in Alrecht and Hahl, *Lebensbild*, 143–4.

14 Paul Tillich, *Christentum und soziale Gestaltung: Frühe Schriften zum Religiösen Sozialismus*, ed. Renate Albrecht (Stuttgart, 1962), 112–14.

15 Paul Tillich, *Die religiöse Deutung der Gegenwart: Schriften zur Zeitkritik*, ed. Renate Albrecht (Stuttgart, 1968), 48–9.

social groups could refrain from using force. He explained that the use of force implied the possibility of not using it, and the use of force could be refused for the sake of justice, love, or even a classless society. A church that refused the use of force would become a true church. Should a whole people do so, Tillich concluded, it would represent a turning point in human history and, perhaps, create a new world.[16]

During the Weimar era, Tillich's views on peace and pacifism were shaped by two considerations. First, as a socialist, he believed in the solidarity of all human beings. Second, as a practicing Christian, he hoped for the solidarity of all churches in safeguarding the peace. Churches and their clergy should no longer serve national policies, he stated, as they had before 1918 and continued to do so afterward. According to Tillich, the ecumenical movement should create an international climate in which nations no longer settled disputes by means of war. Therefore, he believed, church leaders should strengthen international law and cooperation and become responsible for international peace.

Tillich's position in the 1920s could not, however, be characterized simply as Religious Socialism. He might better be described as an ecumenical idealist, a cosmopolitan supporter of international peace. But while he cherished the proposals of radical pacifists in the 1920s, he never subscribed to them completely. In the 1920s he did not explicitly discuss aspects of "total war," but he did address the causes of this phenomenon. In particular, he took up what he considered the main causes of warfare in modern times – chauvinism, national egoism, national expansionism, nationalistic aggressiveness, and the use of military force to pursue national policies.

Tillich was never so close to utopian pacifism as he was in 1931, when he embraced the ideal of peaceful societies whose coexistence did not require the use of force or threat thereof. He could not foresee that a different kind of turning point in human history would occur shortly thereafter. In the spring of 1933 Tillich, like many of his friends, lost his academic position. Unlike many of them, he had the good fortune to be invited to the United States to teach at the Union Theological Seminary in New York City.

In the fall of 1934 Tillich wrote an open letter to Emanuel Hirsch, with whom he had been close before 1918. While Tillich had developed a theory of Religious Socialism in the 1920s, Hirsch devoted himself to *völkisch* political theology. According to Hirsch, the rise of National Socialism was a sign that God had decided, as part of His economy of salvation, to elevate the German people to new greatness. Hirsch thus championed Hitler as

16 Tillich, *Christentum und soziale Gestaltung*, 204–6.

the savior of the German people.[17] In his letter, Tillich asked Hirsch not to reject Religious Socialism altogether. Like Hirsch, he himself had seen the crisis of bourgeois capitalism and had looked forward to the renewal of Germany and Europe once social classes had been abolished. Hence, he had decided to support the workers' movement. Tillich thus accused Hirsch of perverting eschatology into the sacralization of the Nazis' rise to power. He abhorred Hirsch's claim to live in a blessed era, in the divinely ordained spring of the German nation. By contrast, Tillich had never characterized an era as sinful or blessed, for he had always recognized power's demonic side. To him, it was terrifying to see Hirsch claiming political events as a source of revelation, equal in importance to biblical testimony. He could never share such views. Equally wrong, Tillich observed, was Hirsch's equating of the German people with a racial covenant (*Blutbund*) that blurred the separation between the worldly order and Christian socialism. Tillich and his friends among the Religious Socialists had always recognized the difference between religious belief and socialism, and they had tried to give meaning to the bonds among all true Christians.[18]

Living as a political refugee in the United States between 1933 and 1939, Tillich was forced to reconsider his position on international peace. After returning from a trip to Europe in 1936, he observed that Europeans had missed the opportunity to move toward lasting peace. By 1936 the destructive consequences of this failure could no longer be overlooked or avoided. Politicians in France feared rearmament and renewed warfare, as did British pacifists. In his view, both of these attitudes, however morally laudable, would lead to the exact opposite: a new armed conflict. As he analyzed the European situation Tillich noted the omnipresence of fear, uncertainty, and senselessness. By hesitating and making compromises, the ruling political parties in the western democracies were giving support to antidemocratic forces.[19]

In the mid-1930s Tillich lauded the virtues of pacifist groups in the United States and Great Britain. In an essay on "The Social Functions of the Churches in Europe and America," which he published in 1936, he praised the Quakers' spirit of "absolute tolerance," as well as the connection

17 On Emanuel Hirsch, see Robert P. Erickson, *Theologians under Hitler: Gerhard Kittel, Paul Althaus, and Emanuel Hirsch* (New Haven, Conn., 1985).

18 Open letter to Emanuel Hirsch, Oct. 1, 1934, Paul Tillich, *Briefwechsel und Streitschriften: Theologische, philosophische und politische Stellungnahmen und Gespräche*, eds. Renate Albrecht and René Tautmann (Frankfurt am Main, 1983), 142–76.

19 "Eine geschichtliche Diagnose: Eindrücke von einer Europareise 1936," Paul Tillich, *Impressionen und Reflexionen: Ein Lebensbild in Aufsätzen, Reden und Stellungnahmen*, ed. Renate Albrecht (Stuttgart, 1972), 239–42.

between this kind of tolerance and democratic forms of government.[20] But he increasingly realized that in preserving the peace, pacifism could not be the last word.

Reacting to the news of Nazi policies, Tillich became more critical of pacifist ideas. In the speeches and writings of his years in exile, he made clear his conviction that the totalitarian rule of dictators, insofar as it threatened the peace, should not be tolerated. The reality of Nazi Germany forced Tillich to begin to understand the ugly face of total war, which meant total control, total mobilization, total methods of warfare, and total war aims.

In a long essay titled *Religion and World Politics* (*Religion und Weltpolitik*), which he composed in 1938 but did not publish at the time, Tillich laid out his revised position. Now he argued that with the victory of the Enlightenment, genuine cosmopolitanism had replaced medieval theocratic universalism, and lasting peace had been inscribed in the program of all citizens who subscribed to the new ideal. Since the Enlightenment, however, bourgeois nationalism had defeated cosmopolitanism. Worse, in many places aggressive nationalism had taken the form of racial ideologies and the romanticism of blood and soil. Nonetheless, Tillich reminded his readers that pacifism, based on Christian values and humanism, had not ceased to exist. In fact, the aggressive nationalism of the totalitarian dictatorships, which was evident everywhere, lent acute topicality to the ideas that underlay pacifism.[21] In Tillich's view, however, the fundamental weakness of all idealism was that it failed to take changing political conditions into account. Idealism had thus nurtured utopian pacifism, as well as socialism, but it had not done enough to prevent the rise of power-politics based on national egoism.[22] Tillich then considered the possibilities for a world of justice without the use of force. Now, however, he characterized this pacifist ideal as an extreme situation, a state of such angelic perfection that it might even lead to "a kind of dehumanization" (*eine Art Entmenschlichung*).[23]

After Germany invaded Poland in the fall of 1939, and once it was clear that another European war had begun, Tillich admonished American Protestants to distinguish among three political positions. First, he explained, radical pacifism was based on the belief that a political system was possible without recourse to force, even though no power would then resist international aggressors. Second, a position that he called "more moderate pacifism"

20 Paul Tillich, *Das religiöse Fundament des moralischen Handelns: Schriften zur Ethik und zum Menschenbild*, ed. Renate Albrecht (Stuttgart, 1965), 114.

21 Paul Tillich, *Die religiöse Substanz der Kultur: Schriften zur Theologie der Kultur*, ed. Renate Albrecht (Stuttgart, 1967), 144–5.

22 Ibid., 168.

23 Ibid., 177.

(*gemilderter Pazifismus*) demanded, in the present case, that America stay out of the European war; this was a policy of isolationism. Finally, Tillich wrote of a policy of responsibility for Europe and the world. This policy opposed the depredations committed by nationalist dictatorships as well as the irresponsible nationalism of the American isolationists. Tillich argued that, as a Christian and democratic nation, America was responsible for the world's future. Many American Christians had a guilty conscience because the United States had not supported the League of Nations. More important, he noted that since the start of the war the ecumenical movement had produced a new kind of international solidarity among the Christian churches. No longer could these churches lend their moral support to the exercise of national power or the ideology of nationalism. Christian leaders of many countries had instead learned that Christian solidarity, a comprehensive expression of humanity, had to replace divisive nationalism. Thus, despite their weaknesses, Tillich called on the churches to speak out for the equality of all human beings and to do so in the name of the kingdom of God.[24]

By 1941 Tillich was convinced that only the reform of the League of Nations could prevent a third world war. Because national sovereignty remained a demonic force, a genuine confederation of all states (*ein Staatenbund*) must replace the League of Nations. Given the ideal of unity among all peoples, this was a limited goal, he admitted, but unlike the political dreams of pacifists, it was realistic. Such a confederation should thus be the foremost American war aim.[25]

In 1942, in an essay titled "The Word of Religion" ("Die Botschaft der Religion an den heutigen Menschen"), Tillich argued that Christians must defend more than before what he called the *religiosum reservatum*. For Christians it was not enough to defend America against Hitler or to defeat Germany for the second time in the twentieth century. Such victories would serve nothing but cynical opportunism if America failed to shoulder responsibility after the war for rebuilding Europe in a radically new way. As long as Americans did not look beyond the day of victory, the postwar world would witness the renewed defeat of human values. The crusading spirit of 1917, and the spirit of humanism and pacifism predominant in the decades since the war, had created a great number of illusions, Tillich now argued. These illusions had all been destroyed. Religion, by which he meant experts in the field of religion, could perhaps have prevented such illusions about human nature or the progressive course of history. For this reason, he

24 "Der europäische Krieg und die christlichen Kirchen," *Impressionen und Reflexionen*, 271–2.
25 "Kriegsziele," in ibid., 262.

believed it was important for those like himself who taught religion to distinguish between hope and utopia and to ponder the relationship between hope and responsibility.[26]

By 1942 Tillich's flirtation with utopian pacifism was over. More than ever before, as he argued in his essays and speeches, he was convinced that the responsible use of power was necessary to regain and safeguard world peace.

Between 1942 and 1944 Tillich produced more than a hundred short speeches "To his German friends," which were broadcast by the Voice of America. In some of them he recalled the years after 1918 and tried to analyze what had gone wrong. In January 1944 he explained why the Germans had not understood the lessons of World War I:

> Often enough, something has taken shape out of the depths of a historical catastrophe, from which a people has become great. This is admittedly not always the case. The catastrophe of World War I led only a small circle of Germans into these depths. The German people as a whole did not accept the catastrophe as the warning it was, nor recognize it as the threatening verdict [*Gerichtsdrohung*] that it was. The German people deceived themselves after World War I with the claim that they were not even partially responsible for the war, that they had not really been defeated, [and] that certain select political groups were responsible for the defeat. And when those who thought this way were handed power, the German people was cheated of the blessings of defeat. They closed their ears to the verdict that was pronounced in the misfortune of World War I. And in this way, they were driven almost without resistance into the guilt and the verdict of World War II. If the German people had listened to the threatening verdict of World War I, they could have avoided the judgment of World War II.[27]

In July 1942 Tillich spoke of the difference between the idea of a nation and national idolatry (*nationaler Götzendienst*). He explained that the sacralization of the nation, which the Germans had undertaken, cautioned all peoples to free themselves of the poison of nationalism. Nationalism led to hatred; hatred led to aggression and (self-) destruction. Therefore, with the aid of the German example, the peoples of the world could learn that the nation was not God, that there were higher values than the nation.[28]

In another speech, in April 1944, Tillich contended that the turning point for Germany was not the beginning of the war in 1939. The German government had long before attacked small, vulnerable neighbors. In doing so, the Germans forgot that they were not only destroying the freedom of

26 Tillich, *Religiöse Deutung der Gegenwart*, 217–19.

27 Paul Tillich, *An meine deutschen Freunde: Die politischen Reden Paul Tillichs während des Zweiten Weltkriegs über die "Stimme Amerikas"*, ed. Karin Schäfer-Kretzler (Stuttgart, 1973), 309.

28 Ibid., 64–8.

these peoples but also disrupting the international order. Above all, Tillich opined that the Germans forgot that they were attacking the very nations that had defeated them two decades earlier. For the second time in a generation, the Germans had provoked the rest of the world and were headed for catastrophe.[29]

In August 1943 Tillich treated the question of collective guilt.[30] A week later he discussed the questions of guilt and atonement.[31] In these speeches the former Religious Socialist left no doubt about the military means that were necessary to defeat Nazi Germany. While he had always defended the rule of law, his wartime speeches showed how far his thinking had evolved since the 1920s. In the aftermath of World War I, he had condemned the use of military force as a means of pursuing national goals, and he had dreamt of a peaceful world. Once he was exiled in 1933, he began to revise his views on the use of force. Confronted with Nazi aggression, he became convinced that resistance to dictatorships was justified, even if it included the use of force. At the same time, he became increasingly critical of pacifist nonviolence. After Hitler declared war on the United States in December 1941 and the country that had offered him refuge entered the war, Tillich began to envisage a new world order. To be sure, he still wished for a world of peace, but he hoped for a world in which peace could be protected and secured. This position could no longer be characterized as pacifism, although he continued to express the hope that humanity could live in permanent and stable peace.

It is uncertain how many Germans listened to Tillich's political sermons. In any event, because of his adamant refusal to compromise with dictators like Hitler, Tillich gained in these years of exile the moral authority that was documented in the prestigious peace prizes he won after 1945 in a very different world.

29 Ibid., 345–6.

30 Ibid., 246–51.

31 Ibid., 251–5.

5

No More Peace

The Militarization of Politics

JAMES M. DIEHL

On November 11, 1918, World War I came to an end. Although the guns fell silent on the western front, military violence continued. Border wars, civil wars, and armed uprisings became endemic. In addition to such traditional forms of military violence, a new phenomenon emerged and became a hallmark of the interwar years: street violence produced by clashes between the "political soldiers" of opposing social and political "fronts." If in international terms the interwar years represented an era of cold war between defenders and opponents of the order created at the Paris Peace Conference, in domestic terms it was an era of civil war, open and latent, between the (primarily Marxist) left and the (primarily bourgeois) right. Interwar domestic politics opened not with the end of the First World War in 1918 but with the Russian Revolution of 1917 and closed not with the beginning of the Second World War but with its end.[1] If before 1914 war was the continuation of politics by other means, after 1917 politics became a continuation of war by other means, politics in a new, martial key.[2]

I

There were a number of reasons for the postwar militarization of politics. War surplus made the hardware readily available. Arms were ubiquitous,

1 Although the Spanish Civil War came to an end in March 1939, elsewhere the interwar civil wars continued after September 1939 as wars within a war: in the west, this took the form of collaboration versus resistance; in the east, it was played out between contending factions within resistance movements. Cf. Paul Preston, "The Great Civil War: European Politics, 1914–1945," in *The Oxford Illustrated History of Modern Europe*, ed. T. C. W. Blanning (Oxford, 1998).

2 One of the most direct manifestations of this process was the European-wide – indeed, worldwide – emergence of bourgeois militia and civic guard organizations to combat the left. For an insight into this mentality, see the protocol of the meeting hosted by the Swiss *Bürgerwehren* in Lucerne on November 29–30, 1920, to establish an international information center for civic guards. Bayerisches Hauptstaatsarchiv (BHSA), Allgemeines Abteilung, 66159.

and some states lost their monopoly on the means of violence. In addition to military hardware, there was a form of social war surplus that facilitated the militarization of politics: veterans. Many middle- and upper-class officers were unable to find their way in the postwar world, unable to recapture the status and sense of adventure they had enjoyed during the war; for many ordinary soldiers the war was the decisive formative experience of their lives, and they were unable to free themselves from its spell. As a result, every belligerent nation was host to a substantial postwar army of men unable to psychologically demobilize. In dealing with this problem the established democracies had an advantage. While the postwar military forces in Germany and Austria were limited by treaty and in Italy by fiscal considerations, France and Britain could absorb those who wanted to continue their military careers in relatively expanded peacetime armies, ship them off to colonies, or, in the case of Britain, to Ireland.[3] In Germany, Austria, and Italy there were no safety valves for militarized veterans, and they were driven like a poison into the body politic.

Brutalized veterans were not the only problem, however. A universal legacy of the war was the militarization of political mentalities. The massive mobilization of societies for the First World War brought previously passive or marginalized groups into the national economy and political arena. Postwar empowerment of previously disenfranchised groups made mass politics a reality. Wartime sacrifice combined with postwar economic difficulties created widespread disillusionment. As postwar social and political tensions mounted, the wartime practice of dividing the world into friends and foes and demonizing enemies was carried over into peacetime and furthered by the increasingly ideological nature of politics. Postwar politics were seen as a no-holds-barred, zero-sum game in which more people were fighting for a smaller pie. Social and political opponents were seen as an existential threat and delegitimized. Compromise was ruled out. Total destruction of one's enemies was sought. Domestic politics became infused with the attitudes and tactics associated with total war.[4]

3 The possession of colonies helped Britain and France in two ways: first, it allowed them to disperse the costs of the war, thereby reducing postwar tensions; second, militarized veterans were sent to the colonies to maintain or restore order, thereby removing them from the home countries. On this, see Michael Geyer, "The Militarization of Europe 1914–1945," in *The Militarization of the Western World* (New Brunswick, 1989), ed. John R. Gillis. On Ireland, see David Fitzpatrick, "Militarism in Ireland, 1900–1922," in *A Military History of Ireland* (Cambridge, 1996), ed. Thomas Bartlett and Keith Jeffery.

4 The key signifiers of total war, outlined by Stig Förster in his chapter in this book, were total war aims, total methods of warfare, total mobilization, and total control. All had strong analogues in interwar domestic politics. For more on this, see below.

The years before the outbreak of war had been marked by increasing social tension and political polarization. The growth of mass-based socialist parties was countered by mass-based rightist groups. Virtually every European state was wracked by politically inspired strikes on the eve of the war. Although some, especially on the right, saw war as a means to end domestic tension and to secure the status quo, they soon learned that defeat equaled revolution, since prewar polarization was compounded by the war and defeat delegitimized states. The autocratic regimes of the losers, Russia, Austria-Hungary, and Germany, were swept away by revolution, followed by civil war in Russia and latent civil war in Germany and Austria.[5] The well-established, victorious democracies, France and Great Britain, were able to absorb the postwar wave of revolution. Victory had legitimized their governments, and their political systems proved capable of mobilizing an antirevolutionary majority. Although frightened, the propertied classes were not frightened enough to abandon democracy.

It was in Russia that the militarization of domestic politics began, sparked by revolution and then fueled by civil war. After the Bolshevik victory Russian society remained militarized, first by the continuation of "war communism" and then (after the brief NEP interlude) through the collectivization and industrialization programs that were, in effect, a civil war of the government against the peasants.[6] Meanwhile, the violent rhetoric and practice of communist parties outside of Russia exacerbated postwar sociopolitical tensions and helped prompt fascism, which was the clearest organizational manifestation of the militarization of politics in the West. Italy was the first country to go fascist. Although nominally both a democracy and a victor, Italy, like the autocratic losers, also failed the test of war. Italy's entry into the war was not compelled by treaty obligations or invasion, but forced by rightist demonstrations, an extraparliamentary coup. The war remained a contested issue. The strong upsurge of the left after the war was in many ways a belated antiwar protest. In Italy, unlike Britain and France, the government was not strengthened by victory: for the left it was a senseless, unnecessary victory, whose price was too high; for the right it was a "mutilated" victory, tainted by Italy's failure to achieve its territorial ambitions. Although the postwar surge of the left in Italy was contained by 1921,

5 In February 1934 the covert Austrian civil war became overt. On Austria, see F. L. Carsten, *Fascist Movements in Austria: From Schönerer to Hitler* (London, 1977); and C. Earl Edmondson, *The Heimwehr and Austrian Politics, 1918–1936* (Athens, Ga., 1978); Michael Hughes describes the situation in Germany as a "cold civil war." See Michael H. Hughes, *Nationalism and Society: Germany, 1800–1945* (London, 1988), chap. 9. For more on Germany, see below.

6 Cf. the essay by Hans-Heinrich Nolte in this book.

the propertied classes and elites panicked and turned to the fascists, who were waging what was in effect a domestic war of pacification against the left.[7]

The success of fascism depended on a number of factors: the extent of the threat from the left; the confidence of the bourgeoisie in the state's ability to counter leftist threats; the loyalty of civil and military institutions – the bureaucracy, police, and army. In Italy and Germany these institutions were dominated by old elites who distrusted democratic government and consequently forged alliances with the fascists to destroy it. In England the weakness of the communist threat combined with the almost uninterrupted rule of the Conservative Party reassured the propertied classes and checked the growth of fascism. In France the political pendulum swung back and forth. When the Republic's institutions seemed able to protect the interests of the bourgeoisie, as in 1919–24 and 1928–32, fascism waned. When, however, institutions appeared to be captured by the left, after the victory of the *cartel des gauches* in 1924 and 1932, then fascism waxed.[8] Following the victory of the Popular Front in 1936, France was in a state of virtual civil war, a *guerre franco-française*.[9] In Spain war-related polarization and postwar unrest was initially contained by the dictatorship of Primo de Rivera. Following the collapse of the monarchy and the creation of the Republic, Spanish politics, as in France, were characterized by extreme polarization and violent swings of the political pendulum. After being ousted by the victory of the Popular Front, the Spanish bourgeoisie abandoned democratic institutions and sided with Franco and the army. It has often been noted that civil wars are more vicious than international wars. This was especially true for the ideologically charged civil wars of the interwar era. Opponents were delegitimized and demonized; their total destruction, by any means possible, was sought. The interwar domestic civil wars, whether open or latent, did much to prepare the way for the total international war that followed.

Memories of the First World War obsessed Europeans in the interwar years, but the lessons that were drawn from it diverged sharply. Most wanted to avoid another war at all costs. This desire went far beyond traditional pacifist circles. Even those, primarily conservatives, who had romanticized war in 1914 now realized war's cost in an age of mass politics: the warfare state led inevitably to the welfare state and a further erosion of the wealth and power of traditional elites. Democratic regimes, reflecting this broad consensus,

7 For a good local account of this process, see Paul Corner, *Fascism in Ferrara* (Oxford, 1974).

8 Robert Soucy, *French Fascism: The First Wave, 1923–1933* (New Haven, Conn., 1986), and *French Fascism: The Second Wave, 1933–1939* (New Haven, Conn., 1995).

9 Henry Rousso, *The Vichy Syndrome: History and Memory in France Since 1944* (Cambridge, Mass., 1991).

pursued peaceful policies, even appeasement. In contrast, fascists and fascist regimes idealized war and glorified it. For them war was the defining element of human activity. It could not and must not be avoided. For German National Socialists and Italian Fascists the primary goal was to reverse the loss (real or perceived) of the war. The sacrifices of the Great War had to be given meaning. The fascist lesson of the First World War was not to avoid war, but to prepare to wage it more effectively. This had domestic and international consequences. For fascists the militarized wartime organization of society during the First World War became the model for their political movements and for future society. Militarized fascist movements were mobilized to defeat domestic, "internal" enemies, and the militarized societies created by fascist regimes were designed to prepare the nation for confrontation with "external" enemies and the overthrow of the postwar international order.

II

The militarization of politics in Germany began in 1918, long before National Socialism became a significant political movement. All the ingredients were there: defeat and revolutionary change; border wars; a surplus of veterans coupled with a heritage of militarism; above all, armed uprisings from the left and right which resulted in a polarized stalemate and a simmering, sub rosa civil war.

The collapse of the Imperial army created a power vacuum. The vacuum was filled by the creation of volunteer forces, but the new state failed to obtain a monopoly of violence. By forming, and then failing to control, the volunteer forces, the Republic's Social Democratic leaders unwittingly created militarized middle-class organizational counterweights to the socialist working-class movement and laid the foundations for the development of paramilitary politics in postwar Germany. The negative role of the Free Corps (*Freikorps*) in this process is well known, but perhaps overexaggerated. The Free Corps may have been the yeast of paramilitary politics, but the dough was provided by civil guards (*Einwohnerwehren*). It was in the ranks of the civil guards that many ordinary and respectable middle-class Germans first experienced paramilitary politics and came to appreciate the use of armed force to achieve political ends. While the war and the November Revolution were the immediate causes of militarized middle-class political activity, the psychological foundations were laid in the Empire.

Since the founding of the Empire in 1871, German political discourse had revolved around the concept of conflict between two, presumably irreconcilable, camps: one composed of pro-government, state-supporting "national" elements and the other consisting of presumably state-threatening "enemies of the Empire [*Reichsfeinde*]." The process was begun by the founder of the Empire, Otto von Bismarck. The Iron Chancellor had artfully exploited nationalism and the wars of unification to mobilize support for his policies. After unification he was no longer able to use external wars as a means to garner domestic support, and he replaced external wars with preemptive domestic wars against putative internal enemies.[10] The first targets were German Catholics, who were accused of being disloyal and persecuted in the so-called *Kulturkampf* during the early 1870s. After the anti-Catholic campaign was abandoned, the Social Democrats were designated as the new enemies of the Reich. The Anti-Socialist Law of 1878 outlawed the Social Democratic Party (SPD) and subjected its proponents to legal persecution. Although the formal ban was lifted in 1890, Social Democrats continued to be designated as "enemies of the Reich." Social Democrats and their organizations were routinely discriminated against and harassed by the state.[11] In the process a highly articulated *Feindbild* was created, which portrayed the Social Democratic movement (and by implication, the entire working class) as a treasonous, revolutionary mob bent on the destruction of the nation and its "state supporting" elements. The ultimate line of defense against the revolutionary threat, it was repeatedly argued, both officially and unofficially, was the German army.[12] Displays of military readiness directed against the *Reichsfeinde* became an established part of Imperial political culture, both to highlight the presumed revolutionary threat and to reassure "state-supporting" elements of the state's determination to defend their interests.

The continued growth of the SPD produced a state-of-siege mentality in the "national" camp and prompted a debate over who could best lead the fight against socialist enemies of the Empire. Radicalized bourgeois leaders of the emerging mass-based nationalist organizations began to question whether the existing state could do the job, cloaking their challenge to the old order in a presumed higher nationalism.[13] As the war approached,

10 Wolfgang Sauer, "Das Problem des deutschen Nationalstaats," *Politische Vierteljahrsschrift* 3 (1962).

11 Klaus Saul, "Der Staat und die 'Mächte des Umsturzes,'" *Archiv für Sozialgeschichte* 12 (1972); Reinhard Höhn, *Sozialismus und Heer* (Bad Harzburg, 1969), vol. 3.

12 Stig Förster, *Der doppelte Militarismus* (Mainz, 1985), and "Alter und neuer Militarismus im Kaiserreich," in *Bereit zum Krieg: Kriegsmentalität im wilhelminischen Deutschland, 1890–1914*, ed. Horst Dülffer und Karl Holl (Göttingen, 1986); Bernd F Schulte, *Die deutsche Armee, 1900–1914: Zwischen Beharren und Verändern* (Düsseldorf, 1977), chaps. 12, 16.

13 This process is well summarized by David Blackbourn, *The Long Nineteenth Century: A History of Germany, 1780–1918* (New York, 1998), 430–1. Also see Hughes, *Nationalism and Society*, chap. 6. For case studies, see Marilyn S. Coetzee, *The German Army League: Popular Nationalism in Wilhelmine Germany* (Oxford, 1990); Geoff Eley, *Reshaping the German Right: Radical Nationalism and Political*

the efforts to build antisocialist organizations, "Cartels," and "Blocks," the precursors of postwar "fronts," were intensified and political rhetoric became increasingly apocalyptic.

In 1918 the apocalypse came: the German army was defeated and the country was swept by revolution. Germany's external and internal enemies had triumphed. The nation could no longer resist the former and the propertied classes appeared defenseless against the latter. While many hypernationalists did not mourn the passing of the monarchy, they were stunned and outraged that their leftist opponents, not they, had inherited the nation. By coupling the emancipation of the internal enemy with national defeat in an inverted cause-and-effect relationship through the infamous stab-in-the-back (*Dolchstoss*) legend, Germany's traumatized middle classes delegitimized the former and denied the latter. Germany had not been defeated, but betrayed, "stabbed in the back," by the founders of the Republic. The previous "state supporting" elements now became the most vitriolic opponents of the new democratic state. Its legitimacy was denied; its very existence denounced as a threat to the German nation. The Republic and its supporters were to be destroyed by any means possible. Just as many veterans were unable to demobilize psychologically after the war, many on the German right were unable to demobilize psychologically from the shock of defeat and revolution. For them, domestic politics became a form of war carried out by paramilitary means.

Following the Revolution, Germany was inundated with appeals to form organizations for the maintenance of law and order and by the end of 1918 was teeming with armed organizations, official and nonofficial. During the course of 1919 those on the left were suppressed, and centralized, officially sponsored civil guard networks were organized, first in northern Germany and then, under somewhat different conditions, in Bavaria.[14] By the end of 1919 the civil guards had become a mass organization with a membership more than twice that of the Free Corps. Unlike the swashbuckling Free Corps, whose activities involved only limited segments of society, primarily ex-officers and students, the civil guards encompassed a much larger and more diverse group of citizens. Though their military value was not as great as that of the Free Corps, the civil guards promoted a militarized political mentality among both members and supporters that continued long after the guards' dissolution.

Change After Bismarck (New Haven, Conn., 1980); and, above all, Roger Chickering, *We Men Who Feel Most German: A Cultural Study of the Pan-German League, 1886–1914* (London, 1984).

14 On the civil guards, see James M. Diehl, *Paramilitary Politics in Weimar Germany* (Bloomington, Ind., 1977), and David Clay Large, *The Politics of Law and Order: A History of the Bavarian Einwohnerwehren, 1918–1921* (Philadelphia, 1980).

The activities of the civil guards, as well as their propaganda and nascent ideology, had a profound impact on Germany's postwar political culture. The stipulation that the guards were to be nonpolitical organizations was seized upon and perverted by their leaders to serve their own ends. "Political" was defined as "party-political," and, following the practice established in the Empire, party-political activity was ascribed solely to Marxists. In practice, the "nonpolitical" and "above-party" policy of the civil guards meant only that their middle-class leaders and members agreed not to introduce the political issues that divided the bourgeois parties into the ranks of the guards in the interest of maintaining a solid front against the leftist parties. More important was the introduction of armed force into the political arena. It represented not only a repudiation of liberal parliamentary democracy, which is based on the principle of nonviolent resolution of conflict through compromise, but was the domestic political equivalent of the adoption of total-war tactics.[15]

The paramilitary civil guards, described variously as "self-defense" or "self-help" organizations, functioned as middle-class "counterunions," practicing what was in effect a type of social- and regime-control vigilantism.[16] The slogans law and order, national unity, and reconstruction soon became code words for counterrevolutionary activity. According to civil guard ideologues, once order was restored, the Guards would cease being a defensive organization (*Abwehrgemeinschaft*) and become an agency for reconstruction (*Aufbaugemeinschaft*). Through a program of "civic education" (*staatsbürgerliche Erziehung*), the Guards would infuse the German people with the will to unity and sacrifice that would allow them to stand up to their external oppressors. Germany, it was claimed, needed to develop a "true" democracy and a "true" socialism, as opposed to the sham democracy of the West and the corrupt socialism that had emerged in Russia. Parliamentary democracy, it was implied, caused (rather than reflected) divisions, and since the power of the state was inversely proportional to the number of parties, the ideal state had only one party. Similarly, "true" socialism was both anti-Marxist and nationalist, since it meant an end to class

15 See note 4 to this chapter.

16 The concepts of "social-group-control" and "regime-control" vigilantism are developed by H. Jon Rosenbaum and Peter C. Sederberg, "Vigilantism: An Analysis of Establishment Violence," *Vigilante Politics* (Philadelphia, 1974), ed. Rosenberg and Sederberg. Although vigilantism is seen generally as establishment violence, in transitional situations in which new social groups have not yet established themselves and the old elites still command institutional and societal support, the latter may resort to sociopolitical coercion designed to restore an earlier distribution of values by illegally coercing upwardly mobile segments of society (social-group vigilantism) or try to circumscribe the activities of a regime which represents a new distribution of values (regime-control vigilantism).

struggle and strikes in order to further the national good.[17] The ostensibly "nonpolitical" program of the civil guards was, in fact, highly political.

Given the almost exclusively middle-class social composition of the rank and file and the fact that the leadership was composed largely of displaced elites, the civil guards were instinctively counterrevolutionary. Their true political complexion was revealed during the Kapp Putsch, when they proved to be unreliable in the north and when in Bavaria, using the threat of armed force, they forced the resignation of the Social Democratic government and its replacement by a conservative bourgeois government.

In the wake of the Kapp Putsch, the Allies ordered the dissolution of German volunteer forces. This did not mean their end, however. Many Germans, it turned out, did not want to see the volunteer forces disappear completely: Reichswehr officials believed that they were an indispensable reserve in case of foreign attack; civilian officials, even when they deplored the political inclinations of the volunteers, felt they were needed as a supplement to hard-pressed police forces in case of domestic unrest; finally, large numbers of the middle classes wanted them retained as a form of counterunion, organizational counterweights against the better-organized working classes.

Formally prohibited, yet supported by wide and influential segments of the population, the volunteer forces began to develop new organizational forms that would allow them to maintain themselves under the changed conditions. The second stage in the development of Weimar paramilitary formations, which began after the Kapp Putsch and culminated in the Hitler Putsch of November 1923, was characterized by illegal underground activity and the emergence of what came to be known as military associations (*Wehrverbände*).

An important way station in this process was the Orgesch (*Organisation Escherich*), the brainchild of the founders of the Bavarian civil guard, which continued to exist after the dissolution of the northern volunteer forces because of its hold on the Bavarian government. The Orgesch was an attempt to mobilize the remnants of the volunteer organizations and, in effect, secretly extend the Bavarian civil guard to the rest of Germany. Officially, the Orgesch's goal was to create a strong, united Germany able to cast off the yoke of foreign oppression. Privately its leaders were more candid,

17 This summary of the program of the civil guards is taken from *Bericht von der zweiten Tagung der deutschen Einwohnerwehren unter Leitung der Reichszentrale für Einwohnerwehren 20. und 21. Januar 1920 im Reichsministerium des Innern zu Berlin*, especially the presentation by Ferdinand Runkel, "*Die Zukunft der Einwohnerwehren*." A copy of the protocol of the meeting is in Nachlass Escherich 3/4, Bayerisches Hauptstaatsarchiv (BHSA), Kriegsarchiv.

stating that one had to choose between "left – Bolshevism – or right – Reconstruction" and declaring, in the words of its head, that the Orgesch was a "White army against the Red army."[18] The Orgesch's Work Program was shot through with social resentment, anger, and nostalgia for the authoritarian social and political structures of the Empire.[19] Yet to this was added the activism of the Free Corps units, whose members yearned not for a return to the Empire, but the creation of an authoritarian front-soldier state, based on the "community of the trenches." Initially an effort of bourgeois-conservative rightists to preserve the civil guards, the Orgesch served as a melting-pot, bringing together men from all types of paramilitary organizations and right-wing political persuasions, a process which promoted both politicization and radicalization. Whether they looked backward or forward, the members of Germany's bourgeoning paramilitary subculture were united in their rejection of the present and their conviction that force was an acceptable and desirable tool of politics.

The military associations, which emerged in the years 1920–3, were private organizations, composed primarily of veterans of the World War and postwar volunteer associations. Although involved in secret programs of military training, the military associations operated openly as patriotic organizations dedicated not only to the national cause in general but also, in particular, to the preservation and propagation of German military tradition. Uniformed and organized along military lines, the military associations served as a surrogate for the army denied by the Treaty of Versailles. Military activity, however, was not the only interest of the military associations. They also wanted political changes: the replacement of parliamentary democracy with a "National Dictatorship." Despising and thus eschewing traditional political activity, the military associations hoped to achieve their political aims by means of military, rather than political, action.

The ultimate goal of the military associations was a war of liberation against France à la 1813. Such a war against Germany's "external" enemy was considered blocked by the "internal" enemy, a term used initially to describe the Communists, but which soon came to mean virtually all those who supported the Republic. Following the lead of the civil guards and the Orgesch, the military associations covered their social resentment with patriotic rhetoric. The problem for the military associations, as for their predecessors, was how to translate their military strength into political effectiveness. Two possibilities presented themselves: first, a leftist revolt – provoked,

18 *Regensburger Tagung 8–9 Mai 1920*, Nachlass Escherich, 5/3a, BHSA, Kriegsarchiv.

19 See, e.g., Günther Axhausen, *Organisation Escherich: Die Bewegung zur nationalen Einheitsfront* (Berlin, 1921).

if necessary – followed by its suppression, the creation of a military dictatorship, and a war of liberation; second, a war of liberation, triggered by foreign attack, during the course of which the left would be suppressed and a dictatorship established. In the next years the military associations vacillated between the two alternatives. During 1921–2 the first seemed more likely; in 1923 the second.[20]

The emergence of the *Wehrverbände* added a new dimension to German political life. Largely due to the activities of paramilitary formations, political meetings became scenes of angry shouting matches and physical confrontation. The previous organizational hegemony of the left was challenged not only in meeting halls but in the streets. The use of massive street demonstrations as a means of political expression had been a staple of prewar Social Democracy. In the Weimar Republic the scenario was altered. One of the major political functions of the rightist paramilitary organizations was their breaking of the left's monopoly in the staging of mass demonstrations. The military associations underlined their political demands by going to the streets, where their activities presented, as an observer noted, "a picture which before the war we associated only with the demonstrations and marches of the unions."[21] Former patriotic holidays, such as the birthdays of the Kaiser and Bismarck and the date of the battle of Sedan, were celebrated with massive meetings and marches of uniformed men accompanied by military bands. Unpopular decisions of the government were met with protest marches and violently anti-Republican demonstrations, in which paramilitary organizations of all stripes played a leading role. The constant demonstrations, counterdemonstrations, and confrontations frequently led to bloody conflicts and became a surrogate for Germany's unresolved civil war.

The explosive events of 1923, culminating in Hitler's abortive "March on Berlin," seemed to clear the air, as the social and political turmoil of 1918–23 gave way to comparative peace and prosperity. Confronted after 1923 with a "crisis" of stability, the military associations transformed themselves into political combat leagues (*politische Kampfbünde*). Survival in the new political climate required a reversal of priorities. The military associations had put military activity first and had generally perceived political matters in a derivative manner. After 1923 military activity was gradually relegated to a secondary position. Before military activity (that is, the war of liberation)

20 The assassinations of Matthias Erzberger and Walter Rathenau in 1921–2 were carried out by members of rightist paramilitary organizations with the goal of sparking a leftist uprising. In 1923 the French occupation of the Ruhr was seen as the springboard for a "war of liberation."

21 Franz Glatzel, "Wehrverbände und Politik," in *Politische Praxis 1926*, ed. Walther Lambach (Hamburg, 1926), 315.

could again become meaningful, it was reasoned, the existing "system" had to be changed. Previous attempts to accomplish this by force had failed and, in view of the Republic's stabilization, such attempts were even less likely to succeed in the near future. If change by force was impossible, then other, nonviolent means were necessary. In short, putschism had to be replaced by politics.

The change in tactics in no way meant that the combat leagues had come to terms with the Republic. They remained bastions of antidemocratic thought and activity, providing a haven and training ground for gravediggers of the Republic, a role that was expanded through the formation of youth groups, women's auxiliaries, and the development of a vigorous press. The development of ancillary organizations, designed to mobilize all segments of society, can be seen as the domestic political equivalent of total mobilization for total war.[22]

Paramilitary politics was given a new dimension in 1924, when the Social Democrats and Communists created paramilitary organizations of their own – the Reichsbanner and the Rote Frontkämpferbund (RFB).[23] Thereafter virtually every hue of the political spectrum was represented by a paramilitary organization. Thus, just as the Republic appeared to be stabilizing, powerful seeds of instability were sown. As a result of the interplay of the political combat leagues, political life in Germany during the "golden years" became, if anything, more militarized than before. Political violence not only continued but was systematized, and it was during the mid-1920s that the cadres were trained for the enormous outburst of violence that crippled the Republic in its final years.

The newspapers, periodicals, and other publications of the rightist combat leagues provided a heady brew of antidemocratic thought cloaked in the form of a "Front Ideology" that romanticized war and the "Front Experience." The "community of the trenches" was to be transferred to peacetime society, creating a *Volksgemeinschaft* that in turn would become a *Wehrgemeinschaft* that would permit Germany to reverse the defeat of 1918. The attempt to transport the "community of the trenches" into the postwar world and to make it the basis for a peacetime society was, of course, impossible. In the trenches, where men were united in the simple struggle for survival, all else was secondary, and the normal divisions and differences

22 See note 4 to this chapter.

23 On the Reichsbanner, see Karl Rohe, *Das Reichsbanner Schwarz Rot Gold: Ein Beitrag zur Geschichte und Struktur der politischen Kampverbände zur Zeit der Weimarer Republik* (Düsseldorf, 1966). While the Reichsbanner was formed to defend the Republic, the RFB was created to compete with the Reichsbanner and to oppose the Republic.

between them were erased or suppressed. In a peacetime society it was inevitable that such differences would again arise. To refuse to acknowledge this and to try to return to the simpler circumstances which prevailed during the abnormal conditions of the war ultimately led to dictatorial/totalitarian solutions, since all whose interests seemed to conflict with the common good had to be either forced into line or eliminated. The propagation of the ideas associated with the Front Ideology, especially among impressionable young men, did much to undermine the Republic and to create an *intellectual* climate favorable to the Nazis.[24]

Although the putschist tactics of the military associations were eschewed, the political combat leagues brought to politics practices that undermined parliamentary democracy and helped to create a *physical* environment favorable to the rise of the NSDAP/SA. Through the activities of the combat leagues, military attitudes and methods were transferred to everyday politics. Uniforms, massive marches, confrontation, and physical violence became an integral part of everyday political life.[25] The political combat leagues became a familiar part of elections, during which they staged demonstrations and provided troops for the protection (as well as the disruption) of political meetings. Electoral violence also took the form of clashes between rival placard-posting units, called, in the military jargon of the combat leagues, "poster troops" (*Klebetrupps*), which made nightly forays, accompanied by heavily armed defenders, into urban "no man's lands" for the purpose of defacing their opponents' posters and putting up their own.

Election campaigns were not the only occasions during which the combat leagues provoked, confronted, and clashed with one another. Demonstrations and counterdemonstrations in connection with political issues under discussion in the Reichstag were also a familiar part of the agitated political life of the Weimar Republic and an abundant source of political violence. In the absence of concrete issues, there was no lack of opportunities to hold demonstrations or celebrations that provided platforms for political attacks, prompted counterdemonstrations, and promoted violence. National holidays, past and present, real and imagined, became scenes of confrontations, and these were supplemented by demonstrations held in memory of past heroes and martyrs of the respective political causes.

24 On the front ideology, see Diehl, *Paramilitary Politics*, 211–16; Wolfram Wette, "Ideologien, Propaganda und Innenpolitik als Voraussetzung der Kriegspolitik des Dritten Reiches," in *Das Deutsche Reich und der Zweite Weltkrieg*, vol. 1: *Ursachen und Voraussetzung der deutschen Kriegspolitik*, ed. Militärgeschichtlichen Forschungsamt, (Stuttgart, 1979); and Richard Bessel, "The Great War in German Memory: The Soldiers of the First World War, Demobilization, and Weimar Political Culture," *German History* 6, no. 1 (1988).

25 For the following, see Diehl, *Paramilitary Politics*, 190–8.

Annual conventions were held by most of the political combat leagues and were utilized for staging mass political demonstrations. On the local level, the weekly meetings and outings of the combat leagues were a continuing source of confrontation and conflict. Parades of uniformed bands armed with "walking sticks" became a weekly occurrence and frequently led to bloody clashes in the streets. Armed political soldiers, whose uniforms made them human placard columns, were involved in a clandestine civil war. A favorite tactic was to hold parades or other provocative demonstrations in the "citadels" of the enemy, a practice that frequently let to incidents not unlike the gang wars over "turf" that take place in American cities. In 1926 the Reich Commissioner for the Surveillance of Public Order warned of the danger of a "formal guerrilla war of the *Verbände* against one another." Fatal clashes continued, however, in large part because of the "combative mood" (*Kampfstimmung*) that was systematically cultivated among the younger members of the combat leagues, which bred a cult of "street heroism" (*Strassenheldentum*) and prompted members to "distinguish themselves in street fights."[26]

Putschism may have been replaced by politics, but the violent and aggressive hostility of the members of the combat leagues remained. Instead of being focused directly against the state, however, it was directed against rival combat leagues. For the members of the *Kampfbünde*, winning or losing a brawl at a political meeting became a part of everyday politics, which took on a ritualized, stylized, and militarized form governed by an unspoken convention: speeches, rebuttals, and then a fight. The idea that the streets were a political proving ground and that the winning of the streets was a primary political goal was widely propagated during the Weimar Republic, not only by the extremists such as the Nazis and the Communists but by others as well. The widespread acceptance and normalization of political violence during the Republic's middle years did much to prepare the way for the massive onslaught of the NSDAP/SA after 1930.

During the final years of the Republic, the seeds of violence planted by the volunteer forces in its first years and then nurtured by the *Wehrverbände* and *Kampfbünde* sprouted with a vengeance. The NSDAP's stunning victory in the Reichstag elections of September 1930 was accompanied by an enormous surge in SA membership, as the Nazi organization began to absorb the other rightist combat leagues. The SA's earlier liability of being associated with a political party now became an asset. The swelling ranks

26 Mitteilungen des Rechskommisars für Ueberwachung des öffentlichen Ordnung, Nr. 119 (Sept. 1, 1926) and Nr. 122 (July 15, 1927), both quoted in Diehl, *Paramilitary Politics*, 195.

of the "political soldiers of Adolf Hitler" galvanized both the defenders of the Republic and its extremist opponents on the left. Under the slogan "Learn from the Enemy," the Reichsbanner was revitalized and reorganized and the Communists responded with the founding of the *Kampfbund gegen den Faschismus*, which supplanted the banned RFB and functioned as the communist counterpart to the SA during the final years of the Republic.[27] German politics became dominated by two major "fronts": the "Harzburg Front," composed of conservative and fascist opponents of the Republic, and the "Iron Front," representing the Republic's dwindling supporters.[28] Political violence soared. An American visitor to Germany at this time observed that "politics for the German today is no abstract matter, but one of life and death," and he continued:

> In this moment of political as well as economic crisis, when civil war in Germany is weighed as a possibility by even the soberest, it is necessary to take into account not only the voting but the fighting strength of Germany's political parties. The country is more exclusively and intensively organized for domestic conflict than any other on earth.... It is like no other country in the world.[29]

In such an environment the Nazis did not appear all that strange. For many middle-class Germans, schooled in the paramilitary politics of the civil guards, military associations, and political combat leagues, neither the message (suppression of Marxist "internal" enemies, restoration of traditional values, total mobilization to confront "external" enemies) nor the means used to deliver it (paramilitary demonstrations, violence) seemed unusual. In the end, Adolf Hitler proved to be the consummate practitioner of paramilitary politics: creating disorder while promising order; exploiting disunity while preaching unity; and vowing vengeance against Germany's enemies at home and abroad.

III

Following the Nazi seizure of power, much of the brutal paramilitary subculture of the Weimar Republic became mainstream. An orgy of violence accompanied the *Gleichschaltung* of the Third Reich's opponents and SA

27 On communist activities and the violent interplay between Communists and the SA, see Eve Rosenhaft, *Beating the Fascists? The German Communists and Political Violence, 1929–1933* (Cambridge, 1988); Richard Bessel, *Political Violence and the Rise of Fascism: The Stormtroopers in Eastern Germany, 1925–1934* (New Haven, Conn., 1984); and Conan Fischer, *Stormtroopers: A Social, Economic, and Ideological Analysis, 1929–1935* (London, 1983).

28 On the "Iron Front," see Rohe, *Das Reichsbanner Schwarz Rot Gold.*

29 H. R. Knickerbocker, *The German Crisis* (New York, 1939), 132.

atrocities continued until the Röhm purge, when street violence was replaced by the institutionalized terror of the SS state. The militaristic trappings and political style of the *Kampfbünde* formed the core of the Third Reich's political culture. German society was fully militarized as the regime destroyed its "internal" enemies and prepared to confront its "external" foes.

The militarization of politics, which had done so much to prepare the way for the Third Reich, was superseded by the politics of militarization.[30] Invocation of the Front Experience and Prussian military virtues provided the ideological and psychological foundations for the militarization of German society under the Third Reich. The external manifestations were ubiquitous: in the regimentation and uniforming of virtually every segment of society; in the constant rallies and parades; in the profligate distribution of medals and awards, including those given to mothers for their contributions to the "Battle of Births" being fought in the maternity wards of the Third Reich. Even war-disabled veterans, the most tragic victims of the First World War, were mobilized.[31] Through such measures, the regime hoped to resuscitate and institutionalize the "Spirit of 1914" and the *Burgfrieden* of the First World War in a purer, more effective – and, most importantly, more durable – form, a *Volksgemeinschaft* cum *Wehrgemeinschaft* that would enable Germany to reverse the defeat of the First World War. These efforts failed.[32] The German people did not welcome the Second World War as they had the First, and though they fought until the bitter end, Germany's second bid to become a world power, like the first, ended in defeat.

30 On this, see *Das Deutsche Reich und der Zweite Weltkrieg*, vol. 1; Michael Geyer, *Aufrüstung oder Sicherheit: Die Reichswehr in der Krise der Machtpolitik, 1924–1936* (Wiesbaden, 1980); and Jutta Sywottek, *Mobilmachung für den totalen Krieg: Die propagandistische Vorbereitung der deutschen Bevölkerung auf den Zweiten Weltkrieg* (Opladen, 1976).

31 James M. Diehl, *The Thanks of the Fatherland: German Veterans After the Second World War* (Chapel Hill, N.C., 1993), chap. 2.

32 As Stig Förster has noted, the goal of total control, which stems from the goal of total mobilization, more often produces total chaos, which was the case in Germany by 1945. See note 4 to this chapter.

6

The War's Returns

Disabled Veterans in Britain and Germany, 1914–1939

DEBORAH COHEN

The debate over whether World War I should be termed "total" is, in its essence, a scholarly dispute. It hinges on distinctions that only those at a safe remove from the terrible violence of the first half of the twentieth century can draw. For the Great War's victims, the question was not comparative. More than nine and a half million soldiers died during World War I; on average, the war claimed the lives of 5,600 men every day that it continued.[1] Twenty million men were severely wounded; eight million veterans returned home permanently disabled.[2] Casualties of Europe's bloodiest war, disabled soldiers had suffered the worst injuries ever seen. Shrapnel from exploding shells tore a ragged path through flesh and bone, leaving wounds, one British surgeon acknowledged, "from which the most hardened might well turn away in horror."[3] Under the threat of constant shell fire and ubiquitous death, some men lost their minds. Others contracted debilitating illnesses that shortened their lives. Years after their demobilization, disabled veterans still bore the sufferings war inflicted. Like bank clerk Erich Reese, they lived with injuries that robbed independence. Both hands amputated, blind in one eye, Reese found himself unable even to hold an umbrella.[4] Former infantryman Albert Bayliss, gassed in France, could not sleep for his racking cough. Unemployed for thirteen months, his rent severely in arrears, Bayliss

This chapter provides an overview of an argument developed in my book, *The War Come Home: Disabled Veterans in Britain and Germany, 1914–1939* (Berkeley, Calif., 2001). An earlier version of this essay was published as "Civil Society in the Aftermath of the Great War," in Frank Trentmann, ed., *The Paradoxes of Civil Society: Great Britain and Germany* (London, 1999).

1 Martin Gilbert, *The First World War* (New York, 1994), 541; Robert Weldon Whalen, *Bitter Wounds: German Victims of the Great War, 1914–1939* (Ithaca, N.Y., 1984), 38.

2 Francis W. Hirst, *The Consequences of the War to Britain* (London, 1934), 295. International Labour Office, *Employment of Disabled Men: Meeting of Experts for the Study of Methods of Finding Employment for Disabled Men* (Geneva, 1923), 16.

3 Henry Cedar, *A Surgeon in Belgium* (London, 1915), 22.

4 Herr Erich Reese to the Labor Ministry, June 4, 1921, Bundesarchiv Berlin, RAM 7757.

despaired. "I am only 31," he wrote, "what will I be in a few years time."[5] Keen sportsmen became invalids unable to climb staircases. A drummer boy lost both of his hands. Each disabled man brought the war's horrors home with him.

Throughout Europe, the care of disabled veterans posed one of the most important challenges to postwar reconstruction. Although the war's chief belligerents faced the same dilemma, they sought to resolve the problem in strikingly different ways. In Britain, rehabilitation was left largely to philanthropy and the generous public. In Germany, on the other hand, the state embraced the care of disabled veterans as its highest duty, and charity was all but eliminated. In the latter half of the 1920s, Germany's first democracy spent approximately 20 percent of its annual budget on war victims' pensions; in Britain, by contrast, war pensions accounted for less than 7 percent of the annual budget from 1923 onward.[6] Yet the British state's neglect and the German state's attentiveness had paradoxical effects. Despite comparatively generous pensions and the best social services in Europe, disabled veterans in Germany came to despise the state that favored them. In contrast, their British counterparts remained devoted subjects though they received only meager compensation.

Why did those who had profited from a state's generosity become its implacable foes? Why did Britain's heroes, treated so shabbily by successive governments, never force the state to pay for its negligence? The answers to these questions are complicated. The consequences of victory and defeat, on one hand, and the broader political cultures of interwar Germany and Britain, on the other, frame my inquiry. However, the war's resolution and political culture cannot fully account for the very different responses of veterans in Britain and Germany. Veterans' attitudes toward their fellow citizens left an indelible imprint on ex-servicemen's political movements. In both countries, broad public participation in the resolution of the war victims' problems – through voluntary organizations and charities – led

5 Albert Bayliss to Lord Derby, March 31, 1922, Liverpool Record Office, 920 DER (17) 21/5.

6 Approximately 755,000 British men (from a total prewar population of 45,221,000) and 1,537,000 German (from a total prewar population of 67,800,000) were permanently disabled in World War I. See Boris Urlanis, *Bilanz der Kriege* (Berlin, 1965), 354; Jay M. Winter, *Great War and the British People* (Basingstoke, U.K., 1985), 73, 75; International Labor Office, *Employment of Disabled Men* (Geneva, 1923), 15; Katherine Mayo, *Soldiers, What Next* (London, 1934), 555; L. Grebler and W. Winkler, *The Cost of the World War to Germany and to Austria-Hungary* (New Haven, Conn., 1940), 78. On budgets: for Germany, see Peter-Christian Witt, "Auswirkungen der Inflation auf die Finanzpolitik," in Gerald D. Feldman, ed., *Die Nachwirkungen der Inflation auf die deutsche Geschichte* (Munich, 1985), table 9, p. 93; Whalen, *Bitter Wounds*, 16; Reichstag, Reichshaushaltsetat für das Rechnungsjahr 1932. For Britain, see Sir Bernard Mallet and C. Oswald George, *British Budgets: Third Series, 1921–2 to 1932–3* (London, 1933), 558–9. These figures represent the total pension budget for disabled veterans and war dependents.

veterans to believe that their fellow citizens had honored their sacrifices. Voluntarism brought about a reconciliation between the war's most visible victims and those for whom they had suffered. Veterans' demands on the state reflected what they believed they could expect from their fellow citizens.

In the absence of state involvement, British philanthropists brokered a lasting social peace between the disabled and their fellow citizens. Shoddy treatment at the hands of the state never shook disabled veterans' belief that the public had appreciated their sacrifices. Fearful of alienating their fellow citizens, British veterans – alone among their European counterparts – retreated from politics. No such reconciliation between the public and veterans occurred in Germany. It was not, as veterans later came to believe, that the public scorned their sacrifices. State authorities in postwar Germany eliminated most avenues for the country's citizens to demonstrate their gratitude. Intent upon preserving the new republic's monopoly on benevolence for the disabled, German civil servants viewed charities for veterans as a threat to the state's own claim to legitimacy. They closed most philanthropies down, hounding the oldest and most reputable into submission. Yet as a result of the suppression of charity, the Weimar state ended up bearing not only the burden of thanks for the entire Fatherland but the full brunt of veterans' discontent.

This chapter begins with an analysis of care for the disabled in Britain and Germany, focusing on the parallel development of two very different systems of care, one driven by voluntary effort, the other the crowning achievement of a new state. Each system, the second part of the chapter will argue, fostered a particular type of ex-servicemen's movement. In Britain, veterans' associations cultivated the public and considered their fellow citizens the best allies against the negligent state. In Germany, by contrast, veterans turned against a public they believed had scorned their sacrifices. German veterans' sense of alienation fueled their unceasing demands on the state. Part three will assess the benefits and costs to individual veterans of social reconstruction in both countries. As the state's favored wards, German veterans enjoyed a privileged place in the turbulent postwar economy. Left to the mercy of charity, by comparison, British veterans paid a high price for their country's stability and democratic survival.

I

Despite high expectations raised during the war and promises of "a land fit for heroes," the British state offered only modest compensation to its disabled. Civil servants in the Ministry of Pensions, founded in 1917, were more concerned to limit the state's liabilities than to ensure veterans' well-being. Even the seriously disabled were paid pensions that fell short of the minimum they needed for survival. In 1920 a paraplegic received two pounds a week, not even half of what unskilled building (84s.4d.) and coal mining laborers (99s.3d.) could expect that year.[7] As the cost of living fell in the early 1920s, the buying power of pensions increased. However, the amount paid was not enough to allow men to live with a measure of comfort – or enjoy family life. In France and Germany, men received higher pensions when they married and had children. Citing the prohibitively high cost of marital allowances (£30 million), British authorities compensated the disabled only for familial "responsibilities" they had "incurred" before disablement.[8]

Most importantly, successive British governments proved extremely reluctant to institute programs that would provide disabled men with a chance at gainful employment. At the end of the war, the government had few plans for rehabilitation. In early 1920 the British Ministry of Labor trained only 13,000 disabled men, while another 65,000 waited on placement.[9] Less than two years later, with an estimated 100,000 disabled ex-servicemen unemployed, the government closed admission to the rehabilitative training programs altogether.[10] Because of the postwar slump, the Ministry of Labor could not find employment for those disabled who had already been retrained. There was no room for others. In response to the plight of the severely disabled, the German, French, and Italian states mandated the compulsory employment of badly disabled men; in Britain, the war's victims were left to the mercy of their fellow citizens.

Historians often have noted the unwillingness of the interwar British state to intervene in intractable social problems.[11] Less well understood, however, is the role that voluntarists played in assuming duties that many

7 Guy Routh, *Occupation and Pay in Great Britain, 1906–1979*, 2d ed. (1965; London, 1980), 120. See also Oksana Newman and Allan Foster, *The Value of a Pound: Prices and Incomes in Britain, 1900–1993* (New York, 1995), 51, 78.

8 Questions and Answers, Apr. 21, 1921, Mr. Macpherson, Public Record Office, London (hereafter PRO), PIN 14/41.

9 James Currie to the Minister of Labor, Minute Note of July 26, 1919, PRO, Lab 2/523/TDS/5354/1010.

10 *Times of London*, July 25, 1921; *British Legion Journal*, Aug. 1921, 37; Rehabilitation Committee Paper no. V.T. 8, Draft Report on Vocational Training, Sept. 22, 1928, Modern Record Office, MSS 292/146.9/2.

11 See, e.g., James Cronin, *Politics of State Expansion* (London, 1991), chaps. 6, 7; Anne Crowther, *British Social Policy, 1914–1939* (London, 1988), 40–74; F. M. Miller, "The Unemployment Policy of the National Government, 1936–1941," *Historical Journal* 19 (1976); Robert Skidelsky, "Keynes and the Treasury View: The Case For and Against an Active Unemployment Policy in Britain, 1920–1939," in Wolfgang J. Mommsen, ed., *The Emergence of the Welfare State in Britain and Germany* (London, 1981); John Stevenson, "The Making of Unemployment Policy 1931–1935," in Michael Bentley and John Stevenson, eds., *High and Low Politics in Modern Britain* (Oxford, 1983), 182–213.

contemporaries regarded as the state's responsibility.[12] In Britain, the reintegration of disabled veterans proceeded primarily through voluntary and philanthropic efforts. Philanthropists ran most initiatives for the long-term treatment or rehabilitation of wounded servicemen, from the country's largest artificial limb-fitting center at Roehampton to the comprehensive program for the war-blinded, administered through St. Dunstan's Hostel. Before their discharge from hospital, every blinded veteran in Britain received a Braille watch and an invitation to train at St. Dunstan's.[13] Similarly, voluntarists administered all organized employment for severely disabled men, whether in settlements for neurasthenics, through the ten local Lord Roberts' Workshops, or in factories such as Bernard Oppenheimer's specially outfitted diamond-cutting facility in Brighton. Capitalizing on public indignation about the government's inaction, philanthropists raised money as never before. In just six months (July to November 1916), the British Women's Hospital Committee raised £150,000 to build a home for paralyzed men.[14] Every home for the permanently disabled – and there were eight such institutions in the London area alone – owed its founding to private munificence.

Philanthropists did not wish to replace the state. But in essence, their success encouraged the Ministry of Pensions to do even less for its disabled than it had originally pledged. Ministry officials saw no reason why the state should provide for war victims when philanthropists had produced a Lord Roberts', a St. Dunstan's, and a Roehampton. Charitable institutions that themselves reflected the state's unwillingness to provide for the disabled thereby served to justify further governmental neglect.

By relying on charity, the Ministry of Pensions expected to save money. But fiscal conservatism was not its sole consideration. Between 1920 and 1922, when tens of thousands of men waited for rehabilitation, the ministry underspent special Treasury grants for the purpose by more than one-third.[15] What was at stake for the ministry's senior civil servants was their conception of the state's proper sphere. To the Ministry of Pensions' way of thinking, the state did not represent the nation but was only one actor among many, and a

12 Geoffrey Finlayson, *Citizen, State, and Social Welfare in Britain, 1830–1990* (New York, 1994), 201–86; Frank Prochaska, "Philanthropy," in F. M. L. Thompson, ed., *The Cambridge Social History of Britain, 1750–1950*, vol. 3 (Cambridge, 1990).

13 Committee on Employment of the Severely-Disabled Ex-Service Man, Nov. 3, 1920, PRO, PIN 15/37.

14 British Women's Hospital Committee, Final Report, 1918, Star and Garter Collection, British Red Cross Archive.

15 Parl. Papers 1922, xi, 406–7: Report from the Select Comm. on Training and Employment of Disabled Ex-Service Men, Aug. 2, 1922.

beleaguered one at that.[16] The state could not take on too much. The British public, or so ministry officials believed, wanted the state to accept an infinite amount of responsibility for the disabled – whether or not it could afford to do so. By contrast, the ministry's officials thought it their duty to divest the state of as many tasks as they could. Eager to restrict the state's purview, and increasingly subject to Treasury restrictions, senior civil servants in the Ministry of Pensions delegated responsibility for the most severely injured disabled – the most expensive of cases – to voluntary initiative.

The case of disabled ex-servicemen shows that in a period often conceived of in terms of the state, voluntarism proved a more significant force than is generally acknowledged. As the state demobilized between 1919 and 1921, those ex-servicemen to whom successive governments owed the most – the paralyzed, the insane, the tubercular – instead found themselves dependent on the public's philanthropy. Rare was the disabled ex-serviceman who, by the end of the war, had not been served by charitable enterprise. Of course, charities could help only a fraction of the needy over the long term. Total war wrought destruction far beyond the resources of voluntarism. All told, the number of men employed by sheltered workshops may have approached 2,000 at any one time; according to the government's figures, that was only a fraction of those who needed work.[17] Nevertheless, the public's role was prominent and long-lasting. Throughout the 1920s, donations to the charities for the disabled remained strong, and while there was a general decline during the Slump, some institutions actually recorded improvements. In 1932 donations to the Village Centre at Enham, a rehabilitative training colony for neurasthenics and other "difficult" cases, were higher than they had been in 1921; at the height of the Slump in 1933, Enham managed to collect more subscriptions than in the preceding year.[18]

In sharp contrast to its British counterpart, the postwar German state provided its disabled with the best benefits in Europe. Not only did pensions for the most severely disabled approximate the wages of skilled workmen, but they included provisions for wives and children.[19] Unlike the

16 See esp. C. F. A. Hore, "State-Aided Provision of Employment – An Act of Obligation or Charity?" Dec. 16, 1920, PRO, PIN 15/37.

17 Peter Reese, *Homecoming Heroes: An Account of the Reassimilation of British Military Personnel into Civilian Life* (London, 1992), 95.

18 Report on the 1933 Accounts; Minutes, Executive Committee, Enham. As Macadam noted, "Voluntary charities are less liable than public schemes to fluctuations of policy or economy scares" (267).

19 Benckendorff et al., *Kommentar von Reichsversorgungsbeamten zum Reichsversorgungsgesetz vom 12.5.1920* (Berlin, 1929), 748–65; Reichsarbeitsministerium, *Handbuch der Reichsversorgung* (Berlin, 1932), 356–68; for wage statistics, see Gerhard Bry, *Wages in Germany, 1871–1945* (Princeton, N.J., 1960), 341, 352, 379.

British government, which limited its responsibilities to the distribution of pensions, German authorities aimed to return even the most incapacitated to work, preferably to their former occupations. Weimar's National Pension Law (1920) accorded the disabled more than a right to pensions; they were also entitled to an occupational retraining course and free medical care for their service-related ailments. After 1919 severely disabled veterans were practically assured work by the Labor Ministry. Under the Law of the Severely Disabled, most employers were required to hire and keep them.[20] At the height of the Great Depression, severely disabled workers were twice as likely as their able-bodied counterparts to retain their jobs.[21] Despite half a million unemployed, Berlin's welfare office maintained 30,000 of the severely disabled in work. In 1932, 28 percent of the German capital's male workers were unemployed, as opposed to 15 percent of its severely disabled.[22]

The Weimar Republic created Europe's most comprehensive programs for disabled veterans. However, for most of the war, Germany, like Britain, had relied upon voluntary effort. During the war, a dynamic charitable culture thrived in Germany, even briefly surviving the defeat. In most regions, voluntary and local organizations assumed the lion's share of responsibility for the disabled. In Kassel, for example, citizens' committees found work for the disabled, while in Frankfurt am Main a wartime coalition of private charities directed vocational retraining efforts. For blinded men, there were vacation homes and retraining schools, among others, Berlin's School for the War Blinded, founded by optician Paul Silex in October 1914. Those who had lost hands could attend workshops for retraining, including the Saxon One-Armed School founded in 1915.[23] In 1916, the authoritative welfare periodical *Social Practice* reported that in the greater Berlin area alone thirty-four new organizations had been founded to benefit the war disabled, a development that established philanthropists criticized from the standpoint of practicality, but the fact of which nevertheless testified to public enthusiasm.[24]

20 Christopher Jackson, "Infirmative Action: The Law of the Severely Disabled in Germany," *Central European History* 26, no. 4 (1993): 417–55.

21 Dr. Bruno Jung, *Der Einfluss der Wirtschaftskrise auf die Durchführung des Schwerbeschädigten-Gesetzes* (Mannheim, 1932), 32–3, 39.

22 *Statistisches Jahrbuch der Stadt Berlin* (1933), 105, 229.

23 "Die Einarmigenschule zu Dresden," Eine Denkschrift von Gustav Curt Beyer, Dresden, am Sedantag 1917, Sächsisches Hauptstaatsarchiv, Curt Beyer Collection.

24 "Planlose Wohlfahrtspflege," letter from the Zentralstelle für Volkswohlfahrt, die Zentrale für private Fürsorge, and the Bureau für Sozialpolitik, *Soziale Praxis* 25, no. 22 (Mar. 2, 1916): 2. See also "Die Organisation der Kriegsinvalidenfürsorge," *Concordia* 22, no. 24 (Dec. 15, 1915): 427.

Following a 1917 decree by the Bundesrat (Federal Council), however, the state required charities that sought to raise funds or solicit new members to secure the permission of the authorities. Desperate for scarce resources, the rapidly expanding and militarized state demanded a thorough rationalization of philanthropic efforts.[25] Only a handful of charities were granted a permit to raise funds, and only on the condition that they submit to government control of their expenditures. As Germany's authorities gained unprecedented control over charity, many new or small philanthropies folded, and their more prestigious counterparts entered into junior partnerships with the state. In the early Weimar Republic, the regulation of charity proceeded dramatically; in Prussia alone, the newly appointed State Commissioner for the Regulation of Charity refused more than three hundred charities for the war's victims permission to collect in the years 1919–24.[26]

By 1924 nearly every charity for the disabled had been shut down or relinquished its funds to the government. Even the oldest and most reputable of organizations ran into trouble if the methods or aims of their application violated official dogma. On behalf of the Red Cross, no less a personage than the general of the cavalry appealed to the State Commissioner for the Regulation of Charity for permission to sell a commemorative chest priced at 37 marks.[27] On principle, state officials opposed the sale of products to benefit charity, fearing the possibility of fraud; the Commissioner rejected the application. Similarly, state officials vetoed nearly every proposal for veterans' homes. Before 1918 the citizens of the university town of Marburg raised 250,000 marks to build a home for disabled soldiers.[28] They put the foundations in the ground, but could not afford to finish the home without an additional 150,000 marks. Between 1918 and 1922 the authorities consistently refused permission to collect, on the grounds that segregation of the disabled ran contrary to the Labor Ministry's principles. State officials were willing to allow the building to remain unfinished – and the money already collected from the public to be wasted – rather than make an exception.

Historians of the Weimar Republic have generally accepted the restriction of philanthropy's role as self-evident, even ineluctable, a product of

25 Wilhelm Groener, Minutes, National Ausschuss für Frauenarbeit im Kriege, Jan. 29, 1917, Archiv des deutschen Caritasverbandes, CA XIX 15.

26 Index, Rep. 191, Geheimes Staatsarchiv Preussischer Kulturbesitz (hereafter GStAB).

27 Zentralkomitee der deutschen Vereine vom Roten Kreuz [General der Kavallerie v. Pfuel] to the Herrn Staatskommissar für die Regelung der Wohlfahrtspflege, Nov. 1918. Response dated Nov. 20, 1918, GStAB, Rep. 191, 3577.

28 Contributions Lists; Der Regierungspräsident Cassel [v. Hartmann] to the Herrn Staatskommissar, Aug. 9, 1920, GStAB, Rep. 191, 3365 (unfoliated).

the socialist revolution of 1918–19 and the economic exigencies of the 1920s.[29] The causes of charity's eclipse are more complex. Justified during the war as a necessary measure against waste, the regulation of charity became, in the early Weimar Republic, a critical means of establishing the state's authority. To secure the loyalty of its skeptical citizenry, the Weimar state sought to establish a monopoly on benevolence; centerpiece of a compromise among Social Democrats, the Catholic Center Party, and the left-liberal Democrats, Weimar's comprehensive welfare programs included initiatives for youth, the unemployed, and women.[30] In a state that guaranteed the well-being of its citizenry, charity, more than merely a hindrance, threatened the state's legitimacy. Armed with decrees to regulate charity, Germany's civil servants put an end to philanthropic efforts on behalf of the disabled.

Even before the war ended, then – before there were winners and losers – care for the disabled had diverged markedly in Great Britain and Germany. In Britain, the rehabilitation of the disabled remained the business of voluntarists. In Germany, it became a cornerstone of the new democratic order. Unlike British civil servants in the Ministry of Pensions, who deemed disabled veterans an unnecessary burden for the state, German officials regarded the "war victims problem" as an opportunity. They envisioned programs for wounded soldiers, as well as those for youth and the unemployed, as showpieces of postwar social policy. The Revolution of 1918–19 gave their plans for state control of war victims' care new urgency. Wielded by civil servants convinced of the necessity of generous and comprehensive programs controlled solely by the state, the power to regulate philanthropy ended up isolating the very institutions of governance it was intended to protect.

29 Christoph Sachsse and Florian Tennstedt, *Geschichte der Armenfürsorge in Deutschland*, vol. 2: *Fürsorge und Wohlfahrtspflege, 1871 bis 1929* (Stuttgart, 1988), esp. 160–1; Gerhard Buck, "Die Entwicklung der freien Wohlfahrtspflege von den ersten Zusammenschlüssen der freien Verbände im 19. Jahrhundert bis zur Durchsetzung des Subsidiaritätsprinzip in der Weimarer Fürsorgegesetzgebung," in Rolf Landwehr and Rüdiger Baron, eds., *Geschichte der Sozialarbeit* (Weinheim, 1983), 166–71. An important exception and the best account of changes in the private welfare sector is Young-Sun Hong's *Welfare, Modernity, and the Weimar State, 1919–1933* (Princeton, N.J., 1998), esp. 44–75, 181–202.

30 Tennstedt and Sachsse, *Geschichte der Armenfürsorge*, 2: 68–87; Detlev Peukert, *Die Weimarer Republik: Krisenjahre der klassischen Moderne* (Frankfurt am Main, 1987), 46–52; David Crew, *Germans on Welfare* (Oxford, 1998), 16–31; Elizabeth Harvey, *Youth and the Welfare State in Weimar Germany* (Oxford, 1993), 152–85; Hong, *Welfare, Modernity*, 44–75; Ludwig Preller, *Sozialpolitik in der Weimarer Republik* (Düsseldorf, 1978), 34–85; Werner Abelshauser, "Die Weimarer Republik – ein Wohlfahrtsstaat?" in Abelshauser, ed., *Die Weimarer Republik als Wohlfahrtsstaat* (Stuttgart, 1987); Edward Ross Dickinson, *The Politics of Child Welfare from the Empire to the Federal Republic* (Cambridge, Mass., 1996).

II

What were the practical implications of the British and German solutions to the problem of the disabled? Generous pensions and comprehensive rehabilitation programs did not secure German veterans' loyalty. The German disabled came to despise the state that favored them. The British disabled, on the other hand – despite the state's ill-treatment – remained loyal subjects.

British ex-servicemen never received the "land fit for heroes" that Lloyd George had promised them, but they blamed that on the government, not the public at large. Individual philanthropists, supported by the charitable public, had done what they could. As one disabled man wrote the philanthropist Oswald Stoll in 1932, "To lose you, Sir, would be to lose the Greatest Friend the British Soldier ever had," adding that "it is to me Sir very difficult to express in writing my appreciation for your kindness in thinking of my comfort and happiness, also that of my wife and children."[31] Only the wealthy such as Oswald Stoll could build "Homes for Heroes," but there were other sorts of voluntarism, equally appreciated if less spectacular. Patients at the Star and Garter Home reserved their highest praise for the women who accompanied them on their Sunday strolls. It was that kind of personal attention, said one disabled man, remembering the care he had received in a private convalescent home, that made him believe – as he put it – "life was worth living again."[32]

Scholars have often written of British ex-servicemen's hostility toward their fellow citizens, drawing on the writings of the War Generation's literati, Robert Graves and Siegfried Sassoon among them. My research does not support that conclusion. However much the disabled ex-serviceman distrusted the Ministry of Pensions or the government or the state, he believed the charitable public had done their best by him. The enormous sums raised to build the Star and Garter Home for Totally Disabled Ex-Servicemen, the Roehampton Hospital for amputees, Lord Roberts' Workshops (and many others) testified to the public's appreciation. Disabled men directed their anger at the state, usually the Ministry of Pensions, rarely against their families, and almost never against the public at large. The home front could not understand what soldiers had endured in the trenches; however, that did not prevent the public from helping disabled veterans rebuild their lives. Most men appreciated the distinction. They had not wanted charity, of course, but philanthropists conveyed the public's gratitude.

31 Mackenzie to Stoll, Jan. 29, 1932, Box 6, War Seal Mansions, Hammersmith & Fulham Local Record Office.

32 Recording of Bill Towers, taped Nov. 29, 1989, Imperial War Museum – Sound Records, R9.

The British Legion, founded 1921 as the country's largest veterans' organization, erected gratitude to the public as one of its foremost principles. According to the organization's ethos, disabled veterans occupied an honored position in their society, a result not only of their own role in the war but of their fellow citizens' appreciative response to their sacrifices. The Legion filled the pages of its journal with praise for voluntary initiatives. As one commentator noted: "What would these poor fellows do but for the help of the various voluntary associations?"[33] Delegates at the Legion's annual conferences invoked the "generous public" in near-reverential tones. Urging that the Legion's financial transactions be disclosed, a delegate in 1929 referred to the importance of "keeping faith" with the public: "It was impossible to tell the public too much, and the more they were allowed to know the more they would help."[34] In 1931 the Sandhurst delegate expressed his conviction that time limits on pension claims might be overturned if only the public could be "rightly informed."[35] The Duncannon delegate reminded his fellow veterans, "When the public failed them, the Empire, and not only the Government would fall."

As the Legion's leaders recognized, the knowledge that the public was on their side defused veterans' anger toward the negligent state. According to the Legion's officials, the problem of obtaining fair compensation was not "social" in nature. It did not, in other words, reflect the country's denial of disabled men's suffering but had to be attributed to administrative failure, bureaucratic red tape, and official hard-heartedness. The Legion's diagnosis of the problem implied its solution. Demonstrations, boycotts, and veterans' candidates would not improve ex-servicemen's lot, because, as the Legion's officials emphasized, bureaucratic failings required bureaucratic remedies. The best that ex-servicemen could do was to put their faith in the "generous public." Only if veterans defended their society's well-being in peace as in war – by refraining from demonstrations and by proclaiming their "apoliticism" – could they maintain the privileged status gained between 1914 and 1918. Ex-servicemen owed the British public "Service, not Self," as the Legion's motto proclaimed. Instead of mere interest politics, then, the Legion promised ex-servicemen something higher: a moral and patriotic community.

In Britain, philanthropy fostered a sense of belonging among the war's most visible victims. In Germany, by contrast, the disabled grew alienated from the rest of society, depriving the Weimar Republic of a much-needed

33 A. G. Webb, *British Legion Journal*, Aug. 1922, 45.

34 Verbatim Report of the Annual Conference, May 20, 1929, 20, British Legion Archives.

35 Verbatim Report of the Annual Conference, May 25, 1931, 13, British Legion Archives.

source of support. Disabled veterans were among the most embittered of the republic's discontented. In the years 1918–21, they formed scores of local associations to represent their interests. By 1922 there were six national organizations of disabled veterans with an estimated total membership of 1.4 million, largest among them the Social Democratic Reichsbund.[36] In the cities, thousands of disabled marched to secure their rights, but even the smallest towns witnessed protests. Demonstration followed demonstration – for higher pensions, for secured employment, for free or reduced fares on public transportation. Even as pension costs swelled to 20 percent of the Republic's total expenditure, veterans' organizations took to the streets to protest the state's neglect.

Veterans' bitter discontent requires explanation. Although the German disabled received pensions that were as good as their European counterparts, if not better, superior social services, and secured employment, most came to despise the republic. While lauding the state's material provisions as "exemplary," historians have blamed Weimar's welfare bureaucracy for veterans' alienation.[37] If the state succeeded in the realm of material compensation, it failed, in Robert Whalen's words, "to show human sympathy," to consider men's psychological needs, as James Diehl has argued, and to incorporate its intended clients in decision making, in Michael Geyer's formulation. Yet judged by any criterion, the British state was just as inflexible, bureaucratic, stingy, and inhuman as its German counterpart, if not more so. Yet successive British governments not only dodged their responsibilities to the disabled, but remained largely immune from veterans' protests.

What was significant about German veterans' attitudes was not their anger at the state but their antipathy toward the public. At the war's end, many disabled veterans in Germany still believed in the goodwill of their fellow citizens. The public might have to be "enlightened," but once people realized

36 The Social Democratic Reichsbund (founded 1917) had 639,856 members in 1921. The Kyffhäuser Bund, a prewar veterans' organization, followed, with 225,392. The moderate Einheitsverband (founded in 1919) had 209,194 members. The conservative Zentralverband (1919) had 156,320 members; the communist Internationaler Bund (1919), 136,883; Deutscher Offiziersbund, 27,435; the Bund erblindeter Krieger (1916) 2,521. Throughout the Republic, membership in war victims' organizations fluctuated significantly, declining in most cases from 1922. In January 1924, for instance, the Reichsbund had only 245,410 members in 4,075 local branches. By December 1926, it had 324,580 members organized in 5,156 branches. Geschäftsbericht des Bundesvorstandes und Bundesausschusses für die Zeit vom 1. Januar 1924 bis 31. März 1927. *Reichsbund*, 1927, p. 5, 351–10 I, Sozialbehörde I, KO 80.11, f. 42, Staatsarchiv Hamburg. There is a large literature on Weimar veterans. Among others, see Volker Berghahn, *Der Stahlhelm: Bund der Frontsoldaten 1918–1935* (Düsseldorf, 1966); James Diehl, *Paramilitary Politics in Weimar Germany* (Bloomington, Ind., 1977); Karl Rohe, *Das Reichsbanner Schwarz-Rot-Gold* (Düsseldorf, 1966); Kurt Schuster, *Der rote Frontkämpferbund 1924–1929* (Düsseldorf, 1975).

37 Ewald Frie, "Vorbild oder Spiegelbild? Kriegsbeschädigtenfürsorge in Deutschland, 1914–1919," in Wolfgang Michalka, ed., *Der erste Weltkrieg* (Munich, 1993), 564.

how soldiers were suffering, they would respond sympathetically. In 1920 the conservative veterans' organization, the Zentralverband, observed that "the widest sections of the population have full sympathy for the situation of war disabled and war dependents"; it commented particularly on the public's "sense of honor and obligation, and their will" to help war victims.[38] By the mid-1920s hope had turned to hostility. The public, or so veterans believed, was not merely ungrateful but grudged war victims their rightful due. The animosity became mutual: most people thought that the disabled were the favored wards of the welfare state, and could not understand why they should complain so incessantly. Whereas the British disabled could take pride in their fellow citizens' gratitude, German veterans complained that the public did nothing to help them. "It will not be much longer," warned one severely war-disabled man, "and we will be complete outcasts and pariahs, although it was this ruthless society that sent our bodies to be smashed up."[39]

In Germany, the process of state consolidation of war victims' care elided gratitude and compensation. For disabled veterans, the granting of ever higher pensions and better social services signified that the nation was grateful. When social services were returned to the local level (after the hyperinflationary year of 1923) or pensions were cut (as in the Depression), veterans assumed that their fellow citizens had forgotten them, even spurned their sacrifices. In interwar Britain, pensions were nothing more than compensation, inadequate, as everyone acknowledged, to repay what had been lost; the nation's thanks was expressed in other ways, chiefly by means of philanthropy and sympathetic public opinion. When German authorities suppressed private and local initiatives for disabled veterans, they established a monopoly on much more than welfare programs. The state unwittingly ended up bearing the burden of thanks for the entire Fatherland. However, if the state could deliver legitimation in the form of increased pensions and better social services, the peace it bought was fragile, dependent upon the republic's financial prosperity.

III

In Britain, the state escaped veterans' wrath, whereas in Germany a newly founded republic bore its heroes' full fury. And yet, individual British veterans paid a high price for their country's stability. Never reintegrated

38 "Aufruf an das deutsche Volke!" *Zentralblatt für Kriegsbeschädigte und Kriegshinterbliebene*, Feb. 1, 1920, 2.

39 "Zustände beim städtischen Fürsorgeamt für Kriegsbeschädigte," *Arbeiter-Zeitung*, Jan. 11, 1923, Frankfurt City Archive, Mag. Akte V/65.

into the economy, disabled men existed figuratively, as well as literally, on the margins of British society. Although the charitable public championed the veteran's cause, philanthropy did little more than rescue men from penury. It did not promote their return to society. Disabled veterans were segregated: in sheltered workshops, in veterans' homes in outlying suburbs, in rehabilitation centers. They rarely took part in Armistice Day parades. The Great War's most conspicuous legacy, they became its living memorials. When journalists wanted to write about the war's aftermath, they visited the disabled. But not otherwise. Veterans' stories were feature articles, not front-page news. Touching, occasionally also uplifting, they were irrelevant to the economy and politics.

Abandoned to the mercy of charity, British veterans suffered the indignity that those without rights must bear. As the inmates of philanthropic institutions soon learned, they were to eat the food served them, remain compliant on visiting days, and bury their sorrow in embroidery or chess. Dependent upon philanthropic goodwill, disabled veterans in Britain had no choice but gratitude. Above all, the objects of charity had to eschew bitterness and remain cheerful, at least publicly. Philanthropists might appeal on behalf of the war's "human wreckage," but, when visitors arrived, the wreckage had to behave like the brave Tommies of 1914. No one wanted to support a malcontent, a depressive, or an amputee who mourned his lost limb. While some men were good-humored, there were many others for whom helplessness, institutional life, and separation from their families proved intolerable. They got drunk and violent, or retreated into isolation. Unless they committed suicide, few outside of the veterans' homes knew about their despair. The unrepentantly disgruntled were discharged.

In comparison, the German disabled – as individuals – fared well in material terms. Despite the massive upheaval caused by hyperinflation and Depression, the Labor Ministry and its local welfare offices returned the vast majority of disabled to self-sufficiency and family life. In state-sponsored rehabilitative training programs, they learned the skills they needed to return to their prewar occupations or, if necessary, to embark on another career. Local welfare offices ensured that their severely disabled clients secured and kept jobs. For those veterans too badly disabled to work, the state provided pensions that allowed recipients to live at home with their families. Disabled veterans in Germany were integrated into the workplace; they were the welfare state's favored wards; their protest carried power. They became self-confident and assured of the justice of their cause. Their British counterparts – triumphant heroes of Western Europe's bloodiest war – became the objects of charity, relegated to the periphery of their society, bound by desperation to a "grateful public" that diminished daily.

As the memory of the war receded, disabled veterans in Britain began to regret their "apoliticism." In a 1932 *Sunday Express* article, Viscount Castelrosse, who served with the Guards on the western front, condemned the state for neglecting ex-servicemen but acknowledged that he and his comrades also had failed: "We have never demanded our rights. . . . Instead of demanding our rights, we went hat in hand asking for charity. We ought to have gone bayonet in hand demanding our rights. We behaved sweetly, and were swindled accordingly."[40] Philanthropy could go a long way toward easing hard feelings, but it was never enough to provide for disabled men's reintegration. It helped keep the war's victims out of politics, not off of the public assistance rolls.

Scholars have regarded postwar reconstruction as a task for states and their corporate partners in industry and labor, judging its success or failure on the basis of governments' responses to the problems bequeathed by war. But reconstruction after the Great War was not simply a matter of demobilizing armies, rebuilding cities, and reestablishing industry. Equally important were less concrete aspects of reconstruction, including the development of social solidarity. After this century's first total war, there was peace to be made not only abroad but at home as well. It was a peace between those who had fought and those who had stayed at home, between those who lost loved ones and those who were spared, between the disabled and those for whom they sacrificed.

In Britain, voluntarism shielded the state from the consequences of its unpopular policies. Philanthropy bound veterans closer to their society and diminished their rightful claims on the victorious state. In Germany, by contrast, the state's regulation of charity isolated the disabled from their public. As a result of its elimination of voluntarism, the Weimar state became solely responsible for the fulfillment of veterans' demands. In both nations, reconstruction required the full participation of civil society. The Weimar Republic's framers had believed that they could heal the war's rifts through the distribution of generous benefits. Theirs was a terrible error, for the state alone could not promote successful social reconstruction.

40 Quoted in the *British Legion Journal*, Jan. 1933, 235.

7

The Impact of Total War on the Practice of British Psychiatry

EDGAR JONES AND SIMON WESSELY

It is generally accepted that modern warfare has exercised a significant influence on the evolution of psychiatry in the twentieth century. Stone, for example, argued that the identification of shell shock and attempts to treat the disorder were "an important and dynamic episode in the development of psychological medicine in Britain" in that they brought Freudian concepts of neurosis into "the mainstream of mental medicine and economic life and set psychiatry's field of practice squarely within the social fabric of industrial society."[1] Similarly, Merskey concluded from his study of shell shock that "the maturation of psychiatry occurred in the course of World War One; it then became a speciality with potential for the community." Prominent figures like "T. A. Ross, D. K. Henderson and Millais Culpin," he added, "all received an impetus to work outside the psychiatric hospitals from their own wartime experience."[2]

Whilst it was undoubtedly true that World War I drew physicians with an academic interest in psychology into the armed forces and that psychiatric questions became of paramount importance during the conflict, the expertise acquired by these individuals appears to have been dissipated. They did not continue to exercise a great influence over either military or civil medical services once the armistice had been signed. By contrast, World War II, which drew large numbers of civilians into the front line and created a total conflict, saw more lasting effects. Psychiatric specialists were recruited into the services in both selection and training roles, and also for the treatment of psychologically traumatized servicemen. In addition, it was feared that modern bombers would obliterate entire cities, undermining the

1 Martin Stone, "Shellshock and the Psychologists," in W. F. Bynum, Roy Porter, and Michael Shepherd, eds., *The Anatomy of Madness: Essays in the History of Psychiatry*, 3 vols. (London, 1985), 2: 265–6.

2 Harold Merskey, "Shell Shock," in German Berrios and Hugh Freeman, eds., *150 Years of British Psychiatry* (London, 1991), 261.

fighting spirit of the workforce and their families. Psychiatrists were asked by the government to advise on how best to prepare for this onslaught and treat the effects of continuous aerial bombardment. Hence, in this essay we shall argue that although there were important influences on psychiatric practice as a result of World War I, these can be exaggerated and, furthermore, that it was World War II that had the greater and more enduring impact.

WORLD WAR I AND PSYCHIATRIC PRACTICE

The British army entered the European conflict of August 1914 with little formal provision for psychiatric casualties. Although previous campaigns had seen soldiers discharged with unexplained medical disorders, such as "debility," the effects of sunstroke and Disordered Action of the Heart (DAH), their numbers remained relatively small. The acute stress of war was not thought to be a problem for well-trained troops efficiently led, despite accounts in the *British Medical Journal* of soldiers collapsing from nervous disorders in the Russo-Japanese War (1904–5).[3] Such reports appear to have been largely ignored by the British military authorities, who had sent medical observers to the conflict. The intense fighting of 1914 (characterized by the sustained artillery bombardments) led to increasing numbers of "nerve exhausted" soldiers being sent to base hospitals in France and then invalided to the United Kingdom. Reports filtered through in the winter of 1914–15 of men suffering from what would later be called "combat fatigue" or "battle exhaustion." Lord Nutsford, chairman of the London Hospital, was one of the first to draw attention to the problem of nerve exhausted soldiers in November 1914.[4] Overwhelmed by the scale and nature of these disorders, the military medical services were forced to call on civilian specialists to assist with both diagnosis and treatment.

In August 1915 a special edition of the Oxford Primers on War Surgery was published on *Nerve Injuries and Shock.* Designed to fit into the tunic pocket of a medical officer on active service, it opened with the phrase "an outstanding feature of the casualties in the present war is the very large number of cases of nervous exhaustion, neurasthenia and functional paralyses of various kinds which are being met with."[5] The author, Captain Wilfrid Harris, a Territorial officer attached to the 3 London General Hospital, described a disorder then termed "shell fever." He pointed out

3 Anonymous, "Madness of Armies in the Field," *British Medical Journal* (hereafter *BMJ*) 2 (1904): 30–1.
4 Anonymous, "Mental and Nervous Shock Among the Wounded," *BMJ* 2 (1914): 802–3.
5 Wilfrid Harris, *Nerve Injuries and Shock* (London, 1915).

the psychological nature of the symptoms, observing that a soldier in this state "may break down in tears if asked to describe their experiences at the Front. This is especially the case if the man's regiment has been severely handled, and numbers of his comrades and brother officers have been killed."[6]

Harris was sanguine about treatment, arguing that "with proper methods of suggestive treatment, these cases of nervous shock can nearly all be rapidly, or even immediately cured." Lack of experience may have driven his optimism as Harris was a specialist in nerve injuries. He viewed cases of shell fever as analogous to neurasthenia and hence believed in the efficacy of a rest cure in which the influence of the doctor's personality was paramount. Although Harris referred to psychoanalytic techniques, he concluded that they were "practically not required" in the treatment of war neurasthenia. At this stage in the conflict, shell shock and related disorders were primarily regarded as an organic response to cerebral injury.

Captain Charles Myers (1873–1946) was the first doctor to publish a paper in a medical journal that referred to "shell shock," though he did not claim to be the originator of the term.[7] It probably entered into general usage as the war developed as the diagnosis "cerebro-medullary shock" had been employed during the Balkan Wars (1912–13) by Professor Laurant to describe the torpor and functional paralysis seen in some soldiers that had been close to a shell burst but not wounded. Laurant thought that the shock was produced by the concussive effect of rushing air combined with the inhalation of toxic gases released by the explosion.[8] A medically qualified Cambridge psychologist, Myers had traveled to France shortly after the outbreak of war to work as a volunteer registrar in the hospital at Étaples funded by the duchess of Westminster. Once there, he was offered a temporary commission in the RAMC by Sir Arthur Sloggett, the director-general of medical services of the British Armies in the Field. Observing the growing numbers of servicemen admitted with "functional nervous disorders," Myers began to experiment with light hypnosis to treat their memory loss, publishing his findings in *The Lancet*. In January 1915, concerned by the rising numbers of troops said to be suffering from nervous disorders, the War Office sent Lieutenant Colonel William Aldren Turner, a consultant neurologist and Territorial officer, to France to advise on their management. Having assessed the problem, Turner recommended that Myers succeed him and be given responsibility for the selection of "suitable cases of nervous and mental shock and neurasthenia for transference to the appropriate institutions in

6 Ibid., 2.
7 Charles Myers, "A Contribution to the Study of Shell Shock," *Lancet* 2 (1915): 316.
8 A. A. Roberts, *The Poison War* (London, 1915), 24–6.

England for treatment."[9] Given the title "specialist in nerve shock," Myers's role expanded and, in August 1916, he was made consulting psychologist. While Myers was responsible for all neurological and psychological cases within the Fourth and Fifth Army areas, Lt. Colonel Gordon Holmes, the consulting neurologist, looked after the remainder.

Physicians, in general, found themselves faced with complex and sometimes competing demands. They had to try to ensure that those susceptible to stress and who would probably break down in the trenches were removed from active service, while ensuring that such cases were kept to a minimum. At the same time, they had to attempt to make some sense of what they were witnessing. Captain J. E. MacIlwaine, who had been attached to a convalescent depot, described the dilemma. A considerable number of soldiers suffering from functional cardiac disorders such as DAH were referred for assessment. Troops were put on a six-week program of graded exercises and the medical officers forced to judge between those who were fit to return to active service and those who were sent to safe jobs at a base – a process that the men termed "a strafe."[10] "Although the only question of practical importance to the army in the field had been answered [by the tests], the riddle as to the pathological cause of the men's incapacity," according to MacIlwaine, "had not been solved" as they were no closer to understanding the science of DAH. His experience had taught him that "the Army is a school of practical psychology," and demonstrated "how much the psychological element plays in the life of the soldier, and how his natural sporting instinct is manipulated by great therapeutic skill."[11]

Psychiatrists recruited into the army to treat shell shock sometimes found themselves caught between a wish to heal and the military need to deter desertion. Myers, who had set up an experimental "Advanced Sorting Centre," found that he was edged out by Sir Arthur Sloggett, and the unit was promptly closed.[12] Under pressure from the Adjutant General to enforce rigid discipline, Sloggett believed that Myers might resist this imperative.[13] Facing opposition to the "adoption of psycho-therapeutic measure[s]," Myers requested a transfer and moved to the War Office in London, while his responsibilities in France passed to Gordon Holmes. Demoralized by this experience, Myers declined to give evidence to the Southborough

9 Charles Myers, *Shell Shock in France 1914–1918, Based on a War Diary* (Cambridge, 1940), 15–16.

10 J. E. MacIlwaine, "A Clinical Study of Some Functional Disorders of the Heart Which Occur in Soldiers," *Journal of the Royal Army Medical Corps* 30 (1918): 358.

11 Ibid., 376.

12 Myers, *Shell Shock in France*, 107.

13 Ben Shephard, "The Early Treatment of Mental Disorders: R. G. Rows and Maghull, 1914–1918," in Hugh Freeman and German Berrios, eds., *150 Years of British Psychiatry: The Aftermath* (London, 1996), 440.

Committee on shell shock, and later commented of Sloggett that he could be "extremely sympathetic and understanding" but had been "evidently unwilling to take notice of the prime causes of my dissatisfaction."[14]

THE IMPACT OF WORLD WAR I ON CIVILIAN PSYCHIATRY

Psychiatrists in Practice

Once the armistice had been signed, psychiatry returned to its peacetime roots, and the aberration of war, as far as the profession was concerned, soon passed. Specialists recruited into military psychiatry returned to civilian life, some disillusioned by their army experience. Myers went back to Cambridge and marked his withdrawal from medical psychology in a controversial letter to *The Lancet* in which he condemned physical treatments of functional disorders. "During the war," he wrote, "there were certain physicians who could explain to a patient suffering from functional hemiplegia that the cortical cells on one side of the brain were out of order. . . . And they would proceed to tone up the disordered cells by painful faradism. . . . I have always been convinced that such measures are not only needless, but also dangerous."[15] In 1920 he left his academic post at Cambridge to join a London businessman, H. J. Welch, in setting up the National Institute for Industrial Psychology.

William McDougall (1871–1938), who had been the senior clinical officer at Littlemore Hospital, returned to Oxford as Wilde Reader in Mental Philosophy after demobilization from the RAMC, but feeling unwanted emigrated to Harvard and a chair in psychology. He confided in a friend that "I have done my best to serve my country during the war. I have returned to have my laboratory taken from me."[16] W. H. R. Rivers, who had treated servicemen at Maghull and Craiglockhart, had gone back to Cambridge in 1919 as prelector in natural sciences. However, he appeared to have abandoned clinical work, and even research, when he accepted the nomination as the Labour Party candidate for the University of London constituency. He died of a strangulated hernia in June 1922 before the election took place.[17] William Brown, a psychologist who had also qualified in medicine, was one of the few to continue seeing patients and pursuing academic study after the war. During the hostilities he had worked at Maghull before

14 Myers, *Shell Shock in France*, 110.
15 Anonymous, "Obituary Charles Myers," *Lancet* 2 (1946): 622.
16 Anonymous, "Obituary William McDougall," *BMJ* 2 (1938): 1232.
17 Anonymous, "Obituary W. H. R. Rivers," *BMJ* 1 (1922): 977–8.

going to France to treat traumatized soldiers with abreaction under hypnosis and then moved to Craiglockhart. Brown returned to Oxford where in 1921 he succeeded McDougall as Wilde Reader in Mental Philosophy, and from 1925 to 1931 he also practiced as a psychotherapist at King's College Hospital.[18]

If anything, World War I exercised a far greater and more lasting influence on the practice of neurology rather than psychiatry. Before the war, as Craig and Beaton commented, "the neurologist never saw the case of insanity shut up in the mental hospitals and the mental hospital physician, the alienists or psychiatrists never saw the case of nerves."[19] The conflict had blurred these divisions and allowed psychiatrists to shift from being merely alienists and lunacy doctors to having expertise in other forms of mental disorder. Yet the return of medical officers to civilian practice saw many of these conventions return. Although psychoanalysts, a relatively small group, concerned themselves with neuroses, in mainstream medicine these disorders continued to be the preserve of neurologists. Several of the major neurology textbooks were revised during the war and sections on neurosis added, and it was not until World War II that these topics began to disappear.[20]

The Impact of the Ministry of Pensions

In the aftermath of the war, the Ministry of Pensions attempted to provide treatment for the 65,000 veterans awarded pensions for neurasthenia and allied conditions.[21] An out-patient clinic run along psychoanalytic lines was set up at 80 Lancaster Gate, but, by the nature of the therapy, it could address only small numbers. Other centers were established elsewhere in Britain, and it was calculated in February 1921 that 14,771 ex-servicemen were either attending boards for assessment or clinics for treatment. However, the costs proved prohibitive, and this embryonic and rather experimental initiative was wound up. In general, veterans with psychological disorders were left to fend for themselves during the interwar period.

Equally, the regional medical boards set up by the Ministry of Pensions to assess the level of disability suffered by ex-servicemen rarely, if ever, called on expert psychiatric opinion. The medical members were commonly drawn from the ranks of the local practitioners or retired army physicians.

18 Anonymous, "Obituary: William Brown," *Lancet* 1 (1952): 1073.

19 Maurice Craig and T. Beaton, *Psychological Medicine* (London, 1926), 67.

20 David Armstrong, "Madness and Coping," *Sociology of Health and Illness* 2 (1980): 309.

21 W. Macpherson, W. Herringham, T. Elliott, and A. Balfour, *History of the Great War Medical Services: Diseases of War*, 4 vols. (London, 1923), 2: 56.

On occasion, a specialist opinion was solicited but these were usually from the mainstream medical disciplines such as cardiology or ophthalmology and occasionally neurology. Sir Maurice Craig (1866–1935), a consultant in psychological medicine at Guy's Hospital, was a rare exception. Yet it is interesting that his appointment to the Ministry of Pensions was as a consultant neurologist, and later he was the sole psychiatric representative on the sixteen-man War Office committee set up in 1920 to investigate the nature of shell shock.[22]

Indirectly, perhaps, the pensions system played a part in nullifying the achievements of military psychiatry. It had been set up to compensate soldiers who had suffered disability as a result of wounds or disease contracted on military service. It was not designed to deal with psychological disorders. Indeed, it attempted to manage them as if they were organic conditions. Physicians at medical boards, for example, were required to assess the level of pension due to a man suffering from shell shock in relation to a physical disability such as the loss of a finger or toe. Many doctors took psychological disorders seriously only insofar as they led to physical incapacity and tended to dismiss men who presented with functional symptoms that were obviously related to a nervous temperament.[23]

Treatments and Ideas

What then did civilian psychiatry learn from the experience of World War I? Stone argued that the conflict had a major impact on the practice of psychiatry. Doctors recruited into the army were introduced to new ideas. At Maghull, for example, fifty RAMC officers were trained in the techniques of abreactive psychotherapy. T. A. Ross was convinced by his experience of working with traumatized soldiers that psychotherapy was the preferred treatment for neuroses. Fears brought to consciousness, he argued, "may no longer be a source of stress and therefore symptoms."[24] Stone concluded that

> many British doctors received their first practical introductions to the new medical psychology whilst working in army hospitals. . . . They subsequently gained a considerable expertise in handling and treating nervous disorders and were responsible for a prodigious volume of books and articles on psychotherapy and psychopathology published during the early 1920s.[25]

22 Anonymous, "Obituary Sir Maurice Craig," *Lancet* 1 (1935): 119–20.

23 Peter Leese, "Problems Returning Home: The British Psychological Casualties of the Great War," *Historical Journal* (forthcoming).

24 T. A. Ross, *The Common Neuroses: Their Treatment by Psychotherapy* (London, 1937): 131–2.

25 Stone, "Shellshock and the Psychologists," 243.

This impression was supported by the comments of a number of psychiatrists who qualified before World War II.[26] However, Merskey has questioned this interpretation, arguing that "some services existed before World War I even if they were not large and those that emerged between the wars were also not substantial."[27]

Although the extent to which psychological ideas derived from the treatment of shell shock influenced mainstream British psychiatry remains unclear, there is evidence for important theoretical changes, even if these new ideas did not gain widespread acceptance. In essence, it has been argued that Freudian concepts of neurosis were widely dismissed in the United Kingdom before the war but that the treatment of shell shock led to their recognition albeit in a modified form. Whilst this was broadly true, it also appears to have been the case that the critical adoption of psychoanalytic theories predated the conflict. At Manchester University, T. H. Pear, a lecturer in psychology, presented Freud's ideas on dreams to his colleagues, Grafton Elliot Smith, professor of anatomy, Niels Bohr, and Ernest Rutherford, and had listened while Elliot Smith criticized Freud's adoption of "old-fashioned theories of human instinct."[28] William Brown had written on the use of hypnotism in the treatment of psychoneuroses, and Pear himself had worked in a psychiatric clinic in Giessen.

In February 1918 Rivers published a paper on "The Repression of War Experience" that took Freudian concepts and re-applied them to shell shock and other psychological disorders. Rivers argued that "many of the most trying and distressing symptoms from which the subjects of war neurosis suffer are not the necessary result of the strains and shocks to which they have been exposed in warfare, but are due to the attempt to banish from the mind distressing memories of warfare or painful affective states."[29] Rivers believed that these disorders were an expression of the failure of repression. Because most troops were not regulars but had volunteered or had been conscripted into the army and been trained in great haste, they had not had the time to build up an effective repressive mechanism. Faced with "strains such as have never previously been known in the history of mankind," it was "small wonder that the failures of adaptation should have been so numerous and severe."[30] Rivers abandoned the primary role given to infantile sexuality

26 Merskey, "Shell Shock," 262.

27 Harold Merskey, "Post-Traumatic Stress Disorder and Shell Shock," in Roy Porter and German Berrios, eds., *The Clinical History of Psychiatry, 1841–1991* (London, 1995), 494.

28 Quoted from Shephard, "Rows and Maghull," 442.

29 W. H. R. Rivers, "The Repression of War Experience," *Lancet* 1 (1918): 173.

30 Ibid.

by Freud and argued that it was the conflict between the soldier's sense of fear and duty that lay at the heart of war neurosis. For Rivers, who had treated private soldiers at Maghull, this explanation applied equally well to all ranks. Mott, by contrast, believed that officers were more prone to such a conflict, and therefore the symptoms of neurasthenia, because "the prolonged stress of responsibility . . . worn out by the prolonged stress of war and want of sleep, causes anxiety less he should fail in his critical duties. He fears that his memory may fail him at a critical moment, and anxiety weighs heavily upon him; mental preoccupation leads to a continued struggle to overcome such doubts and fears."[31]

Some psychiatrists, like Sir Robert Armstrong Jones, who were antagonistic to psychoanalysis, used this evidence to undermine the movement, and he declared at a meeting of the Medico-Psychological Society in 1920 that "Freudianism was dead in England today."[32] Millais Culpin, professor of medical industrial psychology at the London School of Hygiene, observed that few doctors with any regard for their reputation would mention an interest in psychoanalysis during the 1920s "without the verbal equivalent of spitting three times over the left shoulder, and even to speak about the revival of war memories carried the risk of being accused of advocating free fornication for everyone."[33] Facing open hostility from the U.K. medical profession and an intellectual challenge from the medical psychologists, Dr. Ernest Jones wound up the London Psycho-Analytical Society and formed the British Psycho-Analytical Society in February 1919 with an inaugural group of twelve members. He also introduced more stringent requirements for admission; in essence, all candidates had to meet with his approval.[34] Although Jones was able to attract a number of talented doctors and literary figures, raising the Society's numbers to fifty-four by 1925,[35] psychoanalysis in the United Kingdom retreated into itself. In this beleaguered position, the psychoanalytic community failed to contribute fully to the general psychological debate, developing as a self-contained discipline to the detriment of both psychotherapy and medicine as a whole.

It has also been argued that the great incidence of shell shock, affecting young men of sound constitution, undermined traditional theories of

31 Frederick Mott, *Neuroses and Shell Shock* (London, 1919), 131.

32 R. Armstrong Jones, "Medico-Psychological Association of Great Britain and Ireland, Annual Meeting," *Lancet* 2 (1920): 404.

33 Millais Culpin, "A Criticism of Modern Trends in the Treatment of Psychoneuroses," *The Medical Press* (1952): 71.

34 Phyllis Grosskurth, *Melanie Klein* (London, 1986), 158.

35 Eric Rayner, *The Independent Mind in British Psychoanalysis* (London, 1990), 11.

degeneration.[36] In fact, these ideas were not abandoned but re-framed by the experience of World War I. Captain Julian Wolfsohn, assistant professor of nervous diseases at Stanford University attached to Mott at the Maudsley, studied the relationship between war neurosis and "an acquired or inherited neuropathy." Comparing one hundred soldiers suffering from shell shock, neurasthenia, or battle exhaustion with one hundred soldiers with battle injuries as controls, he demonstrated that the first group had higher levels of unexplained symptoms, such as tremor, headache, insomnia, poor memory, and fatigue. In addition, research into their family histories showed a greater incidence of mood and stress disorders. In 74 percent of the war neurosis group he identified a background of "neurotic or psychotic stigmata, including insanity, epilepsy, alcoholism, and nervousness," while these were present in only 10 percent of the controls.[37] Constitutional factors were closely correlated with breakdown, and in World War II these findings were used to reduce the number or level of awards given to servicemen applying for a war pension. If it could be shown that a man had suffered with nerves before he enlisted, then his military service could not be a cause but at best an aggravation of an existing condition.

MILITARY PSYCHIATRY IN THE AFTERMATH OF WORLD WAR I

Despite the experience of World War I, the British army returned to its prewar professional origins and largely dispensed with the services of its psychiatrists. Why was this the case when they seemed to have shown themselves indispensable in the battlefield? As Elliot Smith and Pear argued in *Shell Shock and Its Lessons*:

> the war has shown us one indisputable fact, that a psychoneurosis may be produced in almost anyone if only his environment be made "difficult" enough for him. It has warned us that the pessimistic, helpless appeal to heredity, so common in the case of insanity, must go the same way as its lugubrious homologue which formerly did duty in the case of tuberculosis. In causation of the psychoneuroses, heredity undoubtedly counts, but social and material environment count infinitely more.[38]

Although later conflicts were to confirm their judgment, this conclusion was not shared by many doctors and a good number of senior army officers,

36 Stone, "Shellshock and the Psychologists," 252.

37 Julian Wolfsohn, "The Predisposing Factors of War in Psycho-Neurosis," *Lancet* 1 (1918): 180.

38 Grafton Elliot Smith and T. H. Pear, *Shellshock and Its Lessons* (Manchester, 1917), 87–8.

who believed that properly trained troops, well led and with high morale, were virtually immune from psychological breakdown. Giving evidence to the Southborough Committee in 1920, Lieutenant Colonel Lord Gort, V.C., suggested that shell shock was practically nonexistent "in first-class divisions" and that prevention was a matter of "training . . . strong morale and esprit de corps."[39] This view is crucial to an understanding of the apparent failure to translate the lessons of World War I to wider practice and also accounts for the disillusionment felt by many forward-thinking psychiatrists. Clearly, if Gort's ideas prevailed, then what was needed were the traditional virtues of leadership, training, and morale. There was no place in this scheme for military psychiatry. This view also dominated in Germany where at the Munich conference of 1916 a consensus formed around the idea that psychological breakdown after combat was a failure of collective leadership and individual moral fiber that, if it were allowed to spread, would lead to compensation claims, bankrupting the exchequer, and lose Germany the war. In the United Kingdom, Elliot Smith and Pear, having urged that the new treatments inspired by shell shock should be more extensively applied "not only for our soldiers now, but also for our civilian population for all time," were justifiably pessimistic even in 1917. In their estimation, the press and public preferred to leave the subject of mental disease "severely alone."[40] Yet the gains of World War I had not, of course, been lost entirely. The fact that Field Marshall Haig and Admiral Beatty were appointed honorary vice presidents of the Tavistock Clinic when it opened in 1920 showed, for example, that a connection had been established between military orthodoxy and psychological treatments.[41]

The neglect of psychological medicine was demonstrated in 1939 when there were only half a dozen regular army officers with varying degrees of psychiatric training in the British army. It was again necessary to recruit from the civilian profession, beginning with the appointment of J. R. Rees, who had succeeded Crighton Miller as director of the Tavistock Clinic.[42] Rees then discovered that in clinical terms matters were worse than he had imagined: "Henry Yellowlees had gone abroad to the B.E.F. with a very excellent team of psychiatrists, and for the time being I was the only other representative of psychiatry in the British Army. There were two qualified

39 Lord Southborough, *Report of the War Office Committee of Enquiry into "Shell-Shock"* (London, 1922), 50.

40 Elliot Smith and Pear, *Shellshock and Its Lessons*, 108.

41 Stone, "Shellshock and the Psychologists," 248.

42 Robert H. Ahrenfeldt, *British Psychiatry in the Second World War* (London, 1958), 15.

psychiatrists in the regular force, but both of them so senior that they were doing purely administrative jobs."[43]

TOTAL WAR: PSYCHIATRY AND WORLD WAR II

Impact on Civilians

To a far greater extent than in previous conflicts, civilians in World War II were drawn into the fighting and hence exposed to stresses previously limited to servicemen. In the interwar period, a belief had gradually gathered force that any future conflict would involve mass civilian casualties. This view appears to have become even more entrenched among civilian than military leaders, Stanley Baldwin coining the famous phrase "the bomber will always get through." Hence, the authorities planned for civilian casualties on a major scale to the extent of building shadow hospitals in the vicinity of conurbations. They also expected high levels of psychological disturbance, and the specter of collapsed civilian morale was debated at every turn.

This pessimistic conviction had grown, in part, because there was so little evidence from previous wars on which to base predictions. Nevertheless, the few reports that existed seemed to contradict this conclusion. In 1917, for example, Percy Smith had studied psychiatric cases following Zeppelin air-raids and observed that despite the intention "to produce a widespread terror" they had in fact resulted in very little effect on the general population. Although a few individuals had been traumatized, large numbers "flocked into the streets or stood on the door-steps watching search-lights and with shells bursting in the air around them. So that one has heard remarks as if the show were intended for the special benefit or amusement of the observers."[44] Reports from the Spanish Civil War published in the *British Medical Journal* for June 1939 were equally reassuring. Emilio Mira, formerly professor of psychiatry at the University of Barcelona, showed that the impact of war, though increasing the incidence of psychological disorders, did not "call for the provision of more psychiatric beds than had been available in peacetime."[45] After a time the inhabitants of "the city became almost indifferent to a bombardment if it did not affect their own district . . . a great part of the population would feel what may be called 'normal anxiety' during an air raid, but never needed psychiatric attention."[46] Surveying the

43 PRO, WO32/13462, J. R. Rees, Untitled typescript (*c.* June 1966): 1–2.

44 R. P. Smith, "Mental Disorders in Civilians Arising in Connection with the War," *Proceedings of the Royal Society of Medicine* 10 (1917): 11.

45 Emilio Mira, "Psychiatric Experience in the Spanish Civil War," *BMJ* 1 (1939): 1217.

46 Ibid., 1218.

psychiatric literature on civilians in 1940, Wittkower and Spillane confirmed that there were few papers and, like Smith in World War I, concluded that the feeling of shared danger "leads to a strengthening of community ties and to a leveling of differences and opposition in social, economic, religious and political spheres."[47]

Driven by fears of mass psychiatric breakdown and an incidence of shell shock on the scale of World War I, the minister of pensions convened a conference under the chairmanship of Lord Horder in July 1939 to advise the government on how best to deal with cases of psychological disorder. Among those called to give evidence were Gordon Holmes, T. A. Ross, W. Aldren Turner, and Professor Edward Mapother, medical superintendent of the Maudsley. One of their key recommendations, published in the *British Medical Journal* for December was for

> the immediate treatment of patients exhibiting nervous symptoms due to fear, anxiety, and other mental factors during and after air-raids is very important, as if they are neglected the morale of the population suffers seriously. *Such terms as "shell shock," which may suggest that these nervous symptoms have a physical basis or are due directly to injury, must be rigidly avoided.*[48]

Uncertain as to how the public would respond to this novel form of warfare, the government organized four specialist hospitals (Mill Hill, Sutton, Isleworth, and Maidstone, with a fifth planned for Essex) in a ring around the capital. Staffed entirely by psychiatrists and neurologists, their role was to treat those civilians so traumatized that they required admission. In addition, they were to provide mobile units to be sent to areas severely damaged by bombing, while a specialist hospital at Watford had been provided for those requiring prolonged psychological treatment.[49]

Psychiatric expertise was thus pressed into service at the outbreak of war, with the specific question of studying civilian morale. In 1942 Aubrey Lewis, clinical director of the Maudsley Hospital, was asked to prepare a report by the Medical Research Council on the effect of the war, and particularly of air-raids, on the incidence of neurosis in the civilian population.[50] A survey of GP practices and psychiatric out-patient clinics in London, Bristol, Merseyside, Birmingham, Coventry, and Manchester led Lewis to conclude that air-raids were not responsible for a striking increase in psychological

47 Eric Wittkower and J. P. Spillane, "A Survey of the Literature of Neuroses in War," in Emanuel Miller, ed., *The Neuroses of War* (London, 1940), 1.

48 Anonymous, "Neuroses in War Time: Memorandum for the Medical Profession," *BMJ* 2 (1939): 1201, emphasis in the original.

49 Anonymous, "Treatment of Neuroses in the Emergency Medical Service," *BMJ* 2 (1939): 1243.

50 Aubrey Lewis, "Incidence of Neurosis in England Under War Conditions," *Lancet* 2 (1942): 175.

disorders. Intense bombing was shown to lead to "a slight rise in the total amount of neurotic illness in the affected area, occurring chiefly in those who have been neurotically ill before. Neurotic reactions may not show themselves for a week or ten days after the bombing; they usually clear up readily with rest and mild sedatives."[51]

In 1942 R. D. Gillespie, a consultant in psychological medicine at Guy's and temporarily recruited into the RAF, published a book whose title, *The Psychological Effects of War on Citizen and Soldier*, reflected the prevailing concerns about the psychological strength of the civilian population. With experience of both groups, Gillespie was able to reassure his readers that

> one of the most striking things about the effects of war on the civilian population has been the relative rarity of pathological disturbances among the civilians exposed to air raids. Guy's Hospital . . . is in one of the most frequently bombed areas of London, and . . . yet the psychiatric outpatient department which still functions there records very few cases of neuroses attributable to war conditions. The patients, who do come, with few exceptions, present mainly the same problems as in peacetime.[52]

These observations were supported by an analysis of in-patient statistics. Of the 2,306 psychiatric patients admitted to Sutton Emergency Hospital between its opening in September 1939 and August 1941, only 283 were civilian and of these a mere 41 were air-raid casualties.[53]

The Ministry of Pensions and the Issue of Compensation

Equally, World War I had generated no equivalent of J. Mackintosh's *The War and Mental Health in England* (1944) which dealt with such a broad selection of psychological topics. These included the influence of the "phoney war" on the morale of civilians; the effect of the blackout on the mental health of the worker; rationing and the mental health of the housewife, and even the student, in wartime; how to deal with mentally distressed air-raid victims; the psychological impact of the arrival of American forces in the United Kingdom; and the mental health of evacuated children.

This episode also contributed a further chapter to the history of how governments addressed the issue of compensation for psychological injury. Because of the large numbers of ex-servicemen that had been awarded pensions for neurasthenia and shell shock after World War I, the Horder Committee sought to avoid a repetition. In 1939 it was decided that war

51 Ibid., 182.
52 Robert Gillespie, *The Psychological Effects of War on Citizen and Soldier* (New York, 1942), 106–7.
53 Ibid., 110–11.

neurosis would not be a pensionable disorder. However, this soon brought the government into conflict with the Trade Unions over the Workmen's Compensations Acts. The National Union of Seamen raised the case of four crew of the *S.S. Athenia* that had been torpedoed while carrying precious cargo to the United Kingdom. Although the sailors had not been physically injured, they were traumatized by the experience, and the unions argued that they were eligible for financial compensation.[54] In addition, GPs had been giving injury allowance certificates to workers who had suffered psychologically when London was bombed in 1940. With these precedents established, the Ministry of Pensions could not then exclude soldiers disturbed by the experience of battle, though psychiatrists were instructed to assess the serviceman's prewar history to discover whether claimants might have a predisposition to psychoneurosis. In this event, their pension was reduced in value and sometimes only temporary.

Group Therapy

The legacy of World War I was, contrary to some views, not ignored. Many of the psychiatrists called into service were themselves veterans of the first war. Aware of the shortage of psychiatrists in the regular army, Rees had in fact begun to build up a list of potential recruits before war had been declared. The difficulty was to get them called up until a suggestion to a member of Parliament led to a question in the Commons late in December 1939. This publicity led to their rapid transfer into the forces. As Rees recalled, he had gathered together "a group of middle-aged, mature established consultants, and quite a tough bunch. The doyen of the group was Emanuel Miller, and then you had Wilfrid Bion wearing his D.S.O. ribbon . . . then Eddie Bennet wearing his Military Cross also won in the First War."[55]

A significant example of innovation in psychiatric practice resulting from total war was the introduction of group therapy, developed in a variety of settings as a response to the need to treat larger numbers of servicemen than could be managed on an individual basis. Pioneering work was undertaken at Runwell Hospital, Wickford, Essex, by Joshua Bierer who had experimented in the early years of the war with short-term individual and group treatments. Openly critical of Freudian techniques, he sought to turn institutional features to advantage by making use of a self-governing social club to give patients a sense of responsibility and control. He set up groups of varying size (from one hundred members to as few as ten) to instill a sense

54 PRO, PIN15/2208, Mar. 1941.

55 J. R. Rees, untitled typescript, 2.

of independence, motivation, and insight.[56] In this respect, Bierer predated the work of Majors Wilfrid Bion and John Rickman at Hollymoor Hospital, Northfield, Birmingham. Early in 1943 Bion and Rickman set up both large (between 100 and 200 men) and smaller groups in the 600-bed training wing to foster a spirit of self-responsibility and cooperative activity.[57] Bion later noted that the objective for the groups had been "the study of the [wing's] own internal tensions, in a real life situation, with a view to laying bare the influence of neurotic behaviour in producing frustration, waste of energy, and unhappiness."[58] The experiment was brought to a halt six weeks later, following a surprise visit by War Office officials who had been alerted to the unconventional treatments. The training wing was then re-organized by S. H. [Michael] Foulkes (who had served in the German army during World War I) and Harold Bridger in a more structured fashion and continued to treat servicemen until the end of the war.[59] Brigadier Rees, director of army psychiatry, commented that "perhaps the most outstanding and lasting thing that happened [at Northfield] was that the therapeutic community came into being, one of the first instances of a real link in the treatment system between patients and doctors and nurses who were looking after them."[60]

Northfield had not, however, been the only therapeutic community set up by the Army. At the beginning of the war Mill Hill Public School had been converted into an Emergency Service Hospital, drawing staff from the Maudsley. A special 100-bed unit was set up for the study of effort syndrome under the joint directorship of Paul Wood, a cardiologist, and Maxwell Jones, a psychiatrist. At the beginning patients, who were all servicemen, were taught about their condition and its symptoms, but this was soon abandoned in favor of a discussion procedure.[61] These groups then evolved along therapeutic lines, and Jones admitted that he later drew on some of the ideas being explored at Northfield.[62] He also believed that the changes in the medical hierarchy and general improvements in communications could not have occurred so rapidly in peacetime given the strength of "hospital traditions." "We were helped by the temporary nature of the hospital and

56 Joshua Bierer, "Group Psychotherapy," *BMJ* 1 (1942): 214–17; Bierer, *The Day Hospital* (London, 1951).

57 Tom Harrison and David Clarke, "The Northfield Experiments," *British Journal of Psychiatry* 160 (1992): 700; Tom Harrison, *Bion, Rickman, Foulkes and the Northfield Experiments* (London, 1999).

58 Wilfrid Bion, "The Leaderless Group Project," *Bulletin of the Menninger Clinic* 10 (1946): 80.

59 Patrick de Maré, "Major Bion," in Malcolm Pines, ed., *Bion and Group Psychotherapy* (London, 1985), 108–13.

60 J. R. Rees, untitled typescript, 3.

61 Maxwell Jones, *Social Psychiatry: A Study of Therapeutic Communities* (London, 1952), 3.

62 Harold Bridger, "Northfield Revisited," in Malcolm Pines, ed., *Bion and Group Psychotherapy* (London, 1985), 100.

of the nurses who were drawn from other professions, together with the general tendency to change which was apparent in many spheres during war-time."[63]

Diagnoses and Treatments

In 1942 J. A. Hadfield, who had run the 41 General (Neuropathic) Hospital, concluded that there had been a rise in the incidence of anxiety states and a fall in the numbers suffering from conversion hysteria (functional blindness, paralysis, and so forth) in contrast to World War I. He thought that this related to the nature of the conflict, suggesting that traumatic cases had been more common in the trenches where men, subjected to horrific bombardments, developed somatic symptoms. "Dunkirk, Norway, and air raids in this country," Hadfield wrote, "have produced some, but they are negligible compared with the thousands of 'shell-shocked' patients who returned from the Somme and other great battles of the last war."[64] He also considered that air raids had brought large numbers "nearer to the front line" and further increased the incidence of anxiety neurosis. The effect may also have been a cultural one, as people in 1939 may have been more ready to admit to the effects of emotions than had been their forebears of 1914. There had been a general education, albeit an incomplete one, of the medical profession and the public in the influence of psychological factors, and this may have had an impact on the nature of psychiatric presentations.

Whereas in World War I concern had grown about the potential decline in the quality of troops as the regular army was progressively replaced by a volunteer and then a conscript army, in World War II, too, a crisis of manpower arose. By 1944 the shortage of troops had become acute. The British army's global commitments simply could not be sustained. As a deliberate policy, many of the best units were retained for D-Day and the Normandy campaign, but high casualty rates created serious shortages as forces advanced deeper into France. It was important, therefore, to find ways to return combat-fatigued troops back to active duty as soon as possible. Drawing on the experience of Myers's work in World War I and the campaign in North Africa, a number of "Exhaustion Centres" were set up close to the front line. Soldiers were given the opportunity to rest in a safe environment and encouraged to abreact, sometimes under hypnosis. Although a very high percentage returned to duty, relatively few actually went back

63 Jones, *Social Psychiatry*, 14.
64 J. A. Hadfield, "War Neurosis: A Year in a Neuropathic Hospital," *BMJ* 1 (1942): 281.

to fighting units. Captain Patrick de Maré, who ran an exhaustion center in France during 1944, calculated that 86 percent of admissions went to a convalescent depot, where the majority were downgraded. Similar treatments had proved effective in the Italian campaign. Major Dugmore Hunter, a psychiatrist attached to 10 Corps, had succeeded in reducing the proportion of admissions invalided to the United Kingdom to under 10 percent, while 30 percent were returned to combat duties.[65]

Post-Traumatic Stress Disorder

The diagnosis of post-traumatic stress disorder (PTSD) was officially recognized in *DSM-III* (1980), having originally been termed post-Vietnam syndrome because so many returning veterans reported its symptoms. Although the current definition has seventeen possible symptoms, it can be summarized as recurrent and intrusive recollections of a life-threatening event, distressing dreams, avoidance of thoughts and activities associated with the trauma, difficulty sleeping, impaired concentration, hyper vigilance, and increased startle reaction.[66] It has been argued that PTSD has always been present in past societies, but its existence has only recently been identified. Young, however, has suggested that it is a culturally determined disorder and cannot have existed in earlier periods: "The disorder is not timeless, nor does it possess an intrinsic unity. Rather, it is glued together by the practices, technologies, and narratives with which it is diagnosed, studied, treated, and represented and by the various interests, institutions, and moral arguments that mobilised these efforts and resources."[67]

Although veterans from World War II now present with the symptoms of PTSD and the same symptoms can be identified in the historical medical records of servicemen engaged in that conflict, they were not at the time considered evidence for a new disorder. Smaller numbers of these symptoms were also reported in the military medical records during World War I, though physicians were then more alert to somatic, rather than behavioral or psychological, presentations. For British soldiers engaged in the Boer War (1899–1902), it would be difficult using their medical records to find sufficient evidence to meet the current diagnostic criteria for PTSD. It appears, therefore, that the twentieth century has witnessed a progressive

65 Dugmore Hunter, "The Work of a Corps Psychiatrist in the Italian Campaign," *Journal of the Royal Army Medical Corps* 86 (1946): 127.

66 American Psychiatric Association, *DSM-IV* (Washington, D.C., 1994), 428.

67 Allan Young, *The Harmony of Illusions: Inventing Post-Traumatic Stress Disorder* (Princeton, N.J., 1995), 5.

evolution of health beliefs one outcome of which is the description of a new disorder.

CONCLUSIONS

In terms of its impact on mainstream psychiatry, World War II seems to have exercised a greater and more lasting effect than World War I. Why, then, had this been the case? First, the conflict of 1939–45 was more "total" than that of 1914–18, and exposed large numbers of civilians to hazardous situations. They were subject to air raids, rationing, and the tight controls of labor and production. As a result, psychiatrists found themselves working at key posts not just in military hospitals but in civilian practice, and in the selection, training, and management of personnel. Important foundations had been laid for psychological medicine during World War I, but it was not until World War II that fundamental changes in treatment and the ways that mental disorders were conceptualized became widely accepted.

The outbreak of war in 1939 saw psychological factors again taken seriously for the selection of officers, training of troops, and treatment in battle. The development of various forms of therapy, whether brief abreaction, occupational, group, or longer-term strategies, were all advanced during the war. Unlike World War I, when so much that had been achieved rapidly disappeared once the country had returned to peace, these proved to be lasting effects. Psychiatry had become more sophisticated in terms of diagnosis, theoretical underpinning, and treatment by 1945. At the beginning of World War I, the war neuroses were scarcely understood, and the old terms *neurasthenia* and *nervous debility* were regularly called on to supplement such diagnoses as *nerves* and *mental exhaustion*. By World War II, new classifications such as personality disorder, anxiety states, and reactive depression were being employed within the framework of psychoneurosis, and psychiatrists were encouraged to search into soldiers' family and personal histories to assess constitutional factors. These reflected a more general change in the way that post-combat disorders were interpreted. In World War I, most of the physicians who served in the armed forces were new to combat, and when they wrote of their experiences one can still detect Edwardian values of courage and manliness. The industrial killing of the western front and the gradual realization that the individual was largely powerless when confronted with this mechanized warfare altered this view. Likewise, the recruitment and training of mass armies became increasingly relevant to the outcome of the conflict. It was, however, a generation before these lessons could be fully assimilated. In World War II, psychiatrists took a more dispassionate view and treated soldiers on their merits with the overriding aim of returning as many men to combat units as possible.

It is perhaps easy to underestimate the resistance that psychiatrists had met when dealing with military and state authorities. As late as December 1942, Churchill expressed serious disquiet about their growing role in the armed forces:

> I am sure it would be sensible to restrict as much as possible the work of these gentlemen, who are capable of doing an immense amount of harm with what may very easily degenerate into charlatanry. The tightest hand should be kept over them, and they should not be allowed to quarter themselves in large numbers upon the fighting services at the public expense. . . . There are quite enough hangers-on and camp followers already.[68]

Earlier in the year the War Cabinet had set up a ministerial committee under the chairmanship of Sir Stafford Cripps, the Lord Privy Seal, to investigate their role. His conclusion that "there was no substance in the criticisms made of the psychologists and psychiatrists in the Army" prompted the setting up of an advisory committee to coordinate the work of the three services and "to study its methods with a view to their post-war application." Still, the prejudice continued and, in March 1943 a senior civil servant wrote to reassure Churchill that "so far as I have been able to discover at present the occasional idiocy or indiscretion of the psychiatrist is being magnified by gossip and rumour into a general Bedlam."

As total war becomes an increasingly distant phenomenon, it is tempting to argue that its impact on medicine is once again in decline. Neurology textbooks that refer to neurosis and even psychotherapy have long since vanished, while psychiatrists, under pressure from the demands of community care, are once again returning to their alienist origins.[69]

68 PRO, PREM4/15/2, Dec. 1942.

69 Simon Wessely, "The Rise of Counselling and the Return of Alienism," *BMJ* 313 (1996): 158–60.

PART THREE

Visions of the Next War

8

Sore Loser

Ludendorff's Total War

ROGER CHICKERING

The scenes in Sweden betrayed his turmoil. Here, during his walks in early 1919, his wife reported that he "was lost in strained concentration. His lips were constantly moving, as he incessantly murmured words and sentence fragments quietly to himself."[1] Forced to flee from revolutionary Germany to Sweden in fear of his life, Erich Ludendorff was beginning a long emotional and intellectual odyssey, whose goal was to make sense of the disaster, both collective and personal, that the armistice of November 1918 had signaled. The quest for discovery and self-justification occupied him for the rest of his life. In the course of this quest, he became one of the most public figures in Germany – as memoirist, journalist, polemicist, political activist, rebel, and folk-hero – until he withdrew, now the embittered visionary, into the company of his most devoted admirers. In this last capacity, he composed a small volume in 1935 on a topic of general interest. Like everything else he wrote after 1918, this was an intensely personal statement, a variation on the private obsessions that had governed his public agenda since the Great War. This treatise, however, also lent broad currency and meaning to the term *total war.*

Had it been frozen in January 1918, Ludendorff's biography might well have been scripted to dramatize the triumph of willpower over material limits.[2] Not the least in his own mind, his rise to leadership of the

1 Margarethe Ludendorff, *Als ich Ludendorffs Frau war* (Munich, 1929), 244.

2 Ludendorff still lacks a scholarly biography, so one must choose among a number of more popular studies: Franz Uhle-Wettler, *Erich Ludendorff in seiner Zeit: Soldat-Stratege-Revolutionär: Eine Neubewertung* (Berg, 1996); Wolfgang Venohr, *Ludendorff: Legende und Wirklichkeit* (Berlin, 1993); Roger Parkinson, *Tormented Warrior: Ludendorff and the Supreme Command* (London, 1978); D. J. Goodspeed, *Ludendorff: Genius of World War I* (Boston, 1966); Correlli Barnett, *The Sword-Bearers: Supreme Command in the First World War* (Bloomington, Ind., 1963), 269–361; Karl Tschuppik, *Ludendorff: Tragedy of a Military Mind* (Boston, 1932). See also Bruno Thoss, "Erich Ludendorff," *Neue deutsche Biographie* 15:285–90; J. W. Wheeler-Bennett, "Men of Tragic Destiny: Ludendorff and Groener," in Richard Pares and A. J. P. Taylor, eds., *Essays Presented to Sir Lewis Namier* (London, 1956), 506–42.

German armies during the war had documented the extent to which energy, ruthlessness, and ferocious determination could overcome daunting odds. The obstacles that he had defied during his professional ascent included prejudices against non-nobles in the German officer corps, the reluctance of the country's military elites to draw the manpower implications of the Schlieffen Plan, the great numerical disadvantage that German troops faced in the eastern theater of the war, and paralyzing material shortages on the German home front, whose management Ludendorff inherited in 1916. The great German offensive of the spring of 1918, which bore the general's name, was calculated to defy the Allied forces in the west and to bring the war to a triumphant conclusion. This campaign represented as well a fitting climax to the autobiographical narrative. In the event, the failure of the Ludendorff offensive meant not only catastrophe for the German war effort, but also a psychological catastrophe for its leading figure. Ludendorff's desperate call in September 1918 for an armistice represented an effort to address the one catastrophe. Repairing the other was a more protracted process, which featured an effort to locate the causes of military defeat and to bring the humiliation of his own ambitions under intellectual and emotional control.

Several temperamental characteristics steered this effort from the outset. Ludendorff was not given to self-reflection, let alone self-criticism; nor was he patient with ambiguity, nuance, or compromise. "I can only love or hate," as he explained his temperamental preferences to Wilhelm Groener in 1915.[3] These proclivities found nurture in the near-omnipotence of his command during the war, but they constrained his analysis in the autumn of 1918, for they rendered him unable to countenance several obvious explanations for his armies' defeat on the field of battle. That he himself bore a degree of responsibility, that he had fallen prey to any sort of political or operational misjudgment, failed to penetrate his intellectual horizons.[4] So did another thought, which would likewise have undercut the premises of his autobiography: he found it unthinkable that Germany's enemies could have put together a military force of such material superiority that it smothered the greatest virtuosity that the German military leadership could boast.

Rescuing his own integrity thus required another explanation. Even as the signs mounted in the spring of 1918 that the German offensive would

3 Bundesarchiv-Militärarchiv, Freiburg im Breisgau (hereafter cited BA-MA), NL Wilhelm Groener (75), "Persönlichkeit und Strategie Ludendorffs," 5; cf. Klaus Scholder, ed., *Die Mittwochs-Gesellschaft: Protokolle aus dem geistigen Deutschland 1932 bis 1944* (Berlin, 1982), 142–6.

4 See Wilhelm Breucker, *Die Tragik Ludendorffs: Eine kritische Studie auf Grund persönlicher Erinnerung an den General und seine Zeit* (Stollham, 1953), 181.

not achieve its objectives, the search for guilty parties was underway. Early candidates included the front-line troops and officers, who were proving unequal to their leader's vision. By the summer of 1918 the search had probed into the upper levels of the army's command structure. As one of his aides noted at the end of August, "Ludendorff [is] terribly excited. Everybody else is to blame."[5] His excitement reached a crisis in September, in what some observers believed to have been a nervous breakdown. By now, however, the general, whom a psychiatrist diagnosed as "self-absorbed and suspicious, full of bad experiences with people," had definitively found his scapegoat.[6]

He found it back at home. Blaming the home front for "spoiling the masterpiece" required no great imaginative leap on the master's part, for charges of inadequate civilian support for the war effort had become common in the army during the second half of the conflict.[7] The charges were hardly implausible. They could build on the growing exhaustion of the home front, which no one denied, and on mutual resentments that had broadened the gulf between the experience of war at home and in the field. In all events, allocating the blame in this fashion provided an account that was compelling to the degree that it exempted German soldiers and their leader alike from responsibility for the defeat.

This analysis informed the memorandum that Ludendorff laid before the emperor on September 29, 1918, which justified the call for an immediate armistice but failed to save his job.[8] The circumstances of the war's end then intensified the strain on the general, who retreated, humiliated, to Berlin. Here, his wife recalled, he sat dejected for days at his desk, "in silent, brooding despair."[9] His flight from revolutionary Berlin to Sweden in mid-November sealed his humiliation in the realization that his "long life's work was destroyed" – a fate that now evoked in his mind the figure of Hannibal, another tragic warrior-hero abandoned by those whom he had once served.[10]

5 Siegfried A. Kaehler, "Zur Beurteilung Ludendorffs im Sommer 1918," in Walter Bussmann, ed., *Studien zur deutschen Geschichte des 19. und 20. Jahrhunderts* (Göttingen, 1961), 249, 254; Parkinson, *Tormented Warrior*, 175.

6 Wolfgang Foerster, *Der Feldherr Ludendorff im Unglück: Eine Studie über seine seelische Haltung in der Endphase des Ersten Weltkrieges* (Wiesbaden, 1952), esp. 71–81; cf. Kaehler, "Zur Beurteilung Ludendorffs," 241–58.

7 Tschuppik, *Ludendorff*, 274.

8 Kaehler, "Vier Quellenkritische Untersuchungen zum Kriegsende 1918," in Bussmann, ed., *Studien zur Geschichte*, 264–6.

9 Ludendorff, *Ludendorffs Frau*, 208.

10 Ibid., 214; Erich Ludendoff, *Vom Feldherrn zum Weltrevolutionär: Meine Lebenserinnerungen von 1919 bis 1925* (hereafter FW) (Munich, 1941), 11–12.

The theme of his own victimization was thus already firmly in place as his emotional recuperation commenced in Sweden. A flurry of manuscripts, memoranda, and correspondence announced that the warrior had found initial catharsis in the act of writing. It also disclosed the terms on which he was negotiating his own recovery from the "inner turmoil" in which he had fled Germany.[11] This process was marked less by intellectual discovery than by the consolidation and systematization of several ideas that he had earlier embraced. "It is essential," as he explained his project to an aide early in January 1919, "to salvage the honor of the fatherland, the army, and my own honor and my name."[12] His priorities among these goals – and his problematic sense of the relationship between the army and the fatherland – were already clear in a memorandum that he had prepared in the middle of the previous month. Here he insisted that "we had to be victorious or be destroyed" in the war. He continued, "there was no such thing as a third way, once the war began at the dictate of our enemies. The war had to be fought to the end. The German people sacrificed a great deal, but it did not make the ultimate sacrifices."[13] The opposition between the army and "the people" blended here into the alternatives of victory and destruction, and they together staked out the basic dichotomies in which this warrior, who could only love or hate, sought to frame the war. A final, fateful motif, which bore on the link between both these oppositions, lurked amid the images of Hannibal. "I have experienced the same things as he did," wrote Ludendorff to a Swedish officer. "He, too, was stranded shortly before reaching his goal, because the home front did not provide the army with what it needed – in fact, it stabbed him in the back [*sogar mit dem Dolch nach ihm stach*]."[14]

While he was in exile, Ludendorff also composed his first extended reflections on the war. These were his war memoirs, on which he began to labor almost the moment he landed in Sweden. The pace of his work, the fury with which he committed his impressions to paper, and the repeated, agitated revisions through which he wrung them, all attested to the emotional significance of the exercise.[15] By the time he left Sweden in late February 1919, a full draft was complete, based largely on his recollections.

11 Ludendorff, *Ludendorffs Frau*, 211.

12 Breucker, *Tragik*, 172. See James Cavallie, *Ludendorff und Kapp in Schweden: Aus dem Leben zweier Verlierer* (Frankfurt am Main, 1995).

13 Breucker, *Tragik*, 165–7; Kaehler, "Vier Quellenkritische Untersuchungen," 279–80; Cavallie, *Schweden*, 36–7.

14 Ibid., 73.

15 Margarethe Ludendorff, *Ludendorffs Frau*, 213–15; Uhle-Wettler, *Ludendorff*, 378.

After undergoing additional revisions in light of documents to which he now had access, the book appeared in the summer of 1919.[16]

Ludendorff's memoirs were an early entrant in a genre that Samuel Hynes has characterized as "*self*-monuments" of this war.[17] Perhaps because it had to keep company with testimonies from other luminaries of the conflict – including Douglas Haig, John French, and Alfred von Tirpitz – the volume almost invited the description "generous" (a word not commonly used in connection with Ludendorff). Its mission was admittedly to assign to its author credit for the army's every success and to deflect from him the blame for its every failure. The bulk of the volume was devoted to the history of operations. These Ludendorff portrayed as a string of triumphs for which a single man was responsible. Hindenburg's conspicuous absence from the account was to be interpreted in this light, as a nod from Ludendorff confirmed: "for four years we worked together, the field marshall and I, in deepest harmony, like one man."[18] The full generosity of this gesture registered only later, in the invective that Ludendorff subsequently poured on the old man.

Ludendorff's analysis of the home front's war displayed some generous features, too. There were, he acknowledged, "countless reasons" for the ebbing of resolve at home, as conditions deteriorated in the wake of bureaucratic confusion, the British blockade, and basic shortages of raw materials. The importance of these material vexations, however, was to encourage among the civilians a compendium of moral weaknesses, for which Ludendorff also professed, at this time at least, a degree of understanding.[19] These included the mounting pursuit of selfish interests, war-weariness, and, most fatefully, a growing receptivity to the illusion of a compromise peace with an uncompromising foe. "The pacifistic idea of a conciliatory peace was for many a device for use against us," the general wrote. "Many [people] meant it honestly, and it testified to high idealism."[20] Above all, however (and here he rehearsed the standard prewar critique of the peace movement), the appeal of this idea testified to "political and spiritual immaturity and a lack of judgment" – to the accumulation of soft, naive, passive qualities that rendered the home front blind to the harsh realities of international relations, pliant to the allurements of enemy propaganda.[21] The spread of these sentiments

16 Erich Ludendorff, *Meine Kriegserinnerungen 1914–1918* (Berlin, 1919) (hereafter cited KE).

17 Samuel Hynes, *A War Imagined: The First World War and English Culture* (New York, 1990), 278–9.

18 KE, 9.

19 KE, 292, 420.

20 KE, 8.

21 KE, 292. See Roger Chickering, *Imperial Germany and a World Without War: The Peace Movement and German Society, 1892–1914* (Princeton, N.J., 1975), esp. 392–410.

testified finally, in Ludendorff's view, to a political failure. The malleability of morale on the home front – one is tempted to say its feminine weaknesses – demanded forceful, "manly action" on the part of the civilian leadership.[22] Instead, Germany's fate fell into the hands of a succession of leaders who "lacked every talent for shaping events, every strong idea that would have gripped the soul of the people and developed its power."[23] Bethmann Hollweg embodied the problem at its most fateful locus; however well-meaning, the chancellor was "not a forceful character," although he shared this deficiency with his successors.[24] The consequence was a "leaderless people," a home front whose want of direction and resolve ultimately corrupted even the troops at the front.[25]

Ludendorff's war memoirs laid down several benchmarks for his subsequent intellectual migration. Evil agents, "destructive elements" dedicated to "underground agitation," were already in evidence. The list included the familiar demons, the Bolsheviks and Independent Socialists, as well as the war-profiteers. That the accusations extended more generally to Jews could be also intimated in a formulaic reference to "certain groups that, by virtue of their entire historical past, only criticize and do not construct."[26] Still, the most remarkable feature of the conspiratorial intuitions in this volume was their muted infrequency. The collapse of the home front was, in Ludendorff's judgment, due less to malevolence than weakness of will.

From this perception followed several basic motifs, which resurfaced in variations throughout his postwar writings. The first was the emphasis on the moral or spiritual dimension of the home front's collapse. The erosion of civilian support for the war effort reflected the entente's superior skills in the arts of propaganda. The German leadership's ineptitude in this critical arena constituted in fact its greatest failure, for Ludendorff's repeated strictures on this subject made clear his view that the principal function of the politicians was the management of civilian morale. His own exertions during the war on behalf of "patriotic instruction" documented the importance that he attached to the same undertaking, as did his demand for a separate ministry of propaganda, whose occupant he described as an *ersatz* chancellor, "a minister or state-secretary, who would oversee the entire military, political, and economic situation, and would be able to guide the mighty weapon of propaganda in a manner that the war required."[27] This project suggested an obvious resolution to the political problem. "Many people were

22 KE, 622.
23 KE, 360.
24 KE, 349, 424.
25 KE, 620.
26 KE, 356–7.
27 KE, 566.

already approaching me with the suggestion that I myself become chancellor," Ludendorff noted. His objection, he claimed, had been practical. "It was not a reluctance to assume responsibility that held me back, but rather the clear realization that the powers of one human being were not sufficient to lead the people at home and the army in the field at the same time."[28] In the event, the fading of this "clear realization" was one index of the radicalization of Ludendorff's views, a process that began shortly after the publication of his war memoirs.

One evening in the spring of 1919, Ludendorff asked Theodor Wolff, the editor of the *Berliner Tageblatt*, to dine with him. That he could welcome the company of this left-liberal Jewish journalist, who had often criticized the conduct of the war, was itself a sign of the general's state of mind upon his return from exile. Wolff encountered "no sign of the rough warrior, nothing of the old war-horse." As the after-dinner conversation turned to the war's outcome, Wolff was treated nonetheless to a "long monologue, in which nothing was forgotten." There was, however, no mention of the racial question, nor of a stab-in-the-back. Instead, Ludendorff's recriminations were directed at "the weak Bethmann, at those who ruled in Berlin, those who had left him in the lurch, and all those who had offered him up for sacrifice." Ludendorff's whole presentation, Wolff recalled, was "permeated by a deep, passionate resentment," which "gnawed at him incessantly, burrowed in him, and had become his dominating impulse."[29] In the next months, the resentments overwhelmed whatever restraints remained, as the warrior's analysis of the lost war underwent a transformation.

He had returned from Sweden as the center of controversy. His efforts to absolve himself of responsibility for the defeat resonated on the political right, but they were anathema on the left, where he had instead become the symbol of the arrogant military and political miscalculation that had prolonged the war. Philipp Scheidemann gave this verdict official sanction when, in a statement on behalf of the government, he called Ludendorff a "brilliant *Hasadeur*."[30] This was among the more flattering judgments in a loud chorus of criticism, which prompted Maximilian Harden in April 1919 to observe that it had become fashionable to "piss on" the former warlord.[31] Ludendorff, whose feelings of martyrdom fed on these attacks,

28 KE, 424–5.

29 Theodor Wolff, "Ludendorff bei Nacht," *Die Wilhelminische Epoche: Fürst Bülow am Fenster und andere Begegnungen* (Frankfurt am Main, 1989), 211–17.

30 Ulrich Heinemann, *Die verdrängte Niederlage: Politische Öffentlichkeit und Kriegsschuldfrage in der Weimarer Republik* (Göttingen, 1959), 23–4.

31 Uhle-Wettler, *Ludendorff*, 384–5.

lashed back in kind at the "petty enviers" on the left, whom he accused of a calculated effort in 1918 to undermine morale in the army and navy.[32]

The publication of Ludendorff's war memoirs in the summer failed to halt the escalation of the rhetoric. The volume was greeted alike with praise and ridicule from the predictable quarters. The admiration expressed by leading French and British officers was gratifying, but it paled in the face of expert criticism from his own country. The most painful came from the pen of the military historian Hans Delbrück, whose withering review of the memoirs raised questions about Ludendorff's military competence as well as his political judgment. Most galling, because it knocked out the central prop in the memoirist's reading of the war, was Delbrück's verdict on Bethmann Hollweg. The historian characterized the chancellor as an essential voice of moderation in the German leadership. "Whatever one might rightfully say against Bethmann, he was better than his successors," wrote Delbrück. Bethmann's dismissal was accordingly "a change for the worse, the great sin for which the Hohenzollern dynasty collapsed and the German people died."[33] In a favorable review of Falkenhayn's memoirs several months later, Delbrück renewed the attack on Ludendorff. "The achievements of our army, particularly of our officer corps on land and at sea, are incomparable in the annals of world history and are assured of eternal glory. The unhappy end of the war should in no way affect our grateful appreciation for them." On this much he and Ludendorff agreed, but Delbrück then left nothing standing in Ludendorff's intellectual edifice. "It was their leader," he concluded, "who could not accommodate himself to feasible objectives and thus rendered all their heroism null and void."[34]

Ludendorff's most famous rejoinder to this sort of abuse did not come from his own lips. When he and Hindenburg appeared together before the parliamentary commission of inquiry in November 1919, they did speak "like one man." The statement that Hindenburg delivered to the panel was from Ludendorff's pen. It suggested the direction in which Ludendorff's thinking was then leading. It contained references to "secret, calculated subversion of the army and navy," the burden of which was born by those "worthy troops who resisted the revolutionary attrition."[35] Ludendorff's use of the term *attrition* in this connection was a slap at Delbrück, who had used

32 FW, 11–12; cf. Bruecker, *Tragik*, 67.

33 Hans Delbrück, "Ludendorff," *Preussische Jahrbücher* 178 (1919): 100.

34 Delbrück, "Falkenhayn und Ludendorff," *Preussische Jahrbücher* 180 (1920): 250–81; cf. Delbrück, *Ludendorffs Selbstporträt* (Berlin, 1922).

35 Heinemann, *Niederlage*, 177–91; Kaehler, "Aufkommen der Dolchstosslegende," in *Vier Quellenkritische Untersuchungen*, 254–6; FW, 76–9.

the same word in describing Ludendorff's misjudgment of the war's operational challenges. It mattered little that Ludendorff's own usage of this term was not even metaphorically consistent with the conclusion that followed.

This conclusion came in the fateful formula, with which an English officer had revived Ludendorff's thinking: "The German army was stabbed in the back." In a series of progressive elaborations, this proposition, which Hindenburg declaimed from Ludendorff's script in November 1919, became the bedrock of Ludendorff's own understanding of the war and the circumstances of its termination.

Whatever its importance to his own intellectual and emotional constitution, the *Dolchstoss* provided an enormously popular explanation for the painful events of 1918. Nowhere did it exert more appeal than in the circles in which Ludendorff had begun to cultivate contacts after his return from Sweden. Bruno Thoss has written of the "Ludendorff Circle" to characterize the central importance of the general in this network of military and paramilitary groups, nationalist political associations, and right-wing journalists.[36] Bonds of ideology and, in the case of many of the soldiers, personal loyalty provided the cohesion, as did the conspiratorial determination of most of them to bring down the new republic by force. To Ludendorff himself, these groups promised a basis of political action, which now figured increasingly, as the complement to his writing, in his campaign for personal vindication. Like many of the officers in this circle, he regarded domestic politics in republican Germany as a civil war, whose outcome required a new regime in which the authority of the soldiers predominated.

An initial attempt to put this vision into practice came in the spring of 1920. Ludendorff's part in the Kapp Putsch remains shadowy, although it well exceeded "benevolent patronage."[37] He was a central figure in the conspiracy that plotted the undertaking, for his contacts in many quarters made him a principal conduit among scheming soldiers and civilians. In his own view, the action offered an opportunity to redress one of the war's lost opportunities, and he himself now professed a willingness, "under certain circumstances," to assume "full responsibility for a national dictatorship." The project required the full subordination of the civilians, for the general insisted that he was "not prepared to play second fiddle."[38] Whether or not

36 Bruno Thoss, *Der Ludendorff-Kreis 1919–1923: München als Zentrum der mitteleuropäischen Gegenrevolution zwischen Revolution und Hitler-Putsch* (Munich, 1978), esp. 3–7.

37 Johannes Erger, *Der Kapp-Lüttwitz-Putsch: Ein Beitrag zur deutschen Innenpolitik 1919/20* (Düsseldorf, 1966); Harold J. Gordon Jr., *The Reichswehr and the German Republic, 1919–1926* (Princeton, N.J., 1957), 91; Erwin Könnemann and Gerhard Schulze, *Der Kapp-Lüttwitz Ludendorff-Putsch: Dokumente* (Munich, 1998).

38 FW, 99.

the other conspirators sympathized with this design, it translated into no specific plans. Ludendorff was not, in any case, immediately involved in the events that precipitated the crisis. But as designs dissolved into recrimination, confusion, and another clear failure of leadership, he sought to distance himself from the adventure.

He was nonetheless sufficiently implicated that he had to flee the prosecutors in the aftermath of the putsch. This time he left Berlin permanently for more cordial political climes in Bavaria, where he could ponder anew the perils that awaited soldiers who deferred to weak civilians in times of national emergency. The publication of another large volume several months later captured this motif, as it announced the deflection of Ludendorff's energies again toward writing and contemplation. This volume, which he had completed in Berlin, represented an appendix to his war memoirs.[39] Several hundred documents, many of them previously published in connection with the work of the parliamentary inquiry into the end of the war, offered testimony to the same reading of the war that Ludendorff had earlier published. Most of these documents were unglossed, but the selection itself was an exercise that invited – or demanded – assent to Ludendorff's convictions: that he himself had been motivated throughout only by considerations of national security, that he had struggled in vain against the irresolute civilians in an effort to steel the home front morally and materially, that a compromise peace was an illusion, that the Supreme Command remained in sovereign control of the military situation, even as it demanded an armistice in September 1918, and that the war had ended amid panic in the civilian government and revolutionary subversion from below. At the conclusion of the volume, with the shambles of the war effort now amply documented, the general's voice intervened directly. The war ended, he noted, in "revolution from above and below." In this connection, he implicated the civilian leaders as well as the revolutionary agitators among the masses. Both had "brought death to the German army as it struggled with the enemy." Under the rubric of "subversion," he subsumed both the "sabotage of victory" – the sin of the leadership – and "the coup [*Umsturz*] itself," which was delivered from below. "When the history of Germany's misfortune is written," he concluded, "it will have to concern itself thoroughly with these phenomena."[40]

Ludendorff thereupon turned himself to just this challenge. His quest began in earnest for the secrets of Germany's misfortune, or, as he himself

39 Erich Ludendorff, *Die Urkunden der Obersten Heeresleitung über ihre Tätigkeit 1916/1918* (Berlin, 1920).
40 Ibid., 581–5.

defined the effort, for "clarity about the many interconnections" in this unhappy story.[41] The key to the plot (in several senses of this word) he now found in racist anti-Semitism. As he announced in December 1921, he was "occupying [himself] with the Jewish question."[42] His occupation drew his attention to an ideological catechism that had been long gestating, foremost at the hands of leaders in the Pan-German League, with whom he had dealt often during the war and who remained his frequent visitors after the conflict. Under their intellectual guidance, the general read in the standard sources, which featured the writings of Dietrich Schäfer, Theodor Fritsch, Friedrich von Bernhardi, Ludwig Schemann, and Henry Ford, as well as "The Protocols of the Elders of Zion."[43] Ludendorff's intellectual discoveries were hence again in no way original; his sources instead provided confirmation and systematization to murky resentments and long-held intuitions. Above all, they offered the conceptual link between the Jews and the revolutionary subversion of the German war effort.[44]

Ludendorff's *Military Leadership and Politics* (*Kriegführung und Politik*) appeared late in 1921.[45] It announced the results of his study and laid bare the ideological veins that the warrior had tapped. It was his most radical and embittered offering to date, as well as the most pretentiously theoretical. Its theme, the relationship between military and political leadership, brought Ludendorff to the first of several confrontations with Clausewitz, whose dictum that "war is the continuation of politics by other means," he rejected. In the twentieth century, the general announced, politics was instead the "fulfillment of necessity."[46] In this connection, he laid out a brutal, Darwinian vision of international politics. Ludendorff's world was riven with conflict, as violent as it was unremitting. War was the basic principle of international relations. In the modern era its comprehensive claims, as well as the titanic demands of armed forces on the domestic economies of belligerent states, defined "the fulfillment of necessity." They rendered the subservience of war to politics obsolete. In an era in which all war had become akin to Clausewitz's "absolute war" or "war in its essential [*wahrhaftige*] form," Ludendorff argued, "war and politics are, in the final analysis, one and the same."[47]

41 FW, 39, 182–3.

42 Breucker, *Tragik*, 182–3.

43 Ibid., 184; FW, 81n, 184, 249; Thoss, *Ludendorff-Kreis*, 48; cf. Roger Chickering, *We Men Who Feel Most German: A Cultural Study of the Pan-German League, 1886–1914* (London, 1984), 230–52. See also Michel Korinman, *Deutschland über alles: Le pangermanisme 1890–1945* (Paris, 1999), esp. 263–84.

44 Breucker, *Tragik*, 183.

45 Erich Ludendorff, *Kriegführung und Politik* (hereafter KP) (Berlin, 1921).

46 KP, 140.

47 Ibid., 1, 6, 11.

Failure to realize this identity – the growing opposition between war and politics – had been the key to Germany's defeat in the Great War. Ludendorff's volume explored the history of this opposition in a survey that rehearsed much of his war memoir. Now, however, the narrative framework was broader and different in significant respects. *Military Leadership and Politics* was an exercise in political eschatology.[48] It told of a fall from grace into cruel punishment; but it offered the prospect of redemption. It began in the era of Moltke and Bismarck, when the identity of war and politics was preserved, Ludendorff explained, in the mutual understanding of soldier and civilian, their constructive cooperation, and an organic balance of priorities. After Bismarck's departure, the identity dissolved around conflicting poles; and into the gap between them trod "the broad masses of the people," the naive subject of Ludendorff's saga. These masses were, he noted, "patriotic and ready for sacrifice, with strong healthy impulses," but they were also "uniquely receptive to muddle-headed influences," "lacking their own secure convictions about our nation's vital requirements," "weak of will and easily influenced when left to their own devices, particularly when aroused by envy, mistrust, and other human weaknesses."[49] That such innocents were encouraged toward "international and pacifistic thinking" in the post-Bismarckian era, that they were, in Ludendorff's suggestive phrase, being "emasculated as human beings and a people," was due, he observed, to the proliferation of subversive influences, whose source he now descried in the machinations of the Jews, who were bent upon world domination. Ultimately, however, this situation signaled the failure of civilian leadership – in other words, of politics. On the eve of war, a heavy debit thus already lay "on the political account": "the ongoing weakening of the state's power," the "neglect of the armed forces and the morale of the people," and the lack of any economic planning for war.[50] Politics had taken on the soft, passive characteristics of the masses themselves.

This analysis prefigured another survey of the war, to which the bulk of the volume was devoted. The story once again featured the determined, ultimately fruitless efforts of the professional soldiers to repair the breakdown of civilian leadership. The central object of Ludendorff's concern was again the *Volksgeist*, the morale of the naïve German masses, as they flirted with the temptations of their own emasculation in the name of a compromise peace and democratic reform. Ludendorff was less inclined now than he had been in his war memoir, however, to ascribe these temptations to the

48 See Günter Hartung, "Völkische Ideologie," in Uwe Puschner et al., eds., *Handbuch zur "Völkischen Bewegung" 1871–1918* (Munich, 1996), 39.

49 KP, 42–3, 48.

50 Ibid., 60.

mounting material burdens of war. His sensitivities had now been honed to malevolence. The agents of subversion proliferated in this account, in the form of "stooges," "corrupters of the people," "traitors," and "accomplices of the enemy."[51] Ludendorff's intellectual feat was to uncover the links among them all – the Social Democrats, Independent Socialists, democrats, pacifists, Catholics, war-profiteers, and behind them, with a hand in every camp, the Jewish *Volk*. The success of subversion testified ultimately, however, to the bankruptcy of civilian leadership, which stood guilty of passivity, incompetence, and possibly, he intimated, of conscious connivance with the country's domestic and foreign enemies.[52] In all these forms, the behavior of the politicians violated a sacred trust, in which the military leadership had committed the *Volksgeist*, the moral foundation of the war effort, to the stewardship of the civilian government. Ludendorff's indictment extended in the end to policies, politicians, and the political process itself. "Politics remained without plan, adrift in the wake of domestic political thinking." *Politik* had betrayed *Kriegführung*. The criminal dissipation of the home front, "the wicked influence of the *Volksgeist*," then spread frontward, corrupting in the end the martial virtues of the front-line soldier.[53]

Ludendorff wrote amid the ruins, in which the German people found itself enslaved, prey to the partisanship and self-serving materialism that its enemies preached, and governed by their agents, the very criminals who had engineered the great humiliation. Yet at the nadir of his tale, Ludendorff offered redemption. It beckoned in a great act of conciliation, transcendence of the oppositions that had bred catastrophe, and the restoration of the identity of war and policy. To preside over it, Ludendorff summoned up a new breed of leaders, "men free of every vanity and selfish instinct," "*Herrennaturen* of strong will and desire," "who are conscious of their Germanness, their racial heritage, their obligations, and the realities of power." A burden of their qualification for leadership, Ludendorff counseled, was to study the Great War, "to delve more deeply than before and to seek out the causal interconnections." Those who did so would embrace, "as the bedrock of civic education," the proper "reciprocal relations between military leadership and politics before, during, and after the Great War."[54]

This description was hardly modest. This volume advertised the general's own credentials for leadership. It documented his voyage of self-realization, his growing understanding of the meaning of the German defeat, and his

51 E.g., ibid., 126, 132, 133–4, 136, 138, 334.
52 KP, 138.
53 Ibid., 155.
54 Ibid., 341–2.

discovery of race, as well as his determination to learn from his own mistakes. Several passages suggested that the war itself had offered a model for the institutional foundations of the new Germany. "Had I understood the situation then as well as I do now," he wrote of his experiences with the civilian leadership, "I would have acted entirely differently." The failure of policy was thus a challenge – unfulfilled – to the soldiers. "The military leadership did not draw the ultimate conclusion and take over the full leadership of the state." A military dictatorship had offered, as he now recognized, "the only possibility for bringing policy into coordination with the military leadership's views about the requirements of the war."[55] The call for military dictatorship was a logical corollary of Ludendorff's understanding of politics; and it was common currency in the circles in which he traveled politically after the war.[56] However, a hint of self-reproach in these several passages of his *Military Leadership and Politics* echoed regrets that he had expressed in his war memoirs and elsewhere; and it suggested that the function of military dictatorship was not uncomplicated in his intellectual universe.[57] It stood as a quiet reminder that the failure during the war was not the politicians' alone. The extent to which these thoughts plagued the general must remain a matter of speculation. In all events, the goal of military dictatorship soon animated another plunge into politics.

Ludendorff's move to Bavaria was part of a general migration southward of right-wing conspiratorial energies. Here the general found himself again at the center of a large network, still the most prominent figure among the nationalist opposition, a major conduit among its many factions. The situation was calculated to keep him occupied with the familiar problems that had dominated both his writings and his earlier misadventure in politics. Conflicts over the definition of military and political authority, the proper roles of soldiers and civilians both in the overthrow of the republican government and in the aftermath, overshadowed his return to political activism in the name of national revolution.

Ludendorff's involvement in this venture brought him into direct contact with the National Socialists. The relationship was built on uneasy foundations from the start, for it involved ideological ambiguities as well as willful misunderstandings, whose nature became clear only in the course of a misconceived political campaign, the highlight of which was the Beer Hall Putsch. Ludendorff represented the sentiments of the paramilitary groups that floated in and out of the National Socialist orbit; and his close ties to

55 Ibid., 143, 328.
56 Thoss, *Ludendorff-Kreis*, 48.
57 KE, 424–5; cf. Ludendorff, *Ludendorffs Frau*, 336.

Ernst Röhm rested on a fundamental agreement about the claim of soldiers to primacy in the movement.[58] The general's attraction to Hitler, whom he first encountered in 1921, was genuine. It reflected the belief that Hitler possessed both the rhetorical skills and an understanding of politics that a succession of German civilian leaders had lacked during the war. Hitler was to be a Bethmann Hollweg of strength and character, the competent "expert in propaganda" and custodian of popular morale, behind whom the masses would rally to the rule of the generals. Hitler's attraction to Ludendorff was likewise genuine, for he admired the general, recognized the political capital that his name still carried, and he subscribed, initially at least, to a vision of collaboration that was to culminate in a national dictatorship headed by Ludendorff himself.[59] The relationship between the two was destined nonetheless to instability, if only because it was based, as Winfried Martini later wrote, on "messianic competition between the two figures."[60] The rift took on an ideological dimension in pace with Hitler's changing conceptions of his own calling, his growing unwillingness to accept subordination to anyone, soldier or civilian.[61] Although Ludendorff and Hitler marched together in Munich in November 1923, it was already clear that neither was fulfilling the expectations of the other. In the fall of 1923 confusion in planning among the civilians and military groups recalled the fiasco of March 1920; and if Ludendorff symbolized the failure of the military to support the putsch, Hitler embodied, in Ludendorff's eyes, the failure of propaganda in its preparation.[62] Even as the two conspirators stood trial together in January 1924, the signs of an ideological break were apparent. The manifesto that Hitler read at the trial was entitled "Politics and Military Leadership," and its pointed inversion of Ludendorff's priorities signaled the parting of ways.[63]

The pathos of Ludendorff's position was laid bare in the aftermath of the putsch. In Hitler's absence, he attempted to reconstitute the movement under his own leadership. The effort enjoyed the support of the loyal Röhm and the paramilitary bands that remained tied to him, but Ludendorff quickly discovered that he himself lacked the skills, ideological vision, or the political presence to bring unity even to the quarreling paramilitary factions among

58 Thoss, *Ludendorff-Kreis*, 52–3; Ernst Röhm, *Die Geschichte eines Hochverräters*, 305, 311–12; cf. Harold J. Gordon Jr., *Hitler and the Beer Hall Putsch* (Princeton, N.J., 1972), 52.

59 Rudolf Olden, *Hitler* (Amsterdam, 1936), 104; and Ian Kershaw, *Hitler, 1889–1936: Hubris* (New York, 1998), 199–200.

60 Winfried Martini, *Die Legende vom Hause Ludendorff* (Rosenheim, 1949), 79; Breucker, *Tragik*, 98.

61 Kershaw, *Hitler*, 264; Albrecht Tyrell, *Vom "Trommler" zum "Führer": Der Wandel von Hitlers Selbstverständnis zwischen 1919 und 1924 und die Entwicklung der NSDAP* (Munich, 1975).

62 FW, 295.

63 Thoss, *Ludendorff-Kreis*, 8.

the many groups into which Hitler's movement had disintegrated in 1924.[64] From prison, Hitler disdained Ludendorff's implicit challenge; and upon his release early in 1925 he repaid his rival in shrewd, cynical generosity. That Ludendorff accepted Hitler's invitation to be the National Socialist candidate in the presidential elections in the spring of 1925 bespoke the depths of the general's self-absorption, as well as his vanity. His humiliation at the polls was no surprise, least of all to Hitler; and it put a final public seal on his political isolation.[65] Robbed of the last vestiges of political credibility and stature, the war hero became an embarrassment even among the nationalist right. "I no longer had anything to do with them," he wrote of his former allies. "I removed myself from the nationalist paramilitary groups, as well as from the associations of officers and troops. With me remained but a few Germans."[66]

The withdrawal that followed was Ludendorff's last. It was also the most problematic. The emotional management of humiliation now drew him into an intellectual world that is probably better explored by a psychoanalyst than a historian. The search for "clarity" about the great "interconnections" now culminated in a vision whose grandiosity, conspiratorial obsessions, and iron dichotomies displayed classic symptoms of paranoia or "delusional disorder," as this condition is clinically understood.[67] This hermetic vision of politics nonetheless offered him a new degree of intellectual security. It would be an exaggeration to describe Ludendorff as a happy man, now or ever, but even as his power and influence receded beyond a circle of devotees, the warrior, whose life had been devoted to the exercise of power and influence, found a sense of contentment that he had never known before.[68] The world had revealed its last riddles to him.

Mathilde von Kemnitz was one of the "few Germans who remained" with him.[69] Like Ludendorff's, the career of this woman was a study in willpower – directed, in her case, against the obstacles that had confronted women who pursued professional careers in Imperial Germany. One of the

64 David Jablonski, *The Nazi Party in Dissolution: Hitler and the Verbotzeit, 1923–25* (London, 1989), 99–122, 145; FW, 338.

65 Kershaw, *Hitler*, 267–8.

66 FW, 401.

67 See Alistair Munro, *Delusional Disorder: Paranoia and Related Illnesses* (Cambridge, 1999). My thanks to Simon Wessely for this reference. No biography of Ludendorff can remain oblivious of this problem, however tentative its analysis must be. It invites reflection on a number of features of the general's life, including his relationship to his mother, his dependency on other strong women, a hand-washing compulsion, and – certainly not least – the possibility that he was plagued by guilt feelings over his role in the outcome of the war.

68 Breucker, *Tragik*, 110, 197; cf. Parkinson, *Tormented Warrior*, 224.

69 Rudolf Radler, "Mathilde Ludendorff," *Neue deutsche Biographie* 15:290–2; Hans Kopp, *Geschichte der Ludendorff-Bewegung* (Pähl bei Weilheim, 1975), 19–37.

few women to enroll in the German universities before the war, she had studied medicine in Freiburg, Berlin, and Munich, where she also worked in the institute of Ernst Kraepelin, before she herself set up practice as a psychiatrist. Her professional interests in the psychology of gender-difference moved her first toward feminism, then to radical-nationalist politics, and finally to philosophical speculation. In this last capacity, in which she had no academic training, she concocted an uneasy, eclectic synthesis of Kant, Schopenhauer, Nietzsche, and racist anti-Semitism. The cloudy intellectual system that emerged from her efforts was a challenge to follow, and it invited the charge that "everything was not right in the head of its author."[70] But it had the virtue of coherence, if not consistency, as it veered toward the conclusion that the goal of human existence was to "become God-like" in freedom, power, and personal autonomy. This goal required, she reasoned, the abandonment of Christianity's moral constraints and the embrace instead of ethical imperatives that corresponded to the German racial heritage (or what she called *Rasseerbgut*).

Gottfried Feder, the Nazi, first introduced her to Ludendorff in 1923. The initial object of their relationship was Ludendorff's unfortunate wife, whose own emotional unrest in the wake of war had found relief in morphine and now required professional treatment. The affinities that then developed between the psychiatrist and the general were at once political, ideological, and emotional; they were warmed, in all events, by Ludendorff's widely remarked attraction to strong women. After his divorce the two married in 1926 and retired to Tutzing, outside Munich.

Mathilde Ludendorff was a more systematic thinker than her new husband. Her intellectual contribution to their union was to provide a quasi-metaphysical framework in which Ludendorff could arrange coherently the various demons that he had identified as Germany's bane. The key to this undertaking was Mathilde Ludendorff's conviction that every form of Christianity was contaminated by its Judaic antecedents. "The teachings of Christianity," the general observed, represented "the fundamental cause of all adversity," the glorification of weakness, the clever modern cloak of the Jews' drive for world domination.[71] This insight allowed him to tie together the myriad forces that had, in his eyes, subverted home-front morale during the war. Bolsheviks, Socialists, war profiteers, democrats, and pacifists, as well as the usual others who were allied with the Jews, now stood in league with the forces of Catholicism, which had supported the Reichstag's Peace Resolution, embraced the Papal peace note, and permitted the Jesuits back

70 Martini, *Haus Ludendorff*, 4.

71 FW, 14, 184–5.

into Germany in 1917. "Was there not something uncommonly calculated and inimical to Germany in all this?"[72] The logic that turned this into a rhetorical question also uncovered additional agents of Germany's misfortune. Protestantism, too, now stood indicted. On this score, the influence of his wife was decisive, for Ludendorff was on record with praise for the patriotism of the Evangelical clergy, and he had himself practiced a personal kind of Protestantism during the war.[73]

One final element completed the array. Ludendorff's animus against Freemasons sat more uneasily alongside his hostility to Catholicism and its principal agents, the Jesuits; and its roots in his thinking were more obscure.[74] Anti-Masonic obsessions were a staple commodity in the circles he frequented after the war – including the Nazis, to whom the rituals and cosmopolitanism of the lodges betrayed links to Judaism. His wife also subscribed to these beliefs.[75] In all events, in Ludendorff's mind Freemasonry now took its place alongside Catholicism and Judaism in an unholy troika of "supranational forces" (*überstaatliche Mächte*) whose object was Germany's ruin. As he himself described the outcome of this, the final phase in his edification:

> I gradually became aware of the sinister forces that had caused the collapse of the German people in the war, and in these forces [I recognized] the true enemies of a German people and its activity. With ever greater clarity, the secret supranational forces appeared to me not only as the sowers of discord among our *Volk*, but also as its rulers. These forces were the Jewish *Volk* and Rome, along with their instruments, the Freemasons, the Jesuits, occult and satanic formations.[76]

Ludendorff's obsessions obeyed a logic of their own; and dwelling on the preposterous inconsistencies that it conjured up serves little purpose. Two points do deserve brief mention, though, for they bear directly on his thinking about war. The first is that little in this vision was new. Most of the sinister agents who populated it had made appearances in his earlier analyses of the Great War; and, except for the Freemasons, all of them were not only present but conspiratorially linked in his mind, as supranational forces, by the end of 1921.[77] His wife merely supplied him with a more abstract, comprehensive, and iron-clad philosophical housing in which to sort out the many enemies.

The second point has to do with the ontology of the supranational forces. His thinking was too muddled and unsystematic, even (or especially) with

72 FW, 41–3.

73 Kaehler, "Zur Beurteilung Ludendorffs," 251.

74 On anti-Jesuitism, see Róisín Healy, "The Jesuit as Enemy: Anti-Jesuitism and the Protestant Bourgeoisie of Imperial Germany, 1890–1917," Ph.D. diss., Georgetown University, 1999.

75 FW, 42–3, 68.

76 FW, 13.

77 KP, 322.

his wife's help, to embrace a consequential theory of race, to argue the materialist case that a biological entity, the Jewish *Volk*, lay at the root of the problem, that it represented the original force of which the others were mere derivatives. For every utterance that implied as much, others suggested that Jews, Masons, and Catholics were coordinate evils – and that they could also be antagonistic to one another.[78] In this reading, the supranational forces were linked less by material than spiritual bonds; they were joined in a unanimity of purpose, which lay in their common hostility to the idea of "the nation" itself – above all, however, to the German nation.

The troubled offspring of this attempt to wed Gobineau and Nietzsche was the conviction, which both Ludendorffs embraced, that the great political issues of the day were spiritual, that they ultimately involved questions of faith. The eschatological elements in the general's thinking survived his abandonment of Christianity. The German people were to be forged anew, he proclaimed, on "the basis of the unity of blood and faith," according to "clear racial laws [sic] and an unimpeachable moral law."[79] The vehicle of this unity was to be a new religion, a "German understanding of God," devotion to a "German idea of God." This proposition raised its own ontological problems. Given the logic of Ludendorff's position, the object of this "idea" could not transcend the German nation without becoming itself implicated in the supranational forces. The German idea of God was thus entirely self-referential and functional; it was the point around which to rally the nation spiritually, the ideal vehicle of "patriotic instruction."

Much as he rejected the proposition that he was founding a religion, Ludendorff began to preach with the zeal and intolerance of a sectarian leader, as the power of his dark vision grew.[80] He left the Evangelical church. The supranational forces had cast a wide net; legions of his friends and acquaintances had, he was convinced, become ensnared in the conspiracy. The list of those with whom he broke included old military comrades. Many of his former political allies, the radical nationalists, turned out to be Masons, who, he now concluded, had wished to spy on him.[81] He fell out with Hindenburg, Tirpitz, and, in a highly publicized incident, with Crown Prince Rupprecht of Bavaria. He broke with the Nazis once he became convinced that Hitler himself had become the pawn of Rome.[82] He broke with his own sister after she had criticized his attack on the Masons.[83]

78 For example, see Erich Ludendorff, *Volkskrieg auf deutschem Boden* (Munich, 1931).
79 FW, 15.
80 BA-MA, NL Groener (75), Ludendorffs "Totaler Krieg," 6.
81 FW, 176, 249.
82 Breucker, *Tragik*, 158; Schwab, "Vom 'totalen Krieg' zur 'deutschen Gotterkenntnis,'" 8.
83 FW, 126.

It is difficult to resist the word "pathological" to describe the determination with which Ludendorff promoted his own isolation or the energy with which he turned, in his search for his enemies' secrets, to the study of mysticism, cabalistic numerology, and occult rituals. His obsessions made him an easy target. Hitler once remarked that if the supranational forces had half the guile that Ludendorff ascribed to them, they could have done no better than introduce the general to Mathilde von Kemnitz. Hitler, for his own part, regarded this woman as the tool of the Freemasons.[84] Kurt Tucholsky made Ludendorff the object of savage poetic ridicule. The poem begins:

> Are you anxious, Erich? Are you scared, Erich?
> Does your heart pound, Erich? Do you take flight?
> Do the Masons, Erich – and the Jesuits, Erich,
> Want to stab you, Erich, what a fright!
> These Jews are becoming ever unseemlier.
> All misfortune is the work of these . . . schemers.[85]

The shrine of the new religion was in the "Ludendorff House" in Tutzing, where the couple held court to the remaining pilgrims.[86] The "Ludendorff Verlag" published a flurry of their pamphlets, as well as several journals. Both Ludendorffs used these as "publications *ex cathedra*" to address an audience that, to judge from the publication figures, comprised perhaps a hundred thousand people.[87] The so-called Tannenberg League, which the general founded in 1925 to promote his views among German veterans of the war, was a satellite that counted some 30,000 members.[88] A comfortable division of labor, which reflected the views of both the general and the former feminist, reigned in the Ludendorff House. Agreement

84 Breucker, *Tragik*, 110.

85 Kurt Tucholsky, *Gesammelte Werke*, ed. Mary Gerold-Tucholsky and Fritz J. Raddatz, 10 vols. (Reinbek bei Hamburg, 1960–75), 6:296–7. Original text:

> Hast du Angst, Erich? Bist du bange, Erich?
> Klopft dein Herz, Erich? Läufst du weg?
> Wollen die Maurer, Erich – und die Jesuiten, Erich dich
> erdolchen, Erich – welch ein Schreck!
> Diese Juden werden immer rüder.
> Alles Unheil ist das Werk der . . . Brüder.

86 Martini, *Die Legende vom Hause Ludendorff*; Kopp, *Geschichte der Ludendorff-Bewegung*.

87 Martini, *Legende*, 10.

88 Kurt Finker, "Tannenberg-Bund: Arbeitsgemeinschaft völkischer Frontkrieger- und Jugendverbände (TB) 1925–1933," in Dieter Fricke et al., eds., *Lexikon zur Partiengeschichte: Die bürgerlichen und kleinbürgerlichen Parteien und Verbände in Deutschland (1789–1945)*, 4 vols. (Cologne, 1983–6), 4:180–3.

extended to all fundamental principles. Mathilde Ludendorff concentrated on theoretical questions of philosophy and religion, while her husband devoted himself to the political and military matters that continued to consume him.

Ludendorff's exertions at self-vindication were freighted with imperatives. The German collapse in the Great War cast its shadow over his life; but given the predominance of international conflict in his worldview, the catastrophic end of this war could represent only a respite and prelude. The great challenge, in the warrior's eyes, was accordingly to draw the proper lessons from the last war in order to wage the next.

In this belief, Ludendorff found himself in a lot of company. Apart from the professional planners in the Reichswehr, who struggled with the operational implications of the German defeat, a more popular literature, much of which fell under the rubric of the "conservative revolution," addressed the broader problems of war, politics, and society. The experience of general mobilization during the Great War, the pervasive intervention of public agencies into society and the economy, the forging of a moral community, however fleeting, and the erasure of the lines that separated the home and fighting fronts, all weighed heavily in this literature. So did the campaigns of new dictatorial regimes in Italy and the Soviet Union to turn the same forms of mobilization into a principle of rule during peacetime.[89] By the time the word "total" had migrated northward from Italy in connection with this discourse, several German neo-Hegelian scholars, foremost among them the sociologist Hans Freyer and the jurist Rudolf Smend, had sketched out a theory of state that invoked the mobilization of society for war as a normative proposition.[90] The most influential voice, however, was that of the writer Ernst Jünger, who in 1930 introduced the term "total mobilization" into the German discourse as he described processes that admitted no distinction between war and society, the realms of the military and civilian.[91] Jünger's rhapsody to the end of the bourgeois era, the dawn of a new martial age whose symbol he hailed in the figure of "the worker," was taken up both in substance and terminology by the jurists Ernst Forsthoff and his teacher,

89 Abbot Gleason, *Totalitarianism: The Inner History of the Cold War* (New York, 1995), 13–50.

90 Hans-Ulrich Wehler, "'Absoluter' und 'totaler' Krieg: Von Clausewitz zu Ludendorff," *Politische Vierteljahresschrift* 19 (1969):220–48; Ludolf Herbst, *Der totale Krieg und die Ordnung der Wirtschaft: Die Kriegswirtschaft im Spannungsfeld von Politik, Ideologie und Propaganda 1939–1945* (Stuttgart, 1982), 36–40; Jerry Z. Muller, *The Other God that Failed: Hans Freyer and the Deradicalization of German Conservatism* (Princeton, N.J., 1987), esp. 88–121.

91 Ernst Jünger, *Die totale Mobilmachung*, 2d ed. (Berlin, 1934), 11; cf. Azar Gat, *Fascist and Liberal Visions of War: Fuller, Liddell Hart, Douhet, and Other Modernists* (Oxford, 1998), 80–90; Thomas Rohkrämer, *Eine andere Moderne? Zivilisationskritik, Natur und Technik in Deutschland 1880–1933* (Paderborn, 1999), esp. 232–3; and Rohkrämer's chapter in this book.

Carl Schmitt, as they embraced a vision of a Germany organized as a "total state," armed materially and morally for war against enemies both domestic and foreign.[92]

Ludendorff's was a singular place in this discourse. Although it bore his superior's name, the "Hindenburg Plan" was acknowledged to have been Ludendorff's achievement; and its ambitious goals figured everywhere in this literature as a model of domestic mobilization.[93] If, however, the word "discourse" is to convey the impression of intellectual exchange, Ludendorff could be no more than a peripheral figure. He read widely in the military literature and was conversant with all the principal arguments.[94] Consistent as it was, though, with the claims being made by other authors about war, politics, and society, his *Weltanschauung* carried thick filters, through which all information had to pass on its way to intellectual absorption. The lessons offered by "totalitarian" regimes in eastern and southern Europe were hence tainted, for the Jewish Bolsheviks ruled in the one state, Catholic Fascists in the other. Carl Schmitt's Catholicism likewise undercut the validity of his teachings.[95] In fact, Ludendorff used the word "totality" principally to characterize the claims made by supranational powers, Catholicism and Judaism.[96] His most cordial point of access to the discourse of totality and war was Jünger, whom he met personally. Jünger's report of their encounter laid bare the problem, however. For all the two had in common, Jünger recalled, Ludendorff "began almost immediately to talk about the Freemasons and would not drop the subject."[97]

Occasional interventions in the popular discussions were likewise cast in the eccentric terms that the general insisted on using. Even a memoir of his early career, which appeared in 1933, contained a coda in which he lashed out against the supranational forces and "the armies that obey them," whose "machinations" had dogged his efforts before and during the war.[98] In 1931 he laid out an elaborate scenario for a war among France, Italy, and the Soviet Union, all of them agents of the supranational powers, which were about to

92 For an introduction to the literature on Schmitt, see Peter C. Caldwell, *Popular Sovereignty and the Crisis of German Constitutional Law: The Theory and Practice of Weimar Constitutionalism* (Durham, N.C., 1997), 85–119.

93 Ibid., 54, 60; Muller, *Other God that Failed*, 118; Jünger, "Totale Mobilisation," 11–12.

94 Finker, "Tannenberg-Bund," 181–2.

95 Karl von Unruh, "Staatsgefüge und Zusammenbruch des zweiten Reiches," *Am Heiligen Quell Deutscher Kraft* 3 (1934–5): 478. I owe thanks for this reference and a great deal of additional help to Markus Pöhlmann.

96 For example: *Am Heiligen Quell Deutscher Kraft* 2 (1933–4): 253, 385–6.

97 Quoted in Uhle-Wettler, *Ludendorff*, 377.

98 Erich Ludendorff, *Mein militarischer Werdegang: Blätter der Erinnerung an unser stolzes Heer* (Munich, 1933), 172–3.

vie for world hegemony on the soil of a defenseless Germany – in 1932, he predicted, citing the cabalistic significance of this year's digits.[99] The failure of this prediction did not diminish his confidence in his judgment. In 1934 he ascribed the German failure at the Marne in September 1914 to the presence of a theosophist, yet another agent of the supranational conspiracy, in the entourage of Hellmuth von Moltke, the commander of the German armies.[100]

Late the next year Ludendorff published the volume on total war.[101] The occasion of this last major intervention was the announcement of German rearmament in the spring of 1935; his object was to describe the conflict for which the new German armies were to prepare.[102] In the event, his *Total War* (*Der totale Krieg*) did nothing of the sort. Instead, it presented yet another brooding meditation on the last war, which retrieved all the usual motifs and differed from the general's earlier offerings principally in the conceptual idiosyncrasies that had by now assumed full control of his thinking.

It began with another slap at Clausewitz. The philosopher's teachings, Ludendorff announced, had to be "thrown overboard," for they failed to account for the changed nature of war, politics, or the relationship between war and politics.[103] The bulk of the volume then presented a survey of the new realities as Ludendorff judged them. Separate chapters addressed moral unity, the mobilization of the economy, the organization and employment of the armed services, and the question of leadership. These chapters made for familiar reading, as a casual perusal of the general's observations was enough to lay bare the extent to which his thinking was frozen, in every respect, to the Great War. He had little but platitudes to offer on operational matters. "The goal of all battles," explained this critic of Clausewitz, was "the annihilation of the enemy."[104] That this goal might be achieved by new tactical or strategic means was beyond the grasp of the commander who had already, in 1922, characterized tactical reforms that he himself had instituted during the last war as "a milestone in tactical development for all times."[105] His thoughts on motorization and the employment of armor and airpower

99 Ludendorff, *Volkskrieg auf deutschem Boden*, 49n.

100 Erich Ludendorff, *Das Marne-Drama: Der Fall Moltke-Hentsch* (Munich, 1934).

101 Erich Ludendorff, *Der totale Krieg* (hereafter TK) (Munich, 1935). Hans Speier, "Ludendorff: The German Concept of Total War," in Edward Meade Earle, ed., *Makers of Modern Strategy: Military Thought from Machiavelli to Hitler* (Princeton, N.J., 1941), 306–22, has long been the standard analysis of the work. See also Wehler, "'Absoluter Krieg,'" 239–45.

102 See Kopp, *Ludendorff-Bewegung*, 129.

103 TK, 10.

104 Ibid., 79.

105 Ludendorff, *Urkunden der Obersten Heeresleitung*, v–vi.

were conventional.[106] Ludendorff's total war was to be waged in the same political constellation, according to the same principles of operations and mobilization, and largely with the same dreary scenario as the previous war.[107] One remarkable passage could have fit as well in his war memoirs as in a forecast of another war:

> In the execution of total war, operations accumulate upon operations, battles upon battles. Perhaps there are shorter or longer pauses to collect strength; perhaps the war degenerates again into a war of position along extended, unassailable lines, which cannot be flanked either, until the war finally reaches its end – not in the defeat of an army, but in the collapse of one of the belligerent nations.[108]

Ludendorff's total war was the Great War done right. Even as he turned to the lessons posed by the mistakes of this conflict, he trod well-worn turf. He treated these mistakes in the chapters that began and closed his survey, as if to confirm that he found less interesting his own intervening observations on economics, military organization, and operations. In the first of these chapters, he returned to the spiritual factors and again emphasized their primacy in war. "Moral solidarity" was decisive, the "foundation of total war."[109] His own program of "patriotic instruction" had represented, he insisted, a step in the right direction, but it came too late and was burdened by its own limited conception. It was insufficiently alive to the "activity of representatives of the Jewish *Volk* and Rome, who sat concealed within the German people."[110] To redress this problem, patriotic instruction required a "devotion to God in a national experience of God, which crowns the awakening of the race."[111] Ludendorff's *Gotterkenntnis*, the worship of a German God who was free of all traces of Christianity, beckoned now as the focus of civic unity, the shield against domestic subversion, and the fundament of home-front morale for the duration of the conflict.

The most remarkable chapter in Ludendorff's *Total War* was the last. Entitled "The Warlord," it dealt with questions of leadership. Here Ludendorff retrieved all his resentments about German civilian leadership in the last war, as well as his anxieties about the weakness and malleability of the civilian masses committed to their charge. The experience of this conflict testified to the perils of fragmented political and military leadership, or what Ludendorff here called a "fateful *Vielköpfigkeit*."[112] In resolving once

106 BA-MA, NL Groener (75), Ludendorffs "Totaler Krieg," 10–11.
107 Ludwig Beck, "Die Lehre vom totalen Krieg"; and Scholder, *Mittwochs-Gesellschaft*, 292–4.
108 TK, 100.
109 TK, 11.
110 TK, 14–15.
111 TK, 20.
112 TK, 109.

and for all the polarities between military and political authority, Ludendorff proclaimed that total war demanded "the warlord at the top," the great soldier whose responsibilities and power extended to every phase of the war's prosecution. Citing the lessons of the previous war, he demanded the superordination of the military leader over "the war minister, the head of the military administration, and the chancellor [*Leiter der Politik*]."[113] These formulations rehearsed the case that he had made at greater length in his volume on *Military Leadership and Politics.* More startling were his observations about the qualities demanded of the warlord. This leader was, Ludendorff noted, a lonely figure, born to the role – a creative genius, who could "read the souls" of all those entrusted to his leadership.[114] His was the power of command over all soldiers and civilians alike. On him lay the heavy burdens of exercising, "in the highest sense of responsibility, formative power and will over the army and the people and every German – in the ultimate commitment of their spirit, soul, and heart."[115] Every facet of the war effort thus required the execution of an omnipotent, all-pervasive will, which was embodied in the nation's leading soldier.

At this point in the account, in describing the obligations born by this soldier, Ludendorff slid into the present tense and first-person singular.[116] That he was again writing about someone like himself would have come as no surprise to anyone who had followed his earlier accounts of the war. More surprising, except perhaps to a psychoanalyst, were the extravagant terms in which he described the warlord. The functions and powers with which the warlord was now fashioned made this figure look remarkably like the object, as well as the high priest of the Ludendorff's idea of the "German understanding of God."

By the outbreak of World War II, two years after the author's death, Ludendorff's *Total War* had sold about a hundred thousand copies.[117] Most of these had found their way into the hands of those who made up the "Ludendorff Movement" and had dutifully consumed everything that the general or his wife served up to them.[118] The volume looked, as Groener remarked, like "a piece of propaganda for the Ludendorff House."[119] In part for this reason, it enjoyed no broader resonance in Germany. The country's leading military authorities ignored it, as did the leaders of the National

113 TK, 111.
114 TK, 112–14.
115 TK, 114.
116 TK, 117.
117 FW, endpiece. Ludendorff's *Vernichtung der Freimaurerei* had sold almost twice as many copies.
118 Walter Löhde, "Der Feldherr und die Politik," in Mathilde Ludendorff, ed., *Erich Ludendorff: Sein Wesen und Schaffen* (Munich, 1939), 527–44.
119 BA-MA (75), Ludendorffs "Totaler Krieg," 2.

Socialist regime. Nowhere, outside the Ludendorffs' house organs, was the book even reviewed.

More significant reasons for the silence lay elsewhere. Ludendorff was being rewarded for his studied efforts to antagonize his former comrades, many of whom now ruled in Germany. He no longer enjoyed access or credibility in the army's officer corps or the Ministry of Defense, which had, by 1935, begun to police the professional journals for heterodox opinions. Ludendorff's break with Hitler in 1925 had been the prelude to a running feud with the National Socialist movement, which continued after the *Machtergreifung*. Ludendorff's *Total War* signaled no retreat. On the contrary, in its insistence that supreme political power be vested in the soldiers, the volume returned to the basic issues over which he and Hitler had split in the 1920s. It also offered scarcely disguised reminders of the general's contempt for the ruling civilian chancellor and his subordinates.[120]

It is thus tempting to dismiss Ludendorff's volume, as well as his understanding of total war, as the eccentric musings of a troubled old crank. To the extent that they escaped the realm of his bizarre obsessions, Ludendorff's ideas on the subject of total war were neither original nor interesting. In this reading, the principal significance of the volume resides in its place in the general's biography. It represented the last in a sustained series of attempts to deal with the crushing psychological burden of Germany's defeat in the Great War. *Total War* offered a late variation on a single theme, a final, megalomaniacal edition of a book that Ludendorff had already published several times – first as his *War Memoirs*, then as *Military Leadership and Politics*.

To leave the issue here would be to ignore the broader import of the volume and the ideas that it contained. These ideas were significant to the very extent that they were uninteresting. If Ludendorff's book rehearsed platitudes, it was because his ideas had become commonplace in extended circles of articulate military and political opinion in Germany, where the contours of his worldview, including its basic dichotomies and eschatological sense of regeneration, framed a powerful ideological guide to the challenges, as well as the perils that the country faced. Certainly among the leading soldiers and political figures of the German right, consensus had long reigned about the premises on which Ludendorff analyzed the Great War: that the German armies were undefeated in the fall of 1918, that the war had ended because of the home front's collapse, that the civilian leadership had failed to rally the spiritual resources of the people, and that Bolsheviks, pacifists,

120 TW, 113.

and Jews had been the agents of subversion.[121] The same was true about the lessons that these military and civilian leaders drew, like Ludendorff, from the German collapse: that defeat was the prelude to another war, which would also be a titanic undertaking, that the conflict would again encompass civilians as well as soldiers, that the spiritual solidarity of the home front was no less essential to the war effort than were the armaments, and therefore that attending to domestic morale by means of propaganda was a cardinal priority.[122]

The question of Ludendorff's influence on the National Socialist vision of total war must be seen in this light. Hitler did not need to read Ludendorff's book. He already knew what was in it – and what he liked and disliked about it. He was determined in 1935 to solve forever the problem of German militarism, the soldiers' claims to political supremacy over civilians – a position to which Ludendorff's latest text represented another paean. Hitler had nonetheless come of age politically in an earlier era, when most of Ludendorff's other ideas about the nature of war in the twentieth century had become articles of faith in the milieu of the nationalist right; and Hitler himself imbibed them in personal contact with the general. For all their disagreements, Hitler and Ludendorff were kindred spirits, products of the same catastrophic defeat and the ideological radicalization that accompanied revolutionary upheaval and successive attempts to destroy the new republic. Hitler was one among multitudes who shared this experience and drew conclusions about war in the twentieth century that resembled Ludendorff's. Many, if not most of the soldiers and civilians who led the country into the next total war did so, too. Before he retreated with his wife into his own spiritual crevice, Ludendorff was the symbol of a major strain of ideological reconstruction in the wake of war, a "coming to terms with the past" that provided intellectual balm and orientation to the legions of the German right as they contemplated another war.

Ludendorff's volume on total war could lay one other, uncontested claim to fame. Its immediate and lasting impact lay in its title. The new regime could not yet prevent the marketing and advertisement of the book, and the public association of its title with the name of the country's greatest living war hero immediately injected the term "total war" into the German popular

121 Gotthard Breit, *Das Staats- und Gesellschaftsbild deutscher Generale beider Weltkriege im Spiegel ihrer Memoiren* (Boppard, 1973), 123–33; Thoss, *Ludendorff-Kreis*, 52–3.

122 See, in particular, Herbst, *Totaler Krieg*, 42–7; Wolfram Wette, "Ideologien, Propaganda und Innenpolitik als Voraussetzungen der Kriegspolitik des Dritten Reiches," in Wilhelm Deist et al., *Ursachen und Voraussetzungen der deutschen Kriegspolitik* (Stuttgart, 1979), 100–73.

discourse.[123] "Total war" thus became a codeword for a broadly accepted set of ideological principles, which far transcended the fantastic obsessions with which the volume's author had tried to endow the concept.[124] In 1935 most of these principles were in power.

123 BA-MA, NL Groener (75), Ludendorffs "Totaler Krieg," 1. The paternity of the expression, in German, does not belong, however, to Ludendorff: cf. "Der 'totale' Krieg," *Militär-Wochenblatt* (October 18, 1934), Sp. 572.

124 Wilhelm Deist, "Auf dem Wege zur ideologisierten Kriegführung: Deutschland 1918–1945," in Wilhelm Deist, *Militär, Staat und Gesellschaft: Studien zur preussisch-deutschen Militärgeschichte* (Munich, 1991), 385–439.

9

Strangelove, or How Ernst Jünger Learned to Love Total War

THOMAS ROHKRÄMER

In World War I, the scale and intensity of destruction gave rise to the term *total war*. Quantity alone did not, however, make World War I the great "seminal catastrophe" of the twentieth century; this great conflict also frustrated intentions, defied attempts to control it, and turned every participant into its sorcerer's apprentice. Individual heroism could not contend with the machine-gun. Military ingenuity could find no productive alternative to the resource-draining stalemate on the western front; and proud idealism counted less in the war's outcome than did technology and production levels.

Under these circumstances the enthusiasm of August 1914 quickly evaporated. The German volunteers of August 1914 experienced a shock. These largely middle-class men had believed that the war would stimulate idealism and unity; instead, they soon experienced unjust treatment from their officers, tensions with soldiers of humbler social backgrounds, war-profiteers, and loud-mouthed beer-hall patriots with simplistic slogans. They searched for adventure and heroism, but instead they found that modern warfare demanded endurance, discipline, and the precise execution of limited tasks within a huge machinery of destruction. Their contacts with home soon taught them that their sacrifice could not protect their loved ones from hardship. Thus for many soldiers, the "ideas of 1914" soon rang false; and defeat after four years of propaganda made it even more difficult for them to find meaning in the slaughter.

World War I undermined old convictions and brought about a fundamental cultural reorientation. Formerly confined to a small intellectual avant-garde, doubts about progress, moral convictions, the benevolence of human nature, and the integrity of public officials gained broad popular currency. The scale of destruction and the experience of slaughter out of human control raised profound questions about modernity, or at least about what had gone wrong.

Revulsion against war was only one possible reaction. A significant number of young Germans joined the Free Corps after 1918, and some veterans began to glorify their front-line experiences, to promote militarism, and even to argue that the comradeship of the trenches should inspire Germany's future. These former soldiers wished to keep Germany in "the shadow of total war," to prepare for an even more total conflict in the future. Even if they did not employ the term, they propagated the idea of "total war," because it represented not only a useful concept to comprehend the new face of warfare, but an ideal as well. They developed a strange love of total war. This essay examines the way some influential Germans understood "total war" and the reasons that underlay their fascination with it. The focus of the essay is Ernst Jünger, the most influential representative of "soldierly nationalism" in Weimar Germany.

Jünger was the "spiritual leader of the young nationalism" in Germany.[1] He was unique not only in the variety of worldviews, convictions, and themes that he employed to make sense of the war, but also in the volume of books and articles that he wrote on the subject throughout the Weimar Republic. His output permits a reconstruction of his twisted intellectual development, and it reveals an unexpected basis for his strange love of total war.

Ernst Jünger as no typical soldier. As an adolescent, he had tried to escape the boredom of grammar school by joining the French Foreign Legion in Africa. While his father quickly put an end to this adventure, a second attempt to energize his life by volunteering for military service in August 1914 had more enduring consequences. He enthusiastically seized the opportunity to find adventure, heroism, and purpose in life. He was motivated less by a sense of duty than a desire to find a more genuine existence outside the confines of civilization. As he put it, human nature "desires games and adventure, hatred and love, triumphs and disasters." It needed physical danger; and it experienced modern society as a prison.[2]

Jünger's critique of modern civilization and his desire to find meaning and excitement in life represented the first premise of his thinking. It shaped all his writing during the Weimar era. Many observers have analyzed his quest for adventure and heroism in industrial warfare – and within industrial society itself – as a flight from modernity. This is a problematic interpretation. Jünger's protest against a society regulated in the name of security and comfort was not "antimodern." It was a central tenet of many other "modern"

1 Kurt Sontheimer, *Antidemokratisches Denken in der Weimarer Republik* (Munich, 1983), 103.
2 Ernst Jünger, *Der Arbeiter: Herrschaft und Gestalt* (Hamburg, 1932), 50.

movements, from the youth movement and avant-garde art at the turn of the century to contemporary alternative cultures and a devotion to outdoor pursuits.

Even as Jünger rejected the artificiality of modernity in favor of a more "elemental" lifestyle, he tried to avoid normative judgments. This refusal represented a second premise of his thinking. It signaled his desire to accept reality unconditionally. In a manner that recalled Nietzsche's *amor fati*, he regarded any rejection of reality as a cowardly, life-denying act. From his wartime experiences, he drew the lesson that denying an all-powerful reality was childish and futile. As he put it, "the emotions of the heart and the systems of the intellect can be disproved, but an object cannot be disproved – and such an object is a machine gun."[3] In the face of this truth, he called for "heroic realism," the strength to embrace the most unpleasant realities.

Foreswearing normative judgments endowed all historical events with ineluctable reality. Thus Jünger confronted the difficult problems of his day, particularly the new power of industrial technology to shape not only warfare but all of human existence. Although it appeared to frustrate his search for heroic adventure, he came to accept the power of technology as a challenge to his personal convictions, as the means to test the validity of his own worldview, and eventually even as an object of fascination.

The critique of the artificiality of civilization and life-denying effects of tradition was also common among the avant-garde and in leftist thought in the 1920s. Jünger, however, was a conservative, who coupled this critique with a search for stable and hierarchical order. While he sought adventure and self-realization, he regarded the military order as an ideal for organizing the nation, and he looked constantly for an objective goal to guide his own activities. He was fascinated by the specter of chaos and catastrophe, but he saw these as transitory phenomena, whose function was to remove outdated structures. His ultimate ideal was a stable, homogeneous society shaped by a single worldview. Like other critics of civilization, he regarded diversity as a sign of decadence, and he dreamed of "consistency in all institutions and actions, security in economic matters, obedience to authority and orders, in short, a life according to the law."[4]

Like many volunteers in the German army, Jünger at first expected that war would fulfill his desires. He regarded the army as a formidable, conservative institution, the front line as a realm of adventure, and combat as a fundamental way of life. Also like many others, however, he found "that the beliefs with which one had gone to the front were eroded and proved to

3 Ibid., 105.

4 Ibid., 217, 233.

be insufficient."[5] He learned that modern war left little room for traditional martial virtues. He found mass-killing "difficult to comprehend," and he was shocked that soldiers "were merely seen as objects."[6] Technology had destroyed heroism. "In this clash," he wrote, "it is no longer, as it was in the days of the sword, the individual who counts, but the big organisms. Levels of production and technology, chemistry, the school system and railway networks: these are the powers that invisibly stand behind the smoke of the battles of material."[7]

Jünger's youthful hope that war would offer a realm of heroic adventure proved futile. An important moment in his personal disillusionment came when troops under his command were hit by a shell before they could even enter the front line; of his 160 soldiers, only 63 were left unharmed.[8] Experiences like this forced him to acknowledge that war offered no escape in the age of technology, that soldiers, too, were at the mercy of modern weaponry.

Still, Jünger did not condemn the war. In his determination to embrace reality, he forced himself to say that "we must believe that everything has meaning, otherwise we end up with all those unfree, broken, or utopian people."[9] He also regarded it as his "holy duty" to his fallen comrades – and probably to his own suffering – to discover meaning in war. His obsessive writing about the world war revealed the difficulty of this task.

Jünger did not dwell on the causes of the war. Given his views about human nature and international competition, he believed it to have been inevitable. He was interested instead in the phenomenology of war and its implications for a realistic worldview. He was convinced that the war's very absurdity and destruction eradicated the idea that rationality and progress were essential features of modernity. In opposition to materialist, utilitarian, or rational explanations of reality, he emphasized aggression and destruction, honor and heroism, the will to power and adventure, and the joy of risking life and inflicting death. He also stressed the ambivalence of the practical means that modernity provided, for these not only improved the standard of living but also served the will for destruction. As proof that a materialist view could only explain one dimension of human existence, he noted that an expensive battleship "was sacrificed in seconds for things that one cannot know but can only believe."[10]

5 This formulation is in the last edition of *In Stahlgewittern*, Sämtliche Werke, vol. 1 (Stuttgart, 1978), 271.

6 Ernst Jünger, *In Stahlgewittern: Aus dem Tagebuch eines Stosstruppführers*, 2d ed. (Berlin, 1922), 17, 231.

7 Jünger, *Sturm*, Sämtliche Werke, vol. 15 (Stuttgart, 1978), 16.

8 Martin Meyer, *Ernst Jünger* (Stuttgart, 1990), 89.

9 Jünger, "Der Wille," *Standarte* 1 (1926): 128.

10 Jünger, "Nationalismus und modernes Leben," *Die Kommenden* 5 (1930): 5.

Jünger thus accepted modern weaponry and industrial warfare as the most current means by which a natural "will to power and to overpower" found expression.[11] Yet the dominance of the material seemed itself to negate his quest for adventure; in war, personal courage seemed to be at best of peripheral importance. His attempt to live a more elemental existence as a soldier had failed, for war itself had proved to be an integral part of the modern industrial age. Moreover, because Jünger rejected the stab-in-the-back legend, Germany's defeat undermined his confidence in the army. During the Weimar era, his writings attempted repeatedly to contend with these painful realizations. The effort to integrate the modern face of warfare into "the wonderful dream" of August 1914 forced him in the end to love total war.[12]

In his first book, *Storm of Steel* (1920), Jünger resorted to a traditional narrative. Here he focused on the heroism of German soldiers, particularly on his own role as leader of a storm troop. The book culminated in his gaining the prestigious medal "Pour le Mérite," which suggests that he still endorsed traditional criteria of success.

In the same book, however, he also wrote of the two sides of war, which he later captured in the terms "blood" and "fire." These denoted, on the one hand, the elemental emotions of the combatants and, on the other, the power of technology. "The warrior," he wrote, "cannot control his emotions." He does not want to take prisoners, he "wants to kill. He has lost sight of all concrete aims and is driven by basic emotions."[13] Here war is still presented as an adventure, in which the soldier lived according to fundamental human instincts. In other passages, though, Jünger admitted that traditional heroism had no place in modern warfare. "One fundamental aspect becomes increasingly apparent in the flood of appearances: the dominant role of material. The war culminated in the battle of material. Machines, iron, and explosives were its components. Even human beings were regarded as material."[14] The power of the material put the soldier at the mercy of a "storm of steel": "You cower together in a little hole in the ground and feel at the mercy of a cruel and blind will of destruction. With horror, you start to realize that all your intelligence, all your skills, all your spiritual and physical abilities have become pointless, ridiculous."[15] The soldier was left only with his moral stamina to face an orgy of destruction. "Why do you hold out, you and your obedient soldiers? No superior sees you, but there is still somebody watching you. Perhaps unconsciously, your moral self is working and holds you in your place."[16]

11 Ernst Jünger, *Das Wäldchen 125: Eine Chronik aus den Grabenkämpfen 1918* (Berlin, 1925), 191.

12 Ernst Jünger, *Das abenteuerliche Herz: Aufzeichnungen bei Tag und Nacht* (Berlin, 1929), 213.

13 Jünger, *In Stahlgewittern*, 205.

14 Ibid., iii.

15 Ibid., 136.

16 Ibid., 137.

In *Storm of Steel*, the power of the material paled in the face of heroism. This process was the book's central theme. Adventure survived despite the weapons of destruction, and technological warfare figured as a negative factor. Jünger could not find value in the modern features of warfare, so he recruited traditional virtues, like "chivalry" and "the feeling of duty, honor, and inner strength" to explain the will to fight and endure.[17]

Jünger had never been terribly patriotic, and he despised normative arguments, so this resolution could not satisfy him long.[18] In addition, as he became increasingly critical of Germany's military and political leadership during the war, a medal no longer seemed like a meaningful reward for wartime service.[19] As a result, he removed the emphasis on traditional virtues in later editions of *Storm of Steel*, as well as in *Battle as Inner Experience*, which he published in 1922 as a revised interpretation of the war.

Avoiding nationalistic or moralistic arguments, he now concentrated on the joy of living out aggressive instincts in combat. In a tone inspired by *Lebensphilosophie*, he argued that war revealed the fragility of modern society, which had suppressed genuine life.

> We lived aimlessly and were even proud of it. As sons of an age intoxicated by material achievements, we believed that progress would bring bliss, that machines would be the key to becoming god-like, that the telescope and microscope would be organs of new insights. But beneath this artificial mask, beneath all disguises in which we draped ourselves as magicians, we remained naked and barbaric.[20]

War started in 1914, he now explained, when human nature at last broke through the artificial facade of modern society in search of true fulfillment. In war "the true human being sought compensation in a wild orgy for everything long missed. There his instincts, long contained by society and its laws, became once again the only and holy motivation, the final cause."[21] These developments had no political causes but instead grew out of "the will to live, the will to fight and the will to power."[22] The true soldier did not seek meaning in war; he simply loved it.

In Jünger's interpretation, war was now inherently opposed to modern civilization. It was an elemental event, in which a small elite ruthlessly used the masses to satisfy its "will to power." But what of modern weapons? Like the Italian futurists, Jünger saw these now as means to increase human

17 Ibid., iv, 18.

18 Hans-Harald Müller, *Der Krieg und die Schriftsteller: Der Kriegsroman der Weimarer Republik* (Stuttgart, 1986), 219.

19 Ernst Jünger, *Der Kampf als inneres Erlebnis* (Berlin, 1922), 3.

20 Ibid.

21 Ibid.

22 Ibid., 116.

power. It made no difference, he argued, "whether one shows claws and teeth, uses primitive axes and wooden bows or whether the finest technology turns destruction into a sublime art," because "humans remain the same."[23] Technology was a modern tool of an eternal will to power. "The battle between machines is so enormous that man is hardly visible," he wrote. And Jünger continued: "Nevertheless, behind it all are human beings. Only they give the machines direction and meaning. They use [machines] to fire projectiles, explosives, and poison. . . . [Human beings] are the most dangerous, most blood-thirsty and most determined beings whom the earth has to bear."[24]

This interpretation disdained moral argument, but it was even more foreign to the reality of industrial warfare than his earlier book, *Storm of Steel*, had been. Jünger's stress on active combat provided no compelling explanation for the need to endure bombardment, the impersonality of modern battle, or the boring routine of daily life in the trenches. Because it undermined the contrast that he drew between war and civilization, Jünger also ignored modern warfare's dependence on industrial production. Nor did this vision satisfy his search for a stable order, for he could not integrate the positive aspects of warfare into a plan of human existence. Instead, the vision cast human history as eternal oscillation between the construction of civilization and eruptions of destructive instincts.

Jünger wrote *Battle as Inner Experience* while he was still employed in the German army. Here he worked on developing infantry tactics appropriate to industrial warfare, and he wrote theoretical articles about warfare in the industrial age. In these circumstances, casting war as the product of human instincts could not satisfy him for long. In addition, as the war receded in time, he increasingly felt the need to demonstrate its relevance to peacetime existence. He still tried to make sense of the war, but he now focused on its significance for the Weimar Republic and the broader development of history. During the next several years he developed a philosophy of history in which he assigned prime importance to World War I and its veterans. He began now to acknowledge the suffering of the soldiers more openly, as he assigned it a positive historical function.

Many readers of Jünger's work in the Weimar era have found in it a celebration of modern technology and totalitarianism. This reading cannot explain the deep skepticism about technology and a powerful state that Jünger adopted soon after the end of the Weimar Republic.[25] The reason

23 Ibid., 8, 115.

24 Ibid., 116.

25 See, e.g., the difference between the first and the second version of Ernst Jünger, *Das Abenteuerliche Herz* (Berlin, 1929; Hamburg, 1938).

for this inconsistency lay in his attempt to find positive meaning in industry and technology, which he forced himself to accept after concluding that the only alternative to these facets of modern life was marginalization. The initial motivation for accepting technology was not fascination but the will to overcome feelings of fear and powerlessness. In December 1925 he wrote of his "deep fear of this technical system, of this witch's broom."[26] Two years earlier, he had voiced negative views about modern warfare. In the unfinished novel *Sturm*, which he later claimed to have forgotten, the protagonist called life in modern society "slavery" and voiced despair that the individual soldier was nothing but an "ant," which a careless giant killed by stepping on it.[27] Modern warfare, the novel argued, produced the same sense of meaninglessness as mass existence in a modern factory town.

Sturm revealed that Jünger's generally positive interpretation of World War I concealed a more ambivalent memory, which reflected his growing confusion about the paralyzing power of industrial war. By "forgetting" this work, however, Jünger suppressed the ambivalence and soon thereafter published his most optimistic assessments of modern warfare. In *Fire and Blood* and *Copse 125*, both of which were published in 1925, he played down the human suffering by stressing its historical necessity. "The brutality of the method appeared irrelevant," he wrote, because the war was about the "creation of a still hidden future world."[28]

In the following years, Jünger argued that the future would give birth to a state that was structured like a modern army at war – "steel-like, dictatorial, and total."[29] This embrace of a totalitarian state, politically wrong though it was, enabled him to address topics that he had previously evaded. Belief in a better future allowed him to accept many negative aspects of the last war. He openly rejected the "stab-in-the-back legend," calling the German defeat a "historical necessity"[30] given Imperial Germany's failure to mobilize its resources as totally as its opponents had, and given widespread social injustice in the army and society. Jünger now also acknowledged the difficulty of reconciling modern technology and traditional concepts of heroism; he confessed that the new weapons of war had a destructive power well beyond the human capacity to resist. Battle, he announced, was no longer a contest between human beings, but

26 Quoted in Klausfrieder Bastian, "Das Politische bei Ernst Jünger: Nonkonformismus und Kompromiss der Innerlichkeit," Ph.D. diss., University of Heidelberg, 1962, 77.

27 Jünger, *Sturm*, 16, 45.

28 Jünger, *Wäldchen*, viii–ix.

29 Ibid., 74.

30 Ibid., 178.

a terrible competition of production, and victory falls to the competitor who produces faster and more ruthlessly. . . . Here the age in which we were born reveals its dark side. The dominance of the machine over human beings . . . becomes apparent, and a deadly opposition, which already started to threaten the economic and social order in peacetime, also emerges in the deadly battles of this age.[31]

Jünger thus came to see war as the most deadly expression of the modern condition, in which technology had become overwhelming. And there was no avoiding this situation, because success in modern war depended on full mobilization. Waging a successful modern war required "the organization and integration of industry, the work of the masses, the national attitude of the financial system, the superiority of science and its connection with life, the development of transportation, the level of general education."[32]

But what of the common soldiers? In contrast to views that he expressed in *Sturm*, Jünger now maintained that the historical significance of war outweighed the individual sacrifice that it called forth. He nonetheless attempted to show that the commitment of soldiers had been crucial to the outcome of the last war. Here he described the war as a learning process. While the initial reaction to the indiscriminate destruction of battle had been fatalism or paralysis, a new elite gradually mastered the terrible weapons of destruction. In a painful process of education, which was marked by many moments of despair, some of the naive volunteers of 1914 had turned into an elite "that builds machines and resists machines, which does not regard machines as dead iron, but organs of power, which it controls with cold rationality and hot blood." "The great pilot, the tank driver and the technically skilled leader of a storm troop were," he concluded, "the representatives of this new human being."[33]

Jünger ordered the experiences of World War I within this narrative. Suffering belonged to the old world. The moments of control promised a future in which a new elite would dominate technology. This view enabled him to acknowledge the power of technology without turning soldiers into its passive victims. Even as modern weapons dominated battle, the soldiers' enthusiasm was of crucial importance, for it provided the motivation to master technology. Accordingly, the "will to power and dominance" had found its adequate expression not in a return to archaic forms of behavior, but in the rational use of modern technology for goals set by "blood." It was hence essential that a new generation had learned to say, "the machine is our creation. . . . It is nothing but a means, but one that demonstrates the

31 Jünger, *Feuer und Blut: Ein kleiner Ausschnitt aus einer grossen Schlacht* (Magdeburg, 1925), 22–4.
32 Jünger, *Wäldchen*, 125ff. 33 Ibid., 3, 19.

power of our will. As we use it in all areas to improve our performance, we also use it to fight."[34]

How did Jünger characterize this new mane? Above all, he was to resemble technology itself. Only if humans adapted to the logic of machines could they hope to control them. Traditional soldiers were not suited to modern warfare, which demanded instead young men who had "grown up in the centers of modern industry" and were used to machines. "Twenty-year-olds, with hard, matter-of-fact faces. . . . They enjoy technology, they control it like an Australian his boomerang. They are used to increasing the intensity of life by using machines."[35]

Jünger appreciated that technology would promote social harmony and reestablish Germany as a world power, but his positive assessment of technology grew largely out of his analysis of World War I. The experience of being at the mercy of destructive weapons for him posed the seminal problem, while his experience as an officer encouraged his hope that dominance over technology was within human reach. Not only airplanes and tanks but also storm troopers had, he believed, challenged the tactical supremacy of the defense by means of speed, precise coordination, and its own modern weapons. The stalemate of the trenches was overcome as a group of men evolved into a fighting machine. He concluded from this spectacle that "there can be nothing so terrible that man will not eventually learn to dominate it."[36]

Having abandoned both his antipathy to technology and his adolescent dreams of escaping modernity, Jünger scorned those who remained suspicious of technology.

> But where is the human being? Is it [World War I] not a soulless game with explosives and steel? . . . Not only the educated German, for whom Weimar is more important than food, asks this, but also the soldier, who sees heroic instincts disappear in this form of warfare. . . . But what do we, the coming generation, care about such questions? . . . For us technology is an indispensable means of power, that is why we approve it.[37]

By the middle of the 1920s, he had thus abandoned his initial distinction between civilized and elemental spaces, concluding that industry and technology shaped the modern world in both war and peace. He had also demonstrated to his own satisfaction that modern warfare could still be adventuresome. But what of civilian society? Lest he flee peacetime existence

34 Ibid., 126, 191.

35 Ibid., 78–9.

36 Ibid., 213; cf. Ernst Jünger, "Feuer und Bewegung oder Kriegerische Mathematik," in Ernst Jünger, *Blätter und Steine* (Hamburg, 1934), 101.

37 Jünger, *Wäldchen*, 126.

in favor of war-fantasies, lest he deny that modern weapons were dependent on industrial production, he had to find adventure in civilian life as well.

This question Jünger confronted in his book, *The Adventurous Heart*, which appeared in 1929. Here he attacked modernity for stifling the nonrational dimensions of human nature. In a purely materialistic society, he wrote, the search for metaphysical meaning, human destiny, and mission was dismissed; emotions and sensuality were ridiculed. Insofar as intense feelings threatened bourgeois society, they were condemned as dangerous expressions of romanticism, as humans were conditioned to embrace materialistic, instrumental attitudes toward life.

This attempt to secure a comfortable life by controlling unsuitable human emotions was bound, Jünger claimed, to fail. It offered no outlet for human ecstasy, dreams, adventures, or the wish to dedicate one's life to a grand vision. Even if, as Jünger had himself learned the hard way, individual escape did not threaten society, widespread dissatisfaction could not be forever accommodated. True visionaries would realize that although the modern condition was ineluctable, they themselves could use rational means to achieve their own ends. In modern society, "every dissatisfaction was banned into empty space if it did not employ rational means and use scientific achievements as weapons." However, "after all, rationality is just another means, and if there were a world that only cared about mathematics, an extremely daring new formula would be the tool for starting a revolution. Because every pebble . . . can be used . . . for murder, everything can become dangerous if the heart makes use of it."[38]

On the surface Jünger now renounced all his skepticism about technology. He insisted that modern technological means could serve all purposes, as they gained meaning and function in accordance with "the deeper life that carries them."[39] While these means had been traditionally employed to build a world of comfort and security, Jünger was now convinced that adventurers and dreamers could exploit them to their own ends. Again, World War I provided the inspiration. The war had made it clear that modern means did not serve material comfort alone, but that they also underpinned the will to power and destruction.

Jünger expanded on this point when he claimed that technology no longer served "bourgeois" society, which was primarily concerned with material well-being. Not only the loss of control experienced during World War I, but also the many economic and social problems after 1918 indicated that the world of the nineteenth century was doomed. Jünger hailed the

38 Jünger, *Abenteuerliches Herz*, 139–40.

39 Ibid., 80.

erosion of the old order, for he believed that regeneration would follow apocalyptic turmoil. Combined with his naïve optimism, his hatred of the Weimar Republic led him to welcome every crisis because it would, he believed, create space for new developments. Absolute chaos, which he saw coming, he called the "magical zero-point," the point at which increasing disorder would turn into the emergence of a new order of adventure and grand human designs. In this connection, Jünger styled himself as "dynamite . . . so that the living space would be cleared for a new hierarchy."[40]

Jünger was one of many who embraced a dangerous apocalyptic vision of destruction and resurrection between the wars,[41] but on a personal level it served him in two ways. First, it overcame his fear of technology, because it promised a future in which humans would regain control of their destiny. Only the decadent parts of society would perish, while the "new man" would prosper. Second, the vision blended his desire for adventure with his wish for stability. He saw himself as a "Prussian anarchist," who destroyed the old order to assist in the birth of a better one.[42]

Still, close scrutiny reveals the persistence of a deep-rooted ambivalence about modern technology. Like many critics of civilization, Jünger continued to regard the modern technical age as suffocating, and he hoped that at the critical moment a social elite would endow technology with a new, constructive function. Hence, about science and technology he wrote that "we have to find a magical meaning in them, if we do not want to be throttled by them."[43] This sentiment represented no glorification of technology, but rather an attempt to tame its destructive powers within a new structure.

Jünger's apocalyptic hopes underlay his political commitments. Before he experienced the Third Reich, he believed that the political situation in Germany could not get worse. In various journals of the radical right, he called for the destruction of the Weimar Republic, and he tried to turn the right-wing veterans' association, the *Stahlhelm*, into a fighting force against parliamentary democracy. He propagated revolution in the name of a new authoritarian, nationalist, socialist, and militarist political order in Germany. But he had neither the patience nor the talent of a political leader. While his ideas were influential within an extremist intellectual milieu, his elitism stood in the way of political success. His ideological purism made him scorn the idea of a mass party, and his inability to compromise led to his own disillusionment. As the Weimar Republic slid into its fatal crisis, Jünger withdrew from political activity. The activistic pathos gave way to detached contemplation of history.

40 Ibid., 223.

41 See Klaus Vondung, *Die Apokalypse in Deutschland* (Munich, 1988).

42 Jünger, *Abenteuerliches Herz*, 257.

43 Ibid., 244.

For Jünger, the key to understanding the present remained, as always, World War I. In this conflict, he believed, the salient feature of modernity had revealed itself in irresistible pressure toward total mobilization. Wars, he reasoned in a social Darwinist way, were the ultimate test of nations. Nations had to accept this challenge in order to survive, and they had to wage war as totally as the challenge demanded. This universal law had led to a new phenomenon in the industrial age – the war-making nation's need to mobilize all its resources. While the army's strength had alone decided the issues of war in the past, military power depended in the twentieth century on the nation's economic strength. The ability to mobilize resources was now the key to victory. "In the last phase," he wrote of this development, which was

> already partially realized at the end of the last war, there is no movement . . . that is not related to the performance in battle. . . . To mobilize these enormous energies, it is not enough to prepare the sword – militarization into the deepest marrow, the finest nerve is necessary. It is the task of total mobilization to realize this: an act which, by operating one switch, redirects the highly differentiated power network of modern society into the current of military energy.[44]

Jünger cited the Hindenburg Program to illustrate the tendency toward total mobilization, but being more cautious than many historians he did not regard World War I as a total war. Instead, he argued that the imperative, not the reality, of total mobilization had become apparent during the war. Every aspect of society, from material capacity to social and political order, was militarily relevant, so preparations for war were bound to reshape the entire society.

Jünger described these processes in *The Worker*, which appeared in 1932. He now accepted Germany's loss in 1918 as proof that thorough preparations for total mobilization were essential. The bourgeois obsession with comfort and security, all romanticism about rural life, and dreams of conserving the past had to be abandoned in favor of the radical modernization that preparation for war required. Unconditional acceptance of the technological age was necessary to maximize national power. The results would revolutionize human existence. "Wherever human beings live within the reign of technology," he remarked, "they are faced with an inevitable either-or. They either accept these means and learn to speak their language or they decline and perish."[45]

Jünger announced that fundamental changes were needed to make effective use of technology. Technology, he explained, was "by no means a neutral power," which could be used at will for any purpose. "The application of

44 Ernst Jünger, "Die totale Mobilmachung," in Ernst Jünger, *Krieg und Krieger* (Berlin, 1930), 14.
45 Jünger, *Arbeiter*, 158.

technical means demands a certain lifestyle,"[46] he wrote, noting that a technological world required a technological way of life. Jünger now accepted the anonymity of the cities, the rise of the masses, cultural uniformity, and a growing distance from nature, because all these features of modern life were essential to total mobilization. While he had a keen sense for the price of these developments, he was prepared to pay it. He now portrayed modern technology as the vital feature of the contemporary world, the means of a modern human "will to power," and the vehicle to reestablish Germany as a world power. Instead of a flight from modernity, which was futile in any case, he urged his readers "not to fight against historical trends, but to risk a gamble with the historical trends."[47]

With this new attitude toward modern technology, Jünger came full turn. He had long protested against the artificiality of the modern world, which seemed to block human adventure. After his protest had proved futile, he took up the opposite strategy, embracing technology and modernity. Now he hoped that unconditional acceptance would infuse human meaning into both modernity and technology, turning them into means of the human "will to power." Only if the antagonism between humans and technology were transcended – even if this effort involved an adaptation of human existence to technology – might a new synthesis be achieved. Jünger's hope was linked to his vision of more control over the economy. At a time when the German right saw the regulated economy of World War I as a model for the future, when technocrats demanded the rule of technical experts and communists idealized a planned economy, Jünger called for the political will to achieve an "organic construction, the close and conflict-free merger of life with all the means at its disposal."[48]

Jünger thus maintained a critical attitude toward the existing system, but he argued that only the radicalization of contemporary developments, by which he meant total mobilization in preparation for total war, could overcome the alienation of modern life. Humans could break their slavery to technology not by resisting it, but by learning to exploit it. Jünger blamed a lack of technological competence for society's problems, and he expected to find their resolution in a hierarchically structured planned economy.

Several factors motivated this reversal of Jünger's views. First, his determined realism compelled him to acknowledge the overwhelming importance of industry and technology. He thus came to regard as romantic escapism his own earlier desire to find adventure in a different realm. This

46 Ibid., 158.
47 Ibid., 44.
48 Ibid., 226.

change left him, secondly, with two options. He could either abandon his earlier criticism of bourgeois society and accept the existing social system; or he could look to a society that used technology not to achieve comfort, but to realize grand military designs. Jünger, who regarded the "will to power" as the central human drive, chose the second option, for it promised both a natural and adventuresome way of employing technology. Finally, accepting the essential role of technology in modern life allowed him to hope that the alienation between humans and modern technological means might be overcome. Against the pluralism of the Weimar Republic, he envisaged a technocratic future characterized by the "unity of one order." "The all-pervasive desire" for a homogeneous state, a just social order, an ideologically unified people, and the cultural production of enduring values would be realized in this new age.[49] Like Carl Schmitt, the conservative Jünger remained convinced that any order was superior to disorder and that technology would produce a stable state.

All these considerations led Jünger to champion a new technocratic order, which clashed in many ways with his earlier vision of the heroic life. The new technological world would itself take on an heroic intensity. He thus proclaimed "the worker" as the "new man," who would be entirely devoted to work and efficiency. The worker demanded no luxury or comfort, only a mission in life. He regarded not only technology, but also his own body and mind, as instruments to shape reality. The worker disregarded his own self, because his only aim was efficiency.[50]

Jünger's worker resembled Max Weber's "last human being," the "mindless specialist," for whom work, performance, and instrumental rationality had, in an era of secular asceticism, become ends in themselves.[51] But while Weber anticipated a "hedonist without reason" as a second future type, Jünger argued that all those who were not committed to functionality would perish. In a world of pure functionality, the desire for luxury, leisure, or dysfunctional hierarchies would threaten efficiency and undermine the individual's ability to survive. According to Jünger, only a life dedicated to work was appropriate to the technical age. In the end, the world would thus be organized according to the "worker's" principles.[52]

Jünger's book was no detached analysis. He was deeply committed to destroying the old society and realizing his grand heroic design for a new order. He portrayed the worker not as a victim, but as a man who had

49 Ibid., 217–18, 225.

50 Ibid., 28, 41, 65, 144, 160, 162.

51 Max Weber, *Die Protestantische Ethik*, Gesammelte Aufsätze zur Religionssoziologie, I (Tübingen, 1988), 204.

52 Jünger, *Arbeiter*, 96, 108, 144, 148.

abandoned the pursuit of happiness in favor of a heroic destiny. The worker would live out his aggressions in the militant destruction of the established order. Then he would realize his will to power and his vision by investing all his energies (and all technical means) into his own new order. As groups of workers realized their ambitions simultaneously, but in different nations, Jünger expected a "series of wars and civil wars" to rage, until one nation's vision would eventually win out.[53] Until that day, the attempt to avoid total wars – with total mobilization and the unscrupulous use of all available means to establish a new world order – was futile. Only after the triumph of a single vision would technology reveal its potential to shape a peaceful global order. "The aim of all these enterprises is global domination, the highest realization of the new worker."[54]

Jünger regarded a series of total wars as inevitable, but he greeted the prospect. Later, when Jünger had rejected his celebration of militarism and total war, he likened himself to a messenger who was blamed for the message he carried. But the tone of *The Worker* and his other texts showed that he enjoyed imagining the destruction of the Weimar Republic as well as imperialist wars of unprecedented intensity. The vision of total war spoke to his fascination with adventure, violence, and heroism. But he was no less determined to show that the new order would, in the end, be static and homogenous. From the struggle would emerge a new harmony. The victorious power would eventually realize "a consistency of institutions, habits and behavior patterns, a secure economy, an acceptance of commands and an authoritarian order, that is in short: a life according to the law." Above all, the new order would institute a productive attitude toward all modern technological means. "In the organic construction of a planned economy" Jünger expected the worker to realize the "perfection of technology."[55] After competition and total mobilization had first claimed the fruits of production, the future would enjoy them, as technology was turned to the service of humanity. At the end of the Weimar Republic, Jünger imagined a world that would progress from destruction and total war to a perfect new order.

The young Ernst Jünger had been filled with the desire for adventure and a grand mission. He condemned modern civilization as an obstacle to these dreams, insofar as it imposed artificial conventions, discipline, and rules. He hoped at first to realize his ambitions in the wildest parts of Africa, then in World War I; but both attempts failed. He could have retreated into some form of escapism or reconciled himself to life in a "boring" reality. Instead,

53 Ibid., 75; cf. 44, 106, 144, 147.
54 Ibid., 291; cf. 277–90.
55 Ibid., 170, 290.

he continued his search for adventure. First he tried to reconcile industrial warfare with heroism, then he sought heroism in modernity. While he was alive to the power of modern technology over human beings, he eventually sought more satisfying meaning in this power. He aimed to overcome the human experience of impotence in a technological world, to find a mission for "adventurous hearts" in modern society.

The solution on which he seized in the early 1930s involved a reversal of many of his initial convictions. His quest for homogeneity, stability, and hierarchy led him to accept technology, because it would dictate the future organization of society. His discomfort with diversity led him to insist that all accept the demands of total mobilization. He envisaged a future of collective, not individual, adventure in wars fought over the future global order.

The motivation for Jünger's thinking is perfectly understandable, but the end result, his strange or even perverse love for total mobilization and total war, meant rejection of the Weimar Republic and ideological affinities to the expansionist and totalitarian ambitions of National Socialism.[56] Furthermore, his belief in technological solutions combined with his glorification of an ascetic heroism and his naïve trust that the future would bring the perfect conservative order made Jünger disregard individual suffering. An allegedly wonderful future seemed to justify every sacrifice. "The number of people suffering" he regarded as "irrelevant" in comparison with his grand vision of a new global order.[57] Jünger's personal desire for adventure completely changed its character when applied to collective entities. It no longer meant individual self-realization and the freedom to choose a risky lifestyle, but a glorification of militarism and future wars. The enthusiastically described monumental future meant in effect propaganda for total mobilization and total war. And despite all this, Jünger even failed in his main ambition of combining adventure, technology, and his ideal of a stable conservative order in one grand design. Although all these components were present in *The Worker*, his most important book of the Weimar era, they are only supposed to exist in different historical epochs. Whereas the creation of a new order would involve battles, big adventures, and heroism, the new order once realized did not offer any space for these desires. Jünger emphatically demanded a society "*created* by a merger of life and danger,"[58] but it is imperceptible how this dangerous dimension could be maintained in his vision of a technocratic society. Thus, Jünger's historical vision contained

56 Ernst Jünger's love of total war makes Stanley Kubrick's film, *Dr. Strangelove, or How I Learned to Love the Bomb* (1963), appear to be very realistic.

57 Ernst Jünger, *Blätter und Steine* (Hamburg, 1934), 224.

58 Jünger, *Arbeiter*, 56. Emphasis added.

adventure and order, but both could not become reality at the same time. In the end, Jünger describes a future order without space for individualism, adventure, and heroism. If he was right to believe that a political order is always threatened if "it does not allow for the realization of a great dream," his future society would not even be stable.[59]

With the experience of National Socialism and Hiroshima, Ernst Jünger's thoughts fundamentally changed. He no longer advocated total war, but suggested ways in which World War II might lead to total peace.[60] He never owned up to his role in celebrating militarism, recasting instead the role he had played as that of a messenger who got blamed for an unwanted message,[61] and he continued to honor the role of all true soldiers (including those in Hitler's army) in building a better world, but he did break completely with the political role he had played. Independent of this question of personal responsibility, his work still provides an exceptional source for reconstructing the strange love for total war many men on the extreme right in the Weimar Republic felt. This love contributed to the rise of National Socialism and to the unleashing of the next world war.

59 Jünger, *Das Abenteuerliche Herz*, 77.

60 Jünger, *Der Friede*, and *Ansprache zu Verdun*, both in Sämtliche Werke, 20 vols. (Stuttgart, 1978), vol. 7. His immediate reaction to Hiroshima is described in *Jahre der Okkupation*, Sämtliche Werke, 3:503–5.

61 Jünger, *Adnoten zum Arbeiter*, Sämtliche Werke, 8:322.

10

Shadows of Total War in French and British Military Journals, 1918–1939

TIMO BAUMANN AND DANIEL MARC SEGESSER

The debate continues over whether World War I can be called a total war.[1] For many of the officers who had survived the war or been commissioned thereafter, however, this great conflict marked a watershed in the development of military theory, doctrine, and organization. The changes that the war had spawned needed to be taken into account as planners made decisions about national security and the defense of territorial integrity in the future. All these decisions were debated in the shadow of the Great War, which some thought at the time to have been a total war.[2] Although no officer went as far as some socialist or pacifist politicians, who claimed that national defense by military means was no longer a viable option,[3] they all tried to digest the manifold practical lessons of the war. Furthermore, they were under strong pressure from politicians and public opinion to avoid another war, or if this option were impossible, to win it with minimal costs in lives and property.

This chapter grows out of a research project on "Military Journals and the International Debate on Past and Future Warfare, 1918–1939," which

1 See Roger Chickering and Stig Förster, eds., *Great War, Total War: Combat and Mobilization on the Western Front, 1914–1918* (New York, 2000).

2 The term *total war* (in French *guerre totale*, *guerre intégrale*, or *lutte totale*) was used infrequently by French officers and not at all by their British counterparts. Among those who used these terms were: Bernard Serrigny, "L'Organisation de la nation pour le temps de guerre," *Revue des Deux Mondes* (hereafter *RDDM*) Septième Période 18 (1923): 586; Lucien Loizeau, "Succès stratégique, succès tactiques," *Revue Militaire Française* (hereafter *RMF*) 40 (1931): 194; Charles de Gaulle, *Vers l'armée de métier* (Paris, 1934), 78; Edouard Dupont, "La Guerre totale par le général Ludendorff," *Revue d'Artillerie* (hereafter *RA*) 117, no. 59 (1936): 194–207; Georges Kitcheef, "Conditions d'éfficacité stratégique de l'aviation," *Revue de l'Armée de l'Air* (hereafter *RAA*) 2, no. 10 (1938): 848.

3 Martin Ceadel, *Pacifism in Britain, 1914–1945: The Defining of a Faith* (Oxford, 1980), 62–75, 87–108; Maurice Vaïsse, "Le Pacifisme français dans les années trentes," *Relations internationales* 53 (1988): 37–52; Jean-François Sirinelli, "La France de l'entre-deux-guerres: Un 'trend' pacifiste?" in Maurice Vaïsse, ed., *Le Pacifisme en Europe des Années 1920 aux Années 1950* (Brussels, 1993), 43–50; François-Georges Dreyfus, "Le Pacifisme en France 1930–1940," ibid., 137–44.

was based at the University of Bern.[4] It examines how British and French officers met the challenges they faced, the answers and proposals they offered, and the responses they received from political and military authorities. It also examines the discussions that took place in military journals and other periodicals in which officers published their views, in order to analyze how new ideas arose and were received. The analysis rests on an investigation of military journals in Great Britain and France, as well as articles that officers published in other, nonmilitary periodicals in hopes of educating the broader public.[5] The *Revue Militaire Française* and the *Journal of the Royal United Service Institution* were the two major opinion-makers among officers in France and Britain.[6] Other important journals included those of the different service arms, including the air forces, and private periodicals or newspapers that were sympathetic to the interests of the armed forces.[7] Although there was no direct censorship of articles – French officers only had to submit articles dealing with the Great War to the Ministry of War for approval[8] – officers did have to submit to some degree of editorial control, if they did not want to endanger their opportunities for promotion.[9] In general, Faris Russell Kirkland's judgment pertains to both France and Britain:

> The degree of editorial control varied; the articles that appeared had to be within varying limits of orthodoxy. Sometimes controversial articles were preceded by editorial disclaimers. Since the journals were sponsored by the armed forces they excluded those ideas that were so far outside the mainstream as to be totally unrepresentative and without influence.[10]

4 The results of the project will be published in Stig Förster, ed., *Totaler Krieg: Militärzeitschriften und die internationale Debatte über den Krieg der Zukunft, 1919–1939* (forthcoming).

5 Hubert Camon, "La 'Motorisation' de l'armée," *Revue de Paris* (hereafter *RP*) 32, no. 5 (1925): 144; Paul Armengaud, *Batailles politiques et militaires sur l'Europe: Témoignages (1932–1940)* (Paris, 1948), 25–36.

6 The *Revue Militaire Française* emerged from the fusion of the three major French journals of the pre-1914 era. It became the leading French military journal in 1924, when the *Revue Militaire Générale*, which had appeared under the patronage of Joffre, Foch, and Franchet d' Éspérey, ceased publication. The *Journal of the Royal United Service Institution* was published by the institution of the same name, whose aim was to promote military science and military thinking within the British Empire. "La Revue Militaire Française," *RMF* 1 (1921): 5–8; "Note de la rédaction," *Revue Militaire Générale* (hereafter *RMG*) 21 (1924): 969–70; Paul Azan, "But et programme de la Revue Militaire Générale," *RMG*, new ser. 1 (1937): 3–8; Rudolf Kiszling, "Hundert Jahre Royal United Service Institution," *Militärwissenschaftliche Mitteilungen* (hereafter *MWM*) 62 (1931): 1162–3.

7 Private journals and newspapers, for which many officers wrote articles, included the *Revue des Deux Mondes*, the *Revue de Paris*, the *Revue Politique et Parlementaire*, the *Revue de France*, the *Times*, and the *Daily Telegraph*.

8 *Réglement du service dans l'armée: Discipline générale* (Paris, 1924), 26–7.

9 Daniel Segesser, "Nur keine Dummheiten: Das französische Offizierskorps und das Konzept des totalen Krieges," in Förster, ed., *Totaler Krieg*.

10 Faris Russell Kirkland, "The French Officer Corps and the Fall of France, 1920–1940," Ph.D. diss., University of Pennsylvania, 1982, 25. The Admiralty abolished censorship officially in 1919, but articles in the *Naval Review* were cleared nonetheless. See James Goldrick, "Naval Publishing the

The great majority of officers who published in French and British military journals came from the medium ranks. Quite a few had studied in the major staff colleges or served in the general staff, the staffs of the individual services, as unit commanders, or in the military administration. Their articles were designed to inform and support fellow officers – principally those who educated future generations of officers, served in the general staff, or were themselves studying at one of the military colleges of the British armed forces, the École Supérieure de Guerre in Paris, or one of the specialized colleges of the French army and navy. These articles treated military history and technical subjects; and they presented information on the development and organization of foreign armies. British officers published articles in hopes of attracting the attention of the staff officers who were responsible for promotions.[11]

The chapter is divided into two major parts. The first deals with perceptions by British officers of the development of warfare and the future of land war, air war, and naval combat, as well as with British military planning in the 1930s. The second part examines the lessons drawn by French officers from the Great War, particularly with respect to national defense, the mobilization of the nation for war, and new weapons and technologies. While in Britain the shadows of the next war dominated the discourse, the shadow of the last war preoccupied French officers.

THE BRITISH OFFICER CORPS AND PREPARATIONS FOR FUTURE WAR

For most of the British officer corps, the Great War did not mark a watershed in the evolution of warfare. Modern forms of war, they believed, had been in evidence since the Napoleonic Wars, which had entailed the total defeat of states, and the Russo-Japanese War, which had revealed the great power of modern artillery and machine guns. Most British officers thus regarded the lessons of these wars as relevant even after the Great War. As a rule, they did not use specific terms to describe the type of warfare prevalent in the Great War, beyond "new warfare"[12] or "modern war."[13] Terms such as

British Way," *Naval War College Review* 45 (1992): 87; and "The Irresistible Force and Immovable Object: The Naval Review, the Young Turks, and the Royal Navy, 1911–1931," in James Goldrick and John B. Hattendorf, eds., *Mahan Is Not Enough: Conference on the Works of Sir Julian Corbett and Admiral Sir Herbert Richmond* (Newport, R.I., 1993), 83–102.

11 "Avant-Propos," *RA* 43, 85 (1920): 6–7; "Revue Militaire Française," 6; "Editorial," *Army Quarterly* (hereafter *AQ*) 4, no. 1 (1922): 1; B. T. Wilson, "Modern War and its Maze of Machines," *Journal of the Royal United Service Institution* (hereafter *RUSI*) 530 (1938): 341.

12 G. W. Williamson, "Some Problems of a Technical Service," *RUSI* 516 (1934): 796.

13 J. C. Dundas, "The Strategy of Exterior and Interior Lines in the Light of Modern War," *RUSI* 461 (1921): 101–13; H. de Watteville, "The Conduct of Modern War," *RUSI* 497 (1930): 70–81.

"unlimited war"[14] or "totalitarian war"[15] were exceptions, while the term *total war*, which was used on the continent, was not used at all.

For general guidelines, the conflicts of the past could hence be exploited in military training, but detailed lessons could not be drawn. No one could foresee precisely the impact of new weapons that had not been fully tested in action. Tanks, airplanes, submarines, and poison gas had all been used during the Great War, but they seemed in retrospect to be crude devices. "It is impossible to foresee what developments may take place in them after a few months of warfare," noted one British officer, "but it is certain that their evolution would be rapid and the types in existence when war breaks out might be obsolete within a few months."[16] Little more could be said of the character of future war than that it was uncertain and needed to be discussed.[17]

British officers nonetheless deliberated about the characteristics of future war. Faster tanks, they predicted, would make mobile warfare again possible; airplanes would increase in range, and submarines would increase their firepower.[18] When they wrote about poison gas, these officers emphasized its more extensive use, not only on the battlefield but also against an enemy's civilian population, which, in this and other respects, would become a central target of military action.[19]

After the war, Basil Liddell Hart began his quest for new concepts of infantry tactics.[20] In November 1919 he presented the tank as the solution to the tactical problem. "It is here suggested," he wrote in the *Journal of the Royal United Service Institution*, "that the solution of the problem lies in

14 A. H. Norman, "Gold Medal (Naval) Prize Essay for 1923: The Advantages and Disadvantages of a Separate Air Force for the Royal Navy," *RUSI* 474 (1924): 264; E. E. Calthrop, "Weapons on War," *RUSI* 514 (1934): 283–4.

15 J. F. C. Fuller, "Totalitarian War: The Threat of Swift Aggression to Collective Security," *Army Ordnance* (hereafter *AO*) 99 (1936): 135–8; Fuller, "The Development of Totalitarian Warfare," *Journal of the Royal Artillery* (hereafter *JRA*) 113 (1937): 441–52; S. M. Noakes, "Co-ordination of the Civil Population with the Services," *RUSI* 526 (1937): 384.

16 L. I. Cowper, "Gold Medal (Military) Prize Essay for 1924: Given that there Is Maintained at Home in Peace Time a Field Army of Five Regular and Fourteen Territorial Divisions, with Army Troops: How Can They Best Be Organised to Provide for Expansion which a War on a National Scale Will Demand?" *RUSI* 478 (1925): 203.

17 J. F. C. Fuller, *War and Western Civilisation, 1832–1932: A Study of War as a Political Instrument and the Expression of Mass Democracy* (London, 1932), reviewed in *RUSI* 509 (1933): 217; D. Prentice, R.N., "Aircraft in Ten Years' Time," *RUSI* 496 (1929): 705–13.

18 W. S. King-Hall, "Gold Medal (Naval) Prize Essay for 1918: The Influence of the Submarine in Naval Warfare in the Future," *RUSI* 455 (1919): 375; R. V. Goddard, "The Development of Aircraft and its Influence on Air Operations," *RUSI* 515 (1934): 457.

19 E. R. Macpherson, "The Development of Chemical Warfare," *RUSI* 478 (1925): 317; W. G. Carlton Hall, "British Re-armament," *RUSI* 515 (1934): 597; D. Colyer, "A Criticism of 'War in the Air'," *Royal Air Force Quarterly* (hereafter *RAFQ*) 2 (1931): 596.

20 John Mearsheimer, *Liddell Hart and the Weight of History* (London, 1988), 26.

the employment of the tank as an actual weapon of infantry. The infantry combat unit should be armed with them in the same way as they are armed with Lewis guns."[21]

In 1920 another officer went further. J. F. C. Fuller, a colonel in the Royal Tank Corps, argued that the tank had brought back the "armoured knight" to the battlefield. "It has, in fact," he announced, "equilibrated movement and fire and by doing so has superimposed naval tactics on land warfare; that is, it now enables the soldier, like a sailor, to discharge his weapon from a moving platform protected by a fixed shield."[22] Placing men "behind half an inch of steel" in the tank would, he pointed out, protect them from enemy small arms fire.[23] Noticing the potential of Fuller's ideas, Liddel Hart came close to the former's concept of the tank in the mid-1920s. In 1929, however, he claimed that he had himself grasped the potential of the tank from the beginning: "Just after the war I wrote an article in this journal [*Journal of the Royal United Service Institution*] on 'The Tank as a Weapon of Infantry.' Ten years later the idea seems to have a prospect of fulfillment."[24]

Both Fuller and Liddell Hart were well aware of the financial obstacles that their ideas would encounter, for the British government did not want to commit scarce resources to the army or navy. The British armed forces were reduced immediately after World War I, and the budgets for military and naval affairs were cut. The army, navy, and air force therefore had to fight with one another, as well as with other government agencies, over what was left in the budget. Fuller and Liddell Hart denied that they were proposing to set up a large, costly fleet of modern tanks. Right from the beginning Fuller claimed that armies of the future would be completely mechanized with almost all fighting units comprised of tanks, whereas Liddell Hart tried to integrate tanks and infantry step-by-step into his vision of the army of the future. The officers of the air force quickly realized the need to respond to these two energetic champions of armor, lest their own claims on resources be threatened. In fact, the threat of dissolution hung over the RAF.

In 1921 the Royal United Service Institution chose an air force topic for its prize essay. C. J. Mackay submitted an article in which he argued that

21 B. H. L. Hart, "Suggestions on the Future Development of the Combat Unit: The Tank as a Weapon of Infantry," *RUSI* 456 (1919): 667.

22 Fuller, "Gold Medal (Military) Prize Essay for 1919: The Application of Recent Developments in Mechanics and Other Scientific Knowledge to Preparation and Training for Future War on Land," *RUSI* 458 (1920): 249.

23 Fuller, *On Future Warfare* (London, 1928), reviewed by A. G. Baird in *RUSI* 492 (1928): 778.

24 Liddell Hart, "Army Exercises 1929," *RUSI* 496 (1929): 793; cf. J. F. C. Fuller, "Progress in the Mechanicalisation of Modern Armies," *RUSI* 477 (1925): 86–8. Timo Baumann, "Die Entgrenzung taktischer Szenarien: Der Krieg der Zukunft in britischen Militärzeitschriften 1919–1939," in Förster, ed., *Totaler Krieg*.

Britain, more specifically London, would be the target of enemy bombers in any future war. Inspired by Colmar von der Goltz's *The Nation in Arms*, which had been published in Germany before the Great War, he foresaw an unlimited war, in which the whole nation would be involved and the civilian population a major target: "In some cases enemy national morale may be also lowered by the defeat of their air forces, and the consequent exposure of their resources and their homes to air attack, that their submission may be obtained by air action alone."[25] Mackay agreed with his chief of staff, Hugh Trenchard, who had been the first British officer to claim that aerial bombing would have a decisive impact on an enemy's civilian morale.[26] British officers did not, however, mention the Italian apostle of air warfare, Giulio Douhet, until after his death in 1930. Many nonetheless supported Mackay's arguments. "THE object of a nation at war," wrote one, "is to stop the enemy's national life, and the strategic plan which either belligerent follows to achieve this end may be divided into three classes, viz., naval strategy, military strategy, and independent air strategy."[27] These officers first tried to convince the politicians to give the air force precedence over the army and its tank corps. They argued that the menace from the air would continue to grow, while tanks would be of value only in a war outside the British isles. Once they had achieved their aim and the air force was firmly established, these officers began to compete with the senior service, the navy, for the largest share of the defense budget. In the long run, they were bound to win, for concern over London's security was paramount.[28] As the RAF secured its survival, it raised important arguments in favor of enlarging the battlefield.

Royal Navy officers such as W. S. King-Hall talked about attacks by enemy submarines in a future war, but their lurid pictures were not as

25 C. J. Mackay, "Gold Medal (Royal Air Force) Prize Essay for 1921: The Influence in the Future of Aircraft upon Problems of Imperial Defence," *RUSI* 466 (1922): 275, 283. Mackay cites Colmar von der Goltz, *The Nation in Arms* (London, 1887 or 1903), on p. 275.

26 Philip S. Meilinger, "Trenchard and 'Morale Bombing': The Evolution of Royal Air Force Doctrine before World War II," *Journal of Military History* 60, no. 2 (1996): 250.

27 C. H. Edmonds, "Aerial Co-operation with the Navy," *RUSI* 462 (1921): 237–8. On Douhet, see L. E. O. Charlton, *War from the Air: Past–Present–Future* (London, 1935), reviewed in *RUSI* 518 (1935): 463–4. On Trenchard, see Scot Robertson, *The Development of RAF Strategic Bombing Doctrine, 1919–1939* (London, 1995), 25–6.

28 Louis C. Jackson, "Possibilities of the Next War," *RUSI* 457 (1920): 81; R. Chevenix Trench, "Gold Medal (Military) Prize Essay for 1922: Discuss the manner in which Scientific Inventions and Science in general may affect, both strategically and tactically, the next great European War in which the British Empire may be engaged. Indicate the Organisation and Training required to Secure the Views which you may have formed as regards the Imperial Military Forces," *RUSI* 470 (1923): 202; W. T. S. Williams, "Air Exercises, 1927," *RUSI* 488 (1927): 745; W. F. MacNeece, "Air Power and its Application," *RUSI* 490 (1928): 253; C. C. Turner, "The Aerial Defence of Cities. Some Lessons of the Air Exercises, 1928," *RUSI* 492 (1928): 693.

vivid as the scenarios of strategic air attacks or of all-out tank battles. A majority of British admirals favored the big battleship and therefore did not back their inferiors who spoke about the possibility of attacking commerce shipping or coastal towns by submarines. In 1923 the Royal United Service Institution chose "The Advantages and Disadvantages of a Separate Air Force for the Royal Navy" as a prize theme. The winner, A. H. Norman, a naval officer, argued that "the two principal weapons of unlimited warfare are gas and the submarine, the extended use of the former having been rendered practicable by the development of aircraft."[29] He then noted that an airplane could carry bombs or poison gas and that bombing factories would bring about the intensification of warfare. Further intensification would come in "indiscriminate bombing and gassing of all persons" in an enemy country.[30] These strategies entailed a deliberate attack on the enemy's morale. "Since enemy airplanes cannot be kept out by defensive airplanes," he observed, "towns and cities in the battlefield area must be equipped with adequate anti-gas measures, if they are to survive. . . . large towns and cities within the extended battlefield area of modern warfare are, under existing conditions, conspicuously weak spots in a country's defensive armament."[31]

An article like this, from one of its own officers, did not help the navy much in the budgetary competition. Even in articles on imperial defense, though, naval officers of the 1920s did not see the need to emphasize the navy's role as the guarantee of the Empire's security or of British commerce throughout the world because they were ill at ease in a world where they had to justify building a single cruiser for £8 million, the cost of twenty air squadrons.[32] The navy suffered the further disadvantage that no naval weapon could directly threaten an enemy's civilian population, nor could the navy protect its own civilian population from direct attack.[33]

By 1930 the international and domestic situations had both changed dramatically. In India, politicians opposed an increase of their country's share in the general framework of imperial defense. At the same time tensions lessened in Europe, in the wake of the Locarno Treaty and the Kellogg-Briand Pact. British military thinking registered these changes. The army and navy were now to be employed primarily for the defense of India and

29 Norman, "Gold Medal (Naval) Prize Essay," 264.

30 Ibid., 265.

31 Ibid., 267.

32 See A. F. E. Palliser, "The Effect of Air Power on Naval Strategy," *RUSI* 486 (1927): 353–4, and the ensuing discussion.

33 John Ferris, "'It is Our Business in the Navy to Command the Seas': The last Decade of British Maritime Supremacy, 1919–1929," in Greg Kennedy and Keith Neilson, eds., *Far-Flung Lines: Essays in Imperial Defence in Honour of Donald Mackenzie Schurman* (London, 1996), 124–70; Orest Babij, "The Royal Navy and the Defence of the British Empire, 1928–1934," in ibid., 171–89.

the Pacific Empire, as well as the protection of shipping lanes throughout the world. The air force, on the other hand, was to play the major role in defending Britain, as well as in any British intervention on the continent.

After 1933, however, as Germany seemed increasingly the major danger to world peace, British thinking again went into flux. In 1934 the British Defence Requirements Committee proposed sending an expeditionary force, consisting of five regular and fourteen territorial divisions, to Belgium and the Netherlands, in order to protect airfields "as a deterrent to an aggressor, [to] exercise an influence for peace . . . [and as an encouragement for] allies for they would recognize that behind it is the whole might of the British Empire ready and determined to wage war."[34] Nevertheless, given the restrictions set by the Treasury and the wholesale shrinking of the defense establishment after the war, the rearmament program set in place by the National governments of Ramsay MacDonald and Stanley Baldwin was slow to take hold. Only after the German occupation of Austria in March 1938 did the government ask industry to give full priority to rearmament.[35] The appeasement policy, which all British governments followed between 1933 and March 1939, was a consequence of this situation, as the assistant secretary of the Committee of Imperial Defence, Henry Pownall, made clear in 1936:

> From a military standpoint, owing to the extreme weakness of France, the possibility of an understanding between Germany and Japan, and even in certain circumstances Italy, and because of the immensity of the risks to which a direct attack upon Great Britain would expose the Empire, the present situation dictates a policy directed towards an understanding with Germany and a consequent postponement of the danger of German aggression against any vital interest of ours.[36]

Liddell Hart, who in 1937 became military adviser to the Secretary of State for War, Leslie Hore-Belisha, would probably have agreed with this judgment. By the end of the 1920s, as his interests had shifted to grand strategy and ancient military history, he became more skeptical about the possibilities of armored warfare.[37] Whereas the necessity to defend British skies became a common topic, Fuller now concentrated on a kind of land warfare in which ground fighter airplanes would dominate. He became increasingly convinced that totalitarian governments would enjoy great advantages over democracies in future warfare, and that in order to compete,

34 David French, *The British Way in Warfare, 1688–2000* (London, 1990), 188.

35 Ibid., 188–9.

36 Quoted in Brian Bond, *British Military Policy between the Two World Wars* (Oxford, 1980), 235.

37 Alex Danchev, "Liddell Hart and Manoeuvre," *Journal of the Royal United Service Institution for Defence Studies* 143, no. 6 (1998): 33; Mearsheimer, *Liddell Hart*, 84–98.

democracies would have to draw from totalitarian models of military and civilian organization. Totalitarian countries would force "totalitarian tactics" on Great Britain, whether the country liked it or not, for whatever was technologically feasible would be exploited in future warfare. Fuller was certain that the totalitarian countries would be more prepared than the democracies for war.[38] One of the officers who reviewed Fuller's ideas therefore called for comprehensive reforms:

> At a time when we are urgently repairing the deficiencies in our defences it is very necessary that we should not merely make good our weapons, but that we should also examine the whole of our organization for war in order to ensure that it is efficient for determining policy, drawing up plans, and so preparing the nation as a whole, and the fighting services in particular, that, if the emergency arises, we shall be ready.[39]

The reviewer recognized that Fuller had given up his fighting for the tank, and now claimed that "the aeroplane is the master weapon." Any time that Fuller talked about weapons, "it is painful to see [his] imagination and enthusiasm running riot."[40] Fuller, however, now realized that his ideas on tanks would never be put into practice in the British army. He concluded that the airplane would take over the job that the tank could not do. In this context Fuller continued to argue in terms of the earlier debate, but again overstated his point. In the meantime weapons had lost their overall importance.

Whereas the mainstream of military thinking had concentrated on new weapons in the 1920s, more and more British officers began to criticize interservice organization. In this context some argued that the rivalry of the services was an important reason for the high number of casualties in the last war. Never again should British forces suffer defeat in a combined operation – as had been the case in Gallipoli in 1915 – because of a lack of preparation or cooperation among the services. In the future, the services were to join in a common effort, for which officers were to be trained: "What appears to be wanted is a military university where young officers of all varieties of service would rub shoulders together and learn as much from each other as in the military schools and colleges."[41] Other officers, such as Lieutenant-Colonel de Watteville, demanded improved coordination of all dimensions of national defense, whether civilian or military. To achieve this

38 J. F. C. Fuller, *Towards Armageddon: The Defence Problem and Its Solution* (London, 1937); Fuller, "Totalitarian War," 135–8.

39 Navarino, "Our Organisation for War," *RUSI* 527 (1937): 520.

40 Ibid.

41 T. H. Holdrich, "Military Education," *RUSI* 457 (1920): 118.

goal, he advocated that a Ministry of Defence supersede the three existing service ministries.[42] Although such a ministry was not in fact set up, the appointment of a cabinet Minister for the Co-ordination of Defence, at the request of Lord Milne,[43] went some way toward the same end. Parallel to concerns about armed forces on the battlefield, a growing number of officers realized that wars would not only bring about harder fighting but that their effects also would spread to civilian life.

National mobilization in wartime had been a topic of discussion among British officers during the 1920s, although the subject had mainly attracted the interest of officers who had, in one way or another, encountered the problem of mobilization during their military careers. The former director-general of Mobilisation and Recruiting in the War Office, B. Burnett-Hitchcock, the officer who had reorganized the mobilization and recruiting service after the war, predicted that all citizens, including women, would be liable in a future war to military service – be it in the armed forces, the munitions industry, or in production for home consumption.[44] In 1924, in a statement that was noted in the British military establishment, the American assistant secretary for war claimed that

> wars are no longer fought by the armed forces alone. Every man, woman and child, every resource, and every dollar in the entire nation must throw its weight towards victory in the time of war. Industry alone cannot win a war, but it can lose a war by failure to supply the armies with munitions vital to their fighting efficiency.[45]

The same year Ernest Fayle claimed that the morale of the civilian population demanded that living standards not fall significantly during wartime.[46] In 1926 two officers, G. MacLeod Ross and W. G. Linsell, called for more efficient organization of the government, in order to ensure the smooth functioning of industrial mobilization from the moment war broke out: "In war, quick action is required; compromise and debate lose their values, and the dictator is necessary to ensure unity of effort toward the attainment of the common object."[47] Linsell demanded total national mobilization in time of war:

42 H. de Watteville, "Intelligence in the Future," *RUSI* 483 (1926): 483–5; H. G. Eady and G. E. Grimsdale, "A Defence Ministry and a Strategic Staff," *AQ* 4, no. 2 (1922): 253–62; [A. H. Taylor,] "A Ministry of Defence: Another Point of View," *Naval Review* (hereafter *NR*) 10 (1922): 444–6.
43 Robin Higham, *The Military Intellectuals in Britain 1918–1939* (Westport, Conn., 1981), 39.
44 B. Burnett-Hitchcock, "Man Power," *RUSI* 461 (1921): 37–40. See Keith Grieves, *The Politics of Manpower, 1914–1918* (Manchester, 1988).
45 "Military Notes," *RUSI* 476 (1924): 785.
46 C. Ernest Fayle, "Carrying-Power in War: Some Lessons from 1914–1918," *RUSI* 475 (1924): 527.
47 G. MacLeod Ross, "Industrial Strategy," *RUSI* 482 (1926): 261.

Our potential officers, our skilled mechanics, our expert chemists, our miners and mental workers, and skilled artisans, must by some means or other have their particular knowledge or mechanical skill directed into the best channel in which to help the nation in arms. Our available man-power and woman-power must be mobilised from the outset.[48]

In 1930 Archibald P. Wavell weighed the balance of efforts in national mobilization and claimed that

the preparation of the whole national strength for war is probably the factor in which greatest progress has taken place since the war. In practically all countries the subject has been studied in great detail, and schemes have been prepared to mobilise on the outbreak of war not only the naval and military forces, but the factories, the Press, and almost every branch of national life.[49]

Wavell noted that during the last war, soldiers had been unprepared to exploit national resources in the most efficient manner. "But in the next war," he predicted, "industrial mobilization – the conversion of the whole civil population, factories and resources to the purposes of war – will be a predominant feature." Victory in a future war would go to the side that more efficiently mobilized its own resources while paralyzing the enemy's efforts to do the same.[50] In an article on the role of chemistry in a future war, F. A. Freeth followed the same path: "Modern warfare amounts practically to an industrial mobilization. Consequently the chemical industry, which plays an intimate part in almost every national industrial activity in peace, is thereby concerned with the production of nearly every material used in war."[51]

In 1934 the *Journal of the Royal United Service Institution* published a translation of an article by Charles de Gaulle, who was then a lieutenant colonel in the French army. Here the Frenchman called for the use of all national resources in a future war.[52] G. W. Williamson was thinking along the same lines when he claimed in November 1934, in a lecture at the Royal United Service Institution, that

war problems are no longer tactical, solved by action on the field of battle; nor strategical, requiring twenty days preparation. They are industrial. In the future, as in 1918, grand strategy means organization of the whole nation for war an

48 W. G. Linsell, "Administrative Lessons of the Great War," *RUSI* 483 (1926): 719.

49 Archibald P. Wavell, "The Army and the Prophets," *RUSI* 500 (1930): 668.

50 Ibid., 669.

51 F. A. Freeth, "The Chemistry of War," *RUSI* 500 (1930): 691.

52 DeGaulle, "La Mobilisation Économique à l'Étranger," *RMF* 51 (1934): 62–88, translated and summarized as "Industrial Mobilisation," *RUSI* 515 (1934): 483–98.

organization that may take five years to perfect. . . . Key men, key operations, key materials, and key machine tools are the weak links in the chain of production of complicated material.[53]

His listeners appeared to agree. In a final comment on the lecture, Sir Robert Brooke-Popham called for Britain's keeping up with international developments in this field.[54] In 1936 Williamson called for the British to begin comprehensive planning for a future war:

"Mobilisation will include everybody"; therefore everybody must be told, in time of peace, what duties will be allotted to them in war. . . . The greatest defect in our defence programme to-day is the lack of a . . . Ministry [similar to the Ministry of Munitions during the Great War], organized and working before the outbreak of war.[55]

Curiously, the mobilization of the Empire's resources in a future war did not figure much in this debate. Few commentators posed the question of how to ensure that supplies from the Empire arrived in Britain during a future war. They demanded little more than that the government maintain a great navy and merchant marine, particularly a fleet of tankers for the transport of oil, in order to guarantee the supply of raw materials from overseas.[56] Ernest Fayle summed up the important points in a lecture to the Royal United Service Institution in May 1934. A country, he argued,

needs adequate Food Supplies, both for the fighting forces and the population; Raw Materials for the industries, in order that these may be able to equip, arm, and munition the fighting Services, and to pay by exports for its requirements from abroad; Fuel as the motive power of its industries and transport; Plant and Machinery, including plant which is either designed for the production of arms and munitions or readily adaptable to that purpose; an efficient system of internal and external Transport to give mobility to its forces and to carry foodstuffs, material, munitions and manufactures to the places where they are required. Finally, its ability to make effective use of these material resources will depend very much on the strength and elasticity of its Commercial and Financial Organization.[57]

Several years later, Archibald Hurd developed the same theme. Without the Empire, Great Britain could not wage war: "After all, there are

53 G. W. Williamson, "Some Problems of a Technical Service," *RUSI* 516 (1934): 780–1.

54 Ibid., 800.

55 G. W. Williamson, "The Need for a Ministry of Supply," *RUSI* 524 (1936): 736, 738.

56 M. F. Groove-White, "Some Aspects of Future Wars on Land," *RUSI* 479 (1925): 475–6; H. G. Thursfield, "The Functions of the Cruiser in Relation to Imperial Needs," *RUSI* 485 (1927): 101–21; Reginald W. Skelton, "Coal versus Oil for the Navy," *RUSI* 513 (1934): 255; W. G. Carlton Hall, "British Re-armament," *RUSI* 515 (1934): 595–9; Andrew Agnew, "Empire Oil Supplies in War," *RUSI* 518 (1935): 278–96; Barry E. Domville, "The Influence of Sea-Power on British Strategy," *RUSI* 519 (1935): 467–85.

57 C. Ernest Fayle, "Economic Aspects of Empire Defence," *RUSI* 514 (1934): 301.

45,000,000 people in the British Isles, most of whose food as well as raw materials for the factories must reach them from overseas, not to mention the oil fuel, which is almost as essential as food since without neither the Army nor Air Force could fight."[58] None of these commentators demanded, however, that the Empire be efficiently organized for war. One reason was that they recognized that an Empire with no great oil reserves was more burden than help in a future war. Thus, by 1934 the decision had been made to give home defense preference over imperial commitments.[59]

For a growing number of British officers the crucial question was how to stop the trend toward ever-increasing battlefield casualties. Because they became convinced that in a land war the superiority of defense – mainly due to antitank guns – would make it impossible to avoid large numbers of casualties when attacking, they were inclined to look for solutions in the air, where a decisive victory might still be possible. Massive air attacks on civilian centers might force an opponent's hand without sacrificing one's own forces. Many RAF writers were unhappy with such a scenario. They believed, rather, that a bloodless victory could be achieved by attacking key elements of the enemy's war economy. Thus, J. A. Chamier was insulted that "airmen" – the former "Knights of the Air" – were now called "baby killers."[60]

To sum up, one can say that British military thought in the interwar period reflected the independence of the three services. David French has noted in this connection that "the three services were in practice planning to fight three different wars, the navy against the Japanese in the Far East, the RAF against the French across the Channel and the army against the Russians on the North-West Frontier [of India]."[61] Like many historians, David French underestimates the fictional character of the discussion. Of course, in practice France was the only great power in the 1920s capable of projecting its airpower all the way to London. But no one at the time thought in terms of a major war breaking out in the near future. Under the "ten year rule" all British governments asked the military not to prepare for war within the next decade. Like Fuller, Trenchard was only interested

58 Sir Archibald Hurd, "British Merchant Shipping Today," *RUSI* 525 (1937): 46.

59 Lothar Höbelt, *Die britische Appeasementpolitik: Entspannung und Nachrüstung 1937–1939* (Vienna, 1983), 30.

60 J. A. Chamier, "Air Bombing and Air Disarmament," *AQ* 27, no. 2 (1934): 94. On Liddell Hart, see Spenser Wilkinson, "Killing Not Murder: An Examination of Some New Theories of War," *AQ* 25, no. 1 (1927): 25. An exception was Martel, who claimed that "warfare to-day [sic] is a hundred per cent business, and we cannot lie back and carry out long range bombing and avoid the portion of the war which we do not like." See G. Le Q. Martel, "Mechanisation," *RUSI* 526 (1937): 299–300.

61 French, *British Way*, 187; cf. John Buckley, *Air Power in the Age of Total War* (London, 1999), 78, 103.

in the technical possibilities of a later, future war. Prior to the German arms buildup of the 1930s British officers rarely named a specific country when discussing the air menace. Yet they were certain that their fictions would become bitter realities in the future war they were thinking about.[62] Because financial resources were limited and the Treasury, at least until 1937, was principally concerned with a balanced budget and the exchange rate of the pound, the services fought over scarce funds. Each service sketched scenarios that emphasized its own role, to the detriment of an overall vision of how best to defend the country's interests. Most of the scenarios that were worked out in the 1920s tended to overemphasize anticipated dangers, and they invited the conclusion that one or another service was best suited to defend the country.[63] Naval policy was partly an exception, of course, because everyone knew that it did not make sense to start building capital ships just before a war.

In the 1930s British politicians, like most officers, became aware of the risks of these parochial practices. Some advocated the adaptation of military organization and doctrine to changed international circumstances. Most, however, did not go as far as Fuller, who argued that Britain should adopt organizational features of the totalitarian countries to win a future war. Other British commentators supported appeasement, because they feared that limited resources would make it impossible for Britain to fight around the world. They never considered mobilizing the Empire for war, probably because they recognized the difficulties of incorporating many different political, economic, and social systems into a single military framework, even if national survival were at issue.[64]

THE FRENCH OFFICER CORPS AND THE PREPARATION FOR FUTURE WAR

When World War I ended, the French government and military leadership were both aware that great efforts would be necessary to avoid another war with Germany or, should such a war have to be fought, to win it. Their preferred solution, the dismemberment of Germany, was rejected by the Allies at Versailles.[65] Thereafter, the government and the high command

62 Hugh M. Trenchard, "Aspects of Service Aviation," *AQ* 2, no. 1 (1921): 10–21.

63 Bond, *British Military Policy*, 24.

64 Paul M. Kennedy, *The Realities Behind Diplomacy: Background Influences on British External Policy, 1865–1980* (London, 1981), 247–51; Paul M. Kennedy, *The Rise and Fall of the Great Powers: Economic Change and Military Conflict from 1500 to 2000* (London, 1988), 315–18.

65 Gabriel Hanotaux, "Le Traité du 28 juin 1919: Les principes et les applications," *RDDM*, Sixième période 52 (1919): 509–39, 755–97.

had to deal with strong domestic pressures to avoid another war, which promised to bring even more ghastly losses in wealth, material, and human life.[66] In these circumstances, the French military leadership and officer corps struggled to define a new defense policy and grand strategy.

In 1920 the French government charged Philippe Pétain, who was named vice-president of the Superior War Council and Inspector General of the Army, with preparing the French army for a future war.[67] Together with two of his collaborators during the Great War, Edmond Buat and Eugène-Marie Debeney (who served successively as chief of the general staff), Pétain set about reorganizing the French armed forces. Their main challenge was to preserve the army as a reliable instrument of national defense while accommodating the country's strained economic resources and public opinion, which had been traumatized by the war just ended. On the one hand, these soldiers had to review strategy and tactics. On the other, they had to assess the impact of the war's technological innovations, such as poison gas, the tank, and the airplane. On the basis of their study, the three concluded that doctrines of maneuver and the offensive were obsolete, that the French army should in the future emphasize firepower and the *front continu*.[68] In 1921 these ideas informed the *Instruction Provisoire sur l'Emploi Tactique des Grandes Unités*:

> 99. The defensive battle is conducted from a covered position of resistance. . . . It rests on the combined use of firepower and organized positions. . . . 102. The High Command conducts a battle with all its forces in this position of resistance. . . . Firepower is the preponderant element of battle. An attack is firepower that advances, defense is firepower that prevents an enemy from advancing.[69]

Although he now occupied the highest position in the French army, Pétain had to convince not only his ministers, but also his fellow officers in the Superior War Council, which was the highest body in the French army. Here his colleagues Ferdinand Foch, Joseph Joffre, and Marie-Louis A. Guillaumat were opposed to abandoning offensive operations. While they agreed with Pétain that the border with Germany should be fortified,

66 Anthony Adamthwaite, *Grandeur & Misery: France's Bid for Power in Europe, 1914–1940* (London, 1995), 59–63; Judith Hughes, *To the Maginot Line: The Politics of French Military Preparations in the 1920s* (Cambridge, Mass., 1971), 7–143; Wilfried Loth, *Geschichte Frankreichs im 20. Jahrhundert* (Frankfurt am Main, 1992), 60–3.

67 See Hughes, *Maginot Line*, 44–7.

68 Jean-Marie Marill, "La Doctrine militaire française entre les deux guerres," *Revue historique des armées* (*RHA*) 184 (1991): 24–26; Ladislas Mysyrowicz, *Anatomie d'une défaite: Cinq études sur les origines profondes de l'effondrement militaire français 1919–1939* (Lausanne, 1973), 19–21, 37–40; Robert Doughty, *The Seeds of Disaster: The Development of French Army Doctrine 1919–1939* (Hamden, Conn., 1985), 91–105.

69 *Instruction provisoire du 6 octobre 1921 sur l'emploi tactique des grandes unités* (Paris, 1921), 62–3.

they proposed to use these fortifications as bases for offensive operations into Germany.[70] René Tournès of the Historical Branch of the General Staff was also critical of Pétain's ideas. He warned against allowing historical analysis, particularly of the Great War, to prejudice decisions about future war. Accurate analysis of history, he insisted, revealed that war was more than a question of managing industrial resources.[71] Tournès' warnings went unheeded. The opposition of Foch, Joffre, and Guillaumat to exclusively defensive border fortifications broke after the Locarno Treaty and the Kellogg-Briand Pact seemed to make offensive operations against Germany unnecessary (and illegal). Pétain's concept became the doctrinal basis of the Maginot Line, and even though his successors, Maxime Weygand and Maurice Gamelin, tried to change some details, the concept remained in force until 1940.[72]

The French military leadership and most officers were convinced that a future war would be long and that under no circumstances could it be fought by an army of professional soldiers. They thus turned not only to questions of military mobilization and operations, but also to the organization of French resources for war. After the Great War, the Superior Council of National Defense[73] took over responsibility for planning military strategy, organizing national resources, industrial production and supply, and the political and military administration of the armed forces. The concept of the *nation armée* changed as a consequence. It stood henceforth not only for the thoroughgoing conscription of young men into the army, but also for the wartime organization of all parts of the nation.[74]

In 1924 the government of Raymond Poincaré submitted a military-organization bill to the Chamber of Deputies, which should have become the basis of all preparation for future war.[75] The bill provided that in time of war the whole French population without distinction of age or sex could be mobilized either as part of the armed forces or for any other duty. Everyone was supposed to help out wherever his or her skills were of greatest use. The government was given the right to obtain all material resources it needed to conduct the war. These resources were to be acquired through negotiation or requisition if the state and the property owner failed to reach agreement. Furthermore, the bill contained provisions concerning responsibility for war preparations, governmental reorganization, and the powers of parliament,

70 Marill, "Doctrine," 26–7.
71 René Tournès, *L'Histoire militaire* (Paris, 1922), v–xiii.
72 Segesser, "Nur keine Dummheiten."
73 See Bernard Serrigny, "L'Organisation de notre défense nationale," *RDDM* (Sept. 1, 1950): 32–3.
74 See Richard Challener, *The French Theory of the Nation in Arms 1866–1939* (New York, 1955).
75 Journal Officiel, Chambre des Députés (JOC), Documents parlementaires, vol. 1:85–99, doc. no. 6949 (Jan. 10, 1924).

and a detailed description of how the economy was to be organized in wartime.

In order to prepare public opinion for the bill, particularly to persuade conservative members of parliament, the secretary of the Superior Council of National Defense, Bernard Serrigny, published an article in the *Revue des Deux Mondes*. Here he stressed that technological innovation guaranteed that great modern wars would in the future be long and that all of society's resources would be involved. Technology had unleashed unprecedented potential for destruction, as well as an insatiable demand for munitions. As a result, industry's demands for resources and workers would rise dramatically, making increased imports necessary. These pressures would result in massive transfers of capital and a severe drain on the employment market. These were lessons of the Great War, and they would mark a future war as well.[76] In this connection, Serrigny also used the term *guerre totale* to describe the Great War. To him, however, the term only meant the total mobilization of state, economy, and society by a more or less centralized government bureaucracy. Unlike later historians, Serrigny did not think of total means of warfare or total war aims.[77] He demanded that every French man and woman, regardless of age, take part in mobilizing the nation's resources. In order to limit the expansion of government, and to ease the fears of conservative politicians, Serrigny – in contrast to the bill later introduced by the Poincaré government – advocated, however, the wartime organization of industry by private associations of entrepreneurs. These associations were in turn to coordinate wartime measures on the national and regional levels. Finally, Serrigny advocated building up and tapping the resources of the French colonial empire. He called for constructing a new railway-line through the Sahara and securing shipping lanes to north Africa.[78]

The Chamber of Deputies first considered Poincaré's bill on wartime organization in 1927. No strong criticism was voiced during its first reading, and only the Communist Party opposed it. In the Senate, however, the bill faced strong opposition. Many conservatives criticized it for obliterating the difference between combatants and noncombatants. The consequence of

76 Serrigny, "Organisation de la nation," 583–601.

77 Ibid., 586; Stig Förster, "Vom Volkskrieg zum totalen Krieg? Der Amerikanische Bürgerkrieg 1861–1865, der Deutsch-Französische Krieg 1870/71 und die Anfänge moderner Kriegführung," in Walther L. Bernecker and Volker Dotterweich, eds., *Deutschland in den internationalen Beziehungen des 19. und 20. Jahrhunderts: Festschrift für Josef Becker zum 65. Geburtstag* (Munich, 1996), 77; Roger Chickering, "Total War: The Use and Abuse of a Concept," in Manfred F. Boemeke, Roger Chickering, and Stig Förster, eds., *Anticipating Total War: The German and American Experiences, 1871–1914* (New York, 1999), 26. See also John Whiteclay Chambers, "The American Debate over Modern War, 1871–1914," in ibid., 241–2.

78 Serrigny, "Organisation de la nation," 587–601.

the duty to serve wherever required would be, they argued, to make the civilian population a legitimate target of air strikes and other military operations. The Senate therefore decided to strike a paragraph that provided for the mobilization of women. Several additional amendments subdued the fears of senators close to leading industrialists, who feared that the bill would threaten economic freedom. These amendments, however, provoked the opposition of the socialists, who argued that they would put the army in control of mobilization. The socialists therefore rejected the amended bill in the second reading in the Chamber of Deputies. As the two chambers were unable to find an agreement, the bill lapsed and with it the first attempt to prepare France for the eventuality of a total war, which most officers expected to take place at some time in the future.[79] Although some deputies shared Serrigny's and Buat's vision of coordinating the industrial capacity of France to support the war effort and saw comprehensive national mobilization as a compensation for the reduction of time in military service, many just used it as a rhetorical device to justify shortening the length of this service.

Discussions among officers about how to organize the nation for war accompanied these parliamentary deliberations and continued after the bill had lapsed. Between 1924 and 1926, two majors, who wished to remain anonymous, published a series of articles on the topic in the *Revue Politique et Parlementaire* and the *Revue d'Études Militaires*. They made it clear that although future wars did not have to be long, they probably would be. It was, in all events, imperative to prepare for this eventuality. The best way to shorten a war, they insisted, was to be prepared for a long war. The more efficient a country's mobilization, particularly of its means to produce modern materials of war, the greater were the chances of rapid success.[80]

After the parliamentary bill had failed in 1927, other officers took up the same topic and stressed the importance of the organization of the nation for war. Julien Brossé, the deputy commanding officer of the military region of Nancy, emphasized the importance of industrial production for national defense. His former subordinate, Julien Faugeron, demanded that the French

79 Volker Wieland, *Zur Problematik der französischen Militärpolitik und Militärdoktrin in der Zeit zwischen den Weltkriegen* (Boppard am Rhein, 1973), 174–85; Eugenia Kiesling, *Arming Against Hitler: France and the Limits of Military Planning* (Lawrence, Kans., 1996), 14–25.

80 Major A. L., "La Civilisation tuera-t-elle la guerre?" *Revue Politique et Parlementaire* (hereafter *RPP*) 119 (1924): 149–89; A. L., "Le Conseil Supérieur de la Défense Nationale et la 'guerre totale,'" *RPP* 120 (1924): 199–218; A. P., "La Préparation du pays en vue de la guerre," *Revue des Etudes Militaires* (hereafter *REM*) 13, no. 16 (1925): 3–14; ibid., 13, no. 17 (1925): 3–15; A. P., "L'Organisation de la nation pour le temps de guerre," *RPP* 127 (1926): 348–63.

high command attend to economic and industrial mobilization.[81] Charles Menu stressed that the wartime importance of industrial production was now known, so it would be inexcusable to allow a repetition of the events of 1914.[82] In 1934 Charles de Gaulle claimed that modern war was to be regarded in the context of total national defense and the mobilization of all national resources. As the Belgian example demonstrated, preparing economic mobilization was, he noted, possible within a democratic framework.[83] None of these articles, however, was concerned with the question of the mobilization of women and the elderly. Rather, they concentrated on economic aspects that were more important to the army.

In 1936 Charles Ailleret again addressed the administrative organization of economic and industrial mobilization. Like Serrigny, he demanded that responsibilities ought to be decentralized to the greatest possible extent. Within the government itself, however, he argued that one minister be made responsible for coordinating all economic preparations for war. Like Pierre Cot, the Air Minister in the first Popular Front government, he also demanded that industrial production in France be decentralized.[84] In the middle of the 1930s, many officers became concerned that responsibility for organizing national defense was still split among three ministries; and they demanded that a Ministry of National Defense be set up.[85] The Popular Front government of Leon Blum responded to this demand, but it failed to give the new ministry power over the service ministries, which remained represented in the cabinet. The new ministry was hence little more than an agency, like the one set up in Britain at the same time, that was designed to coordinate defense.[86]

After the failure of Poincaré's organization bill, the idea of making it a legal duty for women and other civilians to be mobilized in time of war was dropped. Although not even the conservatives in the Senate thought that their wives and daughters could remain untouched by the demands of

81 Julien Brossé, "Le But des opérations de guerre," *RMF* 45 (1932): 341–61; Julien Faugeron, "La Recherche de la décision," *RMF* 43 (1932): 5–28, 169–96, 313–44.

82 Charles Menu, "Les Fabrications de guerre," *RMF* 50 (1933): 180–210.

83 DeGaulle, "Mobilisation," 62–88.

84 Charles Ailleret, "La Mobilisation industrielle," *RMF* 59 (1936): 145–206. On Cot, see Martin Alexander, *The Republic in Danger: General Maurice Gamelin and the Politics of French Defense, 1933–1940* (Cambridge, 1992).

85 Pétain, "Défense nationale et commandement unique," *RDDM*, Huitième période, 33 (1936): 5–17; Jean-Jules Mordacq, *Les Leçons de 1914 et la prochaine guerre* (Paris, 1934); Mordacq: *La Défense nationale en danger* (Paris, 1938); Eugène-Marie Debeney, "Encore l'Armée de métier," *RDDM*, Huitième Période, 28 (1935): 294–5.

86 Kiesling, *Arming Against Hitler*, 29–33.

a war, few commentators, whether politicians or military officers, judged the idea important. Such an unpleasant eventuality would best be organized when a war started and, therefore, the idea was absent in 1935 when the government of Pierre Laval introduced a new wartime organization bill.[87] After parliamentary debate, the bill was enacted in 1938, but its influence on French preparations for war was minimal. This was mainly due to the fact that the person responsible for its implementation was the prime minister, Edouard Daladier, who was also minister of national defense and minister of war. His many responsibilities left him little time to attend to this legislation.[88] Moreover, cooperation among the three service ministries, and between them and the civilian ministries, was difficult, as was demonstrated in the problems that attended the effort to set up the Collège des Hautes Études de Défense Nationale.[89]

During the Great War, the high commands of every army had welcomed new weapons, such as poison gas, the tank, and the airplane, for these promised an escape from trench warfare, which many high military officers did not consider as "real war."[90] Skepticism about the use of new weapons and technologies survived among French officers, especially in the cavalry,[91] but the great majority of these officers acknowledged that chemical warfare, tanks, airplanes, and other new weapons had become part of modern warfare. The French discussion of this topic revolved around the question of how, not whether, these new weapons and technologies should be employed in a future war.

Although the Hague Convention of 1899 had forbidden the use of weapons that dispersed toxic chemical substances, both sides had made use of such weapons during World War I.[92] After the war the French government and military leaders announced that their country would not use

87 JOC, Documents parlementaires, 1:962–9, doc. no. 5483 (June 21, 1935). For the opinion of conservative senators on the question of the mobilization of women in wartime, see Kiesling, *Arming Against Hitler*, 22.

88 Wieland, *Problematik*, 260; Kiesling, *Arming Against Hitler*, 26–38; Alexander, *Republic in Danger*, 133; Bernard Chantebout, "L'Organisation de la défense nationale en France depuis la fin de la deuxième guerre mondiale," Ph.D. diss., University of Paris, 1967, 6–11.

89 Eugenia Kiesling, "A Staff College for the Nation in Arms: The Collège des Hautes Études de Défense Nationale, 1936–1939," Ph.D. diss., Stanford University, 1988, 22–129.

90 Daniel Segesser, "World War I," in Lester Kurtz, ed., *Encyclopedia of Violence, Peace, and Conflict*, 3 vols. (San Diego, 1999), 3:845.

91 Louis-Alexandre Audibert, "Suppression de la cavalerie?" *RC*, Quatrième série, 6 (1926): 301–32; Audibert, "La Division légère," *RC*, Quatrième série, 7 (1927): 117–37, 235–55; Audibert and Eugène-Jean-Baptiste Féraud, "La Cavalerie pendant la guerre," *RC*, Quatrième série, 2 (1922): 377–96; Émile-Louis Brown de Colstoun, "Idées allemandes sur la cavalerie moderne," *RC*, Quatrième série, 4 (1924): 601–20.

92 See Olivier Lepick, *La Grande guerre chimique 1914–1918* (Paris, 1998); and John Terraine, *White Heat: The New Warfare, 1914–1918* (London, 1992), 155–61.

chemical weapons in a future war, unless it were attacked with them, in which case the French reserved the right to retaliate with such weapons.[93] For this reason, the French army continued research in this field. Raymond Grenouillet, who had worked with chemical weapons during the war and continued to do so afterward, speculated in several articles about the future use of chemical weapons. "Future war will be an unlimited war between whole nations," he argued, "and all means available will be used to secure victory; the possibility of distinguishing between permitted means and others remains in the realm of fiction."[94] The Germans' introduction of poison case on the western front in April 1915, he predicted, had been "only a modest preface compared to this new arm, which will in all probability be used in armed conflicts of the future."[95] In a future war, he continued, chemical weapons would not only be used over the front line, but, thanks to the airplane, it would see "an unlimited field of action."[96] Most French officers shared this opinion and volunteered proposals about how France could best prepare itself for gas warfare.[97]

Many officers were convinced that the tank, which had likewise emerged from the Great War, would also become a major instrument of future warfare and that its potential had not yet been fully exploited. The ideas of British officers, such as Fuller, Liddell Hart, and W. D. Croft,[98] and to a greater extent those of the father of the French tank arm, Jean-Baptiste Estienne, were taken up by several officers, among them Charles Chédeville, Joseph-Aimé Doumenc, Pol-Maurice Velpry, Darius-Paul Bloch, Marie-Camille Pigeaud, and Jean Perré. Their primary demand was that tanks be employed in masses, independently of other arms. Offensive operations by such forces, they believed, would make possible strategic penetration, hence attacks on enemy supply lines and command posts.[99] Some French

93 *Instruction*, 7. See also Major Paul Bloch, "La Guerre chimique," *RMF* 20 (1926): 96.

94 Raymond Grenouillet, "Contribution à l'étude de la protection de la population civile contre les gaz de combat," *RA* 102, no. 51 (1928): 183.

95 Grenouillet, "Naissance de l'arme chimique," *RA* 115, no. 58 (1935): 232.

96 Ibid., 265.

97 "Préparation de la guerre chimique dans differents états," *RA* 97, no. 49 (1926): 222–4; Serge de Stackelberg, *La Guerre des gaz: Comment nous defendre* (Lausanne, 1931), reviewed in *RA* 108, no. 54 (1931): lvii; Louis Izard, Jean Marie Lambert des Cilleuls, and René Kermarrec, *La Guerre aéro-chimique et les populations civiles* (Paris, 1932), reviewed in *RA* 110, no. 55 (1932): xxxiii; F. Salmon, "Protection collective: Les abris modernes," *RA* 121, no. 61 (1928): 112–39, 238–54.

98 Croft's ideas received more notice in France than in his home country.

99 Charles Chedeville, "Les Chars de combat actuels et le haut commandement," *RMF* 3 (1922): 182–95, 330–44; [Joseph-Aimé] D[oumenc], "De l'Autochenille pour la protection des transports automobiles," *RC*, Quatrième série, 5 (1925): 567–91; Joseph-Aimé Doumenc, "La Défense des frontières: Leçons des maîtres disparus," *RMF* 37 (1930): 5–28; Pol-Maurice Velpry, "L'Emploi des chars de combats dans la bataille," in *Revue d'Infanterie* (hereafter *RI*) 61 (1922): 41–55, 183–212; Darius-Paul Bloch, "L' Avenir du char de combat," *RMF* 3 (1922): 90–102; Marie-Camille Pigeaud,

commentators echoed Fuller in the belief that a future war would be fought by armored forces alone, according to laws like those of naval warfare.[100]

The high command, however, disagreed. After Estienne left the army in 1923, his followers became less influential, even though two of them, Pigeaud and Perré, retained leading positions until 1928 as successive heads of the tank department in the office of the infantry.[101] Enthusiasm for the tank arm had nonetheless received a decisive blow. Most officers began to adapt to the views of the army's leadership, which insisted that tanks be used only as auxiliaries to the infantry.[102] Few officers continued publicly to advocate the use of tanks in large, independent units. Among these, however, were Émile-Henri Gailliard, who had been the military attaché to Great Britain between 1928 and 1932; DeGaulle, who was then in the Secretariat of the Superior Council of National Defense; and Captain Louis-Joseph Sarton du Jonchay. While Gailliard and Sarton du Jonchay continued to propagate the ideas of the British champions of armor, DeGaulle was interested in alternatives to the strategy of national mobilization that the secretariat was then preparing.[103]

In the 1930s, under Weygand and Gamelin, the French military leadership did not fundamentally change its views about the use of tanks, although it did try to adapt strategy to the technical potential of tanks. Its aim was to enhance the maneuverability of the French army by setting up light mechanical divisions (DLM). Velpry, who was now Inspector General of Tanks, returned to earlier ideas and proposed establishing large tank units.[104] The Superior War Council rejected this proposal, however, as Debeney, the former chief of the general staff and right-hand man to Pétain, claimed that "the infantry will not move if they do not have the support of tanks."[105] The role of tanks in a future war was therefore primarily to support attacking infantry. Although

"L'arme de sûreté," *RMF* 7 (1923): 388–408; Jean Perré, "Les chars dans les préliminaires de la bataille offensive," *RI* 69 (1926): 176–99, 315–36.

100 Velpry, "Emploi," 212.

101 Doughty, *Seeds of Disaster*, 138–41; Segesser, "Nur keine Dummheiten." Neither Pigeaud nor Perré were officers who defended their beliefs very strongly.

102 Velpry, "Chars Blindés et Chars Cuirassées," *RMF* 12 (1924): 92–118; Velpry, "Infanterie et Chars de Combat," *RMF* 26 (1927): 305–28; Marie-Camille Pigeaud, "Le Problème du Char de Combat en 1926," *RMF* 21 (1926): 219–43; Jean Perré, "Chars et Anti-Chars," *RI* 87 (1935): 951–1014; Perré, "Le Char Moderne: Ses Possibilités et ses Servitudes: Son Emploi dans l'Attaque," *RI* 92 (1938): 620–39.

103 Émile-Henri Gailliard, "L'Armée Moderne: Le Retour à la Mobilité par les Forces Cuirassées," *Correspondant* 104, no. 329 (1932): 76–95; DeGaulle, "Vers l'Armée de Métier," *RPP* 155 (1933): 288–301; Charles de Gaulle, *Armée de Métier*, 69–76; Louis-Joseph Sarton du Jonchay, "Réflexions sur l' Emploi de la Cavalerie Blindée," *RC*, Quatrième série, 16 (1936): 345–63.

104 Doughty, *Seeds of Disaster*, 149.

105 Quoted in ibid.

some large tank units were set up before the German attack in 1940, more than two-thirds of the French tanks remained closely tied to infantry.[106]

Airplanes, too, had become a major weapon of the Great War, when they were used mainly for observation and attacks on enemy ground and air forces. Civilian targets were not a priority, and French aviators concentrated on the use of air power for tactical bombing in support of ground forces. The main consequence of using the airplane tactically was that the French air forces remained tied organizationally to the army and the navy; it did not acquire an independent command structure on the British model.[107] On becoming chief of the general staff in 1924, Debeney revoked his predecessor's order to the inspector general of the air forces, to reorganize the air forces. Reorganization would have brought air forces a degree of autonomy, although it would not have divested land commanders of the ultimate control.[108] Strategic bombing was not a serious concern for most officers of the French air forces, who were more interested in the technical details of flying and the use of air power in support of ground forces.[109] Between 1921 and 1928, only two officers published articles in the *Revue de l'Aéronautique Militaire* on the bombing of targets in the enemy's rear areas. One of these articles insisted that such operations were possible only after one's own air force had achieved superiority in the air.[110]

No one took up Douhet's ideas. Although a ministry of the air was created in 1928, nothing much changed organizationally in the discussion of French air power's role in a future war, as the ministers of war and of the navy, as well as Debeney, the chief of the general staff, insisted on retaining control over their respective air forces.[111] Only in the 1930s did the debate about reorganizing the French air force turn to Douhet's ideas on strategic air power. In 1932 the journal *Les Ailes* published substantial

106 Ibid., 177.

107 Terraine, *White Heat*, 274–5; Christian Geinitz, "The First Air War Against Noncombatants: Strategic Bombing of German Cities in World War I," in Chickering and Förster, eds., *Great War, Total War*; Robert Young, "The Strategic Air Dream: French Air Doctrine in the Inter-War Period, 1919–39," *Journal of Contemporary History* 9 (1974): 57–8.

108 Ibid., 60.

109 Marcel Jauneaud, "Servitudes téchniques de l'aviation militaire," *RMF* 8 (1923): 397–418; Pierre Boutiron, "L'Aviation navale et son rôle dans la marine de guerre," *Revue de l'Aéronautique Militaire* (hereafter *RAM*) 4 (1924): 73–80; Paul Canonne, "L'Avion d'infanterie," *RAM* 2 (1922): 25–7, 77–82; Paul Canonne, "L'Aviation et la cavalerie," *RAM* 3 (1923): 35–7; Gabriel Cochet, "À propos de l'aviation d'infanterie," *RAM* 2 (1922): 147–9; Albert Pastier, "L'Experience actuelle: Emploi de l'aviation en liason avec la cavalerie," *RAM* 8 (1928): 14–16.

110 René Keller, "L'Aviation dans la bataille," *RAM* 5 (1925): 49–55; cf. Paul Hébrard, "De l'Aviation de bombardement de nuit," *RAM* 4 (1924): 87–90.

111 Marcellin Hodeir, "La Création du Ministère de l'Air vue par la presse parisienne (Septembre, Octobre, Novembre 1928)," *RHA* 172 (1988): 97–8.

portions of Douhet's book in French for the first time.[112] Shortly afterward, an anonymous officer commented on Douhet's ideas in the Air Ministry's *Revue des Forces Aériennes*. He disagreed with Douhet's views on the priority of strategic bombers, arguing that fighters would play an important role in a future air war. At the same time, he agreed with Douhet that the air force should not be limited to supporting land forces and the navy.[113]

In the French debate on Douhet's ideas, the officer corps split into three groups. The first, the *douhétistes*, were practically in full agreement with Douhet; the second, the *douhétiens*, wished to use the Italian's ideas as the basis for reorganizing the French air force, but did not accept the entirety of his ideas, while a third group rejected Douhet's ideas outright. Major protagonists of the first group were the two air ministers, Pierre Cot and Victor Denain, and Jean-Henri Jauneaud, whom the historian Martin Alexander has called the "high priest of the strategic aviation."[114] The second group comprised Pétain, who had become inspector general of air defense in 1931, his collaborator Paul Vauthier, Émile Mayer, and Jean-Marie Bourget. Many officers in the army and navy naturally opposed Douhet's ideas. Among them were Gamelin and Weygand and Durand Viel from the navy, but this group also included army and naval officers, such as Pierre Guillemeney and Camille Rougeron, who were themselves involved in the development of air power.[115]

Neither Cot nor his successor, Denain, nor their close adviser, Jauneaud, thought it necessary to clarify their ideas in public. They believed that the ideas of Douhet spoke for themselves. Mayer, Bourget, and Vauthier, with the support of Pétain, agreed that Douhet was wrong to claim that a future war would be won in the air alone. They were convinced, nevertheless, that bombers would play an important if not a decisive role in a future war, because the air force was the only service that could fight over land and water simultaneously.[116] Guillemeney and Rougeron argued that it was necessary

112 Albert A. Stahel, *Luftverteidigung – Strategie und Wirklichkeit* (Zurich, 1993), 27–36; Philippe Masson, "De Douhet et quelques marins," *RHA* 172 (1988): 11–13.

113 "Une Analyse des théories du général Douhet," *Revue des Forces Aériennes* (hereafter *RFA*) 4, no. 2 (1932): 1057–63.

114 Alexander, *Republic in Danger*, 153.

115 Thierry Vivier, "Le Douhétisme français entre tradition et innovation (1933–1939)," *RHA* 184 (1991): 89–99; Patrick Facon, "Douhet et sa doctrine à travers la litterature militaire de l'entre-deux-guerres: Une Étude de perception," *RHA* 170 (1988): 94–103; Gaspar de Cugnac, "La Guerre aérienne," *Correspondant* 104, no. 328 (1932): 513–24; Émile Mayer, "Le Général Douhet et l'arme d'espace,'" *RPP* 164 (1935): 295–309; Jean-Marie Bouget, "L'Aviation dans la défense nationale," *RP* 39 (1932): 379–98.

116 Bourget, "Aviation," 381, 393–8; Mayer, "Général Douhet," 301–2; Paul Vauthier, "Principes de la doctrine de Douhet," all in *RAA* 7, no. 1 (1935): 363–82; Vauthier, *La Doctrine du général Douhet* (Paris, 1935). Pétain wrote the preface to this volume.

to have airplanes over the battlefield, because control of the air was central to the success of ground operations. Rougeron warned furthermore that "a doctrine of bomber aviation which closes its eyes to evidence [of the power of air-defenses] and relies on the mysterious virtue of the offensive to protect its bombers, represents the worst sort of irresponsibility."[117] The debate on Douhet's ideas continued until 1938, and although the *douhétistes* were in control of the air ministry, they could not carry the day. By the time the French government realized that its air force was no match for the Luftwaffe, it was too late.[118]

The commanders of French army, navy, and air forces did pay attention to technical developments, but they tended to adapt technologies to preconceived views on future war. Moreover, their ideas about using poison gas, tanks, and airplanes resulted from compromises within the military leadership and between it and the government. The French high command was open to the use of all these new weapons, even if they were forbidden by international law, should an enemy use them against France. It was thus clear that should a war occur, French military leaders would do everything to mobilize the nation's resources and use every weapon in their arsenal. To this extent, the French military authorities were prepared to wage total war should they be forced to do so.

When World War II began in 1939, things boded well for the French. The fact that war began in the east gave the country time to prepare for military operations. In May 1940 the French armed forces were ready to fight the long and bloody war that they had always thought would eventuate. Everything possible had been done to minimize losses. The Maginot Line stood ready, and the French army had prepared an advance into Belgium to stop the enemy from entering French territory. Furthermore, all potential enemies had been warned that France would not shrink from using new weapons.

Nevertheless, the German Wehrmacht overran the Netherlands and Belgium and occupied large parts of French territory in less than six weeks. Politicians of the time and later historians have offered many persuasive explanations for the French defeat.[119] One important reason has nonetheless often been underplayed. The French leadership planned for a future war exclusively in the name of national defense. Waging offensive war for

117 Camille Rougeron, "L'Éfficacité du bombardement aérien," *RAA* 6 (1924): 1243. See also Pierre Guillemeney, "Le Bombardements aériens des installations industrielles: Le Blocus du bassin de Briey," *RFA* 2, no. 2 (1930): 1151–90.

118 Young, "Strategic Air Dream," 72–6; Alexander, *Republic in Danger*, 142–71.

119 See Segesser, "Nur keine Dummheiten."

limited objectives had become almost impossible.[120] This attitude was due to the experience of the Great War, in which many of the French military leaders of 1940 had themselves participated. Even though they did not use the term, they had in this sense already experienced something resembling total war, and they could conceive of war in no other terms. Their aim in a future war was therefore to improve performance in this kind of war.

The debate on how this aim could be achieved was lively, and it produced a variety of views. Most officers – and their chiefs – were convinced that a future war would be long and comprehensive. Pétain, Weygand, and especially Gamelin tried to make their convictions clear to the government, and they signaled that they were ready to wage total war, should the country be forced or the government be willing to do so.[121] The politicians and most of French society were willing to see the military threaten potential enemies with total war. Waging total war again was another matter. Such a scenario, a repetition of war on a scale larger than World War I, was more than what the French political system and French society were willing to accept.

Although the French and British officer corps did not fully agree about the lessons of the Great War, the shadow of this conflict – and, in the case of the British, of earlier conflicts – figured centrally in the reorganization of the armed forces in both countries after 1918. Most officers in both agreed that the development of warfare since the Napoleonic Wars, and particularly the lessons of the Great War, had made necessary the complete mobilization of national resources and the conduct of warfare free of all unnecessary restrictions. Thus, in embracing total mobilization and a vision of unrestricted warfare, these officers foretold a European war that resembled in fundamental ways the "model" of total war.

120 See Debeney, "Encore l'armée de métier," 292–5; Bourret to Daladier, July 21, 1936, *Documents Diplomatiques Français, 1932–1939*, 2d ser. (1936–9) (Paris, 1966), 3:19–23.

121 Gamelin, *Servir*, 3 vols. (Paris, 1946–47), 2:204–12. See Kiesling, "Staff College," 228–46.

11

Yesterday's Battles and Future War

The German Official Military History, 1918–1939

MARKUS PÖHLMANN

At the end of July 1943, at about the time that the strategic air war against Germany reached a new peak with the raids on Hamburg, Alfred von Wegerer, a member of the army's Military History Research Institute (Kriegsgeschichtliche Forschungsanstalt des Heeres), which had been given the responsibility to complete the German official military history of World War I, looked back on more than twenty years of work:

> It seems necessary to me that we break with the old tradition of military history. . . . Instead of separate accounts of the history of operations and politics, we must – in the interest of a better understanding of the totality [*Totalität*] of war and its universal-historical consequences – find a way to comprehend the totality [*Ganzheit*] of war, in all its military and political aspects, as Clausewitz described it. In this way, we should reach a deeper understanding of the interrelationship and complementarity of politics and the conduct of war.[1]

At the same time, however, his colleague Friedrich Solger complained about the same official history's want of practical applicability. "Having seen how fourteen bulky volumes on the First World War have served inadequately to prepare for the Second," he wrote, "we must conclude that the approach was wrong."[2]

Both testimonies spoke to the skepticism with which the authors of the official history viewed their own work during its final days. Today, the term "official history" often provokes an acute intellectual reaction among scholars. Probably no genre of history has existed in such an uneasy triangular relationship as this one, which must negotiate among academic scholarship, politics, and the defense community. Keith Wilson defined the key aspect of this relationship when he noted that "governments and their officials fear

1 Bundesarchiv-Militärarchiv, Freiburg im Breisgau (hereafter BA-MA), W-10/50075, Report von Wegerer, July 31, 1943.
2 Ibid., Report Solger, Aug. 1, 1943.

historians."[3] Hans von Seeckt, the omnipotent head of the German army command between 1920 and 1926, would have agreed. In his understanding, "private authors" of military history "work materially for themselves and only rarely in the interest of the state, often against it."[4] Some of the difficulties that government officials face can be addressed if they employ academic historians, or if the authors of the histories are themselves officials, who – as in the case of military history – literally write their own history.[5]

This chapter deals with the German official military history of World War I, which was contained principally in the series *Der Weltkrieg 1914–1918* (generally known as the *Weltkriegswerk*) and the equivalent series on the war at sea, which was entitled *Der Krieg zur See*.[6] An attempt will be made here to analyze this history within the framework of perceptions and interpretations of total war. Germany's military historiography represented no special case, but two problems make an examination of it particularly interesting. The first is the fact that Germany lost the war; and a lost war posed distinct military questions, whatever the significance of the economic, social, or political advantages that the Allied powers enjoyed. The second problem is that Germany has conventionally been associated with the subsequent development of total war, both in theory and practice.

Two dimensions, one temporal, the other spatial, defined the picture that military planners painted of a future war. On the one hand, they had to reflect on their experience in the last war that they had fought. On the other hand, they were eager to obtain access to a "view across the fence"; they could observe contemporary military developments in other countries. A number of Anglo-American authors have attested to the Reichswehr's high capacity for military innovation, and it will be necessary to inquire as well whether military history played a role in this process.[7]

3 Keith Wilson, "Introduction: Governments, Historians, and 'Historical Engineering,'" in Keith Wilson, ed., *Forging the Collective Memory: Governments and International Historians through Two World Wars* (Providence, R.I., 1996), 2.

4 Bundesarchiv Berlin (hereafter BA-B), R 15.06, Nr. 41, Oberquartiermeisterstelle für Kriegsgeschichte, Denkschrift über die Zukunft der Archive und Kriegsgeschichtlichen Abteilungen des Grossen Generalstabes, Oct. 12, 1919.

5 For an introduction into (official) military history, see the anthologies by Ursula von Gersdorff, ed., *Geschichte und Militärgeschichte: Wege der Forschung* (Frankfurt am Main, 1974); Russell F. Weigley, ed., *New Dimensions in Military History: An Anthology* (San Rafael, Calif., 1975); and Robin Higham, ed., *Official Histories: Essays and Bibliographies from around the World* (Manhattan, Kans., 1970).

6 Reichsarchiv et al., eds., *Der Weltkrieg 1914–1918*, 14 vols., 2 supplementary vols. (Berlin, 1925–1956) (hereafter WKW); Marine-Archiv et al., eds., *Der Krieg zur See 1914–1918*, 22 vols. (Berlin, 1920–1966).

7 For example, James S. Corum, *The Roots of Blitzkrieg: Hans von Seeckt and German Military Reform* (Lawrence, Kans., 1992); Williamson Murray and Allan R. Millett, *Military Innovation in the Interwar Period* (Cambridge, 1996); cf. Wilhelm Deist, "Die Reichswehr und der Krieg der Zukunft," *Militärgeschichtliche Mitteilungen* 45 (1989): 81–92.

During the first postwar decade, Europeans faced a virtual war of historiographies, in both the academic world and the popular media. The war-guilt question lay at the core of a great process of "historical engineering" in the national interest, in which military history played a crucial role.[8] Nearly every participant in the war undertook an official history, even those that, like Switzerland, had not been belligerents. In the race to publish these accounts, the French *Les armées françaises dans la grande guerre* and the *British History of the Great War* secured the pole positions in the early 1920s. They were quickly joined by the German and the Austrian entries. Nothing revealed the competitive character of the whole enterprise more clearly than the first page of the French publication. Here the authors recalled the Franco-Prussian War, warning their compatriots of the enduring detrimental influence exercised by the German official history of the war of 1870–1. This document had, the authors noted, portrayed

> the Prussian command and the German forces invading France, crushing her armies, thereby following a mechanical process like clockwork. The Prussian general staff took – so to speak – the historical offensive in order to establish and send out into the world a legend, which was consecrated to the glorification of the German armies. Because of its early date of publication . . . this work became very influential and beneficial to the reputation of Germany all over the world.[9]

According to the French general-staff officers, this spectacle was not to be repeated. On the German side as well, however, work on an official history started immediately after the armistice. During the following years the Reichsarchiv (Imperial Archive) monitored the progress of its counterparts in Britain and France. In his annual report to the institution's advisory board in 1928, the president of the Reichsarchiv announced that the archive had finally managed to "overtake" the official histories of Germany's former enemies.[10]

The history of the German official history must be seen finally in the turbulent social and political context of Weimar Germany. The debates over the "stab-in-the-back" and the reception of books like Erich Maria Remarque's *All Quiet on the Western Front* were parts of a long struggle, in which the opinion-leadership of the conservative parties and interest groups was challenged – and with it their custodianship over the memory of the "true" war.

8 Wilson, "Introduction," 2.

9 Ministère de la guerre, ed., *Les armées françaises dans la grande guerre: Tome premier: La guerre du mouvement (Opérations autérieures au 14. novembre 1914): Premier volumes: Les préliminaires – La bataille des frontières* (Paris, 1922), i.

10 BA-B, R 15.06, Nr. 352, Tätigkeitsbericht des Reichsarchivs 1927–8.

THE REICHSARCHIV AND THE OFFICIAL HISTORY OF WORLD WAR I

Military history had been an integral part of the work of the Prussian general staff since 1816; and it had taken on increasing importance after German unification in 1871.[11] The military monopolized the field of military history to the near-exclusion of academic historians. Its basic functions were geared to the professional demands of the army. General education remained a peripheral consideration, as military history turned after 1871 into a propaganda tool on behalf of a nation "created by the sword." In addition, military history was an instrument of officer-training. It was designed to provide instruction in the universal laws of war, to serve as an auxiliary to courses on tactics that were taught at the War Academy. Jay Luvaas has aptly characterized this utilitarian approach to military history. "Knowing already what they want to find," he writes of the soldiers, "they tailor the facts of history to fit their preconceived notions. This is not necessarily wrong, nor does this method lead necessarily to false views. But it is not history."[12]

At the end of the century, however, the military's monopoly of military history faced a significant challenge. It came primarily in the work of the contentious Berlin historian, Hans Delbrück, who took on the historians in the general staff in a debate over the strategy of Prussian King Friedrich II during the Seven-Years' War (1756–63). Delbrück then became the soldiers' most dreaded academic antagonist for the next forty years.[13]

World War I emphasized the challenge to the monopoly.[14] As long as the war continued, military history deferred to immediate necessities, as officer-historians experienced the grim face of modern combat themselves. The Franconian major Mertz von Quirnheim, who became the first president of the Reichsarchiv, confided to his personal war diary in October

11 Modern German scholarship recognizes at least three equivalents of the term "military history." *Kriegsgeschichte* (the history of war) implies traditional "drum-and-bugle" historiography. *Wehrgeschichte* (defense history) was a child of National Socialist rule and implies a strictly utilitarian approach. To mark out the historical subdiscipline today, the term *Militärgeschichte* (military history) is common. See Rainer Wohlfeil, "Wehr-, Kriegs- oder Militärgeschichte?" in Gersdorff, *Geschichte*, 165–75; Hans Umbreit, "The Development of Official Military Historiography in the German Army from the Crimean War to 1945," in Higham, *Official Histories*, 160–209; Martin Raschke, *Der politisierende Generalstab: Die friderizianischen Kriege in der amtlichen deutschen Militärgeschichtsschreibung 1890–1914* (Freiburg im Breisgau, 1993); and Reinhard Brühl, *Militärgeschichte und Kriegspolitik: Zur Militärgeschichtsschreibung des preussisch-deutschen Generalstabes 1816–1945* (Berlin, 1973).

12 Jay Luvaas, "Military History: An Academic Historian's Point of View," in Weigley, *New Dimensions*, 34.

13 See Arden Bucholz, *Hans Delbrück and the German Military Establishment: War Images in Conflict* (Iowa City, 1985); and Sven Lange, *Hans Delbrück und der "Strategiestreit": Kriegführung und Kriegsgeschichte in der Kontroverse 1879–1914* (Freiburg im Breisgau, 1995).

14 The military history section of the general staff was disbanded at mobilization in August 1914. Its last head, Colonel General Hermann von Kuhl, became chief of staff of the First Army and soon found himself on one of the most controversial battlegrounds, the Marne.

1914 that "the French losses are colossal, especially the proportion of those killed. Their night attacks cost them masses of deaths. Perhaps the war will end only because all the belligerents are exhausted."[15] Even quartermaster general Baron von Freytag-Loringhoven, who was the doyen of Prussian military historians, railed privately about the "streams of German blood" that were wasted in the autumn battles of 1914 by the German high command "in an irresponsible manner."[16] Attempts by the intelligence and propaganda section (IIIb) of the general staff to instrumentalize history for the army's purposes proved disappointing. The disjuncture between the nature of official history and the totalizing nature of this war became increasingly apparent. In 1916 the flamboyant chief of military propaganda in foreign countries, Major Hans von Haeften, criticized the general staff's unfinished history of the wars of Friedrich II as "useless both historically and for the army's military education." Three years later, he wrote of the "historical inadequacy of all the general staff's publications."[17]

Under the impact of defeat, the self-criticism broke loose. In a confidential memorandum, the interim head of the reorganized military-history section denounced the army's propaganda during the war:

> It must be admitted that we have become dishonest to ourselves, that we have in a way played theater and have believed it, at least in part, ourselves. In this system of self-deception, our great tragic guilt can be found. The system of concealment resulted in great disappointment. This tragedy . . . must be told. The whole enterprise has to be a kind of general confession.[18]

More candid criticism of the army was now, he continued, to inform official publications:

> Writing in this manner, it will be unavoidable that we touch on personal affairs. We do not have to engage in wild criticism; the manner of presentation itself will often leave the reader with an opportunity to reach a final judgement. But whenever, after careful verification in the documents, it becomes necessary, we must not be afraid to make judgments and, if it is unavoidable, even condemnations.[19]

15 BA-B, 90 Me 6, Nachlass Hermann Ritter Mertz von Quirnheim, no. 16, war diary, Oct. 7, 1914 (copy).

16 Freytag-Loringhoven to Wild von Hohenborn, June 8, 1915, Adolf Wild von Hohenborn, *Briefe und Tagebuchaufzeichnungen des preussischen Generals als Kriegsminister und Truppenführer im Ersten Weltkrieg*, ed. Helmut Reichold (Boppard am Rhein, 1986), 68.

17 BA-MA, R61/110, Militärische Stelle des Auswärtigen Amtes (von Haeften), memorandum to Chef des Generalstabes des Feldheeres, Dec. 19, 1916; BA-MA, PH 3/993, Oberquartiermeisterstelle für Kriegsgeschichte (von Haeften), memorandum to Chef des Generalstabes der Armee, Feb. 11, 1919.

18 BA-MA, RH 61/110, Chef der Kriegsgeschichtlichen Abteilung I (Colonel von Sydow), circular, Mar. 19, 1919.

19 Ibid.

Official historians were consequently to abandon their aseptic, uncritical style, which had long been guided by the elder Moltke's insistence on "protecting the prestige" of the military leadership.

This document typified sentiments during the remarkable winter of discontent and self-criticism in 1918–19, but they met an early end. In the spring of 1919, following the motto "attack is the best defense," a hitherto unknown captain by the name of George Soldan, who had been transferred to the military-history section, stressed in a memorandum the significance of official history in an era of political turmoil and widespread pacifism:

> The time will come when the memories of this great experience [of the war] will rise again of themselves. Affectionately and proudly, glances will rest on the Iron Cross, as memories of the beauty and sublimity of war return. These are as much a part of war as are the seamy sides, which vanish more quickly [from memory]. The Germans' propensity for club-life will flourish again, and all kinds of veterans' organizations will march towards a new, bright future.[20]

Soldan warned against the "concentrated pressure of the enemy's historiography."[21] Only a popular (*volkstümliche*), patriotic, and propaganda-oriented history of the war would do. The "stirrings of the people's soul" have to sound, he wrote, then "its inner being will open up and be accessible to influence." Soldan's proposal reached a cynical high point when he described the design of book-covers: "The title of a popular book must promise something, and it must attract the buyer. Hardly a man who has fought, bled, or even been crippled at the Somme will pass by an account of this battle without taking it home."[22] Soldan's candor in demanding a manipulative official history surprised some of his colleagues, but he soon found himself at the head of a newly established section for popular history.

During the Versailles negotiations, it became clear that the Allies would not tolerate the continued existence of a German general staff, which they regarded as the bulwark of German militarism. As a result, the German army command came under immense pressure to turn its more dispensable sections, such as those on railroads, topography, and history, into civilian institutions, in order to keep their personnel in government service. On October 1, 1919, the military history section, with more than one hundred

20 BA-B, R15.06, Nr. 41, George Soldan, Die deutsche Geschichtsschreibung des Weltkrieges: Eine nationale Aufgabe (1919). Parts of this manuscript are reprinted in Bernd Ulrich und Benjamin Ziemann, eds., *Krieg im Frieden: Die umkämpfte Erinnerung an den Ersten Weltkrieg: Quellen und Dokumente* (Frankfurt am Main, 1997), 65–8.

21 BA-B, R 15.06, Nr. 41, Soldan, Geschichtsschreibung.

22 Ibid.

now-retired officers, was transferred to the newly established Reichsarchiv in Potsdam. From the beginning, the new institution fulfilled a hybrid function, as both an archive and research institute, that reflected the political circumstances in which it was founded. While it became the first German national archive, with an initial emphasis on military and demobilization records, it inherited the general staff's assignment to write the official history of the world war. Major General Hermann Ritter Mertz von Quirnheim became president of the Reichsarchiv; the Kriegsgeschichtliche Abteilung, which was responsible for the official history, was headed by retired Major General von Haeften.[23]

The Reichsarchiv fell under the Ministry of the Interior, so it appeared that official military history had come for the first time under democratic, civilian control. An advisory board, composed of prominent soldiers, historians, and politicians, was installed. Nevertheless, the government failed to support the academic historians against the former soldiers in Haeften's section. Between 1920 and 1924, conflicts raged among these factions over the general concept of the official history; and they resulted in the victory of the conservative group around Haeften who had ties to the army.[24] The Reichsarchiv's official history was henceforth established as an anonymous, official, multi-volume publication, which excluded the political and social history of the war and instead emphasized events of a "strictly military" character. By the late 1920s, the advisory board had ceased to be a factor.[25]

With the rearmament of the Wehrmacht after 1933, the military laid claim to its old monopoly, and it engineered the emancipation of the research section, as the *Kriegsgeschichtliche Forschungsanstalt des Heeres*. All the Prussian-German military record groups in the Reichsarchiv were relocated into the new Army Archive (Heeresarchiv), where the bulk of them were destroyed in a RAF air raid on Potsdam in April 1945. Even as World War II ended, however, work on the official history of World War I continued.

23 See Matthias Herrmann, "Das Reichsarchiv (1919–1945): Eine archivalische Institution im Spannungsfeld der deutschen Politik," 2 vols., Ph.D. diss., Humboldt University of Berlin, 1994; Markus Pöhlmann, "Kriegsgeschichte und Geschichtspolitik: Die amtliche deutsche Militärgeschichtsschreibung über den Ersten Weltkrieg 1914–1956," Ph.D. diss., University of Bern, 2000.

24 After 1923 the *Reichswehr* began to press the Minister of the Interior in order to capture responsibility for the official military history. In its own efforts to monopolize jurisdiction over matters that pertained to the war-guilt question, the Foreign Office had already undermined a plan to incorporate the diplomatic and political history of the war into the *Weltkriegswerk*.

25 Prominent members of this *Historische Kommission für das Reichsarchiv* were the academic historians Hans Delbrück, Friedrich Meinecke, and Hans Rothfels, and the ex-generals Baron von Freytag-Loringhoven and Hermann von Kuhl.

GLIMPSES OF TOTAL WAR IN THE OFFICIAL HISTORY

It is easy to criticize the work of the *Reichsarchiv* for a narrow emphasis on operational history and a neglect of the totalization of war between 1914 and 1919. Some of this criticism has been ideologically motivated or has failed to examine the content of the official history. Criticism that dwells on the *Weltkriegswerk* alone invites a warped judgment. The complete media arsenal of the official military history should be analyzed instead. The thirty-six volumes of the popular series, *Schlachten des Weltkrieges*, were as much a part of this arsenal as were the nine volumes of *Darstellungen aus den Nachkriegskämpfen deutscher Truppen und Freikorps* and the roughly 1,000 regimental histories, most of which were private works published under Potsdam's editorial umbrella. A more comprehensive analysis must attend as well to the special reports of the official historians who worked in connection with the parliamentary committee of inquiry or the notorious "stab-in-the-back-trial" in Munich 1925.[26] It must also include the editorial work and articles of military historians in political as well as military journals, the private publications of these historians, the collection and publication of the records of the wartime office for photography and film (Bild- und Film-Amt), and finally the scripts for at least two major UFA movies.

The deficiencies of the *Weltkriegswerk* were obvious. The chronological framework of the series was unbalanced. Of the fourteen volumes, six dealt with the year 1914 alone, fewer than two with 1918. Much as the officer corps had despised trench warfare, the authors of the official history disliked the narrative of this kind of combat with its "fabulous monotony."[27] The dull statistics of industrialized war could not match the drama of open battle. The political history was fragmentary and – especially in the volumes prepared after 1935 – distorted. The account of the prewar arms race ended abruptly: "And then war came." The last volume concluded with a bizarre rendition of the "stab-in-the-back" legend that jars with its content.[28] The detailed history of armaments and economic preparations for war ended in August 1914. A history of German society at war was absent.

26 For the work of the Parlamentarische Untersuchungsausschuss, see Holger H. Herwig, "Clio Deceived: Patriotic Self-Censorship in Germany After the Great War," in Wilson, ed., *Forging the Collective Memory*, 87–127.

27 BA-MA, MSg 131/7, Mertz von Quirnheim, Comments on the Annual Meeting of the Advisory Board, Oct. 28, 1926; Martin Reymann, Die Entstehung des Reichsarchivs und die Bearbeitung des amtlichen Weltkriegswerkes 1914–1918 durch diese (unpublished manuscript, 1943). Another leading historian complained of the "dull humdrum" of trench warfare: Theobald von Schäfer, "Österreich-Ungarns letzter Krieg 1914–1918: V. Band," *Wissen und Wehr* 17 (1936): 409.

28 WKW 1, 1:15; WKW 14:768.

Nevertheless, closer scrutiny of the series reveals the authors' awareness of the structural elements of total war. First of all, the *Weltkriegswerk* recognized the expansion of the war into a global conflict. It treated every theater of operations in which German forces fought. The fact that the history focused on land war and neglected the war at sea was due to the fact that the volume on this other phase was produced by a separate institution. In this respect, the enduring divisions among the branches of the German armed forces were reflected in their historiographies.[29]

The *Weltkriegswerk* was also sensitive to the significance of technology and the industrialization of war. In particular, the descriptions of the early operations in the west – the still-mobile warfare of 1914 in Lorraine, on the Marne, and in Flanders – made clear the consequences of losing control over modern mass armies. The central dilemmas of military leadership were personalized and psychologized, as the official history launched into withering critiques of Moltke and Falkenhayn as commanders.[30] The rapid evolution of technology, the importance of the Germans' underestimating the airplane and tank, were topics as well. The official history emphasized the military and political impact of U-boat warfare, although it dealt delicately with the High Sea Fleet's peripheral role in the conflict. The military and psychological transformation of the individual soldier was traced in the *Schlachten des Weltkrieges*, which focused on small-unit operations. At least in their design, these accounts attempted to document the same heroic myth of the *Frontkämpfer* that nationalist authors popularized during the Weimar era.[31] The new, total character of the war was apparent in the analysis of the Royal Navy's blockade, which the official history portrayed as one of the decisive causes of the German defeat, while the *Marinewerk*'s critical interpretation of the U-boat campaign resulted in a controversy over naval strategy that lasted for years.[32]

Guerilla warfare, counterinsurgency actions in urban theaters, ethnic struggles, and low-intensity conflicts became topics of a separate series that was devoted to postwar operations in Russia, the Ukraine, Poland, the Baltic States, Austria, and revolutionary Germany itself.[33] The official history of

29 The chapters on naval warfare in *Der Weltkrieg 1914 bis 1918* were contributed by the Naval Archive.

30 Moltke was accused of a practical "self-elimination" of the army high command in September 1914 and a general lack of "strength of character" (WKW 4:519, 533–43). The criticism of Falkenhayn focused on his "indecisive conduct of the operations" (WKW 6:405, 438–9).

31 Reichsarchiv, ed., *Schlachten des Weltkrieges*, 36 vols. (Oldenburg, 1921–30).

32 See Arno Spindler, "Der Meinungsstreit in der Marine über den U-Bootkrieg 1914–1918," *Marine Rundschau* 55 (1958): 235–45.

33 See Forschungsanstalt für Kriegs- und Heeresgeschichte et al., eds., *Darstellungen aus den Nachkriegskämpfen deutscher Truppen und Freikorps*, 9 vols. (Berlin, 1936–43).

these wars is often forgotten. The Reichswehr initiated it in the spring of 1934. Not only its title, *Darstellungen aus den Nachkriegskämpfen deutscher Truppen und Freikorps*, was evidently a gesture to Germany's new rulers. The series made clear that World War I had lasted well beyond November 1918. After 1916 the war gradually lost its character as a single enormous industrial struggle among nation-states. Instead, it began to fragment into myriads of new conflicts, which had strong ethnic and ideological components. At most, the armistice brought a shift in the theaters of war. The last year of the world war, which thus might be defined as 1918–19, witnessed the rise of ideological conflicts and a war for "space," a new kind of warfare that was cast more in ethnic and economic than in operational or military categories. The official history anticipated things to come. In the nine volumes that were devoted to the *Nachkriegskämpfe*, the official historians abandoned the rhetorical and judgmental reserve that had characterized the general staff's earlier histories. Instead, the accounts took on the quality of an anti-Marxist and racist polemic, which ignored the international rules of war. The concept of a "strictly military" general-staff history led here ad absurdum, to descriptions of bloody counterrevolution in Bavaria and the Ruhr area, ethnic battles along the frontiers in Slovenia, and archaic modes of conflict in the Baltic.

In several cases, however, the tendency toward disregarding international law and the rules of warfare could be seen in earlier volumes. Because they had to do with the war-guilt question, questions of international law belonged in the Foreign Office's area of responsibility, and Potsdam's assignment lay only in collecting exonerating documents for use by the diplomats. Even given these limitations, the official history contained some surprises. On the subject of Belgian neutrality, the first volume proffered questionable justifications of the German violation in 1914, citing military necessities – such as the siege of Liège – or the demands of a preemptive strategy. It invoked the apologia of the subsequent president of the *Forschungsanstalt*, Wolfgang Foerster, who repeatedly justified the invasion of Belgium in social Darwinist terms, as a "life-and-death struggle."[34]

The difficulties of presenting a "non-political" military history were evident as well in the account of Belgian *franc-tireurs* in August 1914. Because of its sensitive political implications, this problem was not treated as a separate topic, nor did it appear in the volume's table of contents or the editor's introduction. The text itself, however, addressed more than a dozen incidents

34 See WKW 1:53–4; and Wolfgang Foerster, "Graf Schlieffen und der Weltkrieg," *Wissen und Wehr* 14 (1933): 63–70.

in which German troops reported fighting Belgian irregulars. The account contained nearly all the contemporary stereotypes that were generated in the polemic over the *franc-tireurs* – that they were snipers in civilian clothing, who engaged in ambushes, recruited women, and committed atrocities against German prisoners.[35] The research group on the *franc-tireur* war, whose work was secretly financed by the Foreign Office and the Ministry of Defense, thus engaged in a classic example of "historical engineering." The group was led by Robert Paul Osswald, who became the leading figure in the German propaganda war against Belgium during the interwar period.[36]

Another striking example of total war's erosion of legal and moral standards appeared in the account of the Germans' strategic retreat to the Siegfried Line in February and March 1917. In its systematic destruction of the Somme region and the deportation of some 120,000 inhabitants, the operation, which was code-named "Alberich," offered a chilling anticipation of scorched-earth strategies to come later. The account in the German official history focused on the army's technical and organizational skills and its success in achieving strategic surprise. The high command's initial "most serious concerns" about the operation received passing mention, but they retreated into the argument that the enemy's artillery had already destroyed the region. The fact that at least two generals, Crown Prince Rupprecht of Bavaria and Max von Gallwitz, protested against the action for moral reasons, was not mentioned.[37]

The most important feature of total war was the mobilization of society, and the official history could not ignore the decisive role of finance and the economy. The narrow conception of the *Weltkriegswerk* thus required the preparation of several supplementary volumes (*Sonderbände*). The first was published in 1930 and had a lasting impact.[38] Its main thesis was that Germany's armaments had seriously fallen behind its enemies' before 1914 and therefore that the country's leadership had no interest in war in the

35 See WKW 1:110–4, 223, 357–80, 382; ibid., 3:328, 331.

36 See Robert-Paul Osswald, *Der Streit um den belgischen Franktireurkrieg: Eine kritische Untersuchung der Ereignisse in den Augusttagen 1914 und der darüber bis 1930 erschienenen Literatur unter Benutzung bisher nicht veröffentlichten Materials* (Cologne, 1931); cf. John Horne and Alan Kramer, "War Between Soldiers and Enemy Civilians, 1914–1915," in Roger Chickering and Stig Förster, eds., *Great War, Total War: Combat and Mobilization on the Western Front, 1914–1918* (New York, 2000), 153–68.

37 WKW 12:119–46; cf. Jakob Jung, *Max von Gallwitz (1852–1937): General und Politiker* (Osnabrück, 1995), 76, who quotes from Gallwitz's diary entry of Oct. 16, 1916: "What limits to barbarism still exist, what respect for international law and humanity? Have not the Russians done the same in East Prussia, perhaps in Northern Poland – and what wave of disdain has come over them! To become a new Melac – I will not participate in this, I would rather quit" (In fact, Gallwitz did not quit when his protest was rejected).

38 Reichsarchiv, ed., *Kriegsrüstung und Kriegswirtschaft: Die militärische, wirtschaftliche und finanzielle Rüstung Deutschlands von der Reichsgründung bis zum Ausbruch des Weltkriegs*, 2 vols. (Berlin, 1930).

summer of that year. The relevance of this argument to the war-guilt question was transparent; but the destruction of the archives in 1945 has made the volume long a standard sourcebook on German prewar armaments. The publication of a second volume, on armaments and the economy between 1914 and 1918, was prevented by the outbreak of World War II. Whenever politics was discussed, the official historians tended to be critical of Germany's civilian leadership. The historians accepted the arguments of the high command and condemned the alleged inability of Bethmann Hollweg and the Reichstag majority to understand the requirements of "total war" – a term that appeared in the official history for the first time only in 1943.[39]

The supplements were part of a larger story. The head office of the Reichsarchiv was unhappy that the exertions of the home front had not received more attention in the main body of the work. In the late 1920s, Haeften, who was now president of the archive, adopted the advisory board's proposal and installed a research group that was staffed by civilian historians. It was instructed to prepare a broad "cultural history" of the war. A synopsis was developed and the first topics were distributed. The whole enterprise then perished in the political changes of 1933, as Haeften was discharged. Nevertheless, the plans for additional supplementary volumes signaled an important attempt to broaden the self-imposed limitations that had originally informed the official history.[40]

SECRET MILITARY STUDIES: THE BORRIES GROUP

Evaluating the technological, tactical, and operational lessons of wars had been the primary role of the general staff's historiography. After the institutional ruptures at the end of World War I, it seemed as if the role had come to an end. For obvious political reasons, Seeckt himself sought to bar the Reichsarchiv from this assignment in his memorandum of 1919. But in 1924 cooperation between the official historians and the Ministry of Defense was secretly reinstated. Under the command of retired major general Rudolf von Borries, a team of a half-dozen ex-officers was charged with a range of tasks formerly performed by general-staff historians. Borries's team was to provide military studies as requested by the training section of the army office (Truppenamt, Abt. T 4), to support covert courses for staff-officers by furnishing lecturers and teaching-materials on military history, and to handle ad hoc requests from military agencies for information.

39 WKW 13:339.

40 Reymann, *Entstehung*, 325–31.

This cooperation violated the Reichsarchiv's official mission, but it took place with the silent acquiescence of the government. In a sense, the archive thus became part of the Schwarze Reichswehr. The volume of requests from the military grew so much that it interfered with work on the official history. Between May 1930 and February 1932 alone, the Borries group undertook eighty-two studies.[41] These covered a wide range of technical and tactical topics, such as "Indirect Fire with Heavy Machine Guns," "Motorized Troop-Transport," "Fighting Serbian Gangs North of Ueskueb in the Summer of 1917," "Tactical Lessons of the Tank Battle at Villers-Bretonneux," and "Effects of Gas Attacks against American Divisions in 1918." They also included economic subjects, like "Measures of Economic Mobilization" and "The Question of the German Workforce during the World War from an Economic Point of View," and political or historical topics such as "Are there Examples in History of a State's or a Nation's Opening Hostilities without a Declaration of War?" and "Bismarck's Armament Policy."[42] Although a critical evaluation of these studies is still lacking, they demonstrated the Reichsarchiv's interest in many aspects of future war.

FUTURE WAR IN THE MILITARY DISCOURSE

The debate in interwar Germany about future military conflict was vivid and enduring.[43] Because it took place primarily in military journals, not in monographs, the extent of official historians' participation in the debate is sometimes difficult to reconstruct. Two prominent examples suggest the nature of this participation, however. George Soldan had experienced the war on the western front as battalion-commander. In 1925 he published a booklet entitled *Man and Future Battle*, in which he announced that front-line experience was the only valid source of lessons about the war, and that the most important of these was the "victory of material over man." He attested to the "fiasco of mass armies," and he foresaw trench warfare as the dominant mode of future conflicts. In the stalemate of material warfare, mass conscripted armies would no longer be needed:

> After the experiences of the World War, the future of military organizations must lead to smaller front-line armies [*Frontheeren*], whose technical equipment will be superior and which will bring together the best in human potential. One must

41 BA-B, R 15.06, Nr. 1, Gruppe Borries, Kriegswissenschaftliche Aufträge des Reichswehrministeriums vom Mai 1930 bis Februar 1932, Mar. 1, 1932.

42 Herrmann, *Reichsarchiv*, 2:533–42.

43 See Wilhelm Deist's chapter in this book.

agree with Spengler that this future force of *Frontkämpfer* can be composed only of volunteers, who – out of holy, free inner conviction – are imbued with strong patriotic beliefs.[44]

Soldan envisaged permanent formations of storm troopers, like those of 1918, which were simply to be enlarged to the size of an army and motorized. The similarities were obvious to both Seeckt's vision of a *Führerheer* and J. F. C. Fuller's of an all-mechanized, professional army. Although he was wrong in his general prognosis of future warfare, Soldan's thinking represented the opinions of an influential minority within the German army. But attacking universal conscription, which remained a sacred tenet of German military thought, subjected him to harsh criticism and provoked a debate that continued until 1932.[45] The military advantages of a professional army seemed obvious. Such an army promised higher training standards, stronger motivation, and more rapid operational readiness – all vital factors in a conflict that fell short of a multifront general war with full mobilization. Furthermore, the peace treaty limited the Germans' options, and in the short run at least, an elite professional army looked like the best of these. Although Soldan did not allude to it directly, the elite army had an important political dimension. Armed forces based on universal conscription threatened to bring further democratization of the army, and a professional army seemed better suited to resist parliamentary control.

The intellectual limitations of Soldan's vision are clear in retrospect. It was based entirely on the experience of combat on the western front, so it overlooked the military implications of the Great War elsewhere. Fixed on his own personal experience of the last war, Soldan underestimated the pace of technological change and its tactical and strategic implications. He "discovered" the revolutionary impact of the airplane only in the summer of 1940.[46]

The three authors of the 1930 supplementary volume on prewar armaments and economic preparations offer a second example of the military historians' participation in the discourse on future war. In the course of their research, Otto Korfes, Wilhelm Dieckmann, und Hermann Pantlen delved into a topic that the German officer corps had traditionally neglected. In the early 1930s, the army command set out to develop a modern theory

44 George Soldan, *Der Mensch und die Schlacht der Zukunft* (Oldenburg, 1925), 37, 88.

45 The debate took place principally in the journals *Deutsche Wehr*, of which Soldan was co-editor between 1925 and 1932, and *Militär-Wochenblatt*. See Jehuda L. Wallach, *The Dogma of the Battle of Annihilation: The Theories of Clausewitz and Schlieffen and Their Impact on the German Conduct of Two World Wars* (Westport, Conn., 1986), 229–40.

46 Soldan, "Auf den Spuren einer siegreichen Armee," *Deutsche Wehr* 44 (1940): 326–8, esp. 326.

of a war economy (*Wehrwirtschaftslehre*), which was to be a topic of priority in officer education. After 1933 this enterprise became part of what the new regime called the *Wehrwissenschaften*, or "defense sciences," whose ideological implications were clear. Although their own approach tended to be nonpolitical, the three authors became leading experts in their fields, and they strengthened the role of the official history in Germany's planning for future war.[47]

The vision of future war in the official military history was not consistent. The main series, the voluminous *Weltkriegswerk*, reflected the totalization of war only partially. Nevertheless, its authors themselves recognized this conceptual deficiency. The publication of the supplementary volumes was designed to compensate for it, before political and military developments after 1933 set limits to their powers to do so. Still, the series *Der Weltkrieg 1914–1918* offered a multitude of insights into industrialized and "totalizing" warfare, at least to the reader who could read between the lines. Nor were official perceptions of future war formed only by the *Weltkriegswerk*. The discourse of future war took place primarily in a new milieu of media, whose significance was itself one of the most important lessons that the general staff drew from a war that had been fought between societies, not only armies. The official history reflected changing social and political circumstances, as it was called on to perform new academic, propagandistic, and military functions. It thus seized on many aspects of total war, including economic and financial mobilization, the front-line war experience, and the war's broad cultural dimensions. The authors of the official history participated as well in the numerous debates on the World War. Finally, the confidential studies of the *Gruppe Borries* were indispensable for the military education of the German armed forces in an era of military impotence.

The Reichsarchiv clung nonetheless to an antiquated conception of official military historiography, and the reason lay less in corporate conservatism or professional myopia than in the politics of the military in Weimar and Nazi Germany. The Reichsarchiv undertook "strictly military" history, not because such a history had proved suitable. Its deficiencies were well recognized. The key lay instead in the results of the war itself. The long industrial war, which had called for a supreme national effort, had been lost against a

47 All three held doctorates in history or political economy, and their academic training distinguished the trio from the majority of their fellow officers. See Wilhelm Dieckmann, *Die Behördenorganisation in der deutschen Kriegswirtschaft 1914–1918* (Hamburg, 1937); Otto Korfes, *Grundsätze der Wehrwirtschaftslehre* (Hamburg, 1935); and Hermann Pantlen, *Krieg und Finanzen* (Hamburg, 1935).

coalition whose strategic potential was vastly superior. Military history could provide no answer to the question of how such a conflict could be avoided in the future, while a broader history of the war seemed only to emphasize Germany's disadvantages in any such conflict. These perspectives created an uncomfortable dilemma for German official military history, which continued to see itself less as an academic sub-discipline than part of what Arden Bucholz has called a "deep-future-oriented war planning process."[48]

48 Arden Bucholz, *Moltke, Schlieffen, and Prussian War Planning* (New York, 1991).

12

"The Study of the Distant Past Is Futile"

American Reflections on New Military Frontiers

BERND GREINER

> Never in all the world's history has the likes of the present culture developed. . . . The study of the distant past is futile; the answer is not there. . . . Once wars were won by defeating an army. The next war may be won by destroying the people that furnish the army. . . . Surely the enemy will strike not the fortified position but the basis of the whole army – industry and the people. . . . It is more than useless to decry the terrible casualties that aircraft will cause among noncombatants. That feeling comes from the day when warfare had a certain honor, even dignity. Today it has little: tomorrow none. . . . Consequently, our future conflicts will likely be wars of extermination. . . . The human has at hand weapons of immense destructive power; no philosophy or decency to stop him from using them.[1]

In July 1939 Major J. Halpin Connolly offered this vision of the next war in the pages of the *Infantry Journal*, one of the preeminent American military periodicals. Like the *Field Artillery Journal*, the *Military Review* (published by the Command and General Staff School in Ft. Leavenworth, Kansas), and the *U.S. Naval Institute Proceedings*, the *Infantry Journal* was a product of the services' professionalization in the 1920s. Amid the financial pressures of the Great Depression, the *Infantry Journal*, *Coast Artillery Journal*, and the *Cavalry Journal* pooled articles to ensure a wider circulation. By the late 1930s the *Infantry Journal* had become a forum for broad-minded, seminal thought that prompted the others to improve the quality of their content. Even though it did not entirely mature in this role, it came close to offering an "all-Army forum" open to the other services as well, particularly to the air corps, which was still affiliated with the Army. The authors of the articles were active military personnel, academic historians, and foreign military experts. The journal thus provides a valuable window on the history of American military thinking in the early twentieth century; and it can be read as an

1 J. Halpin Connolly, "War in a Mechanistic Civilization," *Infantry Journal* (hereafter *IJ*), July 1939, 306–14.

introduction to the political education of a new generation of military elite on its way to Omaha Beach, Okinawa, and Iwo Jima.[2]

World War I was a central point of orientation for all who contributed to military journals. That war was defined as a turning point, forcing a new agenda on philosophers of war and military strategists alike. Authors portrayed the trenches of Verdun and the Somme as portents of future combat, while their perspectives on war extended well beyond the battlefield to social, political, and civil-military affairs.

When America welcomed its troops back home from Europe in 1918, there was little talk of military doctrine, strategies, future war, or how to prepare for it. Once the victory parades were over, the heroes of the Argonne and Chateau-Thierry were forgotten or ignored. The problems of urbanization, crime, communist agitators, war profiteers, and alien doctrines from abroad seemed much more pressing. Because most of the recent immigrants had come from Slavic or Latin countries, and because they were not accustomed to the discipline of "Anglo-Saxon stock," the idea of "America" seemed itself at issue.

For the authors writing in American military journals, the debate about "Americanism" recalled the sorry record of the past. Whenever the U.S. Army had concluded a successful war, the public quickly turned away, as if to say that citizens might at times make good soldiers, but soldiers could never make good citizens. After the War of Independence, Congress ordered the troops disbanded and authorized a standing army of eighty men. At the end of the war against England in 1814, the Army melted away to 6,000 men. At the conclusion of the Mexican War, it was reduced to 8,000; and in 1915, the Army comprised only 54,000 troops, 20,000 of whom were garrisoned in Alaska, Hawaii, Panama, and overseas. For years, the *Infantry Journal* emphasized these figures as evidence of an eternal historical pattern. After World War I, Congress rejected compulsory military training, as the opposition drew its strength from the rural south, the Midwest, and from members of the National Guard, who cultivated deep resentments against the regular army.[3]

2 These journals are accessible in the main library of the U.S. Military Academy at West Point, N.Y., Bldg. 757, and at Carlisle Barracks, Pa. The titles of the journals changed frequently in the 1920s. A useful guide is Michael E. Unsworth, ed., *Military Periodicals: United States and Selected International Journals and Newspapers* (New York, 1990). For the early navy publications see Armin Rappaport, *The Navy League of the United States* (Detroit, 1962), 1–83.

3 Bloxham Ward, "An Educational Military Policy," *IJ*, July 1919, 22; Edward S. Hayes, "The Aftermath of War," *IJ*, Sept. 1919, 182; C. G. Follansbee, "National Defense 1775–1929," *IJ*, Apr. 1929, 368–72; May 1925, 490–1; cf. *IJ*, July 1920, 26–7; Oct. 1919, 260–1; Herbert S. Duncombe, "Our National Defense Policy," *Field Artillery Journal* (hereafter *FAJ*) 3 (1926): 241–59.

Business thus continued as usual. The military's perimeter of defense returned to the American homeland. Instead of pondering strategies for future wars, America's military elite strove to devise a policy for domestic consumption, to define its mission in terms acceptable to the American people, and to conquer a place in the Republic's imagination. John J. Pershing's notion of a "new Americanism born of sacrifice" soon became the slogan of the day. From the pens of military authors, however, the slogan sounded like a battle-cry against modernity and its attendant evils, such as disrespect for authority, a lack of discipline, social unruliness, and materialism. To stem the tide of these ills, the armed forces portrayed themselves as the ideal institution, particularly after they had integrated soldiers from over fifty nations into their ranks during the recent campaign in France. Military training, these authors argued, would discipline the stubborn. Given the frequent labor strikes of the early 1920s, the working class, particularly its black segment, was an obvious source of concern. The armed services would teach workers good habits, whether they were black or white – particularly, though, if they were immigrants who resisted American traditions and institutions. Immigrants were to be threatened with the loss of citizenship. Suffrage was to be extended only to males who had demonstrated their willingness to die for the republic. Whatever the topic they addressed, the military journals read like the blueprints of social engineers, visions of biological improvement. Health, hygiene, virility, cleanliness, strength, courage, and uprightness dominated the conceptual vocabulary.[4]

After ten years of these exertions, contributors to the military journals drew a sobering balance. Once Congress had turned down universal military training, the Army attempted to recruit young males into civilian summer camps for thirty days of basic training. In 1923 it mailed out 66,000 press sheets and more than 220,000 letters, had printed 60,000 pamphlets and posters, and produced 900 sets of slides for display at the movies. Nonetheless, throughout the 1920s enrollment lagged behind expectations.

4 John Pershing, quoted in *IJ*, Oct. 1919, 262; cf. *IJ*, Apr. 1919, 771–87; July 1919, 21–5; Oct. 1919, 259–65; Feb. 1920, 650–3. Cf. M. W. Ireland, "Universal Military Training," *IJ*, Feb. 1921, 111–13; ibid., 113–15; Garrett B. Drummond, "Citizenship Training," *IJ*, Sept. 1927, 281–3; John B. Barnes, "Junior Citizenship Training," *IJ*, May 1923, 560; *IJ*, Apr. 1919, 774–9; July 1919, 21–2; Feb. 1920, 649, 652–3; Mar. 1921, 214–16; Aug. 1923, 125–6; Feb. 1924, 172–3; John B. Barnes, "Junior Citizenship Training," *IJ*, May 1923, 557; John W. Heavey, "Universal Military Training," *IJ*, July 1920, 27; cf. *IJ*, July 1921, 10; H. A. Drum, "Objects Sought in School Instruction and Future Study by Graduates," *FAJ* 6 (1921): 576–80; Gilbert Totten McMaster, "Business Men's Course in Military Training as an Adjunct to Universal Training," *IJ*, Nov. 1919, 372–3; cf. *IJ*, Dec. 1922, 621; Feb. 1921, 135. On the military's campaign on behalf of "Americanism" during the war years, see David I. MacLeod, "Socializing American Youth to Be Citizen-Soldiers," in Manfred F. Boemeke, Roger Chickering, and Stig Förster, eds., *Anticipating Total War: The German and American Experiences, 1871–1914* (Cambridge, 1999), 137–67.

The highest attendance at the camps was 39,000, reached in 1927. Many universities abolished the Reserve Officer Training programs, and only 66 (out of 426) institutions of higher education continued to require military instruction for graduation. The Army's public esteem fell almost as low as it had been during the prewar years. Military service was again frowned on as a sign of failure to establish a regular career path. Recruitment teams found it difficult to reach out beyond the unemployed because they encountered "calamitous ignorance, apathy, and even aversion," which they illustrated with stories of soldiers in uniform who were mistaken for conductors, doormen, chauffeurs, liftboys, or dog-catchers. In February 1926 *Harper's* wrote that many Americans wondered how their Army might look if stuffed in a warm, well-lit museum.[5]

When military authors reflected on their own self-image in the 1920s, they invoked a strange mix of superiority and impotence. On the one hand, they saw themselves as outcasts who struggled against being condemned to oblivion. Their narrative turned into an indictment of civil society, full of scorn, resentment, and hate. They characterized intellectuals, preachers, playwrights, and politicians as "short-sighted," "blatant creatures" of our "boasted culture"; they referred to journalists as "slush-writers" and dance directors were "nit-brained nonentities" who had "powerful feet and weak minds." These "ambuscaders," who stabbed the Army in the back, were outright "enemies." In spite of their ritual praise for the country's heritage, military officers waged a verbal vendetta that indicted American political institutions. On the other hand, the same authors portrayed the "profession of arms" as "the physician of the body politic." By implication, the military had both the moral right and the mandate of history to represent the core of the polity; the armed forces embodied the basic power and virtue without which the United States would perish, as other nations had before. This dramatic language was replete with religious metaphors, for it reflected a crusade that the military pursued with missionary zeal.[6]

5 William Waller Edwards, "Junior R.O.T.C. in Public Schools," *IJ*, Oct. 1924, 410; H. A. Finch, "Face the Facts," *IJ*, May 1926, 49; cf. *IJ*, Oct. 1921, 368–9; Dec. 1921, 613; May 1923, 555; Jan. 1924, 32; Feb. 1924, 161–3, 172–3; Dec. 1925, 668; Jan. 1927, 8–13; Dec. 1927, 611–15; May 1928, 494–5; Sept. 1928, 236–7; May 1929, 503–11; June 1929, 618–19; June 1930, 620–1.

6 "One Reason Why," *IJ*, Mar. 1921, 215–16; R. S. Boyesen, "Poison For Posterity," *IJ*, Sept. 1923, 210; J. M. Scammell, "What is a Soldier?" *IJ*, Jan. 1921, 9; R. S. Boyesen, "Your Counter Attack," *IJ*, June 1923, 672–3; R. S. Boyesen, "Soldiers as Peace Officers," *IJ*, June 1924, 692; Amos A. Fries, "The Spirit of the American Doughboy," *IJ*, Feb. 1929, 114; "Another Reason," *IJ*, May 1921, 433; cf. "Co-Operation," *FAJ* 1 (1919): 119–22; W. P. Richardson, "World War Observations," *IJ*, July 1920, 7; J. M. Scammell, "What is a Soldier?" *IJ*, Jan. 1921, 9–10; "A Small Beginning," *IJ*, Nov. 1921, 481–5; Amos A. Fries, "The Spirit of the American Doughboy," *IJ*, Feb. 1929, 113–14; R. A. Hill, "Reserve Policies and National Defense," *IJ*, Jan. 1935, 61.

The greatest obstacle facing the armed forces – one more obstinate than an indifferent public – was the U.S. Constitution and its provisions for federalism and states' rights. From the perspective of the military journals, American history read like a war between the states and the central government, which had raged to the detriment of the nation's vital interests. In 1812, for example, the governor of Massachusetts, citing popular unwillingness, refused to follow a congressional request for military support for war against Britain. Insisting that their militias were to protect only the individual states, other states, such as Vermont, had made it illegal to serve the federal government as soldiers. The War of 1812 was therefore fought largely with troops that disbanded once the scene of battle shifted from one state to another. According to the *Infantry Journal*, these troops had represented "a patriotic mob" – not a proper army. The perseverance of this tradition had recently been demonstrated once again. Returning home from France after the armistice, National Guard units received an enthusiastic welcome in their home states, whereas troops of the regular army were all but ignored by the public. When Army recruiters started the campaign for a peacetime army, they often encountered resistance from National Guard officers, who did not want their men "stolen away" into the custody of the federal government. Many in the Army thus agreed that the National Guard "believes more in state rights today than did the South in '60 and '61."[7]

On June 4, 1920, the campaign to upgrade service in the regular armed forces scored a major success when Congress authorized the National Defense Act. The regular army was henceforth fixed at a maximum of 280,000 enlisted men and the National Guard at a minimum of some 500,000. In the event of emergency, the ranks of the ready reserves were to be filled by the draft. Under ordinary circumstances, these reserves would remain a skeleton force of commissioned and noncommissioned officers, trained in the Reserve Officers Training Corps (ROTC) or in Citizens Military Training Camps (CMTC). This arrangement was designed to mobilize up to three million men on short notice and to make twenty divisions ready for combat within a month. For the first time, provisions were made for the peacetime organization of units above the regimental level. Encouraged by sympathetic remarks from President Warren G. Harding, military journalists celebrated the passage of the defense act as if it were their declaration of independence.[8]

7 John W. Heavy, "National Military Policy," *IJ*, June 1920, 1061; cf. *IJ*, Jan. 1920, 580–1; Feb. 1920, 625–9; Dec. 1920, 573; Apr. 1929, 366–72.

8 *IJ*, Jan. 1920, 584; Oct. 1921, 370–1; Dec. 1921, 615; Mar. 1923, 250–9, 274–7; William Bryden, "Possibilities in the Act of June 4, 1920," *FAJ* 4 (1920): 402–11.

In fact, the new structure significantly reduced the role of individual states in national military policy, and it divested the National Guard of its militia character. In the past, the National Guard had been under the control of the governors of each state or commonwealth; henceforth, Congress was, at least in theory, in a position to determine and regulate every detail. And regulate it did. The organization, training, and equipment of the National Guard were placed under federal authority, and guardsmen were required to conform to the regular army's standards. Consequently, the practice of electing officers began to disappear, ending the careers of many National Guard leaders who had been notorious for their lack of military qualifications. Under the new law, officers had to pass federally administered examinations. Gradually, the National Guard grew beyond infantry units to include artillery, cavalry, and special troops. Finally, the power to draft National Guard members in times of emergency passed to federal authorities. As one commentator observed of these changes, "The powers of the Federal Government have been growing until now we may say that they overshadow anything dreamed of at the time of the Constitutional Convention."[9]

Nevertheless, by the end of the 1920s, military journals were permeated with a mood of stagnation and resignation. The politics of institution-building had ground to a halt. Because of fiscal constraints, the regular army failed to reach its projected level of 280,000 men. In 1925 it was, with about 118,000 men, smaller than it had been in early 1917. Altogether, only about 55,000 soldiers were ready for emergency engagement as a mobile defense force. "Reduction of funds," complained one writer, "has caused unit after unit to be relegated to an inactive status until, at the present time, it is only with the greatest difficulty that the Regular Army can serve as a training school for the National Guard." Thousands of men in the regular army lived in rickety, wooden barracks with leaky roofs and sagging floors. The National Guard never approached the 500,000 men envisaged in the National Defense Act. In 1930 it comprised only about 182,000 men. In the early postwar years, the ready reserves relied on veteran officers who had returned to service. But reserve units found no adequate replacements when these seasoned officers retired. To organize their cadres, the ready reserves needed about 95,000 officers and 150,000 noncommissioned officers. If, however, an order for general mobilization had been issued in 1925, one infantry regiment in every four in a division would have been without officers. As one writer complained: "In the entire 27 divisions of the organized reserves there are not enough enlisted reservists to fill a single

9 Laurence Halstead, "Man Power of the Nation," *IJ*, May 1925, 491; L. C. Scherer, "Development of the National Guard," *IJ*, Jan. 1926, 41–4, 164–70; Mar. 1926, 314–17; cf. *IJ*, Sept. 1926, 333; Mar. 1931, 196.

Infantry regiment." In sum, the armed services in the early 1930s included little more than a skeleton force supplemented by paper units. Many in their ranks had lost confidence in national military service. In retrospect, the National Defense Act and the promise of strengthening federal control of the armed forces seemed like hollow gestures.[10]

By the end of the 1920s, the horizons of the military journals had begun to widen. Disturbing news from Europe, which at times brought prophesies of a war in the immediate future, invited reflection on the military lessons of the Great War. In the event of another war, the bulk of the American forces would again be drafted from men who had, time and again, demonstrated their unwillingness to be soldiered; the same men would then be committed to action after only a limited period of training. This prospect made it urgent to open debate on a practical training doctrine to fit the demands of a strategic plan. In a new atmosphere of urgency, the military journals became a forum of controversy and debates.[11]

The overriding lesson of World War I seemed as simple as it was momentous: democracies could not tolerate long wars. Determined to make this point, military experts revisited little-remembered chapters of the 1914–18 war. After their armies had suffered excessive losses on the battlefield, both Russia and Germany underwent political revolution. Democracies seemed, if anything, more sensitive to the human costs of war, at least to judge from the change in the British government after the failure of the Somme offensive or the French army mutinies in 1917, after the bloodshed in the Champagne. American society seemed the most vulnerable of all. Secure in its material abundance, the country nourished the illusion that it could prevail, and it ignored the possibility of being bled white. American military writers were convinced, however, that the blows suffered by the French and British public during World War I would have torn American society apart. Therefore, the first priority was to revise the traditional concepts of protracted war.[12]

American military writers defined the offensive, both tactical and strategic, as the core doctrine for the education of military leaders. "Those of you who were in France," wrote one, "will recall the low ebb to which the

10 Laurence Halstead, "Defense of the Nation," *IJ*, Dec. 1925, 611; "The Reserve Officer and the Citizens' Camps," *IJ*, Sept. 1925, 341; cf. *IJ*, Oct. 1921, 372–3; Feb. 1924, 238–9; May 1924, 651–2; Jan. 1925, 99; Sept. 1925, 244; Dec. 1925, 616–17; May 1931, 268; Raymond Walters, "Field Artillery in American Colleges," *FAJ* 5 (1919): 543–55; E. R. van Deusen, "R.O.T.C. at Princeton," *FAJ* 3 (1925): 255–9; cf. *IJ*, Mar. 1923, 247–59; June 1924, 780–1; Sept. 1925, 246–7, 282–3; Sept. 1931, 403–7; Nov. 1931, 509–13; Nov. 1933, 443; Jan. 1935, 57–62.

11 *IJ*, Dec. 1929, 551–7; Mar. 1934, 156–7; May 1934, 238; John S. Wood, "Prophecy or Fantasy?" *FAJ* 2 (1936): 183–92; Ferdinand Foch, "The Conduct of War," *FAJ* 2 (1929): 139–55.

12 William K. Naylor, "The Principles of War," *IJ*, Jan. 1923, 149; cf. *IJ*, Mar. 1921, 383–5; May 1927, 476; Nov. 1935, 548.

morale of the allies had touched." "The talk, the training and the plans," he continued, "were all for the defensive – barbed wire, concrete pill boxes, hand grenades." As if Allied timidity had contaminated American military leadership, the *Infantry Journal* and the *Field Artillery Journal* called for turning the war's operational legacy upside down. The literature that they recommended for officers included books on Hannibal, Caesar, and Napoleon. They also called for study of German military history, with special emphasis on the writings of Schlieffen and Bernhardi. If we "get down to the meat of what [Bernhardi] says," noted one journalist, "we will be just that much better prepared for the War of the Future." By the early 1930s, articles in the military journals assumed the character of cult-literature on the spirit of the offensive. A "vigorous offensive" ranked as the top principle in every phase of training. It was to be stressed "until it becomes a settled habit of thought."[13]

A group of traditionalists dominated the early debate on strategic doctrine. Anxious about the strategic mission of infantry, these writers portrayed the individual foot soldier as the consummate fighting machine, who possessed qualities unmatched by machines – willpower beyond fatigue, courage beyond fear, and steadfastness in all conditions. A host of case studies – from Genghis Khan and the Roman legions to the Indian fighters of Nebraska and jungle warriors in the Philippines – foreshadowed the epic of the Doughboy in France. These stories celebrated masculinity, and they repudiated the proposition that machine-guns, tanks, and airplanes had turned men into fodder and shell-shocked caricatures. Hand-to-hand combat would forever be the "Queen of Battles," decisive in any military encounter.[14]

In sharp contrast to their colleagues in the air corps, traditionalists in the infantry insisted that, as a supreme strategic principle, war must never be waged against civilians. The principal objective in war was to defeat the enemy's main force, to destroy a hostile army, or, in case of naval warfare, to cut the enemy's trade routes and sink his battle fleet or merchant marine. In this fashion, the traditionalists threw down the gauntlet to unnamed heretics in their own ranks, as well as to prominent British strategists, such as Ian Hamilton, who since the early 1920s had pondered the terrorization

13 Hjalmer Erickson, "Doctrines and Principles of War," *IJ*, Jan. 1922, 48; Harry A. Smith, "Leadership," *IJ*, June 1924, 681; *IJ*, Nov. 1922, 617; cf. O. L. Spaulding, "Preparation and Conduct of Fire," *FAJ* 1 (1920): 19–28.

14 "Tactics and Mechanization: Discussion," *IJ*, May 1927, 468; cf. *IJ*, May 1937, 225–9; July 1937, 318–27; Nov. 1937, 483–92; July 1935, 307–16, 337–9; May 1934, 171–81; July 1928, 3–11; Aug. 1928, 127–36; Sept. 1928, 283–8; Apr. 1927, 407–14; May 1927, 463; Feb. 1925, 130–1; Jan. 1924, 1, 53–5; Mar. 1923, 301–2; H. G. Bishop, "What of the Future?" *FAJ* 5 (1922): 365–76; Debeney, "Modern War and Machines," *FAJ* 1 (1923): 1–10.

of civilian targets. "Total war" was not an option. If strategic points, like railway centers or lines of communication, had to be targeted, the attack was to come from secondary columns and to take place in limited campaigns. Cities, centers of production, and the home front in general were to be spared. However, while the traditionalists sounded self-assured, their attitude rested on shaky foundations; and by the late 1920s, they were already fighting a rear-guard action.[15]

"Principles of war?" asked E. S. Hughes in the April 1929 issue of the *Infantry Journal*:

> Just one generalization after another. Thousands of packages of predigested mental food, which, swallowed at a gulp, make thought unnecessary. Universal and infallible *guides to action*, good everywhere and at all times. Anything that will save us the trouble of thinking. . . . If we would only stop to think and to analyze the situations with which we and others are and have been confronted, we would find that seldom, if ever, is the same ground covered more than once.[16]

Ten years after the end of World War I, a group of critics who had the self-confidence of upwardly mobile newcomers launched an onslaught on the traditionalists' position. In the view of these critics, the ancien régime in the American military was dominated by ultra-conservative dogmatists who had trained in the world war's school of mass armies. Wedded to the principle of defeating an enemy on the battlefield, they were responsible for the stalemate warfare in France, with its millions of needless casualties. The critics wrote of poor leadership, inelastic minds, ignorant senior officers, and the need to subject their own elders to radical remedies. "A firm hard blow between the eyes, and away to the abattoir," wrote one of them. His recommendation was aimed at instructors who taught the principles of land warfare to the infantry. Building on the doctrines of authorities like J. F. C. Fuller and Basil Liddell Hart, the "new generation" promised to purge the old style of war. By the mid-1930s, these self-styled "scientists of war" had established themselves as regular contributors to military journals.[17]

At the core of their agenda lay an old question: would the American citizen-soldier be fit for wars of the future? Certainly, citizen-soldiers would

15 Hjalmer Erickson, "Doctrines and Principles of War," *IJ*, Jan. 1922, 51; cf. *IJ*, Oct. 1921, 388–93; Nov. 1921, 520–1; Feb. 1923, 146–7, 150–7; Conrad H. Lanca, "Commencing a Modern War," *FAJ* 1 (1939): 43–58.

16 E. S. Hughes, "Principles of War?" *IJ*, Apr. 1929, 355.

17 Nathan A. Smith, "The Theory of Mechanization," *IJ*, Nov. 1935, 548, 550; "The Decisive Element in the Attack," *IJ*, Mar. 1936, 155; J. F. C. Fuller, "Tactics and Mechanization," *IJ*, May 1927, 460, 457–9, 461–5; cf. *IJ*, Nov. 1937, 571; Mar. 1936, 51–5; Sept. 1929, 222–3; Oct. 1928, 329–47; July 1927, 7–11; George S. Patton Jr., "Tanks in Future Wars," *IJ*, May 1920, 958–62; Leon M. Logan, "Are We Up-to-Date?" *IJ*, Nov. 1929, 476–81; cf. *IJ*, Nov. 1921, 516–24; Apr. 1929, 365; Feb. 1931, 91–3; Mar. 1934, 94–8; Sept. 1939, 427.

always faithfully follow once the trumpet sounded. But more was needed. "The last war has clearly shown," declared one of the modernizers, "that it is too late to attempt to develop a fighter after war has been declared. The mental shock that results from the declaration . . . permit[s] the ordinary man no opportunity to readjust himself to his new and unfamiliar circumstances." In a war whose speed and scope had been extended by technology, the burdens on the individual soldier would be greater still. Not trusting the citizen-soldiers became an article of faith for the new generation of military writers. They, too, called history as their witness to demonstrate how, at critical moments, the nation had been saved by luck and the enemy's shortsightedness, not by citizen-soldiers. Not even the Doughboys of World War I had suggested otherwise. The analysis culminated in an indictment. As long as Americans held compulsory soldiering to be as unthinkable as compulsory religion, they would never supply "good soldier material." "The very nature of our people is opposed to the nondemocratic type of organization found in all armies." Modern wars could not be won with men who traded fighting spirit for individualism, who wished to substitute business suits for uniforms. "In a generation or so," warned one author, "the problem of producing a force for war will present a grave aspect, for no one can make an army from a society of agnostics, hedonists, and egoists. An army is forged from the iron in the soul of a people."[18]

To judge from a host of articles that appeared in the 1930s, the army's modernizers envisaged a "new" American soldier who was free of burdensome responsibilities and fearless of consequences and who welcomed war as an adventure. This soldier would not turn his back on the military after his discharge, but he defined himself as a soldier even in civilian life. He retained a mental "permanent preparedness," as if the military were his personal frontier. He was emotionally and spiritually committed, to the point of "divine" dedication. Trained for decisive missions, these "new soldiers" would as a group be set apart from the bulk of the forces. Although specifics were lacking, the modernizers issued a plea for a departure from American tradition. The citizen-soldier was to be replaced by the soldier-citizen.

In their commentary on strategy, the authors of the "new generation" began with Sherman's campaign in the Civil War. They hailed the "march

18 Warmoth Thomas Gibbs, "Military Training of the Schoolboy – and His Later Life," *IJ*, May 1929, 511; Thomas R. Phillips, "The Glory of the Soldier," *IJ*, May 1939, 214, 211–21; E. G. Peyton, "The Regular – A Citizen on Detached Service," *IJ*, Mar. 1927, 253–9; John H. Burns, "The Psychologist Looks at the Army," *IJ*, Dec. 1928, 592–602; P. C. Greene, "The Public and Its Army," *IJ*, June 1929, 618–23; cf. *IJ*, Apr. 1929, 366–72; May 1929, 488–95; June 1929, 649; Mar. 1926, 286; R. W. Marshall, "The Philosophy of a Soldier," *IJ*, Mar. 1930, 250–4; Hanson E. Ely, "Moulding Men for Battle," *IJ*, Sept. 1939, 419–27; cf. *IJ*, Nov. 1939, 559.

to the sea" as a model of a "democratic war," and as a solution to self-exhausting positional warfare. Sherman's forces had shown how to wage war without undue costs, how to attain victory without postponing dividends, and how to gain the enemy's surrender before public opinion could protest against brutality. The object was less to commit troops against the enemy's armies than to break a society's will to continue fighting. The war of the future would hence be a war of irregular fronts against the enemy's logistics and economic base. As one writer explained: "We are moving toward a conception of war which says that wherever possible we avoid the risk and the expense of battle; as an alternative to it, wherever possible, we select those objectives in space whose denial to the enemy will bring on him more suffering than the sacrifice we demand of him in our terms of peace."[19]

At the end of the 1930s, the modernizers found a model in the Wehrmacht's *Blitzkrieg* in Poland, which confirmed the increasing vulnerability of industrialized societies. Advances in social organization in fact multiplied economic targets. In November 1939 the *Infantry Journal* invited Hasso von Wedel, a representative of the German general staff, to write an article. The article's message was that the Germans had learned how to put Sherman's political economy of war into practice.[20]

Exploiting "alternative targets" raised the sensitive problem of civilians and cities. For much of the time, military writers who were outspoken on other topics preferred to camouflage this issue and to cite foreign authorities. Liddell Hart, for example, testified in the *Infantry Journal* that soldiers would only defend their country as long as their families were safe. Menacing the home front could thus break the soldiers' will to fight. By contrast, many authors argued that the indiscriminate bombing of a civilian populace convinced of its cause would only stiffen its resolve.[21]

This discussion took place within a broader framework. The new generation of strategic thinkers sought a means for containing total war. Bleeding contestants white was never a possibility in their eyes, genocidal fantasies even less so. Tools of indiscriminate destruction, like chemical or biological weapons, were to be employed solely against enemy troops. Attacks

19 J. M. Scammell, "David or Goliath?" *IJ*, Nov. 1935, 530; B. H. Liddell Hart, "The Signpost That Was Missed," *IJ*, Nov. 1934, 411; cf. ibid., 405–10; Wedel, "The German Campaign in Poland," *IJ*, Nov. 1939, 543–7; C. M. Bundel, "What is Wrong with Our Principles of War," *IJ*, Oct. 1928, 329–47; cf. Rene Altmayer, "The German Military Doctrine," *FAJ* 2 (1935): 181–91.

20 Alan Pendleton, "The Death of a Nation," *IJ*, Nov. 1935, 512; cf. ibid., 511–18.

21 B. H. Liddell Hart, "The Signpost That Was Missed," *IJ*, Nov. 1934, 411; Claire L. Chennault, "Some Facts About Bombardement Aviation," *IJ*, Sept. 1935, 387–93; cf. George H. Dern, "Army-Infantry-Air Corps," *IJ*, Mar. 1934, 95; *IJ*, Jan. 1925, 15; Nov. 1937, 574–5; H. H. Arnold and Ira Eaker, *This Flying Game* (New York, 1936).

on civilian targets were to be restricted to the enemy's vital economic or logistical centers. These strategies were calculated to bring quick surrender by paralyzing the enemy's war-making capacity, not to annihilate a people physically or destroy its social and demographic foundations. American authors calling for indiscriminate terror bombing made up a tiny minority. Most writers were fascinated instead by the prospects of gradual escalation and a fine-tuned war, which would feature precision-guided munitions and the bombing of exactly determined civilian targets. Maximizing destruction at selected times promised the taming of war before it turned into Armageddon. Future wars would be more terrible, but paradoxically more humane, because they would be shorter and less frequent.[22]

Yet the door to total war was open. The escalation of tensions in the 1930s also found expression in the military journals. Articles fell into a Manichean logic. Authors wrote of life or death, triumph or oblivion, all or nothing, in an impending showdown for survival. Many of them were impressed by the imminent breakdown of past rules and regulations, the emergence of an ethical no-man's land without distinctions between acceptable and unacceptable behavior. One essay in 1927 symptomized the shrinking moral horizon, as it advocated mass executions from the sky: "We must divorce war from ethics. . . . Benevolence, humane concepts, chivalric ideas, all of which are basic in Christian thought and all of which have in some degree permeated the philosophy of war, must be banished."[23] Writers ridiculed the rules of land war, the Hague and Geneva conventions, as figments of international legal imagination. Attempts to control weapons of mass destruction with diplomatic means seemed preposterous. In the mix of social Darwinism and fatalism that prevailed in the 1930s, total war looked increasingly like history's inevitable next step.[24]

To contain or unleash total war, to target or exempt civilians, to destroy an enemy selectively or indiscriminately – these issues dominated the literature. The contributors to military journals seemed at times as puzzled by their

22 Claire L. Chennault, "Some Facts About Bombardement Aviation," *IJ*, Sept. 1935, 392; "Our Army and Chemical Warfare," *IJ*, May 1927, 613–17; N. E. Watts, "Chemical Warfare, Treaty Abrogation and the Infantry," *IJ*, Dec. 1928, 609–13; Robert E. Sadtler, "Possibilities in Chemical Warfare," *IJ*, Dec. 1929, 74–5; C. P. Summerall, "New Developments in Warfare," *IJ*, Feb. 1931, 91–3; George J. B. Fisher, "Chemicals – How, When and Where?" *IJ*, Jan. 1935, 33–8; cf. D. S. Sommerville, "The Field Artillery and Chemical Warfare," *FAJ* 2 (1932): 140–5; J. M. Eager, "The Use of Chemical Agents by the Field Artillery in Future Warfare," *FAJ* 4 (1933): 372–80.

23 Joseph H. Grant, "The Modernization of War," *IJ*, July 1927, 8.

24 Thersites, "The Usefulness of Air Power," *IJ*, July 1937, 359; "Our Army and Chemical Warfare," *IJ*, May 1927, 616–17; Thersites, "A Course in Chemical Warfare," *IJ*, Nov. 1928, 455–9; Dallas D. Irvine, "The Misuse of Air Power," *IJ*, May 1937, 255–6; Leon A. Fox, "Bacterial Warfare," *IJ*, Jan. 1933, 22; cf. ibid., 14–22; *IJ*, Sept. 1935, 392; Nov. 1935, 511; Conrad H. Lanza, "Aspects of Modern War," *FAJ* 5 (1938): 341–63.

own prescriptions as they were by the world around them. As the historian Charles A. Beard wrote in 1934: "We are drifting. . . . Whither all this is leading no one seems to know or care to know. . . . What are and should be the relations of civil and military authorities? What are the inner connections between social and economic development and military power?"[25]

Beard's words also describe pressing desiderata of historical research. Much remains unknown about the political biographies of both "traditional" and "new-generation" thinkers, about how their education, mentalities, and experience were transformed into strategy, and about the institutional affiliations and the "generational" dynamics at work on the eve of World War II. Pending further research, J. Halpin Connolly's dystopia, cited at the beginning of this chapter, should therefore be interpreted with care. Not yet built on a solid strategy, it was meant to scandalize. It nonetheless suggested the extent to which the shadow of total war already loomed over American military thinking.

25 Charles A. Beard, "Introduction," in S. B. McKinley, *Democracy and Military Power* (New York, 1934), v.

PART FOUR

Projections and Practice

13

"Not by Law but by Sentiment"

Great Britain and Imperial Defense, 1918–1939

BENEDIKT STUCHTEY

"If the heart of the Empire was threatened, all the members were threatened," said Joseph A. Lyons, the prime minister of Australia, at the last Imperial Conference of the interwar period, emphasizing that war for Great Britain meant war for its dominions.[1] His words laid bare expectations about the Empire as well as fears for its fate. Lyons' auditors included leaders from the principal dominions – the prime ministers and large retinues from Australia, New Zealand, South Africa, and Canada. They gathered in London between May 14 and June 15, 1937, ostensibly to celebrate George VI's coronation.[2] Their attentions were claimed, however, by less glamorous problems – Japanese expansionism in the Pacific, Italian Fascism, and German Nazism, all of which threatened imperial security. The conference was a crucial step in the British government's efforts to mobilize the dominions for strategic support in case of war.

As had been the case in similar critical circumstances in 1911, British claims to leadership in the Empire[3] conflicted with the demands of some of the dominions for greater autonomy in international affairs.[4] These tensions

1 Public Record Office (hereafter PRO), Cab 32/128, Principal Delegates Fourth Meeting, May 22, 1937. See S. R. Ashton and S. E. Stockwell, eds., *Imperial Policy and Colonial Practice, 1925–1945*, British Documents on the End of Empire, ser. A, vol. 1, pt. 1 (London, 1996).

2 The Irish Free State did not send an official representative. See D. Harkness, "Mr. de Valera's Dominion: Irish Relations with Britain and the Commonwealth 1932–1938," *Journal of Commonwealth Political Studies* 8 (1970): 206–28; Keith Jeffery, "The Irish Military Tradition and the British Empire," in Keith Jeffery, ed., *"An Irish Empire"? Aspects of Ireland and the British Empire* (Manchester, 1996), 94–122.

3 The term *commonwealth* came to be used during World War I and was more clearly defined at the 1926 imperial conference as the dualism of the dependent colonies and the mostly autonomous dominions before the era of decolonization. This chapter will use the term *Empire* rather than either *Empire-Commonwealth* or *Commonwealth*.

4 Nicholas Mansergh, *Survey of British Commonwealth Affairs: Problems of External Policy, 1931–1939* (London, 1952); Robert F. Holland, *Britain and the Commonwealth Alliance, 1918–1939* (London, 1981); Lars S. Skalnes, "Grand Strategy and Foreign Economic Policy: British Grand Strategy in the 1930s," *World Politics* 50 (1998): 582–616.

weighed heavily at the conference in 1937. As Reginald Coupland, the renowned historian of the British Empire and a contemporary observer of colonial affairs, posed the problem, "if the nations of the Commonwealth, with so many of the advantages which make concord and cooperation easy, with so much common sentiment and common tradition, cannot live and work together, what chance is there for France, Germany, Russia, and the rest?"[5] Coupland was right to be cautious. The strength of the Empire – its advantages and limitations – had yet to be tested.

Despite the solemn symbolism of the occasion, the Imperial Conference of 1937 symptomized the increasing difficulties of coordinating foreign and defense policy among the leading members of the British Empire. The conference publicly emphasized imperial solidarity in the face of military threats from several quarters, but its vague declarations masked a reluctance to cooperate in plans for imperial defense schemes two years before the outbreak of World War II. Even as he embraced Empire solidarity, Neville Chamberlain, who succeeded Stanley Baldwin as prime minister during the conference, relegated the dominion governments, in the words of one historian, "to a position of passive acceptance of, rather than active participation in, British policies."[6]

This essay investigates British imperial policy between the wars, particularly during the final years of peace. It examines the military and political prerogatives of the dominions, as well as the limits and opportunities that confronted the Empire as a whole.[7] Its sheer size as a potential theater of combat speaks to Roger Chickering's definition of total war, which emphasizes "the growing expanse of warfare . . . the broadening scope of operations." This characterization describes the problems with which British imperial defense policy struggled between the wars, as it confronted the realization that "theaters of operation span the globe."[8]

Although the language of trusteeship and colonial nationalism portended the eventual end of Empire, the colonial administration was, as John Darwin has remarked, "determined nevertheless to postpone the evil hour of dissolution as long as possible."[9] While demands for self-rule and external threats

5 Reginald Coupland, *The Empire in These Days* (London, 1935), 92.

6 Rainer Tamchina, "In Search of Common Causes: The Imperial Conference of 1937," *Journal of Imperial and Commonwealth History* 1 (1972–3): 100.

7 Older literature often describes the dominions in the interwar period as "the four," omitting the Irish Free State. See J. D. B. Miller, *Britain and the Old Dominions* (London, 1966), 104–40, 124ff.

8 Roger Chickering, "Total War: The Use and Abuse of a Concept," in Manfred F. Boemeke, Roger Chickering, and Stig Förster, eds., *Anticipating Total War: The German and American Experiences, 1871–1914* (New York, 1999), first quotation on 26; second quotation on 16.

9 John Darwin, "Imperialism in Decline? Tendencies in British Imperial Policy Between the Wars," *Historical Journal* 23 (1980): 659; see also Kenneth Robinson, *The Dilemmas of Trusteeship: Aspects of British Colonial Policy Between the Wars* (London, 1965).

from Japan and Italy signaled the need for a new definition, if not the dismantling of the British imperial system, radical anticolonial thinking in Britain itself owed more to philosophical traditions than pragmatic considerations of politics.[10] Pacifist sentiment gained a voice after World War I, although it did not exert mass appeal. An impressive number of publications criticized the imperial idea – from J. A. Hobson's *Democracy After the War* (1917) and E. D. Morel's *The Black Man's Burden* (1920) to John Strachey's *The Coming Struggle for Power* (1932) and Leonard Barnes's *Empire or Democracy* (1939). They could not obscure the fact, however, that British policy-makers were not prepared to risk imperial defense by weakening imperial ties.[11]

Nor, by the late 1930s, was the Labour Party.[12] In its advocacy of a firm foreign policy, rearmament, and strong civil defense, Labour committed itself to national security. While the position of Labour's leadership was popular with the public, it was criticized by the socialist wing of the party, which was associated with internationalism, anti-imperialism, and anti-militarism.[13] However, fundamental principles connected with this wing, such as pacifism, lost their appeal as international tensions mounted, the League of Nations proved incapable of dealing with Japanese and Italian imperialism, and the Soviet Union and Nazi Germany rearmed. Thus, although the Labour Party continued to advocate collective security to protect British interests around the globe, it abandoned some of its traditional positions. It remained opposed to conscription, while it supported increased war production and strengthening the armed forces.[14] Opposition to conscription was rooted in defense of a professional army, the conviction that "citizens should be used as war-industry workers not soldiers."[15]

10 Heinz Gollwitzer, *Geschichte des weltpolitischen Denkens*, 2 vols. (Göttingen, 1972–82), 2:313–21; A. J. P. Taylor, *The Trouble Makers: Dissent over Foreign Policy, 1792–1939* (London, 1993), 167–200. On the radical tradition, see Miles Taylor, "Imperium et Libertas? Rethinking the Radical Critique of Imperialism During the Nineteenth Century," *Journal of Imperial and Commonwealth History* 19 (1991): 1–23.

11 Stephen Howe, *Anticolonialism in British Politics: The Left and the End of Empire, 1918–1964* (Oxford, 1993), 27–81; Bernard Semmel, *The Liberal Ideal and the Demons of Empire: Theories of Imperialism from Adam Smith to Lenin* (Baltimore, 1993), 183–9; John Darwin, " 'High Noon' or 'Loss of Confidence'? The British Empire Between the Wars," in Hans-Heinrich Jansen and Ursula Lehmkuhl, eds., *Grossbritannien, das Empire und die Welt: Britische Aussenpolitik zwischen "Grösse" und "Selbstbehauptung" 1850–1990* (Bochum, 1995), 133; John Callaghan, "The Communists and the Colonies: Anti-Imperialism Between the Wars," in Nina Fishman et al., eds., *Opening the Books: Essays on the Social and Cultural History of British Communism* (London, 1995); see also Partha Sarathi Gupta, *Imperialism and the British Labour Movement, 1914–1964* (London, 1975), 93–102, 162–72.

12 Jerry H. Brookshire, "Speak for England, Act for England: Labour's Leadership and British National Security Under the Threat of War in the Late 1930s," *European History Quarterly* 29 (1999): 251–87.

13 See also Ben Pimlott, *Labour and the Left in the 1930s* (Cambridge, 1977); David Goldsworthy, *Colonial Issues in British Politics: From "Colonial Development" to "Wind of Change"* (Oxford, 1971).

14 Brookshire, "Speak for England," 269–70. On the anti-imperialist tradition and Labour imperialism, see also R. Palme Dutt, *The Crisis of Britain and the British Empire* (London, 1957), 346–75.

15 Brookshire, "Speak for England," 275.

In any case, British policy-makers faced a difficult challenge in imperial relations. Economic problems and financial stringency in Britain reduced their room for maneuver.[16] Sensitive issues of immigration and emigration between center and periphery complicated matters.[17] The function of the Imperial Conferences (1911, 1917–18, 1921, 1923, 1926, 1930, 1935, 1937, and 1941) was thus to promote unity between Britain and its dominions, to clarify areas of joint responsibility, and to encourage cooperation toward collective security. Even if the Empire was a "superpower," it was a vulnerable one.[18] Certainly the "strategic frontiers were no less far-flung in 1939 than they had been in 1914."[19] English shores were no less threatened by a German invasion than New Zealand's were by Japanese aggression.

The Imperial Conference of 1923 had already devoted special consideration to questions of defense, strategic cooperation, and mutual military assistance. A resolution provided that each part of the Empire had primary responsibility for local defense, while, to the extent possible, all its members were to adopt a common system of military organization, arms, and equipment.[20] Problems that affected the vital interests of the Empire – such as sea communications and trade – were to be addressed collectively, as was the conduct of foreign affairs.

Aggravated by growing nationalist sentiment in South Africa and the Irish Free State, problems of imperial defense and security stood atop the agenda at the Imperial Conference of 1926.[21] Lord Balfour warned that cutting imperial ties would cause fundamental problems not only for member states, but possibly also for world peace.[22] In his view, the Empire's task was to bind together its parts "not by law but by sentiment . . . on a footing of equality, on a footing of mutual comprehension with a desire to further the mutual interests, and to form in themselves a great league of civilization."[23]

The shared experience of World War I had provided a vocabulary to express this kind of "Imperial kith and kin sentiment," which created the illusion of global strength on the basis of a common foreign and defense

16 David Meredith, "The British Government and Colonial Economic Policy, 1919–39," *Economic History Review* 28 (1975): 484–99; Ian M. Drummond, *British Economic Policy and the Empire 1919–1939* (London, 1972).

17 Stephen Constantine, *Emigrants and Empire: British Settlement in the Dominions Between the Wars* (Manchester, 1990); Keith Laybourn, *Britain on the Breadline: A Social and Political History of Britain Between the Wars* (Gloucester, 1990).

18 Anthony Clayton, *The British Empire as a Superpower, 1919–39* (London, 1986).

19 Darwin, "Imperialism in Decline?" 660.

20 Robert MacGregor Dawson, ed., *The Development of Dominion Status, 1900–1936* (London, 1965), 275–6. The conference is documented in Parliamentary Papers, Great Britain, 1923, Cmd. 1987, 10–17.

21 See Nicholas Mansergh, *The Commonwealth Experience* (London, 1969), 227–31.

22 *Journal of the Royal Institute of International Affairs* (July 1927), 212–13.

23 Ibid., 212.

policy.[24] Balfour's doctrine of 1926 expressed the constitutional equality of the dominions, their right of free association with the Empire, as well as their internal and external autonomy, which could in theory extend to military neutrality in the event that Britain were involved in war. Each dominion was to control its own policy.

Balfour's statement appeared to undermine the fundamental pillars of the Empire's common action, but in reality it was "no more than a polite fiction."[25] London continued to control the dominions' trade, and the City remained their major creditor. However, the Empire offered much financial security to British investors, in particular as far as railways and the expansion of agriculture are concerned, becoming an increasingly important factor for the British capital market in the interwar years. Clearly, pressing economic problems in the late 1920s and the Great Depression exacerbated concerns about imperial security. Debt servicing rather than trade was the crucial beneficial link between metropole and periphery, and also sustaining the Empire market for British-manufactured exports. Because Britain depended on overseas investment, it tried to keep the dominions and colonies solvent. Especially in times of recession the system showed its limits when their governments were becoming less enthusiastic about meeting the financial demands of imperial defense.[26] While formal bonds of subordination and constitutional dependence loosened, informal connections continued to bind the different members. In addition to economic integration and financial linkages, these ties extended to the belief in a common "Britishness," the sentiment that the populations of the dominions would naturally stand by the mother-country in times of danger. To the extent that coercive measures were replaced by common interests and ideals, the connections became more solid, for they were based on one vital aim, the stability and unity of the imperial system.

The Imperial Conferences were but one device that served this aim. Speeches by prominent British political figures, such as L. S. Amery and Maurice Hankey, were likewise calculated to strengthen imperial ties in defense matters.[27] Amery, the dominions secretary and a passionate advocate of empire, was particularly active in this respect. In 1927–8 he spent seven

24 Anthony Clayton, "'Deceptive Might': Imperial Defence and Security, 1900–1968," in Judith M. Brown and William Roger Louis, eds., *The Twentieth Century*, Oxford History of the British Empire, 4 (Oxford, 1999), 281.

25 P. J. Cain and A. G. Hopkins, *British Imperialism: Crisis and Deconstruction, 1914–1990* (London, 1993), 109.

26 Ian M. Drummond, *Imperial Economic Policy, 1917–1939: Studies in Expansion and Protection* (London, 1974).

27 L. S. Amery, *The Empire in the New Era: Speeches Delivered During an Empire Tour 1927–1928* (London, 1928); Ann Trotter, "The Dominions and Imperial Defence: Hankey's Tour in 1934," *Journal of Imperial and Commonwealth History* 2 (1973–4): 318–32.

months touring the dominions. He delivered some 300 speeches, stressing that the Empire was entering a new era, in which partnership was replacing central political control. All its members, he announced, were equal in their autonomy, as well as in their responsibility for the whole: "As subjects of the King all inhabitants of the Empire owe loyalty not only to the King, but, in virtue of their loyalty to him, to each other." "That obligation of mutual support and cooperation," he continued, "constitutes, so to speak, the Common Law of the Empire."[28]

Hankey, who was secretary to the Imperial Defense Committee until 1938, was less interested in financial and economic ties or in cultural and ideological solidarity than in defense policy. In January 1926 he laid a summary of defense policy before the cabinet.[29] This memorandum identified Japan as the strongest naval power in the east, and it warned that this country could be tempted to threaten key positions of the British Empire. Hankey observed further that Germany would become difficult to control, despite its present weakness, and could be expected to seek to regain the losses of World War I.[30] A further danger, which could possibly result in war, Hankey identified in the "Balkanization of Europe," the proliferation of small states in Central and Eastern Europe. Like Amery and others, he was convinced that Britain could meet external threats only by closing links with its dominions. In fact, he envisaged a new imperial organization to underpin a "Pan-Britannia," prevent the break-up of the Empire, and open a new chapter in British history.[31]

This concern with Imperial affairs limited Britain's involvement in Europe during the 1920s.[32] In the words of Michael Howard, "imperial responsibilities rendered her impotent to bring serious influence to bear on those developments in Europe on which her security ultimately depended."[33] Other regions, whose strategic significance bore more directly on the Empire, claimed the attention of the British government despite the warning that the Empire "would become defenceless if England herself were knocked out."[34]

28 Amery, *Empire*, 4–5; cf. L. S. Amery, *My Political Life: War and Peace, 1914–1929*, 3 vols. (London, 1953–5).

29 PRO, Cab 63/38, MO (26), 1 Jan. 1926.

30 Robin Higham, *The Military Intellectuals in Britain, 1918–1939* (New Brunswick, N.J., 1966).

31 Amery, *Empire*, 12.

32 See Michael Howard, *The Continental Commitment: The Dilemma of British Defence Policy in the Era of the Two World Wars* (London, 1972), 74–96.

33 Ibid., 95–6.

34 PRO, Cab 29/148, NCM (35) 3, note by Norman Fenwick Warren Fischer, Apr. 19, 1934; the authoritative contemporary guide is D. H. Cole, *Imperial Military Geography*, 8th ed. (London, 1935).

The Middle East, particularly Egypt and the Suez Canal, had a vital function for the security of the Empire and could not be neglected.[35] Egypt typified the problems that the Empire faced during the interwar period. Imperial security and stability had to be brought into compromise with Egyptian nationalism. This was one of the reasons why Egypt had been granted conditional sovereignty in 1922, while Britain continued to defend imperial communications, retained freedom of military action within Egypt, protected foreign interests, and administered the Sudan. Britain thus remained in indirect control of Egypt, but in exchange it promoted Egypt's membership of the League of Nations, acknowledging that colonial nationalism needed to be reconciled with imperial defense policy. Actions in Egypt ratified views that Amery had voiced in the House of Commons in July 1919. Here he had observed that the threat of imperial dissolution could best be met by granting the fullest possible equality of status among the different parts of the Empire: "The more the principle of equality is openly established to the world, the greater the effective unity of the British Empire."[36] Balfour agreed. Members of the Empire could well share the King, he wrote, but not the House of Commons; and each dominion needed its own parliament.[37] Unity, defense, and international security were indispensable to encourage the development of self-governing institutions within the Empire. As Drummond Shiels, the undersecretary of state for the colonies, noted ten years later, this proposition formed one of the most important fundaments of British colonial policy between the wars.[38]

Defending Iraq and the South Persian oil fields, both of which were closely linked with India, also figured prominently in British policy in the Middle East. According to Darwin, "at almost all times between the 1880s and 1960s, British interests in the Middle East were regarded as of greater political and strategic value, and more deserving of protection than those in almost any other part of the imperial system."[39] In contrast to Britain's vast empire in Africa, which was of limited strategic significance, the Middle East, a new, yet "undeclared Empire," was integrated into the

35 John Darwin, *Britain, Egypt, and the Middle East: Imperial Policy in the Aftermath of War, 1918–22* (London, 1981), 47–137.

36 Speech of July 30, 1919, in *Hansards*, fifth ser., 118, 2172–86. See also I. M. Cumpston, ed., *The Growth of the British Commonwealth, 1880–1932* (London, 1973), 92.

37 Balfour in his foreword to Amery, *Empire*, x.

38 Shiels in a House of Commons Speech, Dec. 11, 1929, in *Hansards*, fifth ser., 233, 611–15; see also Cumpston, ed., *Growth*, 97–8.

39 John Darwin, "An Undeclared Empire: The British in the Middle East, 1918–39," *Journal of Imperial and Commonwealth History* 27 (1999): 160.

imperial system, because British interests required control of this geo-strategic axis. India was the fulcrum of the imperial system in this region, the basis of imperial defense and security plans.[40] The key to these plans was Iraq, whose strategic importance lay in its air bases. In a cabinet memorandum, Lord Passfield of the Colonial Office compared the importance of this country in 1930 to that of the Suez Canal for strategic and commercial communications with India, Australia, and the Far East. Passfield recommended that once the British mandate in Iraq lapsed in 1932, Britain should lease an air-base permanently. Without a British military presence in the region, he argued, "oriental despotism would ultimately take its place."[41]

India itself was not to serve as a base of military operations in the Middle or Far East. The Indian army was intended instead primarily for employment within the Indian empire.[42] The British calculated that the Indian army could not hold Afghanistan, a vulnerable point in Britain's defense plans against Soviet expansion. Under the terms of an agreement between London and Delhi, India covered only the costs of its own defense.[43] Britain invested heavily in the modernization of the Indian military system, which badly needed reform, but still, the Indian army was arguably weaker in 1939 than it had been in 1914.[44] On the whole, the subcontinent was torn by violent aspects of the noncooperation movement, whether the Moplah peasant uprising in South-West India, the 1922 Akali Sikh movement, or the turbulent northeast frontier and Burma. The tension was obvious between numerous regional and local scenes of nationalist violence and Britain's promise of 1929 to grant the dominion status eventually. Firm repression came before constitutional concession. Foreign relations and defense policy remained British prerogatives and in this respect, India continued to depend on Britain. India's "ties of blood, of literature, of language, of common institutions and of common allegiance to the Crown" were so weak, however, that the subcontinent remained a security risk.[45]

40 Daniel Silverfarb, *Britain's Informal Empire in the Middle East: A Case Study of Iraq, 1929–41* (New York, 1986); cf. David Killingray, "Imperial Defence," in Robin W. Winks, ed., *Historiography*, Oxford History of the British Empire, 5 (Oxford, 1999), 347–8.

41 PRO, CO 730/151/10/6, CP 167 (30): May 17, 1930; see also B. Gökay, *A Clash of Empires: Turkey Between Russian Bolshevism and British Imperialism, 1918–1923* (London, 1997).

42 See Brian Bond, *British Military Policy Between the Two World Wars* (Oxford, 1980), 98–126; T. A. Heathcote, *The Military in British India* (Manchester, 1995).

43 See Ashton and Stockwell, *Imperial Policy*, 114.

44 Pradeep Barua, "Strategies and Doctrines of Imperial Defence: Britain and India, 1919–45," *Journal of Imperial and Commonwealth History* 25 (1997): 240–66.

45 PRO, Cab 32/128, E (PD) (37) 5–6.

British strategy in the Far East relied primarily on the naval base in Singapore. Singapore was called the "gateway to the Pacific," for its location allowed control over both the Indian and Pacific oceans. Other ports, such as Hong Kong or Sydney, were less important.[46] The decision to build the base was already taken in 1921, but construction proceeded slowly because of the costs, disputes between the Royal Navy and Air Force over use of the base, and friction with the Commonwealth governments.[47] Political opposition in Britain played a role, too. In 1924, Ramsay MacDonald's Labour Government was more anxious to promote international confidence and disarmament. After the fall of MacDonald's government, the conviction survived that Japan should be regarded as a potential partner rather than an enemy and that, as a government memorandum noted, "aggressive action against the British Empire on the part of Japan within the next ten years [was] not a contingency seriously to be apprehended."[48]

British reluctance in Singapore reflected a broader dilemma, for imperial stability seemed torn among Asian, European, and American interests. Warren Fisher, the permanent secretary to the Treasury from 1919 to 1939, forcefully represented one pole. He recommended that Britain pursue its interests independent of the United States. In 1934 he complained that the naval pact with Washington was unsatisfactory, while he saw Germany as Britain's principal enemy in Europe and warned that Britain could not fight wars in Europe and Asia simultaneously. "The American 'yard arm,'" he said, "may well get us into trouble, but will assuredly never come to our rescue." Consequently, he called for good relations with Japan in order to make resources available where they were most urgently needed, against the "Teutonic tribes, who century after century have been inspired by the philosophy of brute force."[49] Despite Fisher's counsel, the Manchurian and the Shanghai crises of 1931–2 convinced decision-makers in Whitehall to complete the base in Singapore and to seek arrangements with the United States.[50] According to John Gallagher, the arguments over the base reflected the condition of the Empire itself: "Just as the Singapore base had been the touchstone of imperial indecisiveness during the nineteen-twenties, when

46 William Roger Louis, *British Strategy in the Far East, 1919–1939* (Oxford, 1971).

47 W. David McIntyre, *The Rise and Fall of the Singapore Naval Base, 1919–42* (London, 1979); James Neidpath, *The Singapore Naval Base and the Defence of Britain's Eastern Empire, 1919–1941* (Oxford, 1981).

48 PRO, Cab 63/38, MO (26), 1: Jan. 1926.

49 Both quotations are from a note by Norman Fenwick Warren Fisher for the naval conference 1935, PRO, Cab 29/148, NCM (35) 3: Apr. 19, 1934.

50 Christopher M. Bell, "Thinking the Unthinkable: British and American Naval Strategies for an Anglo-American War, 1918–1931," *International History Review* 19 (1998): 789–808.

the going was good, so its reinforcement was an indication of imperial weakness during the late nineteen-thirties, when international pressure had now appeared as the chief threat to empire."[51]

Given the breadth of British imperial commitments or "overstretch," an alliance with the United States and appeasement policies looked increasingly like the only option.[52] Thus, Fisher's opinion won no wider recognition. By 1933 Hankey was convinced that the situation in the Far East was extremely unstable, with a regime in Japan that "respects nothing but force." Now it seemed clear that Britain and the Empire would soon go to war again. In these circumstances, the loss of Singapore would, Hankey claimed, be "a calamity of the first magnitude," which could result in the loss of India and impair trade with Australia and New Zealand.[53] In 1934 Alfred Chatfield, the first sea lord and chief of naval staff, had called for reestablishing a "Two-Power Standard." While the Empire required security against a Japanese attack and protection for its merchant fleet in the Pacific, sufficient forces also had to be kept in the Mediterranean and the Atlantic. Moreover, he argued, the navy's ability to send ships quickly to the region in the greatest danger needed to be strengthened, lest the dominions' and Britain's mercantile interests be threatened.[54] Chatfield's warnings addressed global commitments, but Britain was not yet prepared for a world war.

Chatfield's position clashed, however, with a significant segment of popular opinion, in which the views of Norman Angell, the legendary pacifist, publicist, and Nobel Laureate, found resonance. Angell's position was straightforward. Since men could make wars, they could also cause wars to cease. Together with G. Lowes Dickinson, A. Fenner Brockway, Bertrand Russell, and H. N. Brailsford, Angell protested against the Empire's preparations for war, thereby taking up the nonconformist tradition of intellectuals of World War I and before.[55] Rather than rearmament and the mobilization of its dominions, Britain should, he insisted, employ diplomatic means to resolve international tensions. Mobilizing troops would not prevent war or

51 John Gallagher, *The Decline, Revival and Fall of the British Empire: The Ford Lectures and Other Essays*, ed. Anil Seal (Cambridge, 1982), 132.

52 See E. Ranson, *British Defence Policy and Appeasement Between the Wars 1919–39* (London, 1993); Ritchie Ovendale, *"Appeasement" and the English-Speaking World: Britain, the United States, the Dominions, and the Policy of "Appeasement," 1937–1939* (Cardiff, 1975).

53 PRO, Prem 1/152: Apr. 5, 1933.

54 PRO, Cab 29/148, NCM (35) 1: Mar. 23, 1934.

55 *Kriegsgegner in England: Nach englischen Quellen dargestellt von* [anonymous] (Munich, 1915); Gottfried Schramm, "Minderheiten gegen den Krieg: Motive und Kampfformen 1914–18 am Beispiel Grossbritanniens und seines Empires," *Geschichte und Gesellschaft* 6 (1980): 164–88; cf. Wolfe Schmokes, "The Hard Death of Imperialism: British and German Colonial Attitudes, 1919–1939," in Prosser Gifford et al., eds., *Britain and Germany in Africa: Imperial Rivalry and Colonial Rule* (London, 1967), 301–35.

improve the nation's economic condition: "Military power can do nothing commensurate with its cost and risk for the trade and well-being of the particular states exercising it. It cannot be used as an instrument for seizing or keeping trade."[56] As a pacifist Angell was a critic of empire *par excellence*. He demanded that Britain and the other imperial powers free themselves from the "hypnotizing effect of this 'mirage of the map' "[57] while genuine problems remained to be solved. These problems could not be solved by military means, for Angell was convinced that war had become physically impossible and that cooperation among human communities was the only acceptable alternative in the modern world.[58]

Intellectuals like Angell argued that financial interests profited from imperialism, while the masses were deceived by its glittering. When Leonard Barnes wrote in 1939 that "the failure of the League of Nations is a failure not of the League, but of the nations," he meant that peace was the outcome of more than words, good will, international organizations, or cooperation.[59] In order to prevent war, he believed, "the inward character of nationhood must change."[60] This challenge included a critical examination of both the social structure of nations and the imperialism they practiced.

Official proponents of British imperialism were not impressed by this argument. Military circles and the cabinet turned instead to national defense, the areas that needed special attention and where rearmament was urgent.[61] In December 1936 Neville Chamberlain, who was then chancellor of the Exchequer, drew up a memorandum that laid down the cabinet's priorities. The navy remained the basic component of Britain's national defense, in particular in preserving communications with the dominions.[62] Of no less importance, however, was the rebuilding of the air force.[63] Chamberlain was thinking in imperial terms when he stated that "there are definite limits to the contribution" that Britain could make in the eventuality of a European war. Above all, he counseled, the government "should not lose sight of the fact that the political temper of people in this country is strongly opposed to

56 Norman Angell, *The Great Illusion* (London, 1908); Angell, *The Great Illusion – Now* (London, 1939), 139–40.

57 Ibid., 196.

58 Ibid., 272–3.

59 Leonard Barnes, *Empire or Democracy? A Study of the Colonial Question* (London, 1939), 208.

60 Ibid. For the intellectual tradition before Barnes, see Sheldon Spear, "Pacifist Radicalism in the Post-War British Labour Party: The Case of E. D. Morel, 1919–24," *International Review of Social History* 23 (1978): 193–223; Gupta, *Imperialism*, 93–133, 162–72.

61 See K. Fedorowich, *Unfit for Heroes: Reconstruction and Soldier Settlement in the Empire Between the Wars* (Manchester, 1994).

62 Stephen Roskill, *Naval Policy Between the Wars*, 2 vols. (London, 1968).

63 Malcolm Smith, *British Air Strategy Between the Wars* (Oxford, 1984); David E. Omissi, *Air Power and Colonial Control: The Royal Air Force, 1919–1939* (Manchester, 1990).

Continental adventures."[64] In this respect at least, the government's policy was close to Labour's position, especially in its reluctance to see the army engaged in a European war. At a strength of about 180,000 men, the army was to focus on a possible Soviet threat in India and to secure the Empire against nationalist revolts.[65]

Ten days after Chamberlain submitted this memorandum, Hankey addressed the dangers that confronted the Empire. Germany, Italy, and Japan had all become enemies, he wrote. Britain would have to rely on the navy and air force for its defense. France was weak, although it could keep Germany at a distance. The French suffered from the "pacifist and defeatist disease" and were "inoculated with the virus of Communism." In the event of war, he predicted, the United States would remain neutral unless the Japanese threatened Australia.[66] Hankey's analysis made clear that greatly accelerated British armament was necessary to prevent a disaster. But he also insisted that attending to imperial defense policy required that Britain emancipate itself from the League of Nations, which could not guarantee security. Hankey was not alone in this view of the League. Other officials agreed that it had failed in its basic mission to resolve international disputes peacefully, that, as one wrote, "in its 16 years of existence" the League had "not a single success in a first-class issue to its credit."[67] The conclusion was that Britain and its dominions stood alone. Not the idealism of the League, but political pragmatism and the defense of imperial interests were the only language that Britain's enemies understood.

It was another matter to achieve a consensus within the Empire about using this language. In 1931 the Statute of Westminster guaranteed the dominions' autonomy in foreign affairs. While the Crown retained the right to declare war, the British parliament "forewent its right to legislate for the Dominions without their request and consent."[68] Nonetheless, the dominions did remain dependent on Britain for naval defense; and they continued to rely on one another in many political and strategic matters. In fact, as has been argued, the dominions' exposure to external threats – Japan in the Pacific, Italy and Germany in Africa – "actually enhanced the value of

64 PRO, Cab 24/265, CP 334 (36): Dec. 11, 1936; cf. Robert A. C. Parker, *Chamberlain and Appeasement: British Policy and the Coming of the Second World War* (London, 1993), 58–79.

65 See Clayton, "Imperial Defence," 287–93; David E. Omissi, *The Sepoy and the Raj: The Indian Army, 1860–1940* (Basingstoke, U.K., 1994).

66 PRO, Cab 63/51, MO (36) 10: Dec. 21, 1936.

67 Ibid.

68 Miller, *Britain and the Old Dominions*, 109; see also Arthur Berriedale Keith, ed., *Speeches and Documents on the British Dominions, 1918–1931: From Self-Government to National Sovereignty* (1932; London, 1970), 303–7.

imperial protection."[69] Tensions arose, however, whenever the dominions, which were also members of the League of Nations, asserted their autonomy in foreign affairs.[70] In particular, the Irish Free State, Canada, and South Africa stressed their independence and proved reluctant to accede to British imperial requirements. Their resentments over lingering dependence surfaced during the abdication crisis of Edward VIII, when the British prime minister, Stanley Baldwin, failed to consult the dominions.

Canada exemplified the problem. The famous and much-quoted statement by a Canadian representative, that "We live in a fire-proof house, far from inflammable materials," spoke to the Canadians' perception of their place and role within the imperial system.[71] After Mackenzie King became Canadian prime minister in 1921, isolationist sentiment pervaded the Canadian government, which rejected the principle that London was solely responsible for imperial defense policy. Local interests in North America demanded attention; and the Empire, despite its size (or rather, because of its size), was incapable of solving local problems. Canada's proximity to the United States gave primary importance to political relations with this nation, while the isolationist policies pursued by the United States influenced thinking to the north. Canada, Mackenzie King explained, could understand the USA's policy of neutrality – which Britain condemned – and he sympathized with the Americans' approach to defusing political tension by economic appeasement rather than military force. A "path of conciliation and cooperation, not the path of sanctions and defense of the status quo, should be followed," Mackenzie King told the Imperial Conference in May 1937.[72]

Because he believed that international peace could alone preserve the unity of the Empire, as well as the stability and unity of Canada, Mackenzie King recommended that Britain and the dominions employ peaceful means in response to the threats posed by Germany and Italy. Tensions between the French and the English in Canada played a role in his policy. The consequence was that the Canadian parliament reserved the right to determine whether to participate in a military conflict.[73] Despite the "strong pull of kinship" and the "pride in common traditions" of which Mackenzie King

69 Darwin, "Imperialism in Decline?" 665.

70 D. C. Watt, "Imperial Defence Policy and Imperial Foreign Policy, 1911–1939: A Neglected Paradox?" *Journal of Commonwealth Political Studies* 1 (1963): 266–81.

71 Quoted in Howard, *Continental Commitment*, 75–6.

72 PRO, Cab 32/128, E (PD) (37) 3: Minutes of the third meeting of principal delegates, statements by the dominion leaders on the international situation, Imperial Conference, May 21, 1937.

73 PRO, Cab 32/128, E (PD) (37) 5–6: May 24–5, 1937. See also Charles P. Stacey, *Canada and the Age of Conflict: A History of Canadian External Policies*, 2 vols. (Toronto, 1977–81), 2: 194–236.

spoke at the Imperial Conference, imperial loyalty and imperial patriotism were limited in Canada.

The case of South Africa was similar, although the historical and political background was different.[74] The polarization of official opinion here was reflected in the positions taken by the generals J. B. M. Hertzog and Jan Smuts, who were the most important political leaders of their time. Both men advocated South African neutrality in a European conflict; and both were apologists for Hitlerism, seeing it as a consequence of the Versailles treaty. But while Hertzog was prepared to trust Hitler until the outbreak of war in 1939, Smuts changed his mind after Germany's invasion of Czechoslovakia.[75] In his speech at the Imperial Conference in 1937, Hertzog advocated partial restitution of Germany's colonies, if this gesture would secure peace in Europe.[76] Furthermore, he explained, South Africa could not be expected to fight on Britain's side if Britain continued to "associate herself with France in an Eastern or Central European Policy calculated to threaten Germany's existence; or because of unwillingness to redress wrongs arising from the Treaty of Versailles."[77] The other dominions likewise rejected involvement in a war in Central or Eastern Europe, but they were willing to support Britain in a war in Western Europe. The question of war on Britain's side deepened social divisions between Afrikaner and British in South Africa. As in Canada, international and domestic interests complicated one another. However, South Africa, unlike Canada, was almost entirely dependent on Britain militarily. In these circumstances, far-right nationalists in South Africa called for contracting out of the imperial system in order to preserve neutrality in an eventual war.

The picture was again different in Australia and New Zealand. Given the strategic vulnerability of these dominions, conservative governments in both sought to avoid war. Both advocated strengthening the mechanisms of collective security through the League of Nations, a policy that also allowed them to loosen their ties with Whitehall, although New Zealand usually supported British policy. In Australia, Edward VIII commanded little respect as King and head of Empire. When Prime Minister Lyons telegraphed Baldwin in the midst of the abdication crisis, he expressed concern over the unity and stability of the Empire.[78] The British government concluded that military reinforcement of Singapore was necessary to calm

74 See T. R. H. Davenport, *South Africa: A Modern History* (Toronto and Buffalo, 1991), 295–7.

75 See D. C. Watt, "South African Attempts to Mediate Between Britain and Germany, 1935–1938," in K. Bourne and D. C. Watt, eds., *Studies in International History* (London, 1967), 402–22.

76 The British government later rejected this idea on moral grounds, stating that international opposition could be expected to "proposals involving the handing over from one Power to another of native populations as though they were mere chattels": PRO, Cab 27/623, FP 21 (36) 2: Jan. 24, 1938.

77 PRO, Cab 32/128, E (PD) (37) 3.

78 See Mansergh, *Survey*, 35–48.

the Australians, whose fears were directed primarily at Japan. Yet Baldwin failed to soothe Australian skepticism over Britain's ability to provide naval protection in a short period; and the Australian government refused to share the costs of the naval base, turning instead to the building up of its own defenses.[79] This effort encouraged industrial growth and the development of military technology in Australia to support strategic autonomy within the imperial system. Significantly, during the Ethiopian crisis Australia was ready to contribute ships while the Royal Navy stayed away because Britain feared "that ships damaged in a conflict with Italy would not be available for use against Japan."[80] Nonetheless, both Australia and New Zealand also recognized that their fates were linked with Britain's, for the defeat of the center would mean the defeat of the periphery: "History also showed that in war the fate and future of overseas territories had always been decided by the outcome of the war in the main theatre," said Archdale Parkhill from the Australian delegation at the 1937 Imperial Conference."[81]

When the representatives of Great Britain and the dominions left this conference, they were rightly pessimistic about the future of their defense concepts, observing the growing power of the European dictatorships and Japan. Statements at the conference, both from Britain and the dominions, had been imprecise, calling in vague terms for cooperation. However, this demonstration of unity and cohesion was not strong enough to encourage subsequent peace initiatives or the formulation of concrete strategic principles; nor did it lead to material cooperation, which was a special concern of Whitehall.[82] Moreover, by failing to provide for regional security, the dominions had a share of the blame for perceptions that the League had failed to meet the needs of world security. To this extent, the Empire, which had been envisaged as a possible substitute for the League of Nations, offered cooperation without liability, as ultimate responsibility remained with Britain. Eventually Britain and the Empire had no alternative to war with Germany in 1939. The power-political insufficiency of the mother country could no longer be concealed, but the question of war or peace had become one of British self-respect.[83]

The dominion governments had tried to exercise their influence on British imperial policy, making clear that Britain could no longer pursue a

79 A. T. Ross, *Armed and Ready: The Industrial Development and Defence of Australia, 1900–1945* (Sydney, 1994); Ian Hamill, *The Strategic Illusion: The Singapore Strategy and the Defence of Australia and New Zealand* (Singapore, 1981); John McCarthy, *Australia and Imperial Defence, 1918–39: A Study in Air and Sea Power* (St. Lucia, Queensland, 1976).

80 Clayton, "Imperial Defence," 286.

81 PRO, Cab 32/128, E (PD) (37) 5–6.

82 Tamchina, "Imperial Conference," 97–8.

83 Lothar Kettenacker, *Krieg zur Friedenssicherung: Die Deutschlandplanung der britischen Regierung während des Zweiten Weltkrieges* (Göttingen, 1989), 13.

foreign policy that did not take account of the dominions' interests. In practice, solidarity between Britain and its dominions was "safeguarded without sacrifice of principle."[84] For all the dominions' regard for their autonomy and for all their criticism of British leadership, their bonds of interest and sentiment proved in the end more durable.

In 1939, when the Chiefs of Staff Sub-Committee of the Committee of Imperial Defence put together a long list of precautions that were to be taken in the event of war, they concluded: "Once we have been able to develop the full fighting strength of the Empire, we should regard the outcome of the war with confidence."[85] Another total war was about to demonstrate the grounds for this optimism, and to prove whether the imperial connection was equal to Edmund Burke's famous characterization that the Empire's ties were light as air but strong as links of iron.

84 H. V. Hodson, ed., *The British Commonwealth and the Future: Proceedings of the Second Unofficial Conference on British Commonwealth Relations, Sydney, 3–17 September 1938*, with a foreword by Thomas Bavin (London, 1939), 205.

85 PRO, Cab 16/183A, DP (P) 44: Feb. 20, 1939.

14

"Blitzkrieg" or Total War?

War Preparations in Nazi Germany

WILHELM DEIST

No satisfying and convincing answer to the question posed in the title of this chapter can be offered without reference to World War I. For the military leadership of the Reichswehr and the Wehrmacht, this war posed the basis for analyzing all questions of their military craft, and it dominated all their plans and preparations for a future war.[1] Friedrich von Bernhardi, whose provocative and influential book, *Deutschland und der nächste Krieg* (Germany and the Next War), had appeared in 1913, turned shortly after the end of the Great War to the military consequences of this conflict. In a work that was published in 1920, *Vom Kriege der Zukunft* (On War in the Future), he took it as self-evident that a future war would be fought between mass armies. However, he also adopted the eccentric idea that "the troops" must be separated "inwardly from the home front," in order to avoid a repetition of the situation that arose in Germany at the conclusion of World War I, which Bernhardi interpreted in the light of the "stab-in-the-back" legend.[2] Like all his successors in the interwar period, this conservative cavalryman was preoccupied with World War I, an industrialized people's war, as the model of future warfare.[3] Subsequent military authors differed only in their

1 *Handbuch zur deutschen Militärgeschichte 1648–1939* (Munich, 1979), 5: 529–84; Klaus-Jürgen Müller, *General Ludwig Beck: Studien und Dokumente zur politisch-militärischen Vorstellungswelt und Tätigkeit des Generalstabschefs des deutschen Heeres 1933–1938* (Boppard, 1980), 29–61; Bernhard R. Kroener, "Strukturelle Veränderungen in der militärischen Gesellschaft des Dritten Reiches," in Michael Prinz and Reiner Zitelmann, eds., *Nationalsozialismus und Modernisierung* (Darmstadt, 1991), 267–96; Wilhelm Deist, "Anspruch und Selbstverständnis der Wehrmacht: Einführende Bemerkungen," in Rolf-Dieter Müller and Hans-Erich Volkmann, eds., *Die Wehrmacht: Mythos und Realität* (Munich, 1999), 39–46; Wihelm Deist, "The Road to Ideological War: Germany, 1918–1945," in Williamson Murray, MacGregor Knox, and Alvin Bernstein, eds., *The Making of Strategy: Rulers, States, and War* (Cambridge, 1994), 352–92.

2 Friedrich von Bernhardi, *Vom Kriege der Zukunft: Nach den Erfahrungen des Weltkrieges* (Berlin, 1920), 153–5, 236.

3 Max Schwarte, *Der Krieg der Zukunft* (Leipzig, 1931). See Markus Pöhlmann's chapter in this book.

assessment of specific dimensions of a future conflict.[4] All believed that in addition to human and material resources, the psychological resources of the nation would have to be fully mobilized. The experience of World War I had made them aware of the need to conduct effective psychological warfare, primarily in order to safeguard the *Heimatfront* (home front), the basis of the military's effectiveness in war. In his work *Der Feldherr Psychologos*, Kurt Hesse envisaged the solution of this problem in a charismatic leader to preside over the moral mobilization of the home front.[5]

Initially, however, the Reichswehr confronted far more pressing problems. On January 11, 1923, five French divisions and one Belgian division occupied the Ruhr cities of Essen, Gelsenkirchen, and Dortmund and extended their bridgeheads on the eastern banks of the Rhine. The Reichswehr could offer no response to the invasion. The army leadership saw no way to fulfill its traditional mission to defend the country's sovereignty, because, as Lieutenant Colonel Joachim von Stülpnagel noted in 1924, the Reichswehr's seven divisions disposed over the ammunition to fight but a single hour of battle on a typical day in the Great War.[6]

The consolidation of the Reichswehr as an instrument of national defense began only after the political crisis of 1923 had passed.[7] The vision of Stülpnagel, who was then chief of the Truppenamt's army section, of a "war of liberation," a popular uprising against a foreign enemy, was significant in this connection. It confirmed that given the restrictions of the Versailles Treaty, the Reichswehr stood no chance against its potential opponents, Poland and France. Stülpnagel's vision also outlined the political and psychological prerequisites of a future conflict. He called for focusing all the state's activity on preparing for conflict in both the west and east. As prerequisite for the envisaged psychological warfare, he demanded the "complete transformation" of political conditions in Germany, "the elimination of morbid parliamentary government," a campaign against "internationalism

4 Wilhelm Deist, "Die Reichswehr und der Krieg der Zukunft," *Militärgeschichtliche Mitteilungen* (hereafter *MGM*) 45 (1989): 81–92.

5 Kurt Hesse, *Der Feldherr Psychologos: Ein Suchen nach dem Führer der deutschen Zukunft* (Berlin, 1922). In Hesse's view (206–7), this leader should be "ein Herrscher der Seelen," a "ruler of souls." Hesse lived through the war as an officer and retired in 1928; he also published *Von der nahen Ära der jungen Armee* (Berlin, 1924).

6 Michael Geyer, *Aufrüstung oder Sicherheit: Die Reichswehr in der Krise der Machtpolitik 1924–1936* (Wiesbaden, 1980), 23–38; Carl Dirks and Karl-Heinz Janssen, *Der Krieg der Generäle: Hitler als Werkzeug der Wehrmacht* (Berlin, 1999), 200–1; Heinz Hürten, "Das Krisenjahr 1923: Militär und Innenpolitik 1922–1924," in *Quellen zur Geschichte des Parlamentarismus und der politischen Parteien*, 2d ser., Militär und Politik, vol. 4 (Düsseldorf, 1980), 266–72.

7 On March 1, 1924, on the lifting of the state of emergency, Seeckt ordered the Reichswehr to occupy itself exclusively with military problems in the future. See Militärgeschichtliches Forschungsamt, ed., *Offiziere im Bild von Dokumenten aus drei Jahrhunderten* (Munich, 1964), 236.

and pacifism, [and] against everything un-German."[8] Ten years later, Erich Ludendorff gave more extreme expression to the same ideas. In his opinion, future total war required military dictatorship in peacetime as well as in war. Above all, Ludendorff argued, this dictatorship was to ensure the "psychological unity of the nation [*Volk*]." Appropriate measures, such as protective custody, were to be instituted against the enemies of the militarist and racist *Volksgemeinschaft*. In this connection, Ludendorff mentioned Jews, the Catholic Church, and socialists.[9] Both Ludendorff and Stülpnagel spoke for broad segments of opinion in the German military leadership, as they foretold a future European war as an industrialized people's war, whose preparation required particular attention to its psychological dimensions vis-à-vis one's own nation.

Against this background, and within guidelines laid down in 1925, the army's illegal armament plans took shape, assuming concrete form in the armament programs of 1928 and 1932.[10] The origin of the so-called Great Plan of 1925 was Hans von Seeckt's vision of a wartime army of 2.8 million men.[11] The specifics of the plan were drawn up with utmost care by a group of General Staff officers. The whole project was calculated to serve a political goal, the Reich's reassertion of its status as a European great power. In this respect the Reichswehr could be confident of the support of a majority of the civilian population in Weimar Germany. In the 1920s, however, the project had no chance to be executed and represented only a framework for Germany's subsequent rearmament.[12]

In 1928 a rearmament program was launched as a first step; its military aim was to secure, by 1932, the equipment and ammunition necessary to support a sixteen-division army, as well as limited stockpiling and improved industrial production in the event of mobilization. In 1932, a second rearmament program called for a twenty-one division field army, which was to be operational by the spring of 1938 and have the equipment and stockpiling necessary for six weeks of combat.[13] These planning exercises reflected the Reichswehr's expectation that setting up an effective field army would

8 See Deist, *Reichswehr*, 85–6; Dirks and Janssen, *Krieg der Generäle*, 193–209.

9 Erich Ludendorff, *Der Totale Krieg* (Munich, 1935), 11–28; Deist, "Road to Ideological War," 360–1. In December 1938, ten months after the ill-fated Blomberg-Fritsch crisis, Werner Freiherr von Fritsch shared the views of Ludendorff concerning these three internal enemies. See also Roger Chickering's chapter in this book.

10 Karl-Heinz Janssen, "Der grosse Plan," *Die Zeit* (Mar. 7, 1997), 15–20; Michael Geyer, *Aufrüstung oder Sicherheit*, 188–236; Geyer, "Das Zweite Rüstungsprogramm (1930–1934)," *MGM* 17(1975): 125–72; Wilhelm Deist, "The Rearmament of the Wehrmacht," in Militärgeschichtliches Forschungsamt, ed., *Germany and the Second World War: The Build-up of German Aggression* (Oxford, 1990), 375–404.

11 Dirks and Janssen, *Krieg der Generäle*, 13.

12 Ibid., 11–33, 209–21.

13 Deist, *Rearmament*, 382–4.

take a long time under the republican political system.[14] Moreover, the plans demonstrated the general belief that a future military conflict, should it prove necessary in order to reestablish German power, would be an industrialized people's war.

These plans accompanied experiments with new weapons systems that offered the prospect of restoring movement to warfare. The German army joined armed forces across Europe in the search for operational mobility, after World War I had brought mass armies to stalemate.[15] The Reichswehr's officer corps closely followed developments in other countries. In Britain, J. F. C. Fuller and Basil Liddell Hart envisaged a mobile, operationally independent tank force as the future instrument of war, while the Italian Giulio Douhet called for the deployment of massive bomber squadrons over the enemy's civilian centers. These theorists shared the hope of bringing future wars to a quick end by means of rapid, massive blows against the enemy's communications and command centers, as well as against key industries. The German officers around Heinz Guderian and, later, the powerful state secretary in Göring's air ministry, Erhard Milch, developed the German variants on these ideas.[16] Even as the German army rapidly acquired warplanes and tanks in the late 1930s, however, its leadership continued to assume that a future European conflict would be an industrialized people's war.

With the National Socialist seizure of power, conditions changed for the Reich's armed forces in two fundamental ways. First, the new German chancellor promised, as he put it in a speech to leading Reichswehr officers on February 3, 1933, a "complete reversal of the current domestic political situation" and a "strengthening of the nation's will to defend itself by all means."[17] With these promises, Hitler embraced the ideology of a militarist and racist *Volksgemeinschaft*, which Stülpnagel and Ludendorff had demanded as an essential prerequisite for warfare, and which his own regime thereon propagated with extraordinary success.[18] Second, Hitler described the

14 Dirks and Janssen, *Krieg der Generäle*, 34–48.

15 See Azar Gat, *Fascist and Liberal Visions of War: Fuller, Liddell Hart, Douhet, and Other Modernists* (Oxford, 1998).

16 Ibid., 91–103. On Guderian, see Hans-Heinrich Wilhelm, "Heinz Guderian: Panzerpapst und Genralstabschef," in Ronald Smelser and Enrico Syring, eds., *Die Militärelite des Dritten Reiches* (Berlin, 1995), 187–208; Kenneth Macksey, *Guderian: Der Panzergeneral* (Düsseldorf, 1976). On Milch, see Horst Boog, "Erhard Milch: Der Architekt der Luftwaffe," in Smelser and Syring, eds., *Militärelite*, 349–67; David Irving, *Die Tragödie der Deutschen Luftwaffe: Aus den Akten und Erinnerungen von Feldmarschall Milch* (Frankfurt am Main, 1970).

17 Cited in Wolfgang Michalka, ed., *Das Dritte Reich: Dokumente zur Innen- und Aussenpolitik*, 2 vols. (Munich, 1985), 1:23–4; Deist, *Rearmament*, 408–11.

18 Manfred Messerschmidt, "Der Reflex der Volksgemeinschaftsidee in der Wehrmacht," in Manfred Messerschmidt, *Militärgeschichtliche Aspekte der Entwicklung des deutschen Nationalstaates* (Düsseldorf, 1988), 197–220; Jürgen Förster, "Vom Führerheer zur nationalsozialistischen Volksarmee," in Jost

"reconstruction of the armed forces" as the "most important prerequisite" for the "recovery of political power."[19] He thus opened the way to an unparalleled rearmament of the three branches of the armed forces – the army, navy, and air force. The army's rearmament took place in rapid, successive stages under the initiative of the commander-in-chief, Werner Freiherr von Fritsch, and his chief of the general staff, Ludwig Beck.

A program that was drawn up in December 1933 projected a peacetime army of twenty-one divisions. This program, however, implied military necessities that in turn called for additional measures concerning the recruitment of manpower and the defense of the industrial heartland east of the Rhine – both in violation of the Treaty of Versailles. On March 16, 1935, the regime reestablished universal conscription. A year later, on March 7, 1936, German troops occupied the demilitarized Rhineland. Freed of the last restrictions of the Versailles Treaty, the army's high command presented a new rearmament program on August 1, 1936, which corresponded to the projections of Seeckt's great plan of 1925. It provided for a peacetime army of 830,000 men (as against 761,000 in 1914) and an effective field army of 2,421,000 men (as against 2,147,000 in 1914), which was to be operational by October 1, 1939. In fact, at the beginning of war in 1939, the high command disposed over an army that, with 3,700,000 men organized in 103 divisions (including six tank and four motorized divisions), by far exceeded the contours of the 1925 plan. The navy and the air force underwent similar expansion. The personnel strength of the navy grew more than fivefold, and an ambitious fleet construction program was underway. The biggest gains, however, came in the newly founded Luftwaffe, whose supreme commander, Göring, was the Nazi regime's second most powerful representative. At the end of 1939, the air force included 3,832 serviceable airplanes. Moreover, after the Luftwaffe's existence was made public in early 1935, its officer corps grew thirteenfold, and it commanded more than 370,000 noncommisioned officers and men.[20] This explosive rearmament was financed by a risky state economic policy, as money appeared to play no role in the calculations of the military planners.[21]

Dülffer et al., eds., *Deutschland in Europa: Kontinuität und Bruch: Gedenkschrift für Andreas Hillgruber* (Berlin, 1990), 311–28.

19 Michalka, *Das Dritte Reich*, 23–4.

20 Deist, *Rearmament*, 405–504. For the figures, see Bernhard R. Kroener, "The Manpower Resources of the Third Reich in the Area of Conflict Between Wehrmacht, Bureaucracy, and War Economy, 1939–1942," in Militärgeschichtliches Forschungsamt, ed., *Germany and the Second World War* (Oxford, 2000), 5:787–845.

21 Michael Geyer, "Rüstungsbeschleunigung und Inflation: Zur Inflationsdenkschrift des Oberkommandos der Wehrmacht vom November 1938," *MGM* 30 (1981): 121–86; Deist, *Rearmament*, 436.

Equipping the Wehrmacht in fact caused problems from the start, however. In May 1934 the chief of the army's ordnance office, Kurt Liese, pointed out that an army that "had to throw down its weapons after six or eight weeks because of a total lack of ammunition or fuel" could not be taken seriously as an agent of military or political power. Here he alluded to growing tensions between the planner's programs and economic realities.[22] Within a few years, the massive rearmament had reached the limits of the Reich's economic capabilities, as the military planners were fully aware.[23] Nor did the institution of the Four-Year Plan significantly alter the situation. In August 1936 Hitler ordered the army to be "fit for use in four years" and the economy "ready for war in four years," but translating these goals into practice proved another matter.[24] In 1937 the regime was forced to introduce a system of allocating the raw materials that related to armaments. One consequence of this system was constant conflict over quotas, which in turn bred an "insatiable bureaucracy" within the Wehrmacht; the resulting tangle of agencies encouraged the planning of programs but diminished the prospects of their implementation.[25] In the spring of 1939, the supreme commander of the army, Walther von Brauchitsch, acknowledged the grave disparity between the army's projected wartime strength and its supplies of weapons and equipment; and at the beginning of September 1939, the supreme commander of the navy, Erich Raeder, likewise observed that the navy was "by no means adequately equipped for the great struggle against England."[26]

Thus, in the judgment of the military's own leadership, the arming of the Wehrmacht had not by 1939 reached a level appropriate to the ambitions of a European great power. One might well object that the demands of the military can, as a general rule, never be fully satisfied; but in this case something else was at issue – the military leadership's image of war. In the early stages of the rearmament, in April 1930, the defense minister, Wilhelm Groener, had issued a directive to the chiefs of the army and the navy, in which he remarked that political considerations alone defined the task of the armed forces, and that "definite prospects of success" were a precondition for the employment of the Reichswehr.[27] The program of December 1933 abandoned this principle. Under the direction of Ludwig Beck, the *Truppenamt* assumed that a wartime army mobilized from a peacetime army of 300,000

22 Ibid., 418–20.

23 Ibid., 440–3.

24 Michalka, *Das Dritte Reich*, 188–90.

25 Geyer, "Rüstungsbeschleunigung," 121–86. The reference to the "insatiable bureaucracy" is on 140. In another passage Geyer speaks of the "progessive irresponsibilty of the bureaucracy" (128).

26 Deist, *Rearmament*, 454, 479–80.

27 Ibid., 386–92.

men would be able to fight "a defensive war on several fronts with some prospect of success."[28] In 1935 Beck opposed working out an operational study that the Wehrmacht's supreme command had ordered for a surprise invasion of Czechoslovakia, because he believed that the army had not reached the requisite fighting strength.[29] The debate soon grew into a protracted conflict over the organization of the Wehrmacht's command structure, but for Beck the real point of the controversy was political, the assumption that a conflict between Germany and Czechoslovakia would remain isolated. Beck was convinced that one could not count for "one day" on "an isolated undertaking"; he predicted that a European conflict would result instead, and that unleashing it would represent an "act of desperation" on Germany's part. In the following years, as the striking power of the Luftwaffe and tank divisions grew, and as Beck incorporated them into his plans, he clung nevertheless to the conviction that a German attack on a neighboring state would result in a European war.[30] On the other hand, he did not in principle exclude the employment of the armed forces for the Reich's expansion, even into Czechoslovakia; he merely insisted that there be "some prospect of success" for such a venture. Finally, in 1938 he again rejected an attack on Czechoslovakia and resigned from the general staff, convinced of Germany's inability to survive the European conflict, the "long war," that would inevitably result.[31] As he wrote on July 15, 1938, "We hence confront the fact that military action by Germany against Czechoslovakia would automatically lead to a European or world war," and "that such a war would predictably end not only in a military but a general catastrophe for Germany." A day later, he expressed himself even more clearly. "The idea of a *Blitzkrieg* (Prague in two days?)," he wrote, "is an absurd dream. One ought to have learned from the modern history of war that surprise invasions have rarely led to lasting success."[32] This statement represented Beck's comment on the general staff exercise of 1938, which he himself had initiated. Contrary to his own expectations, the exercise had suggested the feasibility of a quick defeat of the Czechoslovakian army and then the timely transfer of German troops to the west against France.[33] In a way, Beck had only

28 Ibid., 414–15; Müller, *Beck*, 339–44.

29 Ibid., 117–20, 438–44; Deist, *Rearmament*, 512–14.

30 Ibid., 430–6.

31 For a comprehensive interpretation of this episode, see Müller, *Beck*, 276–311, 537–56.

32 Georg Thomas, who was responsible for the armaments economy in the Wehrmacht's supreme command, expressed himself with similar clarity in 1937: "The mistaken orientation towards a short war has already been our ruin once; hence, even in the era of airplane and tank squadrons, we should not allow ourselves to be led by wishful thinking about a short war" (cited in Karl-Heinz Frieser, *Blitzkrieg-Legende: Der Westfeldzug 1940* [Munich, 1995], 13).

33 Müller, *Beck*, 267–9, 279–80, 298–304.

himself to blame, for he had steered an impetuous rearmament campaign that in the end overwhelmed his own strategic judgment.

Beck's memoranda of July 1938 were addressed immediately to the army's supreme command. Ultimately, however, they were directed to Hitler, who on May 30, 1938, had declared his "unalterable decision to destroy Czechoslovakia in the foreseeable future."[34] Until the fall of 1937, the chancellor had rarely concerned himself with rearmament or concrete military objectives. In his programmatic writings, on the other hand, Hitler had examined at great length the problems of war, peace, and Germany's unfavorable geopolitical position; and he had laid out vast plans, which were grounded in a racist vision, for German expansion into eastern Europe and Russia.[35] This soldier of World War I rejected a two-front war and believed that France would remain the Reich's most immediate and determined foe.[36] In February 1933 he had emphasized to the Reichswehr's commanders the danger that France and its allies in Eastern Europe posed to German rearmament. He believed that a preventive strike against Germany was possible from these countries, if France were led by determined and far-sighted statesmen.[37] Finally, in his *Second Book* Hitler had written that "in the future . . . all wars, insofar as they affect great nations, [will] be people's wars of the most gigantic proportions."[38] Hitler's ideas about future military conflicts thus did not differ significantly from those of the military leadership. He did not speak of "lightning" campaigns or *Blitzkriege*. "Conquering new *Lebensraum* in the east and Germanizing it ruthlessly" required a "long" war in new circumstances.[39] On February 28, 1934, in a speech to the Reichswehr generals and high functionaries of the SA and SS, Hitler alluded to one dimension of these new circumstances.[40] Because the Western powers would oppose an expansion of the Reich, he declared that "short decisive and crushing military actions, first to the west then to the east, could become necessary." This declaration was not inconsistent with the projections contained in his *Second Book*, for although their importance later grew in his eyes, "military actions" were not synonymous with the "long war" for *Lebensraum*.

In the meeting that took place in the Reich Chancellery on November 5, 1937, and has become known by virtue of the Hossbach Protocol, Hitler

34 Michalka, *Das Dritte Reich*, 252.

35 See Adolf Hitler, *Mein Kampf*, 58th ed. (Munich, 1933), 317–62, 726–58; *Hitlers Zweites Buch: Ein Dokument aus dem Jahre 1928*, ed. Gerhard L. Weinberg (Stuttgart, 1961), 160–9.

36 Ibid., 145–53.

37 Michalka, *Das Dritte Reich*, 23–4.

38 *Hitlers Zweites Buch*, 140.

39 Michalka, *Das Dritte Reich*, 23–4.

40 Klaus-Jürgen Müller, *Armee und Drittes Reich 1933–1939: Darstellung und Dokumentation* (Paderborn, 1987), 195.

delivered a long-winded assessment of the diplomatic situation, whose validity, he claimed, rested among other things on the "experience of his four and a half years of rule." He designated England and France the country's two principal enemies, for they had rejected "a further strengthening of Germany" in Europe. Hitler calculated "with high probability," however, that "England, and probably also France, has already quietly written off Czechoslovakia."[41] He based this judgment on the previous reactions of the Western powers to Nazi Germany's step-by-step erosion of the Versailles settlement. Thus, with "high probability," he predicted that the Western powers would not take resolute military reaction as Germany embarked on an expansive policy of conquering *Lebensraum* in the east.

Another factor likely contributed to Hitler's confidence. The meeting on November 5, 1937, had originally been called to consider economic problems of the rearmament. It had become clear that neither the Four-Year Plan nor the allocation of raw materials would meet the requirements of the armaments programs that the Wehrmacht's three branches had established. Hence, the second part of the meeting was devoted to a fight over steel allotments. The conference thus symptomized the way the tempo and dimensions of the armaments programs were overtaxing the Reich's limited resources.[42] Enlarging abroad the economic base of Germany's rearmament offered one possible resolution to the problem. Hitler was surely aware of this possibility. Discussions of the "expansion of our limited economic strength for defense" were also being held in circles that were responsible for the armament economy.[43] The *Anschluss* of Austria and the occupation of Czechoslovakia were thus possible consequences of this thinking. In all events, these actions brought impressive gains to the economic foundations of Germany's armament.[44]

Hitler's appraisal of the military situation in 1938 thus grew out of his perception that further infringements against the Versailles system would bring no military sanctions, as well as the threat that a growing economic crisis posed to German armaments. He resolved on the dangerous gamble of prosecuting the war for *Lebensraum* in the east by means of individual, isolated campaigns. Such a course would also create the continental basis for

41 Michalka, *Das Dritte Reich*, 234–6; Manfred Messerschmidt, "Foreign Policy and Preparation for War," in Militärgeschichtliches Forschungsamt, ed., *Germany and the Second World War*, 636–9; Jonathan Wright and Paul Stafford, "Hitler, Britain and the Hossbach-Memorandum," *MGM* 42 (1987): 77–123.

42 Deist, *Rearmament*, 469–72, 498–501, 728.

43 Hans-Erich Volkmann, "The National Socialist Economy in Preparation for War," in Militärgeschichtliches Forschungsamt, ed., *Germany and the Second World War*, 314–49, 728.

44 Ibid., 323–36, 728.

an eventual clash with Britain and the other naval powers.[45] Hitler's analysis of the political situation, his belief in the military passivity of the Western powers, allowed him to maintain – both to himself and to the people around him – that the situation would not develop into another two-front war. The ease with which the *Anschluss* and Czechoslovakia's destruction were achieved only strengthened his confidence in this course of action, which henceforth changed only in the details of its execution.

Although the declarations of war by Great Britain and France on September 3, 1939, meant the political collapse of Hitler's concept, the first phase of the war, from September 1939 to May 1941, appeared to confirm the soundness of the underlying grand strategy.[46] This was, in all events, the conclusion reached by the new chief of the general staff, Franz Halder, who, unlike his predecessor, accepted Hitler's reasoning. In April 1939 Halder had told the generals and general staff officers that the conquest of Poland and the destruction of its armies would be possible within two or three weeks. Furthermore, he implied that Germany as a Central European power enjoyed complete strategic freedom! Specifically, he raised the prospect of turning against either the Soviet Union or the Western powers after the campaign against Poland, and in the latter connection he mentioned air attacks on Paris and London.[47] The behavior of the German military leadership in 1939, its concentration on the operational aspects of the campaign – that is, exclusively on the so-called *Waffenkrieg*, not on war as a broader, grand-strategic phenomenon – comported with a tradition in the general staff's thinking since at least the days of Schlieffen's operational planning. In this way, military leaders increasingly became mere recipients of orders, as their narrow operational thinking, their pointed disregard for grand-strategic aspects of the war, accommodated Hitler's intentions to an extraordinary degree.

The campaigns in the north and west in 1940, as well as those against Yugoslavia and Greece the next year, promoted the view, still common today,

45 Messerschmidt, "Foreign Policy," 680–3, 710–17; Andreas Hillgruber, "Zum Kriegsbeginn im September 1939," in Gottfried Niedhart, ed., *Kriegsbeginn 1939: Entfesselung oder Ausbruch des Zweiten Weltkrieges?* (Darmstadt, 1976), 163–77; Klaus Hildebrand, "Hitlers 'Programm' und seine Realisierung 1939–1942," in ibid., 178–224; Andreas Hillgruber, *Der Zweite Weltkrieg: Kriegsziele und Strategien der grossen Mächte* (Stuttgart, 1982).

46 See Gerhard L. Weinberg, *A World at Arms: A Global History of World War II* (New York, 1995), 34–47.

47 Christian Hartmann and Sergej Slutsch, "Franz Halder und die Kriegsvorbereitungen im Frühjahr 1939: Eine Ansprache des Generalstabschefs," *Vierteljahrshefte für Zeitgeschichte* 45 (1997): 467–95; Klaus Mayer, "Eine authentische Halder-Ansprache? Textkritische Anmerkungen zu einem Dokumentenfund im früheren Moskauer Sonderarchiv," *MGM* 58 (1999): 471–527. Mayer questions the authenticity of the Halder statement with impressive arguments. Nevertheless, the document expresses the general view held by the German military leadership at the time in perhaps exaggerated but applicable formulations.

that the Wehrmacht owed its successes primarily to a special "*Blitzkrieg* strategy." Karl-Heinz Frieser has now convincingly refuted this legend in a comprehensive study of the western campaign.[48] The consequences of the German victory in this campaign were nonetheless far-reaching. Triumph in the west confirmed Hitler's conviction that his goals could be achieved in stages, without the risk of a multifront conflict like World War I. For the German military, victory in the west dissolved traumatic memories of the stalemate battles of World War I. In the euphoria that now reigned, everything seemed militarily and politically possible.[49] The subsequent failure of Operation Barbarossa, which actually had been planned as a short campaign, ended the euphoria in the fall of 1941 before Moscow; but it did not put an end to the German army's refusal to think and act on a broader, grand-strategic basis.[50]

Because *Blitzkrieg* is itself commonly regarded as a grand-strategic concept, its components also have been sought outside the realm of military affairs. Alan Milward in particular has argued that the German military economy corresponded to a *Blitzkrieg* strategy during the first phase of World War II, when "a series of short European wars" or "limited wars" placed only limited demands on the German economy.[51] This conclusion has not, however, survived the comprehensive studies by Rolf-Dieter Müller and Bernhard R. Kroener of the mobilization and steering measures in the Germans' so-called economy of transition.[52] The concept of *Blitzkrieg* in fact bore no realistic relation to Germany's broad intentions. "Limited European wars" were inconsistent with Hitler's vast goal of *Lebensraum* in Eastern Europe, to say nothing of his ambitions to compete with the Anglo-Saxon naval powers for global hegemony.

48 Frieser, *Blitzkrieg-Legende*, esp. 401–41. The success against the Western allies in 1940 was based not on a special "Blitzkrieg Strategy" but on a combination of breakthrough tactics and technically advanced equipment, on the one hand, and commanders in front who acted on their own, looking for opportunities and taking risks, on the other.

49 Jürgen Förster, "Hitler's Decision in Favour of War Against the Soviet Union," in Militärgeschichtliches Forschungsamt, ed., *Germany and the Second World War* (Oxford, 1998), 4:13–25; Karl-Heinz Frieser, "Die deutschen Blitzkriege: Operativer Triumph – strategische Tragödie," in Müller and Volkmann, eds., *Die Wehrmacht*, 182–96.

50 Jürgen Förster, "Der historische Ort des Unternehmens 'Barbarossa,'" in Wolfgang Michalka, ed., *Der Zweite Weltkrieg: Analysen, Grundzüge, Forschungsbilanz* (Munich, 1989), 626–40.

51 See, e.g., Alan Milward, "Der Einfluss ökonomischer und nicht-ökonomischer Faktoren auf die Strategie des Blitzkriegs," in Friedrich Forstmeier and Hans-Erich Volkmann, eds., *Wirtschaft und Rüstung am Vorabend des Zweiten Weltkrieges* (Düsseldorf, 1975), 189–201.

52 Bernhard R. Kroener, "Der Kampf um den 'Sparstoff Mensch': Forschungskontroversen über die Mobilisierung der deutschen Kriegswirtschaft 1939–1942," in Michalka, ed., *Der Zweite Weltkrieg*, 402–17; Rolf-Dieter Müller, "The Mobilization of the German Economy for Hitler's War Aims," in Militärgeschichtliches Forschungsamt, ed., *Germany and the Second World War* (Oxford, 2000), 5, pt. 1:424–563.

Yet the idea of the *Blitzkrieg* continues to enjoy a degree of currency. After the campaign in Poland, journalists lent the concept broad popularity. On September 25, 1939, an article in *Time* called the German military action a "war of quick penetration and obliteration – Blitzkrieg, lightning war." Talk of "surprise, lightning-quick" offensives had surfaced even earlier in the military literature, but only during the early German victories did *Blitzkrieg* become a popular term, especially in English-speaking countries.[53] In 1941 Ferdinand Otto Miksche, one of the most respected commentators, published a book with the title *Blitzkrieg*, in which he offered this definition of the concept: "Using machines instead of masses of men, they attack the whole of the forces of the enemy throughout all the territory held by that enemy; or rather they threaten and disrupt those forces by penetrating deeply into the territory. And they have introduced this same method into the spheres of economics, politics and diplomacy."[54]

This definition implied that the German successes were due to a comprehensive, well-considered grand strategy – a vision that linked political goals, military operations, and appropriate allocation of national resources. This conclusion was wrong from the first. It has nonetheless captivated historians, who continue to popularize the term *Blitzkrieg* and appear to forget that the conflict that began with the attack on Poland did not end in 1941. None of the early German campaigns led to anything that resembled peace or stability. None of these victories enabled the Germans to achieve their war aims. Great Britain, the Soviet Union, and the United States remained undefeated. Historians should heed these facts. With respect to World War II at least, the term *Blitzkrieg* represents a *contradictio in adiecto*. Germany did not fight a series of *Blitzkriege* against individual European states, nor did it ever embrace a comprehensive "*Blitzkrieg* strategy."

Neither the political nor the military leadership of the Reich entertained the illusion of a "short" war in the autumn of 1939. The aim of the Wehrmacht's leadership, like that of the Reichswehr before it, was to restore Germany's supremacy in Europe. Should war result, they expected an industrialized people's war, a total war, but a war of movement made possible by modern weapons systems. Germany's meteoric rearmament after 1933 was directed at waging this kind of war. Nonetheless, the speed and extent of the rearmament, the limits of Germany's national resources, and the inability to gear the armament toward a well defined grand-strategic

53 Frieser, *Blitzkrieg-Legende*, 5–14.

54 Cited in Matthew Cooper, *The German Army, 1933–1945: Its Political and Military Failure* (London, 1978), 114.

goal caused the Wehrmacht to enter the European War unprepared, at least in the eyes of its own leaders.

Before 1937 Hitler's goals appeared to differ little from those of the military. With the program of *Wiederwehrhaftmachung* – Germany's reestablishment of its political and military capacities to fight – Hitler created the essential prerequisites for waging an industrialized people's war, as he freed the military of responsibility for moral mobilization, a task in which it had until then failed. In the autumn of 1937, however, Hitler openly assumed sole responsibility for grand-strategic questions, as Beck's successor confined his own efforts to planning and implementing operations. The declarations of war by the Western powers on September 3, 1939, meant that Hitler would fail to achieve his aim of *Lebensraum* without a multi-front European war. The unattainability of this grand-strategic goal became obvious in December 1941, in the defeat before Moscow. Hitler's war was more than an industrialized people's war, however. From the beginning, it was a racial war. The regime began laying the foundations for this kind of war in 1933 in racist policies, as well as in *Wiederwehrhaftmachung*, which was from the start itself framed in the racist and militarist ideology of the *Volksgemeinschaft*. In these circumstances, the radicalization of warfare came early, and it made Hitler's war a total war from the beginning.

15

The Condor Legion

An Instrument of Total War?

KLAUS A. MAIER

The affinity between the concepts of "total war" and "total mobilization" was evident in Nazi ideology from the early 1930s. In fact, the linkage between these two ideas underlay the alliance between the Nazi regime and a critical portion of the German military establishment. In 1935, in his preface to the German edition of Giulio Douhet's book on total air war, *Il dominio dell' aria*, Hilmer Freiherr von Bülow of the Air Command Office (Luftkommandoamt, later the Luftwaffe's general staff), wrote that Douhet's attacks on the bastions of the old principles of warfare were the military equivalent of the Fascist's March on Rome; both were a reflection of the fascist revolution.[1] Some German writers had already drawn a similar conclusion about the "German revolution." In May 1933 Erhard Milch, the state secretary in the Ministry of Aviation, submitted to Hermann Göring, his boss, a memorandum on the German air force. This document had been prepared by Robert Knauss, the transportation director of Lufthansa and later the commander of the Air War Academy in Berlin. In it Knauss referred to "concentrations of millions of people in large cities" as legitimate targets of air warfare. "Terrorizing enemy capitals or industrial areas will lead more rapidly to a collapse of morale," he wrote, "if the national consciousness of the population is weak and the masses in the big cities have become materialistic and divided by social and partisan conflicts."[2] This prediction reflected the Nazis' belief in the superiority of the German "ethnic community" (*Volksgemeinschaft*) over Western democratic societies.

Nevertheless, the Third Reich never built a strategic air force comparable to the British Bomber Command or the U.S. Army Air Corps. The principal role of the Luftwaffe remained tactical, the product of financial

1 Giulio Douhet, *Luftherrschaft* (Berlin, 1935), 6.

2 Bernhard Heimann and Joachim Schunke, "Eine geheime Denkschrift zur Luftkriegskonzeption Hitler-Deutschlands vom Mai 1933," *Zeitschrift für Militärgeschichte* 3 (1964): 72–86.

and technological difficulties, poor management of production, and, above all, the Nazis' aggressive foreign policy. During the second half of the 1930s, Hitler's foreign policy underwent a fundamental change. He had originally hoped to conquer "living space" (*Lebensraum*) in the east in an alliance with Britain, or at least without direct British intervention. By 1936 Hitler had recognized that the British government was trying to halt his drive to the east by means of a general European peace settlement.[3] Thereafter his ambitions entailed the risk of a wider European war involving Britain and its allies. Hitler, who remained committed to his "program," decided to mobilize German resources as quickly as possible. He envisaged waging a series of short wars, before the Western powers could prepare to intervene. Timing was thus all-important.[4] Within four years the German army was to be ready for action and the German economy ready for war.[5]

This deadline increased the difficulties of building the Luftwaffe and forced the German aircraft industry to concentrate on fast, medium-range, multipurpose aircraft, which were already in production. In April 1937 Göring ordered a halt to the development of nearly all long-range, four-engined bombers. He remarked in this connection that "the Führer will not ask how big the bombers are but only how many there are."[6]

Although Hitler established the Luftwaffe as an independent service under Göring, who became Reich air minister and commander of the air force, he never paid much attention to the theory of air power.[7] With all its implications for air armament, Hitler's program nonetheless basically shaped the Luftwaffe's concept of air war.

In his inaugural address to the Air War Academy in November 1935, Major General Walter Wever, the chief of the Luftwaffe's general staff, defined the first priority in air war as the close cooperation of the air force with the army and navy against the enemy's armed forces. However, he added a strategic role to the Luftwaffe's mission when he demanded, in addition, that the Luftwaffe aim at halting enemy war production. This line of thought also followed a directive titled "Luftkriegführung," which was published in 1935. It not only emphasized air raids against enemy armed

3 Josef Henke, *England in Hitlers politischem Kalkül 1935–1939* (Boppard am Rhein, 1973), 40–69.

4 For a survey of research on Hitler's "program," see Gerhard Schreiber, "Der Zweite Weltkrieg in der internationalen Forschung: Konzeptionen, Thesen und Kontroversen," in Wolfgang Michalka, ed., *Der Zweite Weltkrieg: Analysen, Grundzüge, Forschungsbilanz*, 2d ed. (Munich, 1990), 3–24.

5 Wilhelm Treue, "Hitlers Denkschrift zum Vierjahresplan 1936," *Vierteljahrshefte für Zeitgeschichte* 3 (1955): 184–210.

6 Quoted in Edward L. Homze, *Arming the Luftwaffe: The Reich Air Ministry and the German Aircraft Industry 1919–39* (Lincoln, Neb., 1976), 125.

7 R. J. Overy, "Hitler and Air Strategy," *Journal of Contemporary History* 15 (1980): 405–21.

forces, but also called for offensive action against the "roots of the enemy people's will to resist [*Widerstandswillen des feindlichen Volkes an der Wurzel*]." Even though this directive minimized the idea of terror-bombing, Major Paul Deichmann, the chief of the operations section in the Luftwaffe general staff, delivered a lecture to the Air War Academy in October 1936 on "principles of operative air warfare." Here he claimed that while air attacks should target war production, the Luftwaffe should also seek ways to strike at the morale of the enemy's civilian population.[8]

Hitler's decision to intervene on the side of General Francisco Franco in the Spanish Civil War (1936–9) had additional implications for the development of the German air force. Parts of the German medium-range fleet could now be tested under combat conditions.[9] To this end, a special unit, the Condor Legion, was dispatched to Spain. Lieutenant Colonel Wolfram Freiherr von Richthofen, the chief of staff and last commander of the legion, defined its role in these terms: "Primary mission the fight against the enemy air force. Then, after establishing control of the air by our night bombers, attacks on lines of communications and possibly industry."[10] Because of Franco's lack of heavy weapons, however, the Condor Legion was forced to engage primarily in close air support.[11] For this kind of action Richthofen developed effective tactics, which later contributed significantly to the early victories of the Wehrmacht in World War II. During the campaign against the Republican northern front, the Condor Legion entered battle for the first time under joint command, so it could exert decisive influence on the conduct of the operation.

The most famous event in this campaign, during which the Condor Legion enjoyed complete air superiority, was the destruction of Guernica on April 26, 1937, by German and Italian bombers. Many observers regard this attack as a masterpiece of terror bombing.[12] According to Richthofen, who

8 Klaus A. Maier, "Total War and Operational Air Warfare," in Klaus A. Maier et al., eds., *Germany and the Second World War*, vol. 2: *Germany's Initial Conquests in Europe* (Oxford, 1991), 33–9; James S. Corum, *The Luftwaffe: Creating the Operational Air War, 1918–1940* (Lawrence, Kans., 1997), 124–54.

9 On German intervention in the Spanish Civil War, see Walther L. Bernecker, *Krieg in Spanien 1936–1939* (Darmstadt, 1991), 47–70. On German military involvement, see Raymond L. Proctor, *Hitler's Luftwaffe in the Spanish Civil War* (Westport, Conn., 1983).

10 Bundesarchiv/Militärarchiv, Freiburg im Breisgau (hereafter BA-MA), N 671/1, Nachlass Richthofen, Richthofen diary, Jan. 26, 1937.

11 "Von der span. Führung wird sehr häufig ein *Einsatz als Artillerie* verlangt, weil die Feldartillerie schlecht ist und versagt. Das muss abgelehnt werden, weil . . . der Einsatz der Luftwaffe an oder unmittelbar hinter der Front unzweckmässig erscheint und nach unseren taktischen Anschauungen abzulehnen ist," BA-MA, RH 2/288, Sonderstab W., Hauptmann Heinze, Bericht über Kurierreise vom 22–30.12. [1936] nach Salamanca, Jan. 4, 1937.

12 Günter Grass has called this air raid an "area bombing première [*Flächenbombardement als Uraufführung*]," *Die Zeit*, Mar. 22, 1991.

ordered the attack, the town was bombed because it was an important center of communications in the rear of the Basque-Asturian forces, which were then in full retreat.[13] The bomber group K/88, the experimental squadron VB/88, and Italian bombers[14] were ordered to strike

> the roads and bridge (including the suburb [Renteria]) just to the east of *Guernica*. This [route] *must* be closed off if final success against enemy personnel and materiel is to be achieved. Vigon [the chief of staff of the Francist northern army group] promises that his troops will advance in such a manner that all roads south of Guernica will be closed. If successful, we will have surrounded the enemy in Marquina [*Gelingt das, haben wir den Gegner um Marquina im Sack*].[15]

The payloads used by the Condor Legion comprised high explosive and incendiary bombs, a mixture that the pilots called the "general staff's blend [*Generalstabsmischung*]," because it had proved effective in previous attacks on towns and villages that were presumed to contain enemy headquarters.[16] After a visit to Guernica about a month after the attack, Richthofen wrote in his diary:

> The attack employed 250-kilogram bombs, with fire bombs making up about a third of the load. When the first Jus [Junkers 52 of the K/88] arrived, there was already a lot of smoke (from the VB, which attacked with 3 aircraft); nobody could recognize the streets, the bridge, or suburb targets, and we therefore dropped the bombs right into the midst of things [*warfen nun mitten hinein*]. The 250-kilogram bombs destroyed a number of houses and the water lines. Then the fire bombs did their work. The kind of buildings – the tile roofs, wooden beams, and wooden galleries – accounted for the complete destruction. . . . Bomb craters can still be seen in the streets – it's just terrific (*einfach toll*). The town was completely closed for at least 24 hours. This was in fact the condition necessary for a big success. If only [our] troops had advanced further. Therefore, the only complete technical success was that of our 250[-kilogram bombs] and the EC.B1 [incendiary bombs].[17]

Richthofen's tactical reasoning, which envisaged the encirclement of the Basque-Asturian Army in Marquina, east of Guernica, was plausible given the military situation on April 26, 1937, and the geographical conditions. But the bomber crews deliberately and unscrupulously "dropped the bombs

13 "From the sea to Tellamendi the Basques were in disorganised movement homewards. It looked like the finish," in G. L. Steer, *The Tree of Gernika* (London, 1938), 233.

14 The situation report of the *Aviazione Legionaria* for Apr. 26, 1937, read: "3 apparecchi S.79 ore 5.20: bombardamento de ponte di Guernica, bombe lanciate: 36 da kg 50," quoted in Jesus M. Salas Larrazabal, *Guernica* (Madrid, 1987), 261. The inflight report of the Italian Lt. Col. Chiappini is quoted by Arrigo Petacco in *Corriere della Sera*, May 18, 1981. The Italian air contingent in Spain at that time took orders from the Condor Legion's leadership, although the Germans had no formal command or control over it. See Richthofen diary, Mar. 24, 26, 1937.

15 Richthofen diary, Apr. 26, 1937.

16 Max Graf Hoyos, *Pedros y Pablos: Fliegen, Erleben, Kämpfen in Spanien* (Munich, 1939), 42.

17 Richthofen diary, May 30, 1937; cf. Proctor, *Hitler's Luftwaffe*, 130.

right into the midst of things," once smoke and dust prevented clear identification of the targets that Richthofen had ordered.[18] Indiscriminate, terror-bombing had been "in the air" since the attacks on Madrid in November and December 1936, in which German bomber units had participated. On the night of December 4, 1936, the Condor Legion dropped thirty-six tons of bombs on the Spanish capital. This attack also featured trials with 500-kg bombs dropped by the new German dive-bomber, the Ju 87. Also on December 4, 1936, a group of experts from the Condor Legion completed a study of the "vulnerability of Spanish towns." "For obvious psychological reasons," Richthofen opposed the idea of discussions with Spanish officials about "bombing effects on Spanish towns."[19] In December 1936 the plans of the Condor Legion for offensive operations against the northern Spanish provinces read as follows:

> Operational action in the north (Basque province). A lack of foodstuffs there. According to General Franco, [there] already [have been] overtures in surrender negotiations. Until now, little air defense. No modern fighters yet confirmed, [so] the Ju(s) can be brought into action without fighter protection. Targets: weapons and munitions factories, port installations, food supplies, and possibly terror-attacks to encourage the negotiations.[20]

General Emilio Mola Vidal, the commander of Franco's northern army group, initiated the campaign against the Basques and Asturians with an ultimatum at the end of March 1937: "I have decided to terminate the war rapidly in the north. Those not guilty of assassinations and who surrender their arms will have their lives and property spared. But, if submission is not immediate, I will raze all Vizcaya to the ground, beginning with the industries of war."[21] The ultimatum was no empty threat. When the offensive in the north stalled due to bad weather and Basque resistance, and when the leadership of the Condor Legion became angry about the useless consumption of bombs, Mola resolved to carry out his threat. In a dispute with Richthofen, who accused him of lacking motivation, Mola requested that the Condor Legion shift from close air support to strategic operations in order to destroy Bilbao's industrial plant. Mola's arguments revealed the reactionary, antimodern attitude of Franco's forces. Spain, he declared, suffered from the industrialization of Catalonia and Bilbao. Because the Nationalists could not destroy these industrial regions against the will of the Spanish people once the war was over, the Condor Legion was to undertake the

18 For the ongoing discussion of the destruction of Guernica, see Bernecker, *Krieg in Spanien*, 62–6.

19 Richthofen diary, Dec. 2, 1936.

20 *Heinze report*, 4.

21 Quoted in Hugh Thomas, *The Spanish Civil War* (New York, 1963), 402–3.

task at this time. Richthofen resisted, arguing that it would be pointless to destroy industries that would soon be captured. When he failed to convince Mola of this point, Richthofen insisted on a written order from the general personally. Apparently he received it, for he soon promised to attack the Galdakao powder industry, which lay to the east of Bilbao, once the Condor Legion was available.[22]

Richthofen's resistance was not motivated by humanitarian feelings. The leaders of the Condor Legion were eager to take Spain's Atlantic ports as quickly as possible and intact because the German war economy required sea routes to transport the raw materials with which Franco was paying for German military assistance.[23] Economic and political interests, combined with Richthofen's desire to compensate with a German victory for the Italian debacle at Guadalajara earlier in the year, thus underlay the Condor Legion's ruthless conduct of the air war in the north. After Italian bombers had inflicted casualties among Mola's troops with "friendly fire," Richthofen removed the Italians from close air support and assigned them to operations against towns and villages in the Basque rear area. But the German bomber group dropped its own bombs on these towns and villages as well, whenever crews could not attack their battlefield targets.[24] On April 23, 1937, when the offensive again slowed, Richthofen noted that "considerations arise that recommend bombing Bilbao itself to bits [*in Schutt und Asche zu legen*]."[25] Only the retreat of the Basque-Asturian forces evidently saved Bilbao from total destruction.[26] And on the morning of April 26, a few hours before the attack on Guernica, German bombers did destroy Guerricaiz, about 10 kilometers to the southeast of Guernica.[27]

The political difficulties caused by the Guernica affair evidently persuaded Franco not to allow raids on larger Spanish towns. On May 28, 1937, Richthofen gave orders to stop bombing Bilbao.[28] But indiscriminate bombing did not disappear entirely from the Condor Legion's agenda. In June 1938 an "evaluation of the effects of bombs during attacks" designated

22 Richthofen diary, Apr. 2, 1937; BA-MA, RL 2/v, 3188, Generalstab der Luftwaffe, 8. Abteilung, Arbeitsgruppe "Spanienkrieg," Die Kämpfe im Norden, 51–5.

23 BA-MA, M/1405/80839, Kriegstagebuch des Befehlshabers der Aufklärungsstreitkräfte, May 13, 1937.

24 Richthofen diary, Apr. 2, 4, 24, 25, 1937.

25 Ibid., Apr. 23, 1937.

26 In April 1937 six hundred tons of bombs were dropped on Bilbao. "Das ist eine 5 mal so grosse Menge, als im Verlauf des ganzen [Ersten] Weltkrieges auf England abgeworfen wurde." BA-MA, M 1399/80815, Reichskriegsministerium, Wehrmachtsamt, Sonderstab W., Lagebericht Nr. 176, May 4, 1937.

27 "In Guernicaiz [*sic*!] durch Jus kein Haus mehr ganz," Richthofen diary, Apr. 30, 1937.

28 Facsimile of Richthofen's order in Vicente Talon, *Arde Guernica* (Madrid, 1970), facing 265.

"government and population (towns)" as a continuing priority in bombing targets.[29]

By dint of its air raids on Madrid, its bombing "without regard for the civilian population,"[30] and its deliberate targeting of undefended housing areas, like the Renteria suburb of Guernica, the Condor Legion crossed the border between war against an enemy's armed forces and total war against the enemy's entire populace. Evidence suggests as well that the Condor Legion violated international law. Although attempts during the interwar period to set binding legal limits on air warfare failed,[31] several articles that related to land warfare in the Hague Convention of 1907 were applicable. Article 25 banned bombardment or attacks by whatever means on undefended towns, villages, dwellings, and buildings. In the preamble to the Hague Convention, the so-called Martens clause, the contracting parties declared that, in cases not specifically included in the regulations that were adopted, inhabitants and belligerents alike remained subject to the rule and protection of the principles of international law, as these derived from the practices of civilized peoples, the laws of humanity, and the dictates of public conscience. These principles were to govern the conduct of war until the laws of war could be more completely codified in the future. A moral demand no less emphatic was contained in a nonbinding proposal by the Hague Commission of Jurists of 1923, which prohibited aerial bombardment for the purpose of terrorizing civilian populations, attacking property of a nonmilitary character, or injuring noncombatants.[32]

Indignation and dismay over the destruction of Guernica echoed around the world.[33] The revulsion found lasting expression in the painting "Guernica" that Pablo Picasso undertook for the Spanish pavilion at the Paris International Exhibition in 1937. Above all, the Guernica raid shocked public opinion and Parliament in Britain, where the population had, after

29 The other targets were the enemy's air force, war economy, supply (ports, traffic routes), troop movements, and troop positions: BA-MA, RL 57, Auswertestab "R[ügen]," June 25, 1938. In November 1937, Franco reproached Richthofen for the indiscriminate bombing of Collunga, Villaviciosa, Gangas de Onis, and Gijon: Richthofen diary, Nov. 3, 1937. Richthofen himself admitted that he had behaved rudely during the Guernica episode ("Ich hatte mich aber bei Guernica wohl etwas rüpelhaft benommen"): Richthofen diary, letter of May 25, 1937.

30 BA-MA, RL 57, Auswertung "Rügen," Heft 2, 50–1.

31 W. Hays Parks, "Air War and the Law of War," *The Air Force Law Review* 32 (1990): 1–225; Donald Cameron Watt, "Restraints on War in the Air before 1945," in Michael Howard, ed., *Restraints on War: Studies in the Limitation of Armed Conflict* (Oxford, 1979), 39–77; Geoffrey Best, *Humanity in Warfare: The Modern History of the International Law of Armed Conflicts* (London, 1983), 262–85.

32 Manfred Messerschmidt, "Strategic Air War and International Law," in Horst Boog, ed., *The Conduct of the Air War in the Second World War: An International Comparison* (New York, 1992), 298–309.

33 See Herbert R. Southworth, *La destruction de Guernica: Journalisme, diplomatie, propagande et histoire* (Paris, 1975); Southworth, *Guernica! Guernica!* (Berkeley, Calif., 1977).

the German air raids of 1917, become acutely aware that the country was no longer an island safely isolated from the European continent. The British interpreted the attack on Guernica as a prelude to the Luftwaffe's total war in the air.[34] After Guernica and later attacks on Barcelona,[35] the discussions in the British Cabinet, which had taken place in 1935–6 in the abstract over a possible German air threat to Britain, became agitated. Although the German air raids during World War I had been militarily inconclusive, they were psychologically disconcerting. As one scholar has remarked,

> an Anglo-German war, it was anticipated, would involve attacks on an even larger scale, and avoidance of this horrifying prospect therefore appeared to demand a drastic solution. Without this experience it is difficult to understand how the British Cabinet could have discussed the possibility of bargaining away some of Britain's naval power in return for a somewhat dubious convention on air war limitation.[36]

The fear of a "knock-out blow" from the Luftwaffe had a fatal effect on British foreign policy, particularly during the Sudeten crisis in the autumn of 1938. On September 28, 1938, when the crisis was at its peak, British military intelligence (MI5) circulated a warning that the Luftwaffe would attack London the moment Britain declared war on Germany.[37] Prime Minister Neville Chamberlain shared this view of the German air threat and used it to justify his policy, which led to a bloodless British defeat at the Munich Conference. He told his Cabinet colleagues that "he had flown up the river over London. He had imagined a German bomber flying the same course, he had asked himself what degree of protection they could afford for the thousands of homes which he had seen stretched out below him and he had felt that we were in no position to justify waging a war today."[38]

Ironically, Göring was at the same time warning Hitler not to push too far in Munich, for he was convinced that the Luftwaffe could not hope

34 When the British ambassador to Spain, Sir Henry Chilton, reported the destruction of Guernica to the Foreign Office, Evelyn Shuckburgh, the Third Secretary, commented that "Guernica has taught us what to expect from the Germans" (quoted in Hans-Henning Abendroth, *Hitler in der spanischen Arena: Die deutsch-spanischen Beziehungen im Spannungsfeld der europäischen Interessenpolitik vom Ausbruch des Bürgerkrieges bis zum Ausbruch des Weltkrieges 1936–1939* [Paderborn, 1973], 360n154).

35 The Italian air force attacked Barcelona on Feb. 28, 1938, killing 150 people. Bombing continued until Mar. 18, with some 1,300 civilians killed and 2,000 injured: Thomas, *Spanish Civil War*, 647, 658. The newsreel reports on the Barcelona raids had an immense impact on public opinion in Western Europe. See T. Aldgate, "British Newsreels and the Spanish Civil War," *History* 58 (1973): 160–3.

36 Uri Bialer, *The Shadow of the Bomber: The Fear of Air Attack and British Politics, 1932–1939* (London, 1980), 125–6.

37 F. H. Hinsley et al., *British Intelligence in the Second World War: Its Influence on Strategy and Operations*, 3 vols. (London, 1979–90), 1:82.

38 Quoted in Bialer, *Shadow of the Bomber*, 157.

for decisive results in a strategic air offensive against Britain in 1938.[39] The Luftwaffe itself, in which Göring then ordered a fivefold increase by 1942, also considered its chances poor in an all-out air offensive against Britain. In contrast, assessments were much more optimistic about the Luftwaffe's capability as a deterrent force and, if necessary, a terror weapon. In June 1938 the Condor Legion's evaluation of the use of the bombers reported that, in spite of its unique features that limited its lessons for a European war, the Spanish Civil War had provided valuable knowledge about the moral and physical effects of aerial bombing.[40] The evaluation noted that the discipline and organization of the working-class population were in many respects poor and contributed to "very low powers of moral resistance." The report concluded that constant attacks by smaller units on selected cities had "frightened and made a strong impression" on the population, especially where air defenses were inadequate.

In the contemporary German military literature, authors likewise called for total air war because they believed in the superiority of the Nazi *Volksgemeinschaft* over the Western democracies. Major Erwin Gehrts, the director of the Air Ministry's Department of Instruction and Teaching, advocated air war in order to break the will of the enemy's "home army of workers," in the event that the enemy's armed forces could not be defeated quickly. Gehrts argued that it was less important to destroy the "arsenals of economic technology" in the enemy's lands than to "depopulate" them. Because he assumed that Germany's potential enemies had similar intentions, he called for "total mobilization," the "creation and demonstration of a uniform national consciousness by mobilizing all values, even in peacetime," and by educating the German worker to give him a "soldierly basic attitude." In Gehrt's view, "the [German] worker and the soldier are, in their Prussian-German substance, today cast from the same mold." He thus believed that the Nazi state enjoyed a considerable lead over the Western powers.[41]

German moral superiority also became the premise on which the Luftwaffe's official situation reports were based. On May 2, 1939, Department 5 (Intelligence) of the Luftwaffe's general staff suggested that the Western powers' policy of appeasement during the Munich crisis had reflected the limitations that governments faced under democratic constitutions. These

39 Leonidas E. Hill, ed., *Die Weizsäcker-Papiere 1933–1950* (Frankfurt am Main, 1974), 144, 169, 171–2, 508n140. On the Munich crisis, see Williamson Murray, *The Change in the European Balance of Power, 1938–1939: The Path to Ruin* (Princeton, N.J., 1984), 195–263.

40 BA-MA, RL 57, Auswertung "Rügen," Heft 3; cf. Klaus A. Maier, *Guernica, 26.4.1937: Die deutsche Intervention in Spanien und der "Fall Guernica"* (Freiburg im Breisgau, 1975), 150.

41 Erwin Gehrts, "Gedanken zum operativen Luftkrieg: Eine Studie," *Die Luftwaffe* 2 (1937): 16–39. See also the essay by Markus Pöhlmann in this book.

governments had been less flexible than the German "Führer State" in making political and military decisions. The intelligence report concluded:

On the basis of all available information, we can say that Germany is the only state to have developed a *total* plan for the preparation and conduct of an offensive and defensive air war in the areas of equipment, organization, tactics, and command. This means a general advantage in war readiness and hence a strengthening of Germany's overall military position.

This conclusion led Department 5 to the fateful prediction that although the Western powers were bound by treaties and promises to Eastern Europe, a military conflict in this region could be localized.[42] Hitler shared this view. In his speech to the Wehrmacht commanders on August 22, 1939, he described the impending attack on Poland as a "matter of nerves." He himself was prepared to take a "great risk."[43] Four days later, he wrote to Benito Mussolini that he would not hesitate "to solve the problem in the east even if this involves the danger of a conflict in the west." In grounding his confidence, he alluded not only to the Russo-German nonaggression pact of 1939, but also to his conviction that "we clearly have superiority in the air."[44]

42 BA-MA, RL 2/535, Die Luftlage in Europa, Stand: Frühjahr 1939. For the operative planning and the role of terror bombing against Britain, see Maier, "Total War and Operational Air Warfare," 53–5.

43 *Documents on German Foreign Policy, 1918–45*, 24 vols. (Washington, D.C., 1949–83), series D, vol. 7: nos. 192–3.

44 Ibid., no. 307.

16

Stalinism as Total Social War

HANS-HEINRICH NOLTE

In the 1920s and 1930s the Communist Party of the Soviet Union (CPSU) waged a total war against those whom it defined as the exploiting classes. In theory, this war was directed against a social institution – private ownership of the means of production – not against people. In practice, however, it was often waged against persons who were identified simply as members of the propertied classes. Underlying the whole campaign was the premise that changes in material life would in the long run change consciousness,[1] and therefore that people of the propertied classes would eventually acquire, presumably through physical labor, the appropriate worldview.[2] In this chapter, I explore this proposition in the context of collectivization and the campaign against the *kulachestvo* (well-to-do peasantry). I then offer some thoughts about the resonance in Nazi Germany of the Bolsheviks' war on the kulaks.

Whereas the Bolsheviks in 1917 had hoped to create a world in which there were no standing armies, the possibility of war figured prominently in Soviet domestic politics from the start.[3] The Bolsheviks undertook a class war almost immediately, and Allied intervention in the Russian Civil War only intensified its effects. On May 22, 1918, the Central Committee of the Russian Communist Party observed that "the war to achieve the full power of the proletariat and the poorest sections of peasantry is not even finished in our country," but already "the imperialists of all countries are filled with hatred. From West and East the beasts of prey are preparing to

1 Karl Marx and Friedrich Engels, *Die deutsche Ideologie*, Karl Marx–Friedrich Engels Werke (hereafter MEW), ed. Institut für Marxismus-Leninismus beim ZK der SED, 39 vols. (Berlin 1959–83), 3:27.

2 See Stefan Plaggenborg, "Instrumente des sowjetischen Erziehungsstaats," in Manfred Hellmann et al., eds., *Handbuch der Geschichte Russlands*, 3 vols. (Stuttgart, 1976–91), 3:1492–518; Hans-Heinrich Nolte, "Lehren und Lernen 1917–1941," in ibid., 1622–31.

3 V. I. Lenin, *Staat und Revolution* (Berlin, 1970), 315–420.

fall on us."[4] Lenin provided the theoretical framework, which the CPSU then incorporated into its program. According to Lenin, the global concentration of capital had led to imperialism, the final stage of capitalism, which by its very nature fomented wars for markets, resources, and labor. Prices rose; laborers were enslaved. "All this is leading unavoidably," the program announced, "toward linking the civil wars that are raging in various countries to the revolutionary wars being fought by proletarian countries in their own defense and by enslaved peoples against the yoke of imperialist powers." "Under these conditions," it continued, "slogans of pacifism, international disarmament under capitalism, arbitration, et cetera, are shown to be not only reactionary utopias, but direct deceptions of the workers – aimed at disarming the proletariat and distracting it from the task of disarming the exploiters."

The institutions of the Russian Revolution, such as the Cheka (All-Russian Extraordinary Commision for Combatting Counterrevolution and Sabotage or secret police), thereupon described their assignments in military terms. On June 1, 1918, local Cheka organizations were charged with undertaking: "(1) Ruthless war [*bor'ba*] against counterrevolution and speculation, employing all means that the [police] has at its disposal; (2) Control of the local bourgeoisie and all counterrevolutionary movements arising in its midst."[5]

It came as no surprise to the Bolsheviks that the capitalist countries intervened in the Civil War. The Bolsheviks believed that the bourgeoisie had brought an end to real national sovereignty, as Marx and Engels had remarked in 1848.[6] Following their own retreat in the war against Poland, which led to the peace treaty of Riga in 1921, the Bolsheviks hoped for a respite in the fight against capitalism. When Fascism came to power in Italy, they interpreted it as the last stand of capitalism. The Comintern reacted by forming a special committee and organizing aid for the Italian Communist party, which it advised to establish secret printing offices and undertake armed resistance.[7] Following Hitler's Beer Hall Putsch in 1923, Karl Radek again argued that Communists should engage in armed resistance.[8] The fifth congress of the Comintern resolved in 1924 to form armed formations, the so-called proletarian hundreds, and began to collect money for this purpose.[9]

4 Institut Marksizma-Leninizma pri TsK KPSS, ed., *Kommunisticheskaja Partija Sovetskogo Sojuza v rezoliucijakh i reshenijakh*, 14 vols. (Moscow, 1970–84) (hereafter KPSSRR), 2:30–1.

5 A. I. Kokurin and N. V. Petrov, eds., *Lubjanka* (Moscow, 1997).

6 Karl Marx and Friedrich Engels, *Manifest der Kommunistischen Partei* (MEW, 4), 459–93.

7 N. P. Komolova, ed., *Komintern protiv fashizma* (Moscow, 1999), 87–8, 92.

8 Ibid., 109, 129.

9 Ibid., 141–2; cf. 144–8.

After the Civil War had ended, however, the use of military language decreased within the Soviet Union. The powers of the political police remained nonetheless comprehensive, revealing the dictatorial character of the new government, which knew nothing of legal protections like habeas corpus.[10] On March 24, 1924, the Central Committee redefined the mission of the secret police, which was now renamed the State Political Administration (GPU). "In order to wage war against the criminal activities of persons who are considered socially offensive," the statement read, "the GPU has the right":

(1) to send [these people] out of the settlements where they live and to prohibit them from living there for a period of no more than 3 years;
(2) to prohibit them . . . from living in certain other settlements or provinces for the same period, according to a list established by the GPU;
(3) to order them to live . . . under the control of the local organ of the GPU for this period;
(4) to send them to concentration camps for this period; or
(5) to send them outside the borders of the Soviet Union for the same period.[11]

From the inception of the new regime, the distinction between civil society and state became blurred. While a considerable private sphere was tolerated, little or no room remained for publicly stating sectoral interests or discussing political alternatives. Between 1921 and 1928 this tendency increased. In theory, Marx and Lenin had both envisaged the withering away of state institutions;[12] but in practice, as the enormous powers of the secret police demonstrated, the state took on the capacity to overpower civil society. In the tradition of czarism, a camp-system was organized, albeit on a small scale during the early 1920s, with the aim of reforming people by means of forced labor.[13]

Political pluralism survived only on the left, and only for a few years, until the debate on industrialization.[14] But even as long as it was possible

10 See Ian Kershaw and Moshe Lewin, eds., *Stalinism and Nazism: Dictatorships in Comparison* (Cambridge, 1997); Hans-Heinrich Nolte, *Der deutsche Überfall auf die Sowjetunion 1941* (Hannover, 1991); Eckhard Jesse, ed., *Totalitarismus im 20. Jahrhundert* (Baden-Baden, 1996).

11 Kokurin and Petrov, eds., *Lubjanka*, 179.

12 Lenin, *Staat und Revolution.*

13 See Zygmunt Baumann, "Das Jahrhundert der Lager," in Mihran Dabag and Kristin Platt, eds., *Genozid und Moderne* (Opladen, 1998), 81–99; Dittmar Dahlmann and Gerhard Hirschfeld, eds., *Lager, Zwangsarbeit, Vertreibung und Deportation: Dimensionen der Massenverbrechen in der Sowjetunion und in Deutschland 1933 bis 1945* (Essen, 1999).

14 The Socialist Revolutionaries, who were represented in the first soviets, were crippled by the trial of 1922 and erased by arrests of all members in 1925. See also N. D. Erofeev, ed., *Partija socialistov-revoljucionerov: Dokumenty I materialy 1900–1925* (Moscow, 2000). For the debate within the CPSU on industrialization, see Alexander Erlich, *The Soviet Industrialization Debate, 1924–1928* (Cambridge, Mass., 1967).

to dissent within the system of Soviets (as representations of the working people), this pluralism proved tenuous, unable to put checks on the government of "people's commissars."[15] The central Soviet government neither offered effective power sharing, nor did it compensate those who sat in the representative bodies. Within a few years the pluralism of the left turned into a dictatorship of the Communist Party and, in the end, into the dictatorship of a single person, the *Vozhd*, that is, the leader Stalin.[16]

In foreign policy the danger of Fascism had increased by the end of the 1920s, but the Comintern no longer advocated military action. Under Stalin's prodding, at its sixth Congress, in 1928, the Comintern condemned the thoroughgoing "fascistization" of the capitalist countries, a process that was abetted, it claimed, by the Social Democrats, whom the congress branded "social fascists." Attempts to unite the European left "from above" – in cooperation with Social Democratic leaders – were rejected. The Central Committee of the All-Union Communist Party advised the German Communist Party in 1930 to fight the Social Democrats as hard as they fought the Nazis.[17] The leadership of the Comintern regarded fascism as the prelude to Communism, the last stage of bourgeois society prior to the socialist revolution – a point that Stalin believed was corroborated by the fact that capitalistic countries were turning increasingly into open dictatorships.[18] But at the same time, Stalin and his allies were reluctant to prepare to meet the external threat, for they had by now started a war within their own country.

The decision to undertake the forced industrialization and agricultural collectivization of the Soviet Union, announced in 1928, was itself legitimized by the international threat. "The danger of a counterrevolutionary war against the Soviet Union is the most important concern of our time," read the first message of the Central Committee in the summer of 1927.[19] The Fifteenth Party Congress, which met in December of the same year, concluded that the USSR's "peaceful breathing-space" might be shortened and that it was becoming necessary to strengthen the military.[20] But during the next several years, this "strengthening the military" referred in the first instance to the militarization of Soviet society, for Stalin had concluded that the regime needed a continued "breathing space" in order to focus its efforts on domestic war against the villages.

15 "Soviet" refers here to the representative institutions only. For a sketch of the pyramids of power in the Soviet Union, see Hans-Heinrich Nolte, *Kleine Geschichte Russlands* (Stuttgart, 1998), 343.

16 See ibid., 168–80.

17 See Komolova, *Komintern*, 234–6, 278–84.

18 Ibid., 291–8.

19 KPSSRR, 3:463.

20 KPSSRR, 4:14–16.

When the Fifteenth Party Congress called for a new "period of economic transformation onto a higher level of technology and more rapid industrialization,"[21] it counted on accumulating the necessary capital in three ways – from the profits of state-owned industry, taxes on holdings in savings-banks, and state bonds.[22] The congress rejected the argument that capital accumulation would have to be achieved at the expense of the villages.[23] Rural cooperatives were instead to be promoted by means of reduced taxes, easy credit, and other privileges.[24] The development of agriculture in the Soviet Union, it was maintained, offered the best conditions for the village poor to "fight decisively for restricting the exploitive tendencies of the *kulachestvo*."[25]

Who were these kulaks? It is misleading to consider them simply as capitalist farmers.[26] The *mir* or *obshhina* (village community) system, which was based on the regular redistribution of arable land among village members, survived into the "New Economic Policy" (NEP). This system blocked the concentration of arable land in the villages of central Russia. The same system nevertheless nurtured disparities in possessions among the peasants, because some peasant families owned more livestock and capital than others. The system of redistribution pertained only to land, so a family with little livestock or equipment could be forced to lease part of its land to another in return for the use of horses or machines; it could even be forced to work its own land in service to another family. The system primarily benefited older peasants. Younger couples, who had few assets, had to barter with their elders. Sons often bartered with their fathers.

This system granted a considerable degree of autonomy to the *obshhina*, which as a rule comprised a small village. There were some 600,000 such villages in the Soviet Union. Their average population was two hundred; and a rural Soviet (*Selsovet*) comprised about eight such *obshhiny*.[27] The Communist Party was normally absent at the village level, and even at the level of the rural Soviets, there were generally not many party members.

In the old Marxist debates over whether the Russian commune might constitute a basis for agrarian socialism, Lenin had argued that the Russian agrarian economy had already taken on a capitalistic character.[28] The

21 KPSSRR, 3:362–412, citation on 364; *perestrojka* is in the Russian text.

22 Ibid., 366.

23 See Erlich, *Soviet Industrialization Debate.*

24 Ibid., 428–30.

25 KPSSRR, 3:371.

26 Teodor Shanin, *The Awkward Class* (Oxford, 1972); Alexander Tschajanow, *Die Lehre von der bäuerlichen Familienwirtschaft* (Frankfurt am Main, 1987).

27 D. J. Male, *Russian Peasant Organisation Before Collectivisation* (Cambridge, 1971), 92.

28 V. I. Lenin, *Razvitie kapitalizma v Rossii* (St. Petersburg, 1899); Institut für Marxismus-Leninismus beim ZK der KpdSU, ed., *W. I. Lenin Werke*, vol. 3 (Berlin, 1970). For the history of this debate, see Carsten Goehrke, *Die Theorien über Entstehung und Entwicklung des "mir"* (Wiesbaden, 1961).

strategic intent of Lenin's position was clear. If 80 percent of the population did not yet live in capitalist conditions, a socialist revolution was out of the question. In the discussions that followed the Russian Revolution, the followers of Lenin, most of whom were urban intellectuals, were thus badly equipped to understand the structure of the Russian villages, even as these "aliens in the villages" decided the future of the Russian agrarian economy.[29] Nikolay Bukharin argued in favor of the kulaks, but he represented a minority opinion.

During the October Revolution the Bolsheviks had endorsed the agrarian program of the Social Revolutionaries. By partitioning the estates of the tsar, the nobility, and the church, and by forcing back to the *mir* those peasants who had left during the Stolypin reforms of 1907 (which enabled the peasants to leave without the consent of other peasants), the government enhanced the power of the *obshhiny* and the hold of the small-scale economy. Ultimately, the Bolsheviks wanted large, modern estates; but they feared that the kulaks would become the agents and beneficiaries of such consolidation. Large-scale agrarian enterprises were desirable, but they had to be socialist. So when the policy of forced industrialization ran into difficulties in the wake of the first Five-Year Plan, the Communist Party portrayed the *kulachestvo* as the enemy, the exploiting class.

In 1927 the Central Committee still argued that the greatest difficulty facing Soviet agriculture lay in agrarian overpopulation, and that the "war between socialist and capitalist tendencies" in the countryside could be won by drawing the middle peasants into the socialist camp and by taxing the kulaks excessively.[30] In 1928 the government still regarded detention camps as expensive, and it planned to reduce the number of people being detained. Only in 1929 did this attitude change, once the government decided to put the detainees to work in industry.[31] The war against the kulaks was not planned long in advance, and the main weapon was deportation.

About the same time, however, it became clear that village structures were not going to change voluntarily, primarily because the "*bednjaki*" and particularly the *serednjaki*, respectively the "poor" and "middle" peasants on whom the Bolsheviks had pinned their hopes, were to a large degree themselves the sons and daughters of the *kulaky*. They thus united against the government, as they had traditionally united against those who were alien to the village.

29 Rex Rexheuser, "Der Fremde im Dorf: Versuch über ein Motiv der neueren russischen Geschichte," *Jahrbücher für Geschichte Osteuropas* 25 (1977): 494–512; Hans-Jürgen Bömelburg and Beate Eschment, eds., *"Der Fremde im Dorf": Rex Rexheuser zum 65. Geburtstag* (Lüneburg, 1998).

30 KPPSSR, 3:526–41.

31 Michael Jakobson, "Die Funktionen und die Struktur des sowjetischen Gefängnis- und Lagersystems," in Dahlmann and Hirschfeld, eds., *Lager, Zwangsarbeit, Vertreibung und Deportation*, 207–21.

There were bitter intergenerational disputes, but in these small hamlets of 150 to 250 inhabitants, everyone was related. When the government used its monopoly to raise the price of industrial goods, the villages united in action. The peasants raised their consumption of their own products and brought less to market, under the slogan "eating better, selling less."[32]

The CPSU thus concluded that it was essential to break the power of the villages. The argument that the peasantry was to be the source of capital accumulation does not explain the context, however, because the Bolsheviks had planned to bring more capital goods to the countryside from the start.[33] The issue was instead the power to determine the kinds of industrial products that would be made available to the countryside – and when. The party decided that the central government should have this power. The mechanization of agriculture was expected to be a gradual process because the production of agricultural machinery was slow. Accordingly, the first Five-Year Plan provided for enlarging the "socialist sector" of the agricultural economy from 2 percent to 15 percent.

Acting as centralizing institutions, the agricultural cooperatives became the focus of this effort.[34] Their center was the *Selsovet* (rural "Soviet"), which was located away from the village and attracted primarily the poorest peasants. The CPSU tried to strengthen the cooperatives by several means. Young members of the party and *Komsomol* – the party's youth organization – roamed the countryside to "instruct" the peasants about modern ways of life. This campaign had an antireligious dimension, as young atheists from the towns descended on the villages and tried to persuade believers to turn churches into barns and bells into industrial raw materials.[35] Depending on their classification, the cooperatives were freed in 1928 from the principal agrarian tax.[36] By 1929 half the tax was paid by the 3.9 percent of the farms characterized as *kulachnyj*.[37] In 1931, when only 0.9 percent of the farms

32 Alec Nove, *An Economic History of the USSR* (Harmondsworth, U.K., 1972), 93–6, 105–13; cf. Hans Raupach, *Geschichte der Sowjetwirtschaft* (Reinbek bei Hamburg, 1964), 49–81.

33 Ulrich Weissenburger, "Der Beitrag der Landwirtschaft zur Industrialisierung der Landwirtschaft 1928–1940," in Gernot Erler and Walter Süss, eds., *Stalinismus: Probleme der Sowjetgesellschaft zwischen Kolletivierung und Weltkrieg* (Frankfurt am Main, 1982), 140–66.

34 Georg Brunner and Klaus Westen, *Die sowjetische Kolchosordnung* (Stuttgart, 1970), 124–9.

35 M. Ejnisherlov et al., eds., *Vojnstvujushhee bezbozhie v SSSR za 15 let* (Moscow, 1932). See Hans-Heinrich Nolte, "Budgetakkumulation, Kollektivierungskampagne und Religionsbedrückung im ersten sowjetischen Fünfjahrplan," *Kirche im Osten* 24 (1981): 83–105; cf. Stefan Plaggenborg, *Revolutionskultur: Menschenbilder und kulturelle Praxis in Sowjetrussland zwischen Oktoberrevolution und Stalinismus* (Cologne, 1996), 289–341.

36 M. Ja. Zalesskij, *Nalogovaja politika sovetskogo gosudarstva v derevne* (Moscow, 1940), 77.

37 Ibid., 97–8; cf. N. A. Ivnickij, *Klassovaja bor'ba v derevne i likvidacija kulachestva kak klassa* (Moscow, 1972), 294; I. Ja. Trifonov, *Likvidacija ekspluatatorskikh klassov v SSSR* (Moscow, 1975), 256; N. A. Ivnickij, *Kollektivizacija i raskulachivanie* (Moscow, 1996).

counted as kulak, they paid 16.5 percent of the tax.[38] Whenever problems arose in collecting grain after 1928, they were blamed on the *kulachestvo*, who were accused of trying to make profits at the expense of industrial growth, even of threatening the workers and soldiers with starvation.[39]

Thus, the war against the kulaks began in the countryside. It was a war against the villages, in which the kulaks were singled out. As soon as the CPSU realized that economic measures would not suffice, attacks took place on the kulaks personally and their property.[40] Not everyone in the Politburo agreed with this approach. The vice-chairman of the Commissariat of Finances or Narkomfin, Moijsevich Il'ich Frumenkin, informed the Politburo in June 1928 that "putting the kulak outside of the law is leading to lawlessness among the whole peasantry." He predicted that slogans like Vyacheslav Molotov's – that it was "necessary to beat the kulak so hard that the *serednjak* (peasant of middling status) would prostrate himself" – would not work. "We should not close our eyes to the fact," Frumenkin went on, "that excepting only small segments, the whole village is against us." Instead of violence, he proposed to use taxation as the principal weapon.[41]

Stalin rejected Frumenkin's views and insisted that the alliance between town and village was intact.[42] Even when it finally became impossible to deny that Frumenkin was right, the CPSU placed the entire blame on the kulaks. In December 1929 Stalin formulated the slogan in military terms: "attack (*nastupat' na*) the *kulachestvo*: that means break it and destroy it as class."[43] The next month the Central Committee declared that the goal was now the collectivization of 100 percent of the arable land.[44] This goal was justified in theoretical terms: "Now we have the material base for changing large-scale economies that are based on the kulaks into large-scale economies based on the *kolkhoz*. . . . [This prospect has given] the Party reason to a change of policy from restricting the exploitive tendencies of the *kulachestvo* to destroying it as class."[45]

In 1929 alone, "the village" responded to forced collectivization with more than 1,300 acts of insurrection. The next year the incidents of resistance, including passive protests, the slaughtering of animal-stock, and murdering Communists in the countryside, were even more numerous. In a "peasant war" that remains little researched, in Byelorussia, Russia, and

38 *Otchet Narodnogo Kommissariata Finansov SSSR za 1931 g.* (Leningrad, 1932), 138.

39 KPSSRR, 4:75–88.

40 See Stephan Merl, *Die Anfänge der Kollektivierung in der Sowjetunion* (Wiesbaden, 1985); *Bauern unter Stalin: Die Formierung des sowjetischen Kolchossystems 1930–1941* (Berlin, 1990).

41 M. E. Glavackij, ed., *Istorija Rossii 1917–1940* (Ekaterinburg, 1996), 246–7.

42 Ibid., 247–9.

43 Ibid., 251–2.

44 KPSSRR, 4:383–6.

45 Ibid., 385.

Central Asia (data are not known for the Ukraine), 1,642 mass gatherings were recorded in protest against collectivization in March 1930.[46] On March 2, Stalin retreated slightly in order to provide a short *peredychka* or breathing space for the fall harvest.[47] At the end of the year, however, the war against the *kulachestvo* resumed, as unemployment disappeared in the Soviet Union, and forced labor took on economic significance.

The destruction of the *kulachestvo* was achieved by extending the powers of the secret police. When founding a *kolkhoz* (collective farm), officials of the GPU were allowed to transfer kulaks from their villages to other regions or special settlements and to confiscate their land and capital in the name of the new *Kolkhozy*.[48] This policy was made public on February 1, 1931, in an article in *Pravda*.[49] The transfers and confiscations were enacted by a troika, comprised of the local party secretary, the president of the executive committee of the *Selsovet*, and a representative of the GPU.

In 1929, 1.3 million households were classified as *kulachnyj*. The criteria were whether they employed labor and owned two or more horses or pieces of farm machinery. Including the wives of these kulaks, some 2.6 million people thereby lost their voting rights. Together with their children they constituted a population of well over ten million.[50] They were further divided into subcategories: "counterrevolutionary" kulaks were to be singled out and sent to work camps; "dangerous" kulaks were to be resettled, along with their families, in peripheral regions (where the families of the counterrevolutionary kulaks were also sent); and other kulaks were to be resettled outside the *kolkhozy* on poor land in their home districts (*oblast'*).

According to a list compiled by a special committee on the kulak question, in 1930–1 the families of 365,544 kulaks, a total of 1,679,528 people, were deported: 1,157,007 were considered dangerous kulaks and were sent to far-off places, whereas 522,451 remained within their *oblasti*.[51] The same committee resettled these families for work in the large state-run industrial enterprises, such as *Vostokugol* (coal-mining in the East), *Uralugol* (coal-mining in the Urals), *Vostokstal* (steel mills in the East), *Tsvetmetzoloto* (nonferrous metals and gold), *Sojuztorf* (peat), and *Sojuzlesprom* (wood).

46 O. V. Chlevnjuk, *Politbjuro: Mekhanizm politicheskoj vlasti v 1930-e gody* (Moscow, 1996), 17–19.

47 KPSSRR 4:394–7.

48 V. P. Danilova and N. A. Ivnickij, eds., *Dokumenty svidetel'stvujut* (Moscow, 1989), 315; cf. Glavackij, *Istorija*, 253; Nicolas Werth, "Ein Staat gegen sein Volk," in Stéphane Courtois et al., *Das Schwarzbuch des Kommunismus* (Munich, 1998), 165.

49 Danilova and Ivnickij, *Dokumenty*, 331–4; cf. W. Agolikow, ed., *W. I. Lenin und die KPdSU über die sozialistische Umgestaltung der Landwirtschaft* (Berlin, 1974), 612–16.

50 Merl, *Die Anfänge der Kollektivierung*, 68–9.

51 Glavackij, *Istorija*, 262.

A typical document in this process read: "The request of *Vostokstal* for 18,200 families of special settlers is to be fulfilled for the following enterprises . . . 5,000 families of special settlers from the region of Moscow for Kuznetsk. Dates: July 9–11." Whenever the enterprises did not fulfill the expectations of the committee, requests were turned down:

> Regarding the request of *Tsvetmetzoloto*. . . . Taking into account the senseless accommodation of special settlers' families who earlier came to Aldan, [the fact that] 4,000 people – members of these families – are still not distributed but live along the railway . . . the request for 1,000 [additional] families of special settlers for Aldan is to be turned down.
>
> Regarding the request of *Sojuzlesprom*. . . . Taking into account the poor exploitation of the work-force of special settlers who are already in the custody of *Sojuzlesprom*, the request of *Sojuzlesprom* for 17,000 [additional] families of special settlers for the Northern County is to be turned down.[52]

The object of these policies was not to murder the kulaks, but rather to put them to work in the service of socialism. The workforce was an asset to the party, and it was not to be consumed frivolously. Nevertheless, reports of bad treatment, the loss of life, and escapes were frequent. "The center does not know what is done locally," as one resettled kulak, who lived in camp "km 173" on the railway north of Perm, put it in a letter to the Central Committee. In the letter he also pleaded for better working conditions and the reinstatement of his voting rights.[53]

In 1932 the central registry of the GULAG (Gosudarstvennoe Upralenie Lagerej) listed 1,317,022 kulaks who had been forcibly resettled.[54] Resettling the kulaks in the counterrevolutionary and dangerous categories, as well as the economic exploitation of peripheral regions, made it necessary to significantly expand the secret police's system of special settlements and camps.[55] New personnel was needed.[56] Following the establishment of the All-Union Interior Ministry (Narodnyj Komissariat Vnutrennikh Del or NKVD) in July 1934, the security forces were also centralized.[57] The staff was organized militarily with ranks and badges.[58]

52 Ibid., 262–4.

53 Ibid., 265–7.

54 Stephen G. Wheatcroft, "Ausmass und Wesen der deutschen und sowjetischen Repressionen und Massentötungen 1930 bis 1945," in Dahlmann and Hirschfeld, eds., *Lager, Zwangsarbeit, Vertreibung und Deportation*, 76. It is not known how many of the 212,000 inmates who were counted were kulaks.

55 Mikhail Borisovich Smirnov, *Sistema Ispravitel'no-Trudovykh Lageres USSR, 1923–1960* (Moscow, 1998), 25–74; see also Ralf Stettner, *"Archipel GULAG": Stalins Zwangslager* (Paderborn, 1996); G. M. Ivanova, *GULAG v sistems totalitarnoe gosudarstva* (Moscow, 1997); A. J. Kokurin and N. V. Petrov, eds., *GULAG (1917–1960)* (Moscow, 2000).

56 Kokurin and Petrov, eds., *Lubjanka*, nos. 6–7, pp. 181–3.

57 Ibid., no. 8, pp. 183–5.

58 Ibid., no. 11, pp. 187–96.

The number of inmates in the camps surged in the following years. In the early 1930s, the number of inmates in the NKVD camps of the republics has been estimated at 250,000–300,000, those of the GPU at 95,064. These numbers had grown to more than a million by the beginning of 1935 and to more than two million in 1938.[59] According to the GULAG archives, 1,330,812 inmates were in 1939 living in the GULAG, strictly defined, while an additional 938,552 members of kulak families were living in special settlements.

Many members of the CPSU understood the conditions in 1930 as those of wartime.[60] The resettlements were carried out by institutions of a military or paramilitary character. Given the terrible living conditions in the camps, death rates soared. In 1931, 7,283 people died – 2.9 percent of the inmates of GULAG-GPU camps; in 1933 the number was 67,247, or more than 15 percent of the total camp population.[61] In subsequent years the death rates declined. In 1932–3 most of the peasants who died did so of starvation. During the *golodmor* or famine years, more than ten million people died in the camps and prisons, among them not only peasants but also priests, intellectuals, nobles, engineers – and Communists. Thousands more were shot – 1,118 in 1936 and 353,074 in 1937.[62] Of the Soviet Union's 162 million inhabitants in 1937, some 2.4 million, or 1.6 percent, were to be found in some kind of detention.[63]

There was a territorial dimension to this war (against the people). "Enemies" were shipped or marched to the periphery of the country.[64] The main consideration was not territorial or ethnic, however, but social class. The war against the kulaks was a social war or, in the terminology with which the party legitimated the campaign until the end of the Soviet Union, a class war.[65] It was, in all events, a total war. The CPSU achieved the complete destruction of the enemy, which it defined as the exploiting classes – as collective categories – not as persons born within such groups. Although orthodox Marxists had not regarded kulaks as members of the exploiting classes, Lenin did, and therefore the problem was hardly discussed. The main outcome of this policy was that the Bolsheviks destroyed the old social structure of the communal village. With the new system of *kolkhozy*

59 Smirnov, *Sistema*, 38, 41.

60 See Glavackij, *Istorija*, 254; the circular of Sverdlovsk party committee to have the party militia (*komotrjady*) ready for combat, Feb. 6, 1930. Cf. Ivnickij, *Kollektivizacija*, 52–73.

61 Smirnov, *Sistema*, 32, 35.

62 Ibid., 41.

63 Alec Nove, "Victims of Stalinism: How Many?" in J. Arch Getty and Roberta T. Mannings, eds., *Stalinist Terror: New Perspectives* (Cambridge, 1993), 261–74.

64 Kokurin and Petrov, eds., *Lubjanka*, no.7, pp. 182–3.

65 Trifonov, *Likvidacija*, 239–391.

and a network of machine/tractor stations, the village lost all power to resist the town.

Officially, the reason for the Soviet resettlement program was that socialist industry was ready to supply agriculture with the machinery to build modern, socialist enterprises in the countryside. In fact, the machines necessary for this plan could not be provided. The most compelling reason for proclaiming a *kolkhoz* was to justify the expulsion of rich peasants from the villages so that their capital and land could be expropriated. In a country with rural overpopulation, this policy meant that the ratio of land to labor increased. Productivity should have as well.

In reality, the economic impact of collectivization was catastrophic. Many peasants slaughtered their stock. In other cases the newly founded *kolkhozy* were not able to manage the collectivized animals, and many of them died. Between 1928 and 1933, the number of dairy cows fell by two-thirds, the number of horses by one-half.[66] It was impossible to till and fertilize the soil properly. Given the lack of livestock, the famine of 1932–3 followed logically from the use of an antiquated three-field system. The most disastrous effect, however, was that the social structure and spirit of Russian peasantry were broken. Russian agriculture recovered, but it never compensated for the losses of *dekulakization* (removal of kulaks).

Although the Bolsheviks won the war against the *kulachestvo*, they could not control the logic of violence that they themselves had legitimated and unleashed. The victory over the kulaks also was politically destructive. Mass terror not only broke the capacity of the villages for economic self-determination, but it also established mass terror as an instrument of politics. In a dictatorship with no checks or balances, nobody could later stop this instrument from being turned against other groups.[67]

Paradoxically, one of these targeted groups was the military. Within the framework of renewed class war, Soviet society was militarized, but not by the military. The result was not militarism in the classical Western sense of this word. Instead, the CPSU was the agent of change. Ever alive to the danger of "Bonapartism," the party then purged the military itself after 1936.[68]

The Bolsheviks harbored no doubts about the international consequences of their policies. During the Civil War, foreign intervention had made these implications obvious. The failure of international revolution at the conclusion of World War I resulted in the decision to build "socialism in

66 Merl, *Die Anfänge der Kollektivierung*, 229. 67 Werth, "Ein Staat gegen sein Volk," 165.
68 See O. F. Suvenirov, *Tragedija RKKA 1937–1938* (Moscow, 1998), 373–494.

one country," that is, in the Soviet Union. During the 1920s, the Soviet Union gradually became a European power, and it used external threats (real or imaginary) as instruments of domestic politics. But the extent and reach of Bolshevik power made this regime unique. In no Western society (and no fascist society) were leaders able to mold conditions to the degree that the Communists did in the Soviet Union.

How did the total social war influence developments outside the Soviet Union, particularly in Nazi Germany?[69] In *Mein Kampf*, Hitler expressed his "Angst um Deutschland" – his anxiety that Germany was losing not only power but its sovereignty.[70] The Jews, he claimed, were undermining the country by promoting the emancipation of women, Sinti and Roma, homosexuals, and other groups, and by advocating free trade. The other important instruments of the Jews were the parties of the left, the Social Democrats and especially the Communists. "When I discovered that the Jews were the leaders of Social Democracy," Hitler wrote, "it was a revelation." He added, "A long struggle within my soul had come to an end."[71] As a young man in Vienna, when he was not yet an ardent anti-Semite, Hitler had heard that the leftist movement was a tool of international Jewry.[72] The idea recurred to him during the failed German revolution of 1918. He concluded that Bolshevism was an instrument in the Jewish fight against national sovereignty in the name of world government: "The most abhorrent example is Russia, where [the Jew] killed about three million people with fanatical barbarity and partly under unhuman torments, or let them starve, just in order to establish the power of a few Jewish intellectuals and stock-exchange robbers over a great nation."[73]

Hitler wrote this passage in 1927, but he was not referring to the class war that accompanied Soviet industrialization. Instead, he was talking about the casualties of the Russian Civil War. As Klaus Theweleit has shown, the experience of revolution and counterrevolution in Germany was of decisive importance to Hitler's generation.[74] Hitler, like many others on the political right, was not afraid of the violence that went along with revolution – on the contrary, he welcomed violence as providing an opportunity to fight as

69 Hans-Erich Volkmann, ed., *Das Russlandbild im Dritten Reich* (Cologne, 1994); Wolfram Wette: "'Rassenfeind': Die rassistischen Elemente in der deutschen Propaganda gegen die Sowjetunion," in Hans-Adolf Jacobsen et al, eds., *Deutsch-russische Zeitenwende* (Baden-Baden, 1995), 175–201; see also Ernst Nolte, *Der Faschismus in seiner Epoche* (Munich, 1963), 486–512.

70 Eberhard Jaeckel, *Hitlers Weltanschauung: Entwurf einer Herrschaft* (Stuttgart, 1991).

71 Adolf Hitler, *Mein Kampf* (Munich, 1938), 64: original: "fiel es mir wie Schuppen von den Augen."

72 Brigitte Hamann, *Hitlers Wien: Lehrjahre eines Diktators* (Munich, 1997), 437–503.

73 Hitler, *Mein Kampf*, 358.

74 Klaus Theweleit, *Männerphantasien*, 2 vols. (Frankfurt am Main, 1978–8).

part of really living.[75] But he dreaded leftist and revolutionary sedition or *Zersetzung*. This was believed to be typical for Jews, and for that reason the most compelling obligation, he pronounced, was to rid Germany of Jewish influence.[76] Emphasizing Bolshevik violence during the Russian Revolution had a legitimizing function in his mind: because all were using violence to establish power, the Germans must do so, too. "Nature does not know political boundaries," Hitler announced. "She puts her creatures onto the globe and then waits for the free game of power [to play out]. The strongest one in spirit and diligence will receive the Lord's position as her most beloved child."[77]

After the *Machtergreifung* (seizure of power), the Nazi government deployed Stalinist violence as an argument against pacifism and Christianity. The famine of 1932–3 was widely remarked in Germany, as Mennonite German peasants made their way to Moscow and asked for exit visas.[78] The Soviet government's religious policies, which destroyed the Lutheran Church in Russia, were also well known in Germany.[79] Possibly as a direct consequence, Bolshevik violence became an argument in the German government's campaign against the Confessing Church. The government used the argument that the "Reds" would have liquidated Protestant pastors as had the Bolsheviks in Russia and therefore pastors should be grateful to the Führer.[80] Bolshevik terror was in all events a welcome argument for the German fascists, but not the backbone of their ideology. Soviet atrocities legitimized Nazi violence, but they did not cause it.

The indirect consequences of Bolshevik power in Russia were more significant. Because Hitler believed that Bolshevism was a tool of international Jewry, the Russian Revolution adumbrated the coming of a second world war. Because he reasoned that Jews were parasites who could conquer a state from within by *Zersetzung* but not lead it, he regarded "Jewish" power in Russia as an opportunity for Germany:

75 For the structural importance of fighting in fascist thinking, see Ernst Nolte, *Der Faschismus in seiner Epoche* (Munich, 1963), 494–5. Hitler's slogan, "Who wants to live is both to fight and who does not want to fight in this world of eternal battle is not worthy of life" (Wer leben will, der kämpfe also, und wer nicht streiten will in dieser Welt des ewigen Ringens, verdient das Leben nicht), together with a woodcut of the "Führer," was on the walls of many German homes. A reproduction of the woodcut is in Eberhard Aleff, *Das dritte Reich*, 17th ed. (Hannover, 1970), 105.

76 See Michael Ley and Julius H. Schoeps, eds., *Der Nationalsozialismus als politische Religion* (Mainz, 1997).

77 Hitler, *Mein Kampf*, 147.

78 Wilm Stein, "Hunger in Russlands Kornkammer," *Vossische Zeitung*, May 27, 1932; Karl-Heinz Grotjahn, "'Moskaus Kampf ums Brot': Sowjetische Agrarpolitik 1927–1933 in der Darstellung Berliner Tageszeitungen," M.A. thesis, University of Hannover, 1989; cf. Robert Conquest, *The Harvest of Sorrow: Soviet Collectivization and the Terror-Famine* (New York, 1986), 308–21.

79 K. Cramer et al., eds., *Das Notbuch der russischen Christenheit* (Berlin, 1930).

80 Hans Krieger, "Nicht alle wollen Noltes sein!" *Das Schwarze Korps*, July 15, 1937, 14.

By delivering Russia up to Bolshevism, [fate] robbed Russia of the intelligence which until then had organized and guaranteed the state-character of Russia.... Today this may be seen as almost completely destroyed. The Jew has taken this place.... It is as impossible for the Russians to throw off the Jewish yoke by their own power as it is for the Jew to maintain the Empire for long. The Jew is no element of organization, but an element of decomposition. The giant Empire in the East is ready for collapse.[81]

The Wehrmacht followed closely the purge of the Soviet military.[82] The poor performance of the Red Army during the Finnish War (1939–40) showed that it was unable to employ its enormous material superiority adequately on the battlefield. Instead of initiative, the Wehrmacht saw little but predictable behavior in the Red Army.[83] This dismissive judgment was one of the reasons why the German military leadership believed that it could destroy the Soviet Union relatively quickly. Franz Halder and his followers believed in the decisive superiority of the German strategy of *Panzer vorn* (tanks upfront) in a new version of massive envelopment.[84]

In several ways, the total social war that the Bolsheviks fought against the *kulachestvo* was a way station on the road to total international war in the 1940s. First, the Soviet experience eroded the distinctions between national and international developments. The Soviet government embraced the proposition that "the workers have no fatherland." The success of the Soviet Union was supposed to vindicate the predictions of Marx and Engels and represent the prelude to the extinction of differences among nations. The Russian experience also contributed to the blurring of distinctions between civil and military affairs. The victory over the village during collectivization created unbroken lines of command from Moscow to the last hamlet in the Far East, as the CPSU accumulated great powers to mobilize society from above.[85] The capacity to wage total war against a domestic enemy made it easier to wage total war against a foreign enemy. Moreover, the Bolsheviks created a system that produced enormous quantities of weaponry and was materially well equipped to wage war. After the first Five-Year Plan was declared a success, the regime turned toward producing increasing amounts of armaments. Defense expenditures grew steadily, from

81 Hitler, *Mein Kampf*, 742.

82 Bernd Bonwetsch, "The Purge of the Military and the Red Army's Operational Capability during the 'Great Patriotic War,'" in Bernd Wegener, ed., *From Peace to War: Germany, Soviet Russia, and the World, 1939–1941* (Providence, R.I., 1997), 395–414.

83 Ernst Klink, "Die Rote Armee im Urteil des Heeres im September 1939," in Militärgeschichtliches Forschungsamt, ed., *Das Deutsche Reich und der Zweite Weltkrieg*, vol. 4: *Der Angriff auf die Sowjetunion* (Stuttgart, 1983), 121–202; cf. 286–99.

84 Heinrich Nolte, *Vom Cannae-Mythos: Tendenzen und Katastrophen* (Göttingen, 1991).

85 Cf. Marina Fuchs, "Die grauen Zonen der Sowjetisierung oder die sozialkulturellen Nischen in der sowjetischen Gesellschaft," *Zeitschrift für Weltgeschichte* 2, no. 1 (2001): 107–24.

3.4 percent of the budget in 1933 to 32.6 percent in 1940. The manpower strength of the armed forces doubled between 1934 and 1939.[86] The rearmament of the 1930s led to the great material superiority that the Soviet Union enjoyed in 1941.[87] Industrialization also created the Ural-Kuzbas industrial complex, without which the Soviet defense industry would have lacked the steel to continue building the T-34 tank in the winter of 1941–2.[88]

Of great importance in this respect, too, were the effects of Bolshevik rule on the West. The Bolshevik revolution convinced the Nazis that Russia would be easy to conquer. The exercise of Bolshevik power in Russia persuaded them that "Jewish Bolshevism" would bring the downfall of Russia and abet Germany's fight for living space – *Lebensraum*.[89] The purge of the Soviet military in 1937 convinced the German general staff that the Red Army lacked professional leadership, and this view was confirmed in the performance of the Red Army in Finland. The terrible conditions that attended collectivization, especially the famine, fed German hopes for a rapid military victory. Finally, Soviet terror against its own citizens tended to legitimate Nazi rule in Germany, although the Nazis' resort to violence predated Soviet collectivization.

Ernst Nolte, who called Boshevik violence the "logical and factual premise" of Nazi violence,[90] did not sufficiently take into account the indigenous traditions of violence in European societies in general and in Germany in particular.[91] The genocidal program of Ukrainian anti-Semites murdering whole villages of Jews (1919) and National Socialism (Hitler, *Mein Kampf*, 1925–6) predated collectivization and *golodmor*.[92] Both Ukrainian anti-Semitism and Nazism make reference to the violence in the

86 Hellmann, *Handbuch*, 836.

87 Joachim Hoffmann, "Die Sowjetunion bis zum Vorabend des deutschen Angriffs," in Militärgeschichtliches Forschungsamt, ed., *Das Deutsche Reich und der Zweite Weltkrieg*, 75.

88 J. E. Chadaev, *Ekonomika SSSR v Gody Velikoj Otechestvennoj Vojny* (Moscow, 1985), 172.

89 Andreas Hillgruber, *Hitlers Strategie: Politik und Kriegführung 1940–41* (Frankfurt am Main, 1965).

90 Ernst Nolte, "Vergangenheit, die nicht vergehen will," *Frankfurter Allgemeine Zeitung*, June 6, 1986; Nolte, *Das Vergehen der Vergangenheit: Antwort an meine Kritiker im sogenannten Historikerstreit* (Frankfurt am Main, 1987). Cf. Dan Diner, ed., *Ist der Nationalsozialismus Geschichte? Zu Historisierung und Historikerstreit* (Frankfurt am Main, 1987).

91 Hans-Heinrich Nolte, "Die Qualen ihr erdachtet nach Barbaren Art: Der Historikerstreit, die 'Asiatiche Tat' und die Sowjetunion," *Forum Wissenschaft* 1 (1987): 10–16; cf. the genocidal actions in the American West, Armenia, and European colonies (e.g., Namibia) before 1917: Dabag and Platt, eds., *Genozid und Moderne*; Stig Förster and Gerhard Hirschfeld, eds., *Genozid in der modernen Geschichte*, special issue of *Jahrbuch für historische Friedensforschung* 7 (1999).

92 Hans-Heinrich Nolte, "Inwieweit sind russische und deutsche Massenmorde vergleichbar?" in Niedersächsische Landeszentrale, ed., *Von der Verdrängung zur Bagatellisierung? Aspekte des sogenannten Historikerstreits* (Hannover, 1988), 49–58; for the Ukrainian genocide, see Zvi Y. Gitelman, *A Century of Ambivalence: The Jews of Russia and the Soviet Union, 1881 to the Present* (New York, 1988), 96–108.

revolutions of 1917–18, but they only count the deaths of "whites" in the civil wars in Russia, Hungary, and Bavaria. Moreover, German propaganda after 1941 exploited traces of Bolshevik terror, for example, in the cases of Lvov and Katyn.

A history of the twentieth century must include the spiral of violence, for which Georges Sorel's famous book *Réflexions sur la violence* (1908) was perhaps an early indicator. The Soviet war against the kulaks was certainly another decisive marker. In the Convention on Genocide promulgated by the United Nations in 1947, article II, section b refers to "causing serious harm" and article II, section c refers to "deliberately inflicting on the group unbearable circumstances of life."[93] Both would have applied to the dekulakization campaign. As a permanent member of the UN Security Council, the Soviet Union had prevented the inclusion of socially defined groups as possible victims.[94] Comparison of the Soviet and German mass murders is a relatively recent undertaking for historians. The Soviet archives have been open for only the last ten years. However, editions of archival material are now being produced at an impressive rate, and the work of comparing these events is moving ahead with contributions from both sides.[95]

In sum, the Russian Revolution and the Soviet experience of collectivization bore centrally on the character of the war that began in 1939. The Soviet Union was well practiced in the mobilization of society, and it had laid the foundations for winning an industrial war. It also defined a category of its own people as domestic enemies, and then proceeded to annihilate them as a social group. The Germans were deceived by the Soviet experience into thinking that they would encounter little military resistance, as they themselves set out to annihilate a category of people whom they had defined as enemies.

93 *Bundesgesetzblatt*, 1954, pt. II, 730.

94 Otto Luchterhandt, "Bekämpfung von Völkermord: Konzepte des Völkerrechts," in Dabag and Platt, eds., *Genozid und Moderne*, 355–6.

95 Dahlmann and Hirschfeld, *Lager, Zwangsarseit, Vertreibung und Deportation*; Klaus-Dieter Müller et al., eds., *Die Tragödie der Gefangenschaft in Deutschland und der Sowjetunion 1941–1956* (Cologne, 1998); cf. Hans-Heinrich Nolte and Pavel Poljan, "Massenverbrechen in der Sowjetunion und im nationalsozialistischen Deutschland," *Zeitschrift für Weltgeschichte* 2, no. 1 (2001): 125–47.

17

Total Colonial Warfare

Ethiopia

GIULIA BROGINI KÜNZI

Like no other Italian city, Rome symbolized the Fascist experience. The past was evoked by a huge monument with the inscription "Mussolini Dux" near the sports center Foro Italico, and by a series of architectural reminders in the form of bombastic buildings, large avenues, and spacious squares, which formed an ideal background for military parades and mass meetings. Even the Italo-Ethiopian War of 1935–6 left its footprint in the old capital of the *Impero dell'Africa Italiana.* One of the famous Axumite monoliths, which dates from the fourth century, still stands next to the ruins of the Baths of Caracalla, although the Italian government has now promised to return it to Ethiopia as soon as possible. The obelisk was transported to Rome as a war trophy in 1937. Rome's northeastern districts also display reminders of colonial times. "Viale Eritrea," "viale Etiopia," "viale Somalia," "via Adua," "via Dessiè," "via Tembien," "via Endertà," and "Piazza Addis Abeba" all refer to geographical locations in eastern Africa, which were sites of major battles in the Italo-Ethiopian War.

Even though the signs of the colonial past are still manifest, historians and the general public have until recently suppressed memories of the Italo-Ethiopian War.[1] In contrast to the interwar commentary, Italian historiography has since 1945 been reticent about the Italian colonial experience and the colonial wars on the African continent, even though these conflicts had exercised a formative influence on the young nation-state for seventy-five years. The subject was long regarded as unworthy of mention. Defeat in World War II and the resulting loss of the Italian colonies as a status symbol led to this state of affairs.[2] As a result, Italian historiography remained

1 Angelo Del Boca, "Il mancato dibattito sul colonialismo," in Angelo Del Boca, ed., *L'Africa nella coscienza degli italiani: Miti, memorie, errori, sconfitte* (Rome, 1992), 111–27.

2 The colony *Africa Orientale Italiana* (AOI) was founded in 1936 and comprised 1.73 million square kilometers and 11.45 million inhabitants. With the addition of this territory to its other holdings in

relatively unaffected by the turmoil of decolonization in the 1950s and 1960s. Even the Roman Catholic Church, particularly Pope Pius XI and his advisers Monsignor Pizzardo and Monsignor Tardini, never officially criticized the war in Abyssinia, despite ancient diplomatic relations between the Coptic Church and the Vatican. Fascism never hesitated to cooperate with as many supporters as possible. Moreover, the church and its missionaries were well versed in the game of imperialism. The exponents of the *consolata* order were literally mobilized to promote the war, and the fascist party exploited the idea of Italy's "civilizing mission" in Africa to justify the cause. Thus, both clerical and secular authorities supported the seizure of Ethiopia.[3] In most European historiographies, imperialism has registered as a narrative of colonial warfare. Italian expansionism provides no exception to this rule. But while the colonial histories of other imperialist powers featured wars of nation-states against stateless societies,[4] Italian expansion in East Africa in the 1930s featured a war between two states. Both were members of the League of Nations, although they differed profoundly in their political, economic, and military development.

One telling example illustrates the disparity in military strength. In March 1929 young Ras Tafari challenged his last rival, Ras Gugsa Wolie. He achieved final victory thanks to a mysterious weapon, a single airplane that bombarded his enemy's army. Soon after the victory, Ras Tafari was proclaimed emperor of Ethiopia and adopted the name Haile Selassie, "Power of Trinity."[5] Even as he did so, several hundred Italian officers, engineers, and scientists deliberated about the character of future war, its proper objectives and methods. In this connection, they seized on the idea of a "nothing-but-air war." The enemy's civilian population, not its armed forces, was to be targeted.[6] In earlier wars civilians had been involved in military action and suffered attack, but never as directly, massively, or on such a sustained basis as the Italian advocates of air power now recommended.[7] The employment

North Africa, Italy became the third-ranking colonial power on the African continent. In 1939 the Italian empire comprised 11.7 percent of the territory and 9 percent of the population of Africa. Wolfgang Reinhard, *Die Geschichte der europäischen Expansion*, 4 vols. (Stuttgart, 1990), 4:86–7.

3 Agostino Giovagnoli, "Il Vaticano di froute al colonialismo fascista," in Angelo Del Boco, ed., *Le guerre coloniali del fascismo* (Rome, 1991), 112–31; and Emilio Gentile, *Il culto del Littorio: La sacralizzazione della politica nell'Italia fascista* (Rome, 1933), 136–8.

4 See Trutz von Trotha, "'The Fellows Can Just Starve': On Wars of 'Pacification' in the African Colonies of Imperial Germany and the Concept of 'Total War,'" in Manfred F. Boemeke, Roger Chickering, and Stig Förster, eds., *Anticipating Total War: The German and American Experiences, 1871–1914* (New York, 1999), 415–35.

5 Harold Golden Marcus, *A History of Ethiopia* (Berkeley, Calif., 1994), 128–9.

6 Giulia Brogini Künzi, "Die Herrschaft der Gedanken: Italienische Militärzeitschriften und das Bild des totalen Krieges," in Stig Förster, ed., *An der Schwelle zum totalen Krieg: Militärische Fachzeitschriften und die Debatte über den Krieg der Zukunft 1919–1939* (forthcoming).

7 John Buckley, *Air Power in the Age of Total War* (London, 1999), 2.

of fleets of bombers represented one of several doctrines that emerged during the interwar period, but it was a central feature of the next European war.

The central question in this essay pertains to the character and significance of the Italo-Ethiopian War in the military history of the twentieth century. Was it an unlimited war of conquest, fought with all available financial, economic, and military means? Or was it a traditional colonial war, with limited expenditures and restricted war aims? Do lines of continuity extend from the first Italian expansion into East Africa, which culminated in the disaster of Adowa in 1896,[8] to the Italo-Ethiopian War of the 1930s; or are there significant disjunctures between these two imperial episodes?

Statistics are lacking about the total number of those killed, injured, or imprisoned during this second East African war. Nor is it clear how many people starved to death, were dislodged or raped, or were crippled for life. The Italian historian Angelo Del Boca has estimated that on the Ethiopian side, 55,000 to 70,000 combatants were killed on the two fronts of the war – the southern, Somali front and the northern, Eritrean front.[9] According to the files of the Central Archive in Rome, the Italians lost some 9,000 men.[10] These numbers cover the period between October 10, 1935, and May 5, 1936, which marked out the official duration of the war. In addition, 500 Italian workers, who had been recruited for road construction in Africa, were killed. The soldiers and officers killed in action were generously decorated with medals. On average, every fourth fatality earned a medal.[11]

In this "war of seven months," mass armies fought one another. While the Italian armed forces comprised five hundred thousand combatants, the Negus managed to mobilize only half that number. In addition, the Ethiopians lacked modern equipment, weapons, and ammunition, as well

8 The decisive battle took place near the village of Adowa. The Italian army counted 17,000–20,000 metropolitan soldiers and Eritrean ascaris, the Abyssinian army had around 70,000–100,000 men. Romain R. Rainiero, "The Battle of Adowa on 1st March 1896: A Reappraisal," in J. A. De Moor and H. L. Wesseling, eds., *Imperialism and War: Essays on Colonial Wars in Asia and Africa* (Leiden, 1989), 189–200.

9 Angelo Del Boca, *Gli italiani in Africa orientale: La conquista dell'Impero* (Rome, 1979), 720. Official Ethiopian sources estimated the total losses of combatants and civilians at 275,000. The same sources assessed the financial costs of the war at £26,800,000.

10 In his report to the general staff in East Africa, General Gariboldi wrote that from October 10, 1935, to May 5, 1936, the number of those killed in action, seriously injured, or missing was 9,106. Of them, 3,964 were Italians and 5,142 were ascaris. Archivio Centrale dello Stato (ACS), Fondo Graziani 48/66, busta 23, fasc. 29, sottofasc. 5. It is worth mentioning that these figures exceed the data presented in earlier accounts. See Del Boca, *Gli italiani in Africa orientale*, 716–25.

11 The macabre comparison to the awards presented during World War I, which accounted for 680,000 losses, shows that one medal was awarded for every five dead. Monika Kiffer, *Mussolinis Afrika-Feldzug 1935/36 im Spiegel von Literatur und Propaganda der Zeit* (Bonn, 1988), 2.

as the financial resources to provision a larger army. There was thus a great material imbalance between the opponents. In spite of the discrepancies, Haile Selassie decided to confront his enemy with regular armies. He rejected the idea of a guerilla warfare, which would presumably have brought him a tactical advantage, for such a people's war might have jeopardized his own claim to the imperial throne. In most of the five principal battles of the war, the Ethiopians were thus the weaker party, not only numerically but also technologically and logistically. In the fall of 1935, shortly before the conflict began, there were 170,000 soldiers, 65,000 ascaris, and 38,000 workers ready for war in Africa on the Italian side. In May 1936 there were twice as many – about 330,000 soldiers, 87,000 ascaris, and 100,000 workers. Ninety-thousand pack animals and 14,000 motor vehicles of various categories, from automobiles to trucks, supported the Italian forces. The effective Italian armaments included 10,000 machine-guns, 1,100 artillery pieces, 250 tanks, and 350 warplanes, most of which were reconnaissance planes and bombers. The daily petrol consumption of these machines exceeded Italy's total petrol consumption during World War I. The Italian navy transported soldiers, building materials, and arms to the African colonies. Altogether 900,000 soldiers and civilians, as well as several hundred thousand tons of goods, were shipped to the colonies and back.[12]

The most evident consequence of the Italo-Ethiopian War, and later the Spanish Civil War, was the loss of military effectiveness. Manpower and arms were exhausted. Fifteen hundred airplanes were lost during the two wars – about 20 percent of the air force's entire capacity. In the aftermath, Italy had to increase exports of its own warplanes in order to finance imports of critical raw materials. The backwardness of Italy's military technology on the eve of World War II was the product of the conflicts of 1935–6 and 1936–9. Diminished productive capacity and the expense of technological innovation impeded the modernization of the Italian military until the outbreak of World War II.[13]

According to the initial plans, the Italo-Ethiopian War was supposed to cost 1.5 to 2 billion lire. But the financial burden amounted to 1 billion lire per month. Including the preparation of the campaign and the period of reconstruction shortly after the war, Italy spent about 57,303,000,00 lire from 1935 to 1940.[14] The short-term effect of the Italo-Ethiopian War was to

12 Giorgio Rochat, "Badoglio e le operazioni contro l'Etiopia 1935–1936," in Giorgio Rochat, ed., *Guerre italiane in Libia e in Etiopia: Studi militari 1921–1939* (Padua, 1991), 105–6.

13 James J. Sadkovich, "The Development of the Italian Air Force Prior to World War II," *Military Affairs* 51 (1987): 132.

14 Giuseppe Maione, "I costi delle imprese coloniali," in Boca, ed., *Le guerre coloniali del fascimo*, 400–20.

encourage Italian heavy industry, particularly the armament industries, and to reduce unemployment. But the country's financial reserves diminished rapidly. From 1935 to 1940 some 77 billion lire were consumed by the costs of the wars in Ethiopia, Spain, Albania, and the pacification campaigns in East Africa. This sum corresponded to two-thirds of the military budget of that period.[15]

The first serious plans for the campaign were initiated by Emilio De Bono, the minister of colonial affairs. He ordered two complementary studies. Within three months, the military experts in Asmara had prepared a memorandum dated September 8, 1932, which described a scenario for offensive war against Ethiopia. In December 1932 the second plan, an analysis of a defensive war, had been completed, too. The plan for the offensive war assumed that Europe was at peace and that Italy had arranged a diplomatic agreement with France and Great Britain, the two other powers that were interested in stability in the African Horn. The second memorandum, on the defensive war, posited an Ethiopian attack during a period of instability in Europe, during which the metropolitan army's movement to Africa would be impeded.[16] The first of these plans assumed that on the Italian side a colonial army of 35,000 regular soldiers and 50,000 mercenaries would suffice. Within one month, the Ethiopian army was supposed to mobilize 50,000 to 60,000 soldiers. Within three months, however, Ethiopian mobilization was to comprise between 200,000 and 300,000 men. The maximum force available on the Ethiopian side was supposed to reach 500,000 men. In the second plan, nearly all the manpower on the Italian side had to be provided by the colonies of Eritrea and Somalia. About 60,000 to 80,000 Eritreans would be called to arms. The equipment had to be imported from Italy, but the quantity and quality of the requested material was to depend on the military situation in Europe. In order to be prepared for any of the alternatives, offensive or defensive, on November 29, 1932, De Bono called for the deployment of at least a hundred airplanes, which the aircraft industry was to supply.[17] He thus based his plans on the speed of Italian mobilization and on the destructive potential of warplanes, for he knew that the Ethiopian side possessed only a handful of airplanes and antiaircraft guns. De Bono planned to invade the Ethiopian plateau from the north. A second attack, from Italian Somaliland, was not considered at this time,

15 Brian R. Sullivan, "The Italian Armed Forces, 1918–40," in Alan R. Millet and Williamson Murray, eds., *Military Effectiveness*, 2 vols. (Boston, 1988), 2:717.

16 Archivio Storico Diplomatico (ASD), Archivio Segreto Ministero Africa Italiana (ASMAI) II, busta 181/1, fasc. 2 and 3.

17 Giorgio Rochat, *Militari e politici nella preparazione della campagna d'Etiopia: Studio e documenti 1932–1936* (Milan, 1971), doc. no. 1, 276–91.

because environmental conditions were regarded as too harsh for Europeans and Eritrean ascaris alike.[18]

In 1932 Pietro Badoglio, the chief of the Supreme General Staff and governor of the North African colonies, became De Bono's rival for leadership of the campaign. The rivalry grew in the ill-defined competencies of the Fascist bureaucracy. As governor of Libya, Badoglio was the colonial minister's subordinate, but in military affairs De Bono was Badoglio's. As chief of the Supreme General Staff, Badoglio coordinated the three branches of the armed forces and held the higher rank. The bureaucratic jungle encouraged the accumulation of important positions, however, and in this case, the issue was complicated by the involvement of Mussolini himself in his drive to institutionalize his own military power. In July 1933 he took over the War Ministry. Four months later he took over the Air Ministry and the Navy Ministry. The undersecretaries in the three ministries acted respectively as chiefs of the general staff of the army, the air force, and the navy. In the autumn of 1933, however, Mussolini designated De Bono, informally and secretly, as the military leader of a future African campaign, which both men anticipated would begin in 1935. Ignorant of the agreement, Badoglio worked out his own operational schedules for a campaign that carried special emotional significance for him: He had seen service at Adowa in 1896. However, he reckoned with a longer mobilization, which would conclude only in 1936; and he warned that the campaign would drastically weaken Italy's military force in Europe. He expressed these concerns in a letter to Mussolini on January 20, 1934.[19] A war against Ethiopia, he wrote, would not be one of the "usual colonial ventures." It would be real war. It would catch the eye of the whole world and take place under completely different circumstances than the war of 1896. As Haile Selassie's incipient modernization of the Ethiopian army made clear, that country was well aware of Italy's desire for revenge for Adowa. In addition to the regular armies of his vassals, he had built up an Imperial Army, a kind of personal guard of several thousand men, all of whom were well equipped and well trained by Belgian instructors. Badoglio stressed that many Ethiopian officers had been trained in European military academies. Finally, Badoglio emphasized that the war would be fought by Italians, for he did not regard the Eritrean ascaris as reliable.

With countless problems waiting for solution, preparations continued secretly and at high speed after August 1934. The Italian ports in the Red

18 Until 1935 the military role of Italian Somaliland, whether offensive or defensive, was undefined. The commanders decided at the last moment to wage a two-front war.

19 Rochat, *Militari*, doc. no. 7, 301–4.

Sea, Assab and Massawa, were enlarged, war materials were built up, pack animals bought, camps constructed, and the whole infrastructure improved. In addition, several landing fields were constructed. The colonial administration in Eritrea recruited most of the people who had earlier served in the Colonial Army. The training of the ascaris took place in special camps in Libya. Suddenly, at the end of 1934, Mussolini's role became known, when he issued an appeal for war and explained to Badoglio the special features of the campaign he intended to "dictate" from Rome.[20] He had become a convinced supporter of the campaign, for he recognized Ethiopia's military inferiority. He wanted a decisive, powerful takeover, and he wanted it to happen quickly. The timing was crucial. A war 4,000 kilometers from home was feasible only while peace survived in Europe. The dictator trusted that a Franco-Italian diplomatic arrangement, which was imminent, would at least temporarily stabilize the European continent. In his memorandum of December 30, 1934, he scheduled the beginning of operations for October 1935. The goal of the war was to "destroy the Ethiopian Army and achieve the total conquest of the land" in a minimum amount of time.[21] The sooner the war was over, he reasoned, the less resistance would arise in Europe, mainly from Great Britain and France.

In the view of the historian Giorgio Rochat, this memorandum held the key to Italy's military policy in the interwar period.[22] Rochat argued that Mussolini regarded the Ethiopian war as an opportunity to win broader support from the Italian middle classes. Ethiopia was hence, in Rochat's opinion, no prelude to the conquest of other regions in Africa or Asia. Rochat's interpretation of the war did not differ substantially from the analysis that he himself offered of the first Italian expansion into East Africa in the nineteenth century.[23] In 1935 the proportions of the conflict were merely more vast. Nonetheless, Mussolini called his Ethiopian war a "national war." The transition from colonial to national war was also analyzed by Esmonde Robertson.[24] Like Rochat, he interpreted the war as an Italian response to an opportunity. He attributed the campaign in East Africa to an "improvised decision," not to a systematic line of policy. Robertson's interpretation portrayed the Italo-Ethiopian War as the last venture of European imperialism.

20 Ibid., doc. no. 29, 376–9.

21 Ibid., 377.

22 Giorgio Rochat, "L'aeronautica italiana nella Guerra d'Etiopia 1935–1936," in Rochat, *Guerre italiane*, 124.

23 Giorgio Rochat and Giulio Massobrio, *Breve storia dell'esercito italiano dal 1861 al 1943* (Turin, 1978), 211–12.

24 Esmonde M. Robertson, *Mussolini as an Empire-Builder: Europe and Africa, 1932–1936* (London, 1977), 112–13. See also Renzo De Felice, *Mussolini il duce: Gli anni del consenso 1929–1936* (1974; Turin, 1996), 597–757.

Historians are nowadays extending the investigation of modern military history. The "master narrative of total war" has itself been challenged and enlarged.[25] Analysis is turning to neglected aspects of total warfare, such as the specific methods of war, mobilization, and the attempt to keep warfare under control – to make total war "practical."[26] If total war is conceived as the totalization of all these elements, the concept can be useful in comparing the world wars in Europe with the colonial war that was fought in East Africa in the 1930s.

However, two objections can be raised to this comparison straightaway. The first is the utter incomparability of the civilian casualties. The second is the fact that purists among the military thinkers in interwar Italy did not use the term *guerra integrale* to describe war overseas.

Giulio Douhet was one of the first to define the distinction between *guerra totale* and *guerra integrale*. The term *guerra totale* implied a war fought with all means against combatants. *Guerra integrale*, by contrast, implied a war fought against noncombatants as well. Other contemporary thinkers took up Douhet's arguments and elaborated on the difference between the two concepts. Thereafter, strategists in Italy and elsewhere were not content to restrict their plans to land warfare or decisive battles among regular armies. Airplanes and noncombatants had become central in their thinking. Future wars would take place everywhere and encompass everyone. The morale of civil populations, friendly and enemy alike, would be essential. As formulated by Douhet and his disciples, the concept of a *guerra integrale* in Europe emphasized a war against civilians. In his pioneering writings on air power, Douhet noted in 1921 that the enemy's urban centers should be destroyed. He considered aerial bombardment an effective and efficient solution to the stalemate of land warfare. He worked out the doctrine of the "command of the air," which represented the prize of aerial warfare among technologically advanced nations. The tools of strategic bombing were explosives, incendiary bombs, and poison gas.[27] Paradoxically, Douhet wrote, the annihilation of the enemy's cities and industrial production would shorten the war and spare the lives of soldiers.

Living conditions in the colonial world, where there were few cities or areas of industrial concentration, hardly conformed to this vision.

25 Roger Chickering, "Total War: The Use and Abuse of a Concept," in Boemeke, Chickering, and Förster, eds., *Anticipating Total War*, 13–28.

26 See the introduction to this volume.

27 Douhet's book on command of the air was edited by the War Ministry and published in 1921. In 1927 a second and enlarged version was published. The most cited edition is Giulio Douhet *Il dominio dell'aria e altri scritti* (Milan, 1932). See also Ferruccio Botti and Mario Cermelli, *La teoria della guerra aerea in Italia dalle origini alla seconda guerra mondiale (1884–1939)* (Rome, 1989), 315–59.

Nonetheless, colonial warfare resembled European war in the twentieth century in at least one respect, which might not be immediately apparent. Beginning with the Italo-Turkish War in 1911–12 and through the Great War, the "pacification" of Libya in the 1920s, the Italo-Ethiopian War, the Spanish Civil War, the invasion of Albania and finally World War II, Italy experienced war, both in Europe and overseas, almost without interruption for more than three decades. While theorists such as Douhet, Amedeo Guillet, Ugo Fischetti, and Ernesto Coop pondered the question of war in Europe, colonial officers, such as Rodolfo Graziani, Riccardo Barreca, and Ambrogio Bollati, focused on colonial warfare. Italian military doctrine evolved in the exchange of ideas and experiences between these two camps, primarily through the medium of the military journals.

De Bono moved to Eritrea in early 1935 in order to supervise the preparations for the campaign. As war broke out in October, De Bono, who was supposed to invade the Ethiopian plateau, hesitated. As soon as Mussolini became aware of the old general's behavior, he dismissed him and named Badoglio his successor. Meanwhile, Badoglio had developed a series of new operational plans, which testified to his aggressiveness and enthusiasm for the campaign. The fact that he had also dropped his demand to delay the war until 1936 convinced Mussolini to choose him.[28] In his operational plans Badoglio relied on air power, which was to bomb enemy combatants and to destroy the Ethiopian military infrastructure, including lines of strategic communication and supply centers. Badoglio assumed that the enemy troops would operate in masses, so bombers could locate objectives and inflict great damage. "200 kilometers south of our borders, our aircraft could cause such devastation that an army of 300,000 soldiers would be forced to withdraw," he wrote.[29] His strategy featured a colossal march over more than 800 kilometers, from Eritrea to the capital of the Ethiopian Empire, Addis Ababa. Passing through Adowa, the invading column was to advance steadily southward by foot or on motor vehicles. Warplanes were to precede the convoy and "prepare the territory," bombing every city and intimidating the country's population. Everything of importance was to be bombed with explosives and incendiaries. Terror was to reign. Badoglio's war plans exceeded the traditional dimensions of limited colonial warfare. Indeed, Badoglio's plans appear to have absorbed much of Douhet's vision of future warfare. The totalization of warfare had become a necessity. Italy could not stand a long war, for Mussolini's military advisers feared a deterioration of the political situation in Europe after 1936.

28 Rochat, *Militari*, doc. no. 35, 392–404.

29 Ibid., 400.

In November 1935 Badoglio assumed command of all the armed forces on the Eritrean and Somali fronts. Some three-quarters of the mobilized soldiers and officers thus came under his direct command. In Mogadishu, the other quarter of the Italian forces was commanded by general Rodolfo Graziani, who oversaw his part of the campaign with great autonomy and was more answerable to Mussolini than Badoglio, his immediate superior in the chain of command.

The war was fought against an enemy who was from the beginning at an enormous disadvantage. In fact, the war presented the Italians with a unique opportunity to practice aspects of modern warfare with little risk. Logistics were put to a severe test, because nearly everything had to be imported from Italy. Thousands of soldiers, officers, blackshirt volunteers, and workers were mobilized; and even the ascaris were allowed to demonstrate their reliability.

Immense effort went into the propaganda of war in Italy, the colonies, and the Ethiopian regions close to the borders. A Ministry of Propaganda was established in 1935 to confront its first challenge in the Italo-Ethiopian War. Critics were to be silenced by means of coordinated official communiqués. Censorship of written correspondence, telephone calls, telegraphic communications, and the radio was to do the rest. Journals, literary and scientific reports, and books were full of war propaganda, which extended to the theatre, cinema, songs and poetry, museums, research centers, exhibitions, postcards, and stamps, even into comics and children's books. Imperial expansion and war were portrayed as necessary. In the illustrated reviews, photography and printing depicted the color and exoticism of colonial life. The subjects of the propaganda were the heroic Italian soldiers, militiamen, and workers, who were fighting for the glory of the new empire in the distant colonies.

In Africa, De Bono set up rudimentary offices of censorship, in Asmara and in Mogadishu, in January 1935. Thereafter the flow of military and personal information from the front to families in Italy or abroad, and from families to the front, was put under increasing control. The censors read the reports of hundreds of Italian and foreign correspondents. Journalists were gathered together in an elaborate media center, which was established in an old camp near Asmara, far from the front. The center included a dining room, a settlement of huts for lodging, and a special office that supplied journalists with photographs and documentation, as well as a post office and a telegraph and telephone station. Within eight months, 80,000 meters of film were recorded, and some eight thousand official photos were shot, to be reproduced more than three hundred fifty thousand times.[30] In addition, special newspapers and radio transmissions went out to the soldiers and road-builders. The purpose of all this effort was to keep up the morale of listeners and readers and to promote a ruthless policy.

The correspondence carried by airplane or ship to and from Eritrea and Italian Somaliland amounted to two million letters and postcards monthly. The censors selectively read two hundred thousand pieces of civilian correspondence and a similar amount of military correspondence. Reports from the front were read with special attention, and letters that contained sensitive information were censored. This procedure allowed the political and military leaders to keep abreast of the general situation in other countries, as well as the Italian people's feelings about the invasion of Ethiopia and reactions to the sanctions that the League of Nations imposed. Of greatest importance was the correspondence to and from Italy. Surveys of censored correspondence were transmitted to the ministries, secret services, and the secret police, who could use it to reconstruct regional patterns of resistance to the war.[31]

The army's secret service (Servizio Informazioni Militari, SIM), the navy's secret service (Servizio Informazioni Segreti, SIS), and the information service of the air force (Servizio Informazioni Aeronautiche, SIA) decoded telegraphic correspondence within Ethiopia, including messages sent to and from the emperor and telegrams among the Ethiopian military commanders. In this way the Italians were normally well informed about the enemy's armament, mobilization, and, later in the war, about crucial troop movements. A staff of translators and spies kept information and rumors flowing. As the process took on a certain momentum, the mass of news to be controlled and censored (or the rumors to be spread) increased. Errors and misinterpretations were impossible to avoid. Sometimes secret information on Italian military operations leaked out. But on the whole, the "information front" underwent totalization in this war.

Neither Badoglio nor Graziani shied away from using chemical weapons. Although Italy had in 1928 ratified the international convention forbidding the use of chemical and bacteriological weapons, this document proved to be no obstacle. The "pacification" of Libya in the 1920s concluded as Italians employed chemical agents, although military operations in Libya did not find much echo in public opinion. In the case of Ethiopia, the use of

30 Istituto Storico della Resistenza in Provincia di Novara "Piero Fornara," ed., *Si e no padroni del mondo: Etiopia 1935–36: Immagine e consenso per un impero, a cura di Adolfo Mignemi* (Novara, 1982).

31 ASD, ASMAI II, busta 181/11, fasc. 51.

chemical agents was long planned. The documents that related to chemical weapons were treated with great discretion, and use of gas was often only implied. In his memorandum of December 1934, Mussolini ordered "absolute superiority in artillery and gas weapons."[32] The commander of the chemical services in Eritrea had already completed studies of gas warfare by the spring of 1934. He concluded that the terrain, meteorological conditions, and an enemy who would be unprepared all favored the use of gas. His report recommended its employment as soon as the Ethiopian Army came within range of the air force. The results would be effective if the Ethiopians' routes and rallying points were properly contaminated.[33] Nor were Ethiopian soldiers to be the only people targeted. E. Venditti, the chief of the chemical services in Asmara, wrote in February 1935 that the air force should also use fire-bombs, in order to destroy Ethiopian huts, which were built of highly flammable materials such as tree branches, twigs, and straw.[34]

In his correspondence with Badoglio in February 1935, Giuseppe Valle, the undersecretary in the Air Force Ministry and chief of staff of the air force, also proposed the use of chemical agents in bombing Ethiopian cities, such as Addis Ababa, Gondar, and Harrar.

Chemical weapons, above all mustard gas, were in fact used during the Italo-Ethiopian War. Gas was not, however, released over the capital. It was instead employed in remote areas, over provincial towns, against the armed forces, and later against the guerillas. Rochat, who pioneered research on the gas war in Ethiopia, calculated that before January 1936 about 300 tons of mustard gas were used on the northern front. On the southern front, 30,500 kilograms of mustard gas and 13,300 kilograms of phosgene were put to use.[35] On the variety and quantity of bombs used in the following months, there is little information.

Bacteriological weapons were not used in the campaign, although De Bono had suggested the idea in February 1935 and Mussolini had welcomed it early in 1936.[36] The Italian failure to employ these weapons was not due to Badoglio's humanitarian feelings. It was rather a question of political rationality. The overwhelming superiority of the Italian Army after the

32 Rochat, *Militari*, doc. no. 29, 378.

33 Com. R. Corpo to Ministero delle Colonie, Asmara 7. 3. 1934, ASD, ASMAI I, busta 181/6, fasc. 28.

34 E. Venditti, promemoria to Ministero delle Colonie, Asmara 5. 2. 1935, ibid.

35 Giorgio Rochat, "L'impiego dei gas nella guerra d'Etiopia 1935–36," *Rivista di Storia Contemporanea* 1 (1988): 74–109.

36 De Bono, Promemoria sull'impiego degli aggressivi chimici to Ministero delle Colonie, Asmara 18. 2. 1935, ASD, ASMAI II, busta 181/6, fasc. 28.

battle of Endertà had altered the situation. Badoglio did not want to attract the animosity of the local population by needlessly harming Italy's future subjects. Particularly in the Tigray region, the official policy became one of reparation in 1936, as the Italians tried to make amends for the damage they had caused. This policy, too, was part of the propaganda effort to win the confidence of the local elites, above all the clergy. Between February and April 1936 at least 476,000 leaflets, printed in Amharic, Tigrine, and Arabic, were dropped by airplane over villages and towns. In some cases buildings and Coptic churches were reconstructed, indemnities were paid, and village chiefs were allowed to lodge complaints about marauding troops at the newly established bureaus of the *unità politiche*.[37]

Many aspects of the war against the civilian population are waiting to be examined. While there is a good paper on the attitude of the International Committee of the Red Cross, we know little about the treatment of Ethiopian civilians in the north and south.[38] Given the rivalry between Badoglio on the northern front and Graziani on the southern, we can speculate about different military priorities and their effects on combatants as well as noncombatants. The impact of the Italo-Ethiopian War on civilians deserves an important place in the totalization of war in the twentieth century. The employment of forbidden weapons is but one dimension of this story. Another is the perception of the enemy, combatants and noncombatants alike. The Italians' representation of the Ethiopian enemy was deeply influenced by fascist ideology. Racism became a prominent feature in it, as the mass media celebrated the beauty of war, and millions of Italians professed adoration for the Duce. The Italo-Ethiopian War was thus of fundamental significance in the regime's pursuit of two goals: the militarization of society and the fascistization of the army.

While the ruling Ethiopian elites fought for survival, for Ethiopia's independence, and the preservation of their own social and economic positions, Italy's war aims were more limited. Unlike Libya, Ethiopia was not to become a settlement colony for Italian peasants. The goals of the Italian leadership were to destroy the Ethiopian army and to conquer the land in a short period of time. Officially the war lasted seven months. But the conquest of Ethiopia was by no means complete. Italian propaganda misrepresented the situation, as it spread the news that Italy had accomplished its "total" aims.

37 ADS, ASMAI II, busta 181/8 and busta 181/9.

38 Rainer Baudendistel, "Force Versus Law: The International Committee of the Red Cross and Chemical Warfare in the Italo-Ethiopian War 1935–1936," *International Review of the Red Cross* 3 (1998): 81–104.

Nor did the conflict approach "total war" in other respects. Although a huge army was supplied for the first time with motor vehicles and from the air, the tactical and strategic lessons of the war were modest. Italian leaders were aware that they could not have waged war in the same fashion against an enemy that was armed with a comparable air force, artillery, and antiaircraft guns, or one that could exploit the same kind of mobilization and propaganda machinery as the Italians enjoyed.

Nonetheless, the enormous financial, propagandistic, and military exertions caused by the Italo-Ethiopian War vastly exceeded the parameters of nineteenth-century imperialism. The doctrines and techniques of warfare, the mobilization of society, and the attempt to establish total control over the war effort all reached dimensions unknown in the previous century.

Military violence, new weapons systems, and the full powers of propaganda were used against noncombatants as well as combatants. Involving civilians in war in this fashion admittedly resembled practices in earlier wars of colonial conquest, but it also conformed no less to the futuristic vision laid out in Europe's military academies, military journals, and general staffs.

The Italian mobilization for war was impressive. Several hundred thousand tons of war material and some nine hundred thousand men were transported to Africa. In addition, the war had had a tremendous impact on the minds of the Italian people, as it forged a kind of community feeling. As Italian historians emphasized in the 1970s, the war served in this way the purpose for which it was launched, to legitimize the Fascist regime.[39] Growing popular self-esteem went hand-in-hand with the expansion of the Fascist Empire.

During the war the populace was increasingly subjected to government control. The incessant repetition of the message that Mussolini and the military commanders in the colony had the situation well in hand created a climate of stability and faith in the régime. Propaganda pervaded nearly every sphere of life – schools, youth organizations, trade unions, leisure time, women's organizations, and, to a certain extent, even the church, as well as the armed forces. Above all in its methods, in its wholesale mobilization of the population, the attempt to establish total control, and the systematic waging of war on civilians, the Italo-Ethiopian War represented an important way station on the road to total war.

39 De Felice, *Mussolini*; and Del Boca, *Gli italiani in Africa orientale*.

18

Japan's Wartime Empire in China

LOUISE YOUNG

For Japan, World War II began with an effort to secure imperial interests in China. Even as Japan's escalating imperial ambitions on the Asian continent precipitated military conflicts with the Soviet Union, with the United States, and with the British Empire, China remained at the center of Japan's vision and experience of total war. The occupation, in 1931, of Northeast China and the transformation of what had been a Japanese sphere of influence into the puppet state of Manchukuo signaled a turning point in the methods and goals of Japanese imperialism. The challenge of Chinese nationalism placed Japan on the defensive, triggering a shift from diplomacy to militarism and helping forge a domestic consensus behind the need to defend the imperial "lifeline" in China at all costs – even at the risk of war with the Western imperialists in Asia. But what began as a small war in Manchuria in 1931 expanded into the titanic naval battles in the Pacific and ended in the hellfires of Hiroshima and Nagasaki. Throughout the fifteen years of warfare, each stage of escalation, each opening of a new war front was necessitated by the perceived need, on the Japanese part, to defend imperial interests in China. In other words, China remained the center of Japan's total war effort.

The central place of China in the war effort meant that for Japan World War II was in large part a colonial war. Much of the war effort was dominated by colonial concerns: subjugating an alien population, instituting regimes of economic expropriation and mechanisms of social control. The colonial nature of the war also profoundly affected the mechanisms of home-front mobilization and the metropolitan impact of the war. It meant that cultural, demographic, and economic resources were targeted for mobilization in order to meet the demands of empire-building as much as the strategic needs of prosecuting the war. Moreover, war aims were largely articulated in terms of imperial goals and ideologies of empire deployed as a rallying cry to mobilize the social body behind the war effort. Thus, World War II in Asia was at heart a war of empire; what would become the mass and multidimensional mobilization of the home front signaled the construction of a total empire as much as it did a total war.

This chapter deals with the process of building a total empire in the 1930s and 1940s by examining two examples of home-front mobilization. The first concerns the role of the mass media in rallying popular support behind the military occupation of Manchuria and confrontational diplomacy. The second deals with the business community's escalating commitment to the empire, and its concomitant support for the army's territorial advance. Both constitute examples of the domestic effects of empire-building in the 1930s, two ways in which the metropolis registered Japan's shift in direction to a new military imperialism after 1931.[1]

THE NEW IMPERIALISM OF THE 1930S

The immediate forces behind Japan's shift in gears emerged out of the breakdown in the late 1920s of the system of imperialist diplomacy in China. On the Chinese political front, the character of the civil war changed as the corrosive warlord conflicts gave way to a struggle between nascent Nationalist and Communist organizations to mobilize popular support and lead the unification of the country, with critical implications for foreign powers. Placed on the defensive, foreign powers in China reacted with confusion, breaking ranks in a series of flip-flops from appeasement to military suppression and back again. Such desperate and largely ineffectual attempts to protect their own traders and manufacturers from the ire of anti-imperial boycotts and strikes ignored the impact their actions might have on fellow imperialists. Coordinated imperialist activity was a casualty to such confusion, as individual national interests overrode advantages of collective action and bilateral negotiations swept aside the cooperative diplomacy prescribed by the unequal treaty system in China.

The collapse of the American stock market in 1929 and the ensuing shock wave of global depression dealt the interimperialist alliance another profound blow. All parties responded to the economic crisis with economic nationalism. As they sought to barricade their own interests against any competitors, the imperatives of economic survival seemed to leave less and less room for compromise. To Japanese policy makers this meant sealing off their extensive investments in Manchuria from the rest of China, for special steps

1 The research on which this essay is based is presented at greater length in my book, *Japan's Total Empire: Manchuria and the Culture of Wartime Imperialism* (Berkeley, Calif., 1998).

seemed necessary to secure a sphere of interest from the forces of Chinese nationalism. Thus, it was the twin crises of a rising anti-imperial nationalism and a globally spreading economic depression that compelled the search for new formulas to deal with imperial rivals and manage imperial interests.

The catchphrase of Japanese foreign policy of the early 1930s, "autonomous diplomacy," announced the direction these new formulas were to take. In a striking departure from past practice, "autonomous diplomacy" meant liberating imperial interests in Asia from a consideration of relations with the West. In the past, fearing diplomatic isolation, Japanese policy makers took careful stock of how a potential move in Asia was likely to be received in the West. Interventions were preceded by judicious multilateral negotiations. After 1931, however, the "Manchurian problem," the "China question," and the "advance south" all were decided unilaterally and in the face of Western opposition. The stand-off between Japan and the great powers in the League of Nations in 1932–3 signaled this change in direction. In the spring of 1933, failing to gain Western endorsement for its actions in Northeast China, Japan left the League and isolated itself diplomatically. Of their own volition, Japanese statesmen withdrew from the great power club to which they had labored so long to gain entry.

Second, autonomy betokened a new independence for the colonial armies. In this sense the origin of the new phase of imperialism in a Kwantung Army conspiracy was of more than passing importance. Indeed, military faits accomplis followed one upon the other, as aggressive field officers took their lead from the success of the Manchurian Incident. Since Meiji times, imperial expansion began with military conquest. But by the 1930s, the imperial garrisons had multiplied and the institutional complexity of the armed services opened new possibilities for subimperialists. The trigger-happy proclivity of the garrison armies turned the boundaries of the empire into a rolling frontier. And as the army gained influence over political institutions both at home and in the empire, the tendency to resort to force when negotiations stalled only grew stronger.

This "shoot first; ask questions later" approach to empire-building drew Japan into a series of military conflicts. At first, China and the Soviet Union responded to Japan's go-fast imperialism with concessions. In the early 1930s, the Nationalists were too busy fighting the Communists to resist the takeover of Manchuria. Stalin, preoccupied with agricultural collectivization, the five-year plans, and purging the party, decided to sell off the Chinese Eastern Railway in 1935 and retreat before Japan's advance into north Manchuria. But after the formation of a united Chinese Communist-Nationalist front in 1936 and the Soviet fortifications of the

Manchurian-Soviet border, both China and the Soviet Union began to stand their ground. War broke out with China in 1939 and with the Soviet Union in 1938 and 1939.

Similarly, American and European interests in Asia were initially consumed with domestic economic problems and the dissolution of the international financial system. The day before the Manchurian Incident, Great Britain went off the gold standard; there was little attention to spare for the Far East. Although after 1937 the United States did oppose Japan indirectly by supplying Jiang Jieshi with war materiel, only in 1940, after the outbreak of war in Europe and the Japanese advance into Indochina, did the United States begin embargoes on strategic materials to Japan. The tightening of the economic screws led to the decision, once again, to attack; from December 1941, Japan was fighting a war against Britain and the United States, and the boundaries of the empire became an endless war front. In the process, the empire and the war grew indistinguishable. From a small war in Manchuria to the titanic naval battles of the Pacific, the hallmark of the new imperialism of the 1930s was a perpetual state of war.

While the unleashing of the army and the turn to a diplomacy of brinkmanship made Manchuria the starting point for a new imperialism that set Japan on a collision course with the West, Manchukuo became the centerpiece and testing ground for a new wartime empire whose security and defense constituted Japan's most fundamental war aim. In Manchukuo, Japanese officials crafted an ideology for the puppet state that sought to depict Japan as an ally of anti-colonial nationalism. To this end they touted Manchukuo's origins in a Sino-Japanese liberation movement that claimed "Manchuria for the Manchurians," and trumpeted "racial harmony" [*minzoku kyōwa*] as the official slogan of the puppet state. Japanese plans for Manchukuo envisioned a multiracial polity in which Chinese, Manchus, Mongols, Koreans, and Japanese would cooperate to bring about an ideal of "coexistence and coprosperity." The model pioneered in Manchuria was later applied to occupied Southeast Asia, as Japan legitimated their takeover in the language of "liberating" Asia from white imperialists and justified the establishment of puppet states under the slogan "Asia for the Asiatics." As vacuous and self-serving as these declarations seem in retrospect, at the time they were initially effective in mobilizing support both among Japanese at home and among the Asians who helped Japan create the new colonial institutions that constituted the puppet regimes.

Strategies of mobilization were also part of the Manchurian formula. Military, political, economic, and cultural institutions were created or reshaped to organize new communities of support for Japanese rule. Ambitious young Chinese found the Manchukuo Army and military academy a route of advancement, as did their counterparts throughout the empire. Military institutions formed in the late colonial period in Burma, Korea, and elsewhere became the training ground for postcolonial elites. Similarly, Japanese established mass parties such as the Putera in Indonesia and the Kalibapi in the Philippines, patterned on Manchukuo's Kyōwakai. Throughout the empire, Japanese created joint ventures with local capital. Sometimes this was a mask for Japanese control, sometimes a cover for appropriation of native capital, and sometimes, as in Korea, a means of cultivating a collaborative elite and splitting the nationalist movement.[2] Assimilationist cultural policies were widely applied over the course of the thirties and forties in an attempt to create an elite cadre of youth loyal to Japanese rule. These went furthest in Taiwan and Korea, where the *kōminka* (imperialization) movement sought to erase native cultural traditions, replacing them with the Japanese religious practices of shrine Shinto, the use of the Japanese language, and the Japanization of given names.[3]

It was not just colonial state institutions, but also the experiment with economic autarky in Manchukuo that became the guiding spirit of the wartime Japanese empire. The integrated industrial and trading unit formed with the Japan-Manchuria bloc economy was extended first to include north China, then the rest of China, and finally Southeast Asia in a self-sufficient yen bloc. In Korea, Taiwan, and north China this involved industrialization and heavy investment, as it did in Manchukuo. The lessons of economic management learned in Manchukuo, including currency unification, production targets, semipublic development companies, and other tools of state control, were also applied in these new economies.

In all these ways the experiment in Manchukuo marked the beginning of a new imperialism, made necessary by the upsurge of revolutionary nationalist movements throughout the empires of Asia. European powers responded to the rise of Asian nationalism with a policy of appeasement, attempting to shore up the crumbling colonial edifice through political concessions in the Middle East and India. Japanese dealt with the same challenge by claiming a unity with Asian nationalism. They tried to co-opt the anticolonial movement by declaring the Japanese colonial state to be the agent of nationalist liberation.

2 Carter J. Eckert, "Total War, Industrialization, and Social Change in Late Colonial Korea," in Peter Duus, Ramon Myers, and Mark R. Peattie, eds., *The Japanese Wartime Empire, 1931–1945* (Princeton, N.J., 1996), 3–39.

3 Wan-yao Chou, "The Kōminka Movement in Taiwan and Korea: Comparisons and Interpretations," in Peter Duus, Ramon H. Myers, and Mark R. Peattie, eds., *The Japanese Wartime Empire, 1931–1945* (Princeton, N.J., 1996), 40–68.

MOBILIZING CULTURE

These dramatic departures in the empire itself were matched by a transformation in the domestic institutions that supported empire-building. Over the course of the 1930s, as Japan attempted to absorb the vastness of China into its imperial territories, empire-building at home also entered a new and intensive phase of growth. The vast escalation of the military presence in the empire (in Manchuria alone the Kwantung Army grew from a single division in 1931 to a peak strength of twelve divisions in 1941) and the rising power of the army within colonial government institutions was paralleled by the militarization of government at home; recurrent war fevers over the course of the 1930s sanctioned both developments. At the same time, Japanese undertook an enormous expansion in the economic investment in China (between 1932 and 1941, 5.9 billion yen in Manchuria alone, more than the 5.4 billion yen accumulated in the entire overseas empire by 1930), a project underwritten by the domestic financial community and supported by an unprecedented mobilization of Japanese business organizations behind the new empire.[4] Although these developments represented but a tiny fragment of the multidimensional project that constituted the new wartime empire in China, they offer a glimpse into the process of building a total empire. What is revealed is one of the myriad ways that empire in China reshaped the landscape of Japanese history over the 1930s, as Japanese set about building the political and social structures to mobilize the resources essential to the success of the imperial project.

The militarization of both empire and metropolis that marked Japan's shift to "go-fast imperialism" began with the Manchurian Incident of 1931–3. News of the outbreak of fighting on the continent touched off the first of a series of war fevers that punctuated the decade. The mass media played a central role in stimulating the Manchurian Incident war fever, in the process promoting the militarization of popular culture and encouraging the proliferation of social organizations for total war. Popular Japanese stereotypes of the "dark valley" of the 1930s conjure up images of a militaristic police state which exercised unlimited powers of political repression to coerce an unwilling but helpless populace into cooperating with the army's expansionist designs. One of the key subplots in the dark-valley version of the 1930s concerns the deliberate deception of the Japanese people through

4 Kaneko Fumio, "Shihon yushutsu to shokuminchi," in Ōishi Kaichirō, ed., *Sekai daikyōkōki* (Tokyo, 1987), 337; Hayashi Takehisa, Yamazaki Hiroaki, and Shibagaki Kazuo, *Nihon shihonshugi* (Tokyo, 1973), 250; and Hikita Yasuyuki, "Zaisei, kin'yū kōzō," in Asada Kyōji and Kobayashi Hideo, eds., *Nihon teikokushugi no Manshū shihai: jūgonen sensō o chūshin ni* (Tokyo, 1986), 866, 889.

expurgated and even mendacious news reports of the military events on the continent. The role of the press and publishing industry in the government disinformation campaign is usually explained by reference to the notorious Peace Preservation Law of 1925, which gave the Home Ministry widespread powers of arrest and censorship. A closer look at the reaction of the mass media to the outbreak of the Manchurian Incident, however, reveals some inaccuracies in this picture of a press muzzled by government censors and publicizing with great reluctance the official story of Japan's military actions in Manchuria. In fact, without any urging from the government, the news media took the lead in promoting the war. Publishing and entertainment industries volunteered in cooperating with army propagandists, helping to mobilize the nation behind the military occupation of Northeast China. They did so, in large part, for a very simple reason: imperial warfare offered producers of mass culture irresistible opportunities for commercial expansion and profit.

For the press, the war fever provided the chance to expand from the largely saturated urban market to a more thorough penetration of the rural market. The drive to expand circulation was pursued through innovations in format, production, and marketing techniques. Leading the way were the *Mainichi shinbun* and *Asahi shinbun* newspaper chains, which dominated the national news market. The *Mainichi* and the *Asahi* deployed recently purchased fleets of airplanes and cars and mobilized the latest printing and phototelegraphic machinery in their drive to win the news war. They used their airplanes to shuttle teams of correspondents and equipment back and forth between Japan and Manchuria.

The use of new technology to accelerate the speed of news production was also apparent in the latest developments in the "extra" (*gogai*) war. In 1931 victory in the race to break the news was decided by two new machines, the high-speed cylinder press and the wire photograph transmitter. With their capital advantages, the *Asahi* and *Mainichi* dominated the field in this new technology. Hence, they were able to overwhelm smaller papers through sheer numbers of costly extras – sometimes putting out two separate multipage extras between the morning and evening editions – and by featuring the latest photos from the front.

Unfortunately for the large dailies, their weaker competitors were not the only contenders in the news war of 1931–2. No sooner had the fighting broken out on the continent than the newspapers found themselves face to face with an upstart rival in the battle for the "scoop": radio. The fierce competition between radio and newspapers was a new development. Since its founding in 1926, Japan's national broadcasting monopoly, Nihon hōsō kyōkai (NHK), had taken a back seat in news production and concentrated its efforts on pursuing an educational mission. During the Manchurian Incident, however, NHK changed all that, moving aggressively to carve out a new position for itself in the news industry.

Radio competed with the press by increasing regular news programming from four to six times a day, as well as through *rinji nyūsu* – special unscheduled news broadcasts, or news flashes. This device was employed, appropriately, to scoop the big dailies on the events of September 18. In a special report that interrupted the early morning calisthenics program, a six-minute news broadcast broke the story of the "clash between our railway guards . . . and the (Chinese) First Brigade." In addition to its use of the news flash, NHK expanded its role in news production through the introduction of live broadcasts. In 1931 and 1932 radio began participating in public ceremonials such as troop send-offs and welcome parades, funerals, military reviews, collection drives, and armament christenings. NHK's efforts to cover the Manchurian Incident were rewarded with a dramatic expansion in radio listeners. Between 1930 and 1933, the number of radio contracting households rose from 778,948 (6.1 percent of the population) to 1,714,223 (13.4 percent).[5]

Led by the news media giants, an increasingly one-dimensional interpretation of the events in Manchuria expanded into other areas of mass culture. Books, magazines, movies, records, and other forms of popular entertainment took the sense of national crisis primed by the press and radio, and infused it with the boisterousness of a carnival, as Manchuria became the theme for vaudeville acts, Kabuki tragedies, and even restaurant menus. Flooding the marketplace with Manchurian-theme products, mass culture industries disseminated a specific package of information and a set interpretation of events on the continent. They glorified military action, heroized the colonial army, and extolled the founding of Manchukuo. Telling and retelling the epochal moments of the Sino-Japanese conflict in every conceivable cultural form, the mass media helped shape public memory of the Manchurian Incident. When representations of Manchuria moved from the factual, if selective, reportage in the news to fictionalized dramatizations on stage and screen, the complex realities of the military occupation were reduced to the simple and sanctifying patterns of myth.

5 Eguchi Keiichi, "Manshū jihen to daishinbun," *Shisō* 583 (Jan. 1973): 100–3; Ikei Masaru, "1930 nendai no masu media: Manshū jihen e no taiō o chūshin toshite," in Miwa Kimitada, ed., *Saikō Taiheiyō sensō zen'ya: Nihon no 1930 nendairon toshite* (Tokyo, 1981), 144; Minami Hiroshi and Shakai shinri kenkyūjo, *Shōwa bunka, 1925–1945* (Tokyo, 1987), 262; and Abe Shingo, "Manshū jihen o meguru shinbungai," *Kaizō* (Nov. 1931): 36–9.

The crisis in the empire, the heroism of battle, and the glory of sacrifice were the messages of the Manchurian Incident theme products that poured forth from Japan's culture industries, dominating the mass media in 1931 and 1932. These messages dovetailed beautifully, of course, with what the army wanted its public to hear about the Manchurian Incident. But the culture industries needed no arm-twisting to advertise the army's cause: they became unofficial propagandists because crude militarism was all the crack. Audiences flocked to watch the dramas of death in battle; consumers bought up the magazines commemorating the glories of the empire.

Critical to the effectiveness of this informal propaganda was the popular conviction that what audiences were viewing was live history. Songwriters and dramatists lifted their material straight from the pages of the newspaper, moving from fact to fiction without skipping a beat. In dramatizing history as it unfolded, they shaded the line between news and entertainment and presented audiences with a pseudohistorical version of the events on the continent. The production of what today might be labeled "infotainment" was, at the time, another conspicuous feature of the war fever. Rendering the brutality of war in the comforting conventions of melodrama and popular song, the entertainment industry obscured the realities of military aggression even as it purported to be informing audiences about the national crisis.

Newsreel screenings sponsored by the big dailies had already begun the process of transforming history into an entertaining public spectacle. Widespread shooting on location by movie companies further blurred the line between fact and fiction. All the film studios sent actors and technicians to do double duty in Manchuria, entertaining the troops one day and shooting film the next. Film productions of the military campaigning in Northeast China turned the epochal moments of the Manchurian Incident into nationalist metaphors, symbolically rendering the takeover of the Northeast in the familiar language of imperial mythology – where a heroic Japan stood tall against Western bullies and easily routed the cowardly Chinese.

In its myth-making capacity, the entertainment industry created a gallery of Manchurian Incident heroes out of army reports on the outcomes of successive military operations. Kawai Pictures sensationalized the battlefield death of Captain Kuramoto in *The Big-hearted Commander*, while Tōkatsu Films memorialized his bravery in *Major Kuramoto and the Blood-stained Flag*.[6] The story of Private Yamada, captured by the Chinese during a reconnaissance mission and later rescued by a Korean interpreter, was made into the movie *Scout of North Manchuria*, the play *The Occupation of Qiqihar*, and

6 "Sensō eiga," *Eiga to engei* (Apr. 1932).

recorded on the Victory label as the minstrel chant "Private Yamada and Mr. Tei."[7] All seven Japanese movie companies produced versions of the sensational suicide of Major Kuga Noboru, who was apotheosized by Shinkō as *The Perfect Soldier*, by Kawai as *The Yamato Spirit*, and by Tōkatsu as an *Embodiment of the Way of the Warrior.*[8] Injured and left behind when the Japanese force withdrew after a failed assault, Kuga was taken prisoner by the Chinese. After he was released, he returned to the battlefield where he had fallen. He then shot himself to expiate the shame of capture. Announcing Kuga's suicide on April 2, 1932, Army Minister Araki Sadao praised Kuga's martial spirit: "Soldiers of the Imperial Army go to the battlefield to win or to die. Choosing the course of death, Major Kuga displayed the highest military spirit. We will treat him as a battlefield casualty, honoring him as if he died in battle."[9] Even the death of an Osaka *Mainichi* newspaper reporter in the course of covering the front became the stuff of heroic drama. Nikkatsu pictures' *The Blood-stained Pen* glorified the daring and zeal of the reporter when he rushed off behind enemy lines to pursue a scoop. Describing his martyrdom, *Screen and Stage* wrote that he was struck down by an "enemy of unparalleled violence."[10]

The significance of media sensationalism went beyond the manufactured fame of a few military heroes. When the media flooded popular consciousness with images of war and empire, it helped to mobilize popular support for the army's policy of military aggression against China, and in the process influenced foreign policy and the politics of empire. Popular support gave the army a free hand in China, helped silence voices in and out of government that were critical of Kwantung Army action, and provided strength to the army's bid for political power at home.

MOBILIZING CAPITAL

The expansion of Japan's military presence in Manchuria in the early 1930s was quickly followed by a dramatic rise in the level of economic commitment to the Northeast. There the Japanese inaugurated the grand plan that would become a cornerstone of total empire – the scheme to create an autarkic production and trading sphere through the planned and state-controlled industrialization of Japan's colonial territories. What began under the rubric

7 *Eiga to engei* (Jan. 1932): 22, *Eiga to engei* (Feb. 1932): 44; *Rekōdo* (Feb. 1932): 74.
8 *Eiga to engei* (May 1932): 16; "Gunji eiga," *Eiga to engei* (June 1932): no page.
9 On media sensationalism of Kuga's suicide, see Eguchi Keiichi, *Jūgonen sensō no kaimaku* (Tokyo, 1989), 150. For Araki's statement, see ibid., 157–8.
10 "Sensō eiga," *Eiga to engei* (Apr. 1932), no page.

of "Manchurian development" involved an enormous financial outlay – 1 billion yen between 1932 and 1936 rising to 4.7 billion yen between 1937 and 1941.[11] Investment in a colonial economy on this scale was unprecedented in comparative terms as well as in the history of Japan's own colonial empire. And while Japan did fund economic development in the 1930s, the expense of the project evoked political conflict over Manchukuo, as different groups disagreed on what the scale and the nature of the investments should be. The resolution of these disputes occurred within the framework of a growing cooperation between government and business over economic foreign policy. Sharing a common agenda on international questions of economic security and economic expansion, as well as domestic issues of economic and social stabilization, business executives and government officials increasingly worked together to make economic policy. But though the exigencies of the international economy threw public and private interests together, this did not necessarily mean that a smooth cooperation or harmony of interests was the necessary result. The prospect of developing Manchuria brought the big business community and the Kwantung Army together – but fundamental disagreement over the direction of economic policy meant that their partnership remained an uneasy one, a Japanese corporatism riven with internal contradictions. Yet perhaps even more striking than the points that divided them was the unity of faith in Manchurian development: both saw in the new empire the salvation for economic crisis. Facing obstacles in the domestic and global market, Japan's economy was, in the idiom of the day, "deadlocked." Colonial development in Manchukuo became the economic panacea for an uncertain age, the lifeline for a nation set adrift in the stormy waters of the global economy. That the uneasy partnership between soldiers and capitalists endured over the course of Manchukuo's lifetime was testament to the binding power of their shared dreams for the new empire.

In Japan, business leaders began to express excitement about the economic potential of Manchukuo in early 1932. With the establishment of the puppet state in Manchuria, businessmen moved quickly to set up organizations to coordinate, lobby for, and generally advance their interests in Manchukuo. Within weeks of Manchukuo's announcement, Tokyo businesses pressured the city assembly to appoint a committee to "look at the prospects for the city's commerce and industry in the Manchurian economy." The results were

11 Kaneko Fumio, "Shihon yushutsu to shokuminchi," in Ōishi Kaichirō, ed., *Sekai daikyōkōki* (Tokyo, 1987), 337; Hayashi Takehisa, Yamazaki Hiroaki, and Shibagaki Kazuo, *Nihon shihonshugi* (Tokyo, 1973), 872–7; and Hikita Yasuyuki, "Zaisei, kin'yū kōzō," in Asada Kyōji and Kobayashi Hideo, eds., *Nihon teikokushugi no Manshū shihai: jūgonen sensō o chūshin ni* (Tokyo, 1986), 866, 889, 890.

published in 1933 in a four-hundred-page guide to the Manchurian export market, including a digest of Japanese businesses in Manchuria and exporters in Tokyo.[12] Over the summer, the city's chamber of commerce sponsored the formation of a Tokyo Manchuria-Mongolia Export Union.[13] The China Problem Research Committee of the Osaka Chamber of Commerce sent a mission to Manchuria; their findings were published in "A True Picture of the Manchurian Economy."[14] The influential Japan Chamber of Commerce sent a team of business leaders to meet with Kwantung Army officials and tour Manchuria in February 1932.[15] From May to December that year, banking and industrial leaders from Tokyo and Osaka met to formulate a business community position and make recommendations on industrial, tariff, finance, and other policy for Manchuria.[16]

This flurry of activity sent a clear signal that within the domestic business community there was considerable enthusiasm for the economic prospects of a Japanese-occupied Manchuria. While the domestic business community worked to translate this enthusiasm into a national-level organization to advocate their interests in the new puppet state, the Kwantung Army and the Manchukuo government had been putting together a policy for economic penetration of the four provinces of Northeast China that were now under military occupation. In the initial phases of policy formation, the Kwantung Army sent mixed signals to the private sector about their role in Manchuria's new economic regime. On one hand, the Kwantung Army made sporadic efforts to court the goodwill of businessmen, inviting the Japan Chamber of Commerce to send delegates to a conference on economic policy in January 1932, and making army representatives available to meet with businessmen and discuss their concerns.[17] On such occasions spokesmen professed the Kwantung Army's desire to cooperate with private industry, and businessmen frequently came away feeling sanguine about working with the army. As one member of a Japan Chamber of Commerce economic mission reported to the press on his return from Manchuria in late March 1932, "We talked with all the key military authorities there as well as important

12 Tōkyō shiyakusho, *Manmō keizai chōsasho* (Tokyo, 1933), 1.
13 Tōkyō shōkō kaigisho, "Tōkyō Manmō yushutsu kumiai setsuritsu ni kanshi enjokata irai no ken shingi kiroku" (Aug.–Oct. 1932), Tōkyō shōkō kaigisho microreel 139:286–319; and Toda Shin'ichirō, *Manmō e no yushutsu annai* (Tokyo, 1933), 210–14.
14 Ōsaka shōkō kaigisho taiShi mondai chōsa iinkai, ed., *Genchi chōsa: Manmō keizai no jissō* (Osaka, 1932).
15 Nihon shōkō kaigisho, *Nihon shōkō kaigisho shusai Manmō keizai shisatsudan hōkoku narabini ikenshō* (Tokyo, 1932).
16 "Nichiman sangyō teikei ni kansuru iinkai" (1933), Tōkyō shōkō kaigisho microreel 107:329–655.
17 William Miles Fletcher, *The Japanese Business Community and National Trade Policy, 1920–1942* (Chapel Hill, N.C., 1989), 78.

people in and out of government. The military authorities really welcome the investment of domestic capital, and I did not see evidence of the army oppressing capitalists. We at home will take the opportunity to give as much financial support as possible to the construction of the new Manchuria."[18]

Yet this warm show of welcome was shaded by information appearing in the press about Kwantung Army hostility to capital. In a meeting with business leader Yamamoto Jōtarō in December 1931, Army Minister Araki Sadao reportedly declared the army's intention to "exclude monopoly profits of capitalists" from Manchuria and require that earnings be "reinvested in Manchurian development." Even while Kwantung Army Commander Honjō was toasting the fortunes of his corporate guests, he was being quoted as saying, "We want to use Manchuria as the means to renovate [*kaizō*] Japan. Even if this is impossible, at the very least we intend absolutely to exclude finance capital and the influence of political parties from Manchuria." Shared by the right wing and national socialists in Japan, these opinions were summarized in what became known as the Kwantung Army's unofficial slogan for Manchurian development: *zaibatsu wa Manshū ni hairu bekarazu* – big business must not come into Manchuria.[19]

Such mixed messages introduced fissures into the government-business partnership – tensions that were only exacerbated by the further articulation and elaboration of each partner's specific goals for Manchurian development. In the blueprints of the Kwantung Army–dominated Manchukuo government, planners would create a new form of state capitalism, a model to be imported into Japan for the reform of a bankrupt Japanese capitalism. The army envisioned that the Japan-Manchuria bloc economy would create an autarkic trading sphere that would provide for self-sufficiency in wartime. For its part, the domestic business community dreamed of the relief from economic depression that a guaranteed and mythically expanding market for Japanese exports would secure – Manchukuo as the savior and preserver of the existing system of private enterprise. The army's vision of a strategic production sphere was based on studies of economic mobilization during World War I; the business community's concept of a peacetime trading sphere drew, rather, on the more recent experience of global depression. The views of the two partners diverged sharply in other ways as well. The army wanted to industrialize Manchukuo and create state-managed enterprises under their

18 The interview was originally published in the Tokyo *Asahi* on April 2, 1932. This remark was quoted in Suzuki Tōzaburō, "Manmō shinkokka to Nihon no kin'yū shihon," *Kaizō* (May 1932): 66.

19 Suzuki Takashi, "Manshū keizai kaihatsu to Manshū jūkōgyō no seiritsu," *Tokushima daigaku gakugei kiyō (shakai kagaku)* 13, supplement (1963), 99. For typical media treatments see Suzuki Takeo, "Nichiman burokku keizairon no saikentō," *Kaizō* (Jan. 1933): 53–67; Suzuki Tōzaburō, "Manmō shinkokka to Nihon no kin'yū shihon," *Kaizō* (May 1932): 64–71.

control. Big business strongly opposed the industrialization of Manchuria, hostile to the creation of competitive enterprises that would reduce their own market dominance. The army wanted to develop Manchurian mineral and energy resources for heavy industry and military production; the business community desired to promote agricultural development in order to increase the purchasing power of Chinese consumers and expand the market for Japanese goods.

Despite their conflicting visions of economic development, the Manchukuo government and the domestic business community did manage to jointly create a new economic empire in Manchuria. While army bureaucrats laid the plans and oversaw construction, private financiers supplied capital, and private industry purveyed the goods and material necessary to keep the new regime of colonial state capitalism afloat. Although businessmen disagreed fundamentally with the course the army was pursuing in Manchukuo, they were willing to lend economic support that, if withheld, would have brought empire-building to a grinding halt. They did so not because they feared the stick of government coercion, but because the carrot of benefits was sufficiently enticing.

The formation of the trading sphere known as the yen bloc comprised one key project of the joint venture. For the army, the formation of the Japan-Manchuria bloc economy was a first stab at an autarkic production sphere. For the business community, it represented an attempt to develop a protected export market. Over the course of the 1930s, as both sides pursued their independent agendas, the yen bloc gradually took concrete institutional form. In 1933 and 1934, tax and currency initiatives created a new framework for trade between Japan, its colonies, and Manchukuo. In 1935 and 1936, these initiatives were expanded to include north China. After 1937, with the onset of the China Incident, the extension of Japanese military control brought more and more of China into the embrace of the yen bloc. Finally, with the advance south into the European colonies of Southeast Asia, the dominion of the yen spread into the so-called Co-prosperity Sphere. From its origins in Manchukuo to its embrace of greater East Asia, the yen bloc charted a rocky course. At every stage implementation was impeded, first, by problems created by the conflict of public and private interests, and second, by the essential inability of an imperial trade bloc to overcome Japan's economic dependence on Western markets for imports, exports, and capital.

While Japanese exporters traveled the course from giddy optimism at the beginning of the 1930s to grim despair at the decade's close, investors who supplied the capital for Manchurian development followed a different path to the same conclusion. Unlike prospects for the export market, business leaders were initially skeptical about the army's plans to industrialize Manchukuo. Yet despite these sentiments, when they could be insulated from the risks and guaranteed a profit, capitalists were willing to underwrite the army's development project. The unprecedented export of Japanese capital to the Northeast over the course of the 1930s gave meaning to the rhetoric of an inseparable relationship, over time committing Japan to a strategy from which it could not easily withdraw. It also demonstrated the extent of private-sector support for the army experiment that business leaders allegedly condemned.

The quid pro quo between businessmen and the army worked well enough during the first phase of Manchurian development. As the thirties wore on, however, the results of army management began to tell not only on the Manchukuo economy, but on Japan's as well. In the early days, the rush of capital to Manchukuo had financed a boom in Japanese exports to the region and helped pull the domestic economy out of depression. But by the mid-thirties, danger signs began to appear in the Manchurian-controlled economy. In 1935 economists reported that progress in Manchukuo's development had come to an impasse. The Manchukuo government's Economic Construction Program was about to run aground due to a lack of capital, and the small amount of direct private investment was in "deep trouble."[20] Meanwhile, the flow of funds into Northeast China was starting to affect the domestic economy adversely, and Finance Minister Takahashi issued a public warning against the "continuation of unrestrained financing of Manchukuo."[21] A competition for funds by Manchukuo bonds and domestic industry had led, by 1935, to a shortage of capital. Becoming increasingly acute as the decade wore on, by the late 1930s the capital shortage led to an inflationary spiral as the government began to print money to make up the shortfall.[22]

Though historians have endorsed the view of business analysts at the time that inexperience and the misplaced priorities of army planners created the problems in the controlled economy, private capital played an equal role

20 For representative contemporary comment, see "Mantetsu no kokkateki shimei to sono jitai," *Ekonomisuto* (Sept. 11, 1935): 24–5; Ōkura Kinmochi, "Manshū keizai no tokushūsei o saguru," *Ekonomisuto* (July 11, 1935): 12; and "Shinsetsu kaisha no genkyō ni miru Manshū keizai kōsaku no shinten jōkyō (I)," *Ekonomisuto* (Nov. 21, 1935): 35. For a historical analysis, see Kaneko Fumio, "Shihon yushutsu to shokuminchi," in Ōishi Kaichirō, ed., *Sekai daikyōkōki* (Tokyo, 1987), 337–9.

21 Kojima Seiichi, "Manshū kaihatsu seisaku to Nihon infure keiki no zento," *Ekonomisuto* (Apr. 1, 1935): 51–3.

22 Hara Akira, "Senji tōsei keizai no kaishi," in *Kindai 7*, vol. 20 of *Iwanami kōza Nihon rekishi* (Tokyo, 1976), 220, 231.

in setting the direction of Manchurian development. Their investments gave the army the capital resources essential to set in motion and sustain state capitalism in Manchukuo. The decision to channel funds into low-risk, state-controlled ventures instead of private enterprise strengthened the position of the state in the Manchurian economy. Thus, the formation of state capitalism in Manchukuo was dramatic testimony not to the power and vision of the army, but to the impact of imperial corporatism of the 1930s. Private industry supplied the capital, the army made policy, and Japanese taxpayers assumed the risk.

In July 1937 the outbreak of what was called the China Incident kindled Japan's second war fever of the decade. As in the Manchurian Incident five years earlier, the mass media played a major role in mobilizing popular support for militarism on the continent. Triumphant headlines reported success after military success, as the Japanese Army drove south from Beijing and spread out over north China and Inner Mongolia, moving into Shanghai, the Chang River Valley, and Nanjing in the fall of 1937.[23]

The same combination of victory euphoria and anxiety over domestic and international economic crises infused the public mood of 1937–9. Just as they had five years before, people turned eagerly to the economic promise that opened up on the continent. Books, newspapers, magazines, and radio programs buzzed with excitement over the possibilities of the China market in Japanese hands and applauded the Konoe cabinet's dramatic unfurling of the "New Order in East Asia" (*Tōa shinchitsujo*) in November 1938. A day scarcely passed without the invention of a new name to describe the transformation of the empire. The "Japan-Manchuria bloc" became a relic of an earlier era, replaced by "management of the continent" (*tairiku keiei*), "East Asian league" (*Tōa renmei*), "East Asian cooperative community" (*Tōa kyōdōtai*), "Japan-Manchuria-China bloc economy" (*Nichimanshi burokku keizai*), the "East Asian coordinated economy" (*Tōa sōgai*), and the "new economic structure" (*shinkeizai taisei*).

The new thicket of slogans that grew up around the China Incident promoted the belief that Japan's economic security was linked to continental expansion over the whole of China. Under its multiple labels, the New Order in East Asia was essentially a reformulation of the Manchurian solution on a grander scale. The vision of the New Order invoked the two key elements of the Manchurian program: the trade bloc and the controlled economy. Extending the purview of the bloc to include China, the New

23 Ikei Masaru, "Nitchū sensō to masu media no taiō," in Inoue Kiyoshi and Etō Shinkichi, eds., *Nitchū sensō to Nitchū kankei: Rokōkyō jiken gojusshūnen Nitchū gakujutsu ronka kiroku* (Tokyo, 1988), 211–23.

Order continued the pursuit of a guaranteed market for exports and raw materials. Like before, this aimed to mitigate Japan's economic vulnerability to the vagaries of the global marketplace and political interventions by Western countries in the markets under their control. The New Order also appropriated strategies for state management of the economy that had been developed for Manchukuo, making Japanese-controlled puppet states throughout China the agents of planned and regulated economic development of industries important to Japan.

Both these formulas emerged out of the particular history of Japan in Manchuria. The plan to develop the Northeast, where Japanese had at their service the extensive operations of the South Manchurian Railway, was now expanded to an area of vastly greater size, vastly more dense population, and where investments were limited to the treaty port operations of Japanese shipping lines, trading houses, and textile mills. With little or no thought to its applicability to the whole of China, Japanese simply expanded formulas devised for Manchukuo to encompass first north China, then Inner Mongolia, then central and south China. Etched in people's minds as a remedy for economic ills, the experiment which had produced such mixed results in Manchuria nevertheless became the blueprint for the New Order in East Asia. This virtually seamless transition from Manchuria to China highlights an often overlooked dimension of Japan's thrust in China in the 1930s. We tend to think of the "China quagmire" in military terms: the relentless logic of military expansionism bogged Japan down in an unwinnable war. But the logic of economic expansionism was equally powerful. In this sense, a "pathology of security" that prescribed the perpetual enlargement of the perimeter of defense paralleled a "pathology of development" that drew Japan incrementally southward into the same territories.

The character of Japan's continental expansion in the 1930s has been captured by one historian in the title *The China Quagmire*.[24] As the phrase implies, imperialism in China in the 1930s entangled Japan in a morass from which there was no easy escape. It was not a sudden leap that landed the nation in the middle of the bog, but a large number of small steps taken by a host of independent agents of empire. Each step by one limited the choices of another, gradually cutting off exit routes from the imperial quagmire. This dynamic made Manchukuo the first of a succession of territorial appropriations and the starting point for the series of wars that took place over these years.

24 James William Morley, ed., *The China Quagmire: Japan's Expansion on the Asian Continent* (New York, 1983).

The process began with the Manchurian Incident. The initiatives of Kwantung Army officers to engineer the clash of Chinese and Japanese forces in September 1931 provided cabinet members with a limited set of options. The reaction of the mass media and the political parties further narrowed those choices. The continued escalation of military action by the Kwantung Army subverted the Foreign Ministry's negotiating position at the League of Nations. Pinned between League pressures to cease the military action and army resistance to foreign pressure, diplomats stalled, gambling on a favorable finding by the Lytton Commission. When this failed to materialize, the cabinet was forced to choose between staying in Manchukuo or staying in the League. Japan withdrew from the League, plunging deeper into the China quagmire.

In a different venue, another series of steps moved Japan from the first plans for a bloc economy toward the runaway inflation of the 1940s. Year after year public and private sources poured increasing amounts of yen into Manchuria. Paralleling the widening flow of capital were steady rises in Japanese exports to Manchukuo. Thousands of new Japanese-owned businesses opened every year as the Japanese population in Manchuria rose by over three-quarters of a million between 1930 and 1940. Whether measured in terms of the thirty-two new rail lines or the forty-eight new urban centers, or in increasing capital, commodity, and population flows, by the end of the decade the Japanese commitment to Manchukuo had escalated to a scale and complexity that left policy makers with few options for retreat.

By the advent of the Pacific War, Manchukuo was clearly destroying itself from within. Yet because their commitment to Manchuria proscribed retreat, Japanese chose to go forward. In the process they accumulated a total bill for empire that cost the nation dearly. The occupation of Manchuria set in motion a perpetual expansion of the perimeter of defense, fueled by a preoccupation with securing Japan's ever-expanding territorial commitments. The price of military occupation proved to be an endlessly expanding war front, as war in Northeast China spread in all directions. In the interim, the Japan-Manchuria bloc became a sinkhole for financial, industrial, and human resources. By the 1940s the continued flow of capital, goods, and services into Manchuria was crippling a domestic economy already stressed by the demands of war. Equally critical, the shift toward an exclusive trade and production sphere in China helped follow diplomatic isolation with economic isolation. First tariffs shut Japan out, then export controls cut Japan off from European and American markets. Eventually this economic isolation threatened the nation's very survival.

When all this began in 1931, no one knew that the total bill for empire would run so high. With the clarity of hindsight, it is possible to appreciate the terrible price the Japanese paid for their empire in Manchukuo. But at the time, there was no master strategist coordinating the disparate agendas, no master accountant watching over the bills and charges – no single hand at the helm. Rather, decisions to push forward in Manchuria were narrowly focused; they were made piecemeal and without coordination. The process was thus plural rather than totalitarian. Only in their cumulative force did these thousands of independent initiatives provide the momentum for a total empire. And if the decisions were multitudinous, then the responsibility was also widely dispersed. There was, in short, plenty of blame to go around for the brutality, hubris, and tragedy of total empire.

Index

Lightning Source UK Ltd.
Milton Keynes UK
UKOW05f1805120114

224439UK00001B/35/P